KING'S GATE MEDIA PRESENTS THE WORKS OF:
SAMUEL ROWBOTHAM & WILLIAM CARPENTER

TESTING THE GLOBE
A ZETETIC INVESTIGATION
VOLUME I

REFORMATTED WITH INTRODUCTION AND COMMENTARY BY
ROB SKIBA

He that answers a matter before he hears it, it is folly and a shame unto him.
– King Solomon (Proverbs 18:13)

*It is the mark of an educated mind to be able to
entertain a thought without accepting it.*
– Aristotle

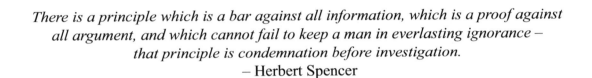

There is a principle which is a bar against all information, which is a proof against all argument, and which cannot fail to keep a man in everlasting ignorance –
that principle is condemnation before investigation.
– Herbert Spencer

This book is dedicated to those willing to hear the whole matter; to those daring enough to entertain a thought, even without first accepting it and who have the guts to actually take the time to investigate the matter before condemning it.

TABLE OF CONTENTS

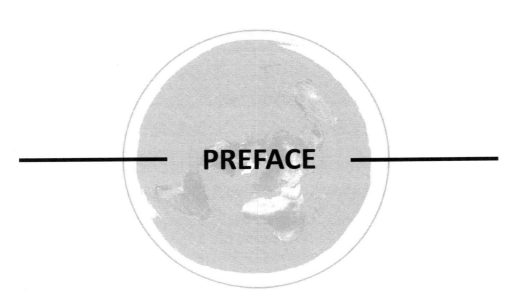

PREFACE

WHY am I writing/publishing this book? To be perfectly honest, I had to think long and hard about this question myself, because... the topic is *flat Earth*. Yes, in the 21st Century, we're actually talking about flat Earth of all things. Although, I firmly believe after you finish reading this series of books, you will at least begin to understand *why* I decided this topic is important enough to be addressing. Furthermore, you will also begin to see why it is coming to the forefront, trending so high on Google and YouTube and why, believe it or not, you may actually know some "Flat Earthers" yourself (if indeed you are not already one too).

Most of us were led to believe this topic "was settled over 500 years ago"—some going so far as to claim it was settled several hundred years before Christ with the likes of Pythagoras and Eratosthenes (among others). While it is true the vast majority of the population has considered the issue to be settled for quite some time now, there appears to have always been a remnant of believers in the old ways. Their ancient Scriptures and sages—and indeed their own senses—told them the Earth was something other than a spinning, heliocentric, globular world, hurling through the vast and ever-expanding vacuum of space. Most of these contrarians kept silent. However, this book will focus on a couple of them who were brave enough to speak out and boldly take a stand against the *status quo*.

This book is volume one in a series. It includes an Introduction from myself as well as some additional commentary on the writings of two outspoken men from the late

19th century: Samuel B. Rowbotham (a.k.a. "PARALLAX"), and William M. Carpenter. These men were among the first who caught my attention and whose works I consider to be quite valuable as an introduction for a new way of looking at this Earth and its place in the cosmos apart from what we have all been taught.

Are your beliefs just based on what others *told you to believe*, or rather on a firm foundation, of well researched facts—on *both sides* of the issues at hand? For those who already believe the Earth is not a spinning, heliocentric globe hurling through space, hopefully this series will further inform and inspire you. For those who are skeptical, on the fence, or already think they are quite set in their beliefs to the contrary, my hope is that this series will at the very least challenge and provoke you to want to know more. Either way, I believe it is important to know *why* we believe what we believe. Hopefully, this series will, in some way, aide in that pursuit.

The collection of literary works contained within this series have been reformatted to fit the larger dimensions and format of this book. The pictures and diagrams have also been scanned, cleaned up a bit and better placed within the content. Many of the on-line archives of these books have the imagery placed in mid-sentence. In such instances, we've appropriately placed them either before, after or beside the paragraphs, which reference them. Additionally, we've reformatted each new chapter in these collections to reflect a uniform style throughout this work, with each chapter always beginning on the right-side.

The paragraph structure has also changed from the tighter format, with indented first word, which all four books originally had, to the more open format you see here. In some cases, we have broken up a paragraph after a sentence completes in order to better place a diagram, so it is easier to follow along with what the author is saying. However, with but a few exceptions for accommodating graphics, we have for the most part preserved the lengths of the paragraphs as they were originally written (note: Rowbotham seemed to like writing *very long* paragraphs).

Regarding figures and diagrams, occasionally we have replicated some of them in order to place them on the same page(s) where they are being discussed. This is not a formatting error. We did this so the reader doesn't have to keep flipping pages back and forth to see what the author is talking about. We have also taken the liberty to add a few photographs of various, famous people to go along with what is being said.

We have tried to make every effort to preserve the text as it was originally written, to include giving emphasis in italics, where the authors did. In some cases, we have put such emphasis in bold, to further draw your attention to what is being said.

The original texts were done in a smaller font and book sizes. In this series, we have standardized the font size to 12 point Times New Roman and have reformatted all of the content to fit the template for this book size. So, naturally, the page count of the original books has had to change too. Not just because of the new, larger font and format size, but also due to the fact that this is a compilation work. So, where the author originally referred to a specific page number in his book, such instances have either been modified to show the appropriate reference page in this new compilation or in some cases, just either the chapter is referenced or a specific diagram instead. In such cases, the changes are shown [in brackets like this] so you can see where an edit has been made.

Likewise, the Footnotes have been completely reworked. Instead of the format in which they originally appeared, they now begin with number "1" and go through to the end of each book in sequential order, with each Footnote appearing on the same page they are mentioned. The numbers then reset with the start of each new book so that all Footnotes are specific only to the work being read and not a continuation of the preceding work.

There may be a *few* new Footnotes that I have added along the way. However, for the most part, where ever I have decided to give commentary...

> ...it will appear in a box like this one in an Arial style font in order to differentiate my thoughts from those of the authors.

Occasionally you may find references made by the authors to other books and page numbers contained therein, such as this one from William Carpenter's *100 Proofs*:

96. If we refer to the diagram in "Cornell's Geography," page 4, and notice...

In such cases, obviously it is up to the reader to seek out the sources being referred to in order to see such diagram as the one Carpenter describes here.

Other than the above format changes, the content remains as originally published. The content contained in this work was taken from various on-line archival sites. Every effort has been made to clean up errors in the archived scans, but it is possible the occasional typo or stray page number may appear every now and then, having been missed in the proofing process. Please note however, that some words are left with the spelling of the day and were not corrected to our modern spelling. For example, you will see words like "centre" and "labour" and "vapour" and "levelled" and "theorise" and "enquiry " among other such words spelled differently from the way we spell them today. These spellings were preserved in this collected work. That said, if you happen to find any stray page numbers or other errors and artifacts, which we may have missed, please bring it to our attention at info@kingsgatemedia.com so we can correct future editions of this book.

And finally, in an effort to bring this content up to the 21ˢᵗ century, I have included a number of Quick Response Codes (QRCs) in some of my commentary. So, if you have a smart phone or an iPad or other comparable device, which can read them, just point it at the QRC and go directly to the website or video I am referring to for more information.[1] If you'd like to try it out, by way of example, you can use the one below to go directly to my TestingTheGlobe.com website:

ACKNOWLEDGMENTS

This book would never have been possible were it not for the dedicated efforts of a number of people. First and foremost, the authors Samuel Rowbotham and William Carpenter. Naturally, they are the ones who put in the bulk of the labor. Then, long after their deaths, their works were preserved by a number of archival institutions to include, but not limited to: sacred-texts.com, archive.org, Google.com, the scanned, digital library collections of Oxford University, Cornell University Library (with funding from Microsoft Corporation, scanning performed by Kirtas Technologies and OCR by Internet Archive), and the Library of Congress. Additional compiling, editing, typesetting and formatting were done by Zen Garcia, Joy Garcia and Cathy Dunson of Sacred Word Publishing. This was all before we at King's Gate Media ever even put our hands to the task. When it comes to this finished product however, I owe a tremendous debt of gratitude to my extremely talented and supportive wife Sheila Skiba (with appreciation to Wendi Yokum, Jacqueline Lamar, Christina Kinman and Jeremiah Skiba for their added assistance). Sheila worked *very hard* to proof read and reformat the available data to fit the dimensions of this book (often having to retype large sections) and to provide the templates needed for me to complete the work with some added commentary along the way. So, to all of the above and to those who have loved and supported us on our ongoing journey of discovery and research, I give my deepest love, thanks and heartfelt appreciation.

---

1 **PLEASE NOTE:** All web pages and videos referenced in this work were accessible at the time of publication. Unfortunately, they may not always stay that way. Such is the nature of the Internet. One day the information is there, the next it could be gone. Naturally, such things are outside of our control.

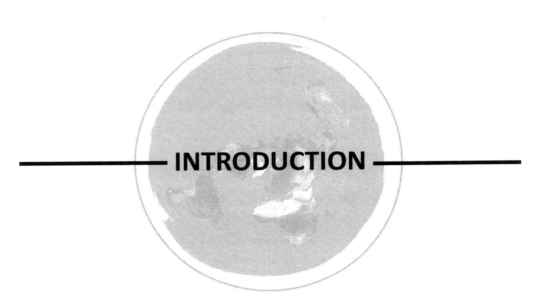

INTRODUCTION

The word "zetetic" is not a very common word you hear these days. In fact, until just a few years ago, I had never heard it used before. In the first chapter of the book *Zetetic Astronomy*, Dr. Samuel Rowbotham describes the word as having been "derived from the Greek verb *Zeteo*; which means to search, or examine; to proceed only by inquiry; to take nothing for granted, but to trace phenomena to their immediate and demonstrable causes. It is here used in contradistinction from the word "theoretic," the meaning of which is, speculative--imaginary--not tangible,--scheming, but not proving." Later, he says it is "the most natural method of investigation. Nature herself always teaches it; it is her own continual suggestion; children invariably seek information by asking questions, by earnestly inquiring from those around them."

As I have traveled the world speaking on the topics this book will address, I've often cited Herbert Spencer's quote about condemnation before investigation being the height of ignorance. I would then typically put a few books up on the PowerPoint screen, suggesting that if people haven't *at least* taken the time to read these books, they have not even begun their investigation. The books I show are the *Holy Bible, Zetetic Astronomy* by Dr. Samuel Rowbotham, *100 Proofs Earth Not a Globe* by William Carpenter, *Terra Firma* by David Wardlaw Scott and most recently, I've added *Kings Dethroned* by Gerrard Hickson (replacing *The Greatest Lie on Earth* by Edward Hendrie, which although I still consider it to be recommended reading, I think *Kings Dethroned* should be read first). Naturally, since I've been talking so much about these books, it seemed logical to publish them together in a collection where I could give some commentary. So, it is with the above definitions in mind that I have titled this collected work *"Testing the Globe: A Zetetic Investigation,"* of which this is Volume I.

While I have read all of the books I just mentioned, I must confess that I still went kicking and screaming into this subject. Like everyone else, I laughed, mocked, ridiculed and wanted nothing to do with it. I raised all the same objections and asked the same questions everyone does when first confronted with the whole idea that the Earth might not be a spinning globe.

Just to give you a little bit of my background: growing up, it was my life's ambition to become an astronaut. I had books on the early days of NASA and the Mercury, Gemini and Apollo programs. I had a signed photograph of Jim Irwin, allegedly standing on the moon from the Apollo 15 mission, telling me to *"Reach for your dreams. Aim high!"*

In fact, until only a few years ago, that picture always hung somewhere in my room or office as a tremendous source of inspiration. Having received it at a young age, I was determined to one day leave the Earth myself as an astronaut. I bought a 150 power telescope and star charts and spent many a night gazing up at the heavenly luminaries. I later upgraded to a 300 power telescope, with a whole kit of lenses, which even enabled me to observe the sun. I *loved* everything to do with space!

I did well in school and I joined the Army in order to learn how to fly helicopters. I went through Basic Training within weeks of graduating from High School and within two years I was following in my dad's footsteps as an Army aviator, flying scout helicopters.

One of the reasons I wanted to fly helicopters (in addition to wanting to be like my dad) was because I had heard/read somewhere that the astronauts had to learn how to fly them as part of their training to operate the Lunar Lander. So, by age 20, I was on track, with ambitions of eventually crossing over to the Air Force to learn how to fly jets and then to submit my application to NASA. I made a good effort in all of that, and had even been accepted four times for the next level of training I desired to go through. But in every case—and always for reasons outside of my control—I was blocked from doing so. It would not be until many years later, with the writing of my first book, *Babylon Rising: And The First Shall Be Last* that I would come to realize it may have been Divine protection, which prohibited me from reaching my goals.[1]

In addition, I was raised on *Star Trek* and *Star Wars* as well as a host of other science fiction movies and TV shows, which all contributed toward constantly reinforcing my belief in and support for the standard cosmological world view we were all taught to believe in school.

In short, I was thoroughly convinced— *without a doubt in my mind*—that I lived on a spinning ball, hurling through space around a sun, which was just one of countless others in an ever expanding universe. So trust me when I say... flat Earth was the last thing I ever in a million years thought I would even consider, much less endorse.

---

1 For more on that, see Chapter 4 of Babylon Rising, which you can read for free here:
http://www.babylonrisingbooks.com/PDFs/Chapter4_OneNationReduced.pdf

Then came April 13, 2015. That was the date I listened to Mark Sargent on a *Canary Cry Radio* interview.[2] At first, I rolled my eyes and thought the whole thing had to be a joke. But by the end of it, I had to admit, some of what he said made sense to me. So I listened again. Then, I made the mistake of watching Mark's *Flat Earth Clues* series on YouTube.[3] At the end of each video, Sargent left his contact information, so I called him. The following day, April 15, 2015, I had him on my radio show[4]... and from that fateful day forward, I've been tumbling down the deepest rabbit hole I've ever been in (for those who have followed my work for the past decade or so, you know that's saying a lot). And I'm only partly joking when I refer to that date as *"The day Mark Sargent ruined my life."*

As you might imagine, I was quite content in my cosmological world view. So much so that I even allowed my personal biases to color the way I read the Bible. Like many, I often quoted Isaiah 40:22 and Job 26:7, while proudly proclaiming, *"See! Even the authors of Scripture knew the Earth was a globe, floating in the NOTHINGness of space."*—all while remaining willfully ignorant of the fact that a circle is *not* a sphere and even in the model I claimed to believe, the Earth is *not* "hanging on nothing," but rather it *is* "hung" on the gravity of the sun in the Copernican-Newtonian system! Not only that, but Genesis 1 *clearly* states the sun, moon, and stars were placed **_in_** the firmament, not outside and around it—as the Kent Hovind/Carl Baugh "canopy model" (which I once likewise taught myself) demands. And it just gets worse from there. When one takes an honest look at the Scriptures—which we *claim* to take "literally"— the picture it paints is actually quite different from what we say we believe. Speaking of painted pictures...

At some point in my early conversations with Mark, he challenged me. He said, *"OK. You believe we live on a spinning ball. I get it. Prove it Rob. But do so without using, NASA, the government or the military as your source."* Now, why would he give those restrictions? Well, let me ask you: what government of any nation can you name as being absolutely trustworthy? For instance, would you consider the governments of the United States, Russia and/or China to be trustworthy sources of truth? I do not. And of course, the military and space programs of any nation all take their orders from the government that sponsors them. Anyone who joins the military is literally trained and required—even at the lowest ranks—to be able to keep secrets. This is obviously because for a soldier to give up any military secrets, it would jeopardize his friends, his unit, and ultimately his country and those he loves back home. So, we've just established that no government is trustworthy. Those who serve in the military take orders from these untrustworthy governments and are trained to keep secrets. And if you do any real research into the founding of organizations like NASA, you will see the astronauts are either current or former military personnel, and many are also members of secret societies such as the Freemasons. And of course, secret societies... keep secrets.

2 http://www.canarycryradio.com/2015/04/11/ccr-089-flat-earth-with-mark-sargent/
3 http://enclosedworld.com/videos.html
4 https://www.youtube.com/watch?v=tenoUrC4pSE

Although Mark's challenge was a reasonable one, naturally I ignored it like most people and said to myself, *"But we've all seen the pictures! We have lots and lots of pictures and videos from space, showing the Earth to be a globe."* Then came the wake up call. I started actually looking into these pictures and videos. The most obvious place to start was the one we've all seen in our text books:

This is the famous picture allegedly taken by the crew of Apollo 17. But after watching a video from a "hyper-realist" painter named, Mathew Boyland (a.k.a. Math Powerland) on YouTube[5] wherein he was doing a stand-up comic routine challenging his audience with the question, *"Is it real or a painting?"* I honestly had to take a moment and think about it.

Being a gifted artist myself, having won numerous awards for artwork I had done while in school back in the 80s, I thought Math was asking a very reasonable question. How

---

5 Mathew Powerland was talking about flat Earth several years before Mark Sargent or anyone else I had seen back in 2015. You can watch the above referenced here: https://youtu.be/0xYwMjAXna8 (caution: foul language).

would you know? The picture looks real enough. But then, we have no frame of reference here *on Earth* to know if that's really what it looks like. We just trusted the government institution of NASA and therefor accepted it. But let's put this into perspective. Take a few minutes to do a simple Google search on "photorealism" and spend some time looking at the artwork people are actually capable of creating. Yigal Ozeri[6] is arguably the best out there when it comes to both nature scenes and portraits. His work is so amazing, there is almost no way to tell if you are looking at a painting or a photograph.

As you start looking for images of Earth from space, you will keep running into small print, using words like "image" instead of photo or "composite" or "artist rendering" or "CGI" or something telling you that what you are looking at is not an actual snapshot taken of the Earth with a camera. In fact, the most famous "Blue Marble" picture was the one released in 2002 by Robert Simmons,[7] the Lead Data Visualizer and Information Designer for NASA. This 3D model can be seen just about everywhere. It was the default background for iPhones and iPads. It's used in countless documentaries. It is constantly being used in print and video media. But it is not an actual photograph. It is a heavily photoshopped image, allegedly stitched together from "satellite" data.

 If you take these images and bring them into Photoshop or some other comparable image processing program and you start zooming in, you will see *many* of the clouds have been created using the "clone tool", which replicates portions of the image (see picture on the next page). Notice also the backward "c" shaped cloud formation off the east coast of the U.S.. Now that I've pointed it out, start looking for it whenever you see any imagery of the globe on television. It shows up over and over and over again.

6 http://www.yigalozeriartist.com/
7 https://www.nasa.gov/centers/goddard/about/people/RSimmon.html

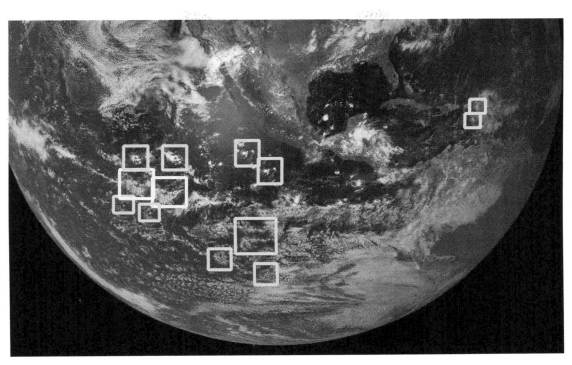

If you keep looking for images of the Earth from space, you find anything but consistency:

The last image showing all the different "Blue Marbles" over the years is much more disturbing in color. In it, as you compare one globe to the next, the colors of the oceans and continents are all drastically different. But even in the black and white image posted here, you can see that the continents are also different sizes from year to year. At this point in my research, my eyes were beginning to open the way they do when one takes the proverbial "red pill" and you start to realize how real eyes see real lies.

Then, I saw a video on the Jet Propulsion Laboratory website.[8] It was allegedly shot from the Galileo space probe back in December of 1990, showing a time-lapse of a 25 hour period of Earth's rotation. The problem is, none of the clouds are moving, or changing shape. I could point my camera up at the sky for an hour, speed it up in the computer and see them doing all sorts of things. But this didn't happen on Dec. 11, 1990 apparently anywhere on Earth.

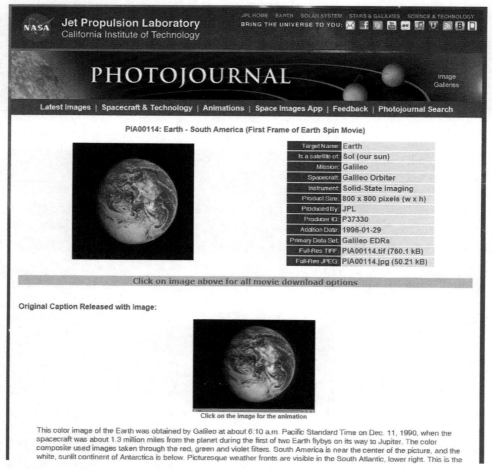

Needless to say, I found all of this to be quite disturbing. And it only seemed to get worse the more I looked into all of this.[9] So, at that point, I began to question everything.

---

8 https://photojournal.jpl.nasa.gov/catalog/PIA00114

9 If you'd like to take the same journey I took, please visit my website: http://www.testingtheglobe.com

ALLOWING THE BIBLE TO SPEAK FOR ITSELF

As someone who claims to be a "Bible believing Christian" I probably should have consulted the Scriptures first. I didn't because as I noted earlier, I was convinced the Bible supported the globe Earth. I mean, we had Isaiah 40:22 and Job 26:7 to prove it, right? Wrong!

I will now present a number of Bible verses without commentary. Unless otherwise noted, all of the Scriptures are taken from the KJV. For the sake of an intellectual exercise, let's pretend you have never heard of a globe or even a flat Earth before. Let's just allow the Bible to speak for itself.

Read these verses over a couple of times, and if you consider the Scriptures to be divinely inspired, begin by asking the Holy Spirit to reveal to you what they mean. Without ***forcing an interpretation based on preconceived notions***, meditate on them and ask yourself, *"What is the Bible really showing me concerning the nature of the heavens, the earth, the sun, moon and stars?"*

These Scriptures are arranged by topics in order to set the stage for what will follow. I have placed the book of Job before Genesis as many (if not most) scholars believe it is the oldest book of the Bible. And I have also emphasized words in bold for us to consider as we read. This is by no means an exhaustive list of Scripture. It is essentially just a first run attempt to show what the Bible actually teaches concerning the nature of the Earth and its place in the cosmos. I'm quite certain if one were to seriously dedicate a substantial amount of time looking through the Scriptures (focusing on the Hebrew, Aramaic and Greek as well as the English), there are probably *many more* verses that could be added to this list. But for now, the following should more than suffice to prove the point.

SCRIPTURES CONCERNING
THE NATURE OF THE HEAVENS/THE SKY ABOVE,
AND THEIR RELATIONSHIP TO THE EARTH

Job 9:
6 Which ***shaketh the earth out of her place, and the pillars thereof tremble***.
7 Which ***commandeth the sun***, and it riseth not; and ***sealeth up the stars***.
8 Which alone ***spreadeth out the heavens***, and treadeth upon the waves of the sea.

Job 22:14 (KJV) Thick clouds are a covering to him, that he seeth not; and he walketh ***in the circuit of heaven***.

Job 22:14 (HCSB) Clouds veil Him so that He cannot see, as He walks ***on the <u>circle</u> of the sky***.

Job 22:14 (ASV) Thick clouds are a covering to him, so that he seeth not; and he walketh *on the <u>vault</u> of heaven*.

Job 26:

7 *He stretcheth out the north over the empty place*, and hangeth the earth upon nothing.

8 *He bindeth up the waters in his thick clouds*; and the cloud is not rent under them.

9 He holdeth back the face of his throne, and spreadeth his cloud upon it.

10 *He hath compassed the waters with bounds*, until the day and night come to an end.

11 *The pillars of heaven tremble* and are astonished at his reproof.

12 He divideth the sea with his power, and by his understanding he smiteth through the proud.

13 *By his spirit he hath garnished the heavens*; his hand hath formed the crooked serpent.

Job 37:18 Hast thou with him *spread out the sky, which is strong, and as a molten looking glass*?

Genesis 1:

1 In the beginning God created the heaven and the earth.

2 And the earth was without form, and void; and darkness was upon the face of the deep. And the Spirit of God moved upon the face of the waters.

3 And God said, Let there be light: and there was light.

4 And God saw the light, that it was good: and God divided the light from the darkness.

5 And God called the light Day, and the darkness he called Night. And the evening and the morning were the first day.

6 And God said, *Let there be a firmament in the midst of the waters, and let it divide the waters from the waters*.

7 And *God made the firmament, and divided the waters which were under the firmament from the waters which were above the firmament: and it was so*.

8 And *God called the firmament Heaven*. And the evening and the morning were the second day.

Genesis 7:11 In the six hundredth year of Noah's life, in the second month, the seventeenth day of the month, the same day were all the fountains of the great deep broken up, and *the windows of heaven were opened*.

Genesis 8:2 The fountains also of the deep and *the windows of heaven were stopped*, and the rain from heaven was restrained;

2 Samuel 22:8 Then the earth shook and trembled; ***the foundations of heaven moved and shook***, because he was wroth.

Psalm 19:1 The heavens declare the glory of God; and ***the firmament sheweth his handywork***.

Psalm 29:10 The LORD ***sitteth upon the flood***; yea, the LORD sitteth King for ever.

Psalm 78:
21 Therefore the Lord heard this, and was wroth: so a fire was kindled against Jacob, and anger also came up against Israel;
22 Because they believed not in God, and trusted not in his salvation:
23 ***Though he had commanded the clouds from above, and opened the doors of heaven***,
24 And had rained down manna upon them to eat, and ***had given them of the corn of heaven***.
25 ***Man did eat angels' food***: he sent them meat to the full.

Psalm 104:
1 Bless the Lord, O my soul. O Lord my God, thou art very great; thou art clothed with honour and majesty.
2 Who coverest thyself with light as with a garment: ***who stretchest out the heavens like a curtain***:
3 ***Who layeth the beams of his chambers in the waters***: who maketh the clouds his chariot: who walketh upon the wings of the wind:

Psalm 148:4 Praise him, ye heavens of heavens, and ***ye waters that be above the heavens***.

Proverbs 8: (KJV)
27 When ***he prepared the heavens***, I was there: when ***he set*** {Hebrew: "chaqaq"} ***a compass*** {Hebrew: "chug"} ***upon the face of the depth***:
28 When he established the clouds above: when he strengthened the fountains of the deep:

Proverbs 8: (NASB)
27 When He ***established the heavens***, I was there, When ***He inscribed a circle*** on the face of the deep.
28 when he ***made firm the skies above***, When the springs of the deep became fixed,

Isaiah 13:13 Therefore ***I will shake the heavens, and the earth shall remove out of her place***, in the wrath of the Lord of hosts, and in the day of his fierce anger.

Isaiah 40:22 (KJV) It is he that sitteth upon the circle of the earth, and the inhabitants thereof are as grasshoppers; that ***stretcheth out the heavens as a curtain, and spreadeth them out as a tent to dwell in***:

Isaiah 40:22 (ISV) He's the one who sits above the disk of the earth, and its inhabitants are like grasshoppers. He's the one who ***stretches out the heavens like a curtain, and spreads them like a tent to live in***,

Isaiah 44:24 Thus saith the Lord, thy redeemer, and he that formed thee from the womb, I am the Lord that maketh all things; that ***stretcheth forth the heavens alone; that spreadeth abroad the earth*** by myself;

Isaiah 45:12 I have made the earth, and created man upon it: I, even my hands, have ***stretched out the heavens, and all their host have I commanded***.

Isaiah 48:13 Mine hand also hath ***laid the foundation of the earth***, and ***my right hand hath spanned the heavens***: when I call unto them, they stand up together.

Isaiah 66:1 Thus saith the Lord, ***The heaven is my throne, and the earth is my footstool***: where is the house that ye build unto me? and where is the place of my rest?

Ezekiel 1:26 And above the ***firmament*** that was over their heads ***was the likeness of a throne***, as the appearance of a sapphire stone: and ***upon the likeness of the throne*** was the likeness as the appearance of a man above upon it.

Amos 9:6 (KJV) It is he that ***buildeth his stories in the heaven***, and hath ***founded his troop in the earth***; he that calleth for the waters of the sea, and poureth them out upon the face of the earth: The LORD is his name.

Amos 9:6 (ASV) it is he that buildeth ***his chambers in the heavens, and hath founded his <u>vault</u> upon the earth***; he that calleth for the waters of the sea, and poureth them out upon the face of the earth; Jehovah is his name.

Amos 9:6 (ESV) it is he that ***buildeth <u>his chambers</u> in the heaven, and hath founded his <u>vault</u> upon the earth***; he that calleth for the waters of the sea and poureth them out upon the face of the earth; the LORD is his name.

Amos 9:6 (Darby) It is he that ***buildeth his <u>upper chambers</u> in the heavens, and hath founded his <u>vault</u> upon the earth***; he that calleth for the waters of the sea, and poureth them out upon the face of the earth: Jehovah is his name.

Amos 9:6 (NASB) The One who builds ***His <u>upper chambers</u> in the heavens And has founded His <u>vaulted dome</u> over the earth***, He who calls for the waters of the sea and pours them out on the face of the earth, The Lord is His name.

SCRIPTURES CONCERNING THE NATURE OF THE EARTH BELOW THE FIRMAMENT

Job 9:6 Which shaketh the earth out of her place, and the ***pillars thereof tremble***.

Job 26:7 He ***stretcheth out the north*** over the empty place, and ***hangeth the earth upon nothing***.

Job 26:10 He hath ***compassed the waters with bounds***, until the day and night come to an end.

Job 28:24 For he looketh ***to the ends of the earth***, and seeth under the whole heaven;

Job 37:3 He directeth it ***under the whole heaven***, and his lightning unto ***the ends of the earth***.

Job 38:
1 ***Then the Lord*** {Hebrew: "YHWH" is talking here} ***answered Job out of the whirlwind***, and said,
2 Who is this that darkeneth counsel by words without knowledge?
3 Gird up now thy loins like a man; for I will demand of thee, and answer thou me.
4 Where wast thou ***when I laid the foundations of the earth***? Declare, if thou hast understanding.
5 Who hath ***laid the measures thereof,*** if thou knowest? or ***who hath stretched the line upon it***?
6 ***Whereupon are the foundations thereof fastened? or who laid the corner stone thereof***;
7 When the morning stars sang together, and all the sons of God shouted for joy?

Job 38:
13 That it might take hold of the ***ends of the earth***, that the wicked might be shaken out of it?
14 It is ***turned as clay to the seal***; and they stand as a garment.

Genesis 1:
9 And God said, ***Let the waters under the heaven be gathered together unto one place, and let the dry land appear***: and it was so.
10 ***And God called the dry land Earth; and the gathering together of the waters called he Seas***: and God saw that it was good.
11 And God said, Let the earth bring forth grass, the herb yielding seed, and the fruit tree yielding fruit after his kind, whose seed is in itself, upon the earth: and it was so.

12 And the earth brought forth grass, and herb yielding seed after his kind, and the tree yielding fruit, whose seed was in itself, after his kind: and God saw that it was good.

13 And the evening and the morning were the third day.

1 Samuel 2:8 He raiseth up the poor out of the dust, and lifteth up the beggar from the dunghill, to set them among princes, and to make them inherit the throne of glory: *for the pillars of the earth are the Lord's, and he hath set the world upon them*.

2 Samuel 22:16 And the channels of the sea appeared, *the foundations of the world were discovered*, at the rebuking of the Lord, at the blast of the breath of his nostrils.

1 Chronicles 16:30 (KJV) Fear before him, all the earth: *the world also shall be stable, that it be not moved*.

1 Chronicles 16:30 (ESV) tremble before him, all the earth; yes, *the world is established; it shall never be moved*.

1 Chronicles 16:30 (NASB) Tremble before Him, all the earth; Indeed, *the world is firmly established, it will not be moved*.

Psalm 18:15 Then the channels of waters were seen, and *the foundations of the world were discovered* at thy rebuke, O Lord, at the blast of the breath of thy nostrils.

Psalm 75:3 The earth and all the inhabitants thereof are dissolved: I bear up *the pillars* of it. Selah.

Psalm 93:1 The Lord reigneth, he is clothed with majesty; the Lord is clothed with strength, wherewith he hath girded himself: *the world also is stablished, that it cannot be moved*.

Psalm 96:
9 O worship the Lord in the beauty of holiness: fear before him, all the earth.
10 Say among the heathen that the Lord reigneth: *the world also shall be established that it shall not be moved*: he shall judge the people righteously.
11 Let the heavens rejoice, and let the earth be glad; let the sea roar, and the fulness thereof.

Psalm 102:25 Of old hast thou *laid the foundation of the earth*: and the heavens are the work of thy hands.

Psalm 104:
5 *Who laid the foundations of the earth, that it should not be removed for ever.*
6 *Thou coveredst it with the deep as with a garment: the waters stood above the mountains.*
7 At thy rebuke they fled; at the voice of thy thunder they hasted away.
8 They go up by the mountains; they go down by the valleys unto the place which thou hast founded for them.
9 *Thou hast set a bound that they may not pass over; that they turn not again to cover the earth.*

Psalm 136:6 To him that *stretched out the earth above the waters*: for his mercy endureth for ever.

Proverbs 8: (KJV)
27 When he prepared the heavens, I was there: when *he set* {Hebrew: "chaqaq"} *a compass* {Hebrew: "chug"} *upon the face of the depth*:
28 When he established the clouds above: when he *strengthened the fountains of the deep*:
29 When *he gave to the sea his decree, that the waters should not pass his commandment*: when he appointed *the foundations of the earth*:

Proverbs 8: (NASB)
27 When He established the heavens, I was there, When *He inscribed a circle* on the face of the deep.
28 when he made firm the skies above, When *the springs of the deep became fixed*,
29 When He *set for the sea its boundary* So that the water would not transgress His command, When He *marked out the foundations of the earth*;

Isaiah 11:12 And he shall set up an ensign for the nations, and shall assemble the outcasts of Israel, and gather together the dispersed of Judah from *the four corners of the earth.*

Isaiah 13:13 Therefore *I will shake the heavens, and the earth shall remove out of her place*, in the wrath of the Lord of hosts, and in the day of his fierce anger.

Isaiah 40:22 (KJV) It is he that sitteth *upon the circle of the earth*, and the inhabitants thereof are as grasshoppers; that *stretcheth out the heavens as a curtain, and spreadeth them out as a tent to dwell in*:

Isaiah 40:22 (ISV) He's the one who sits *above the disk of the earth*, and its inhabitants are like grasshoppers. He's the one who *stretches out the heavens like a curtain, and spreads them like a tent to live in*,

Isaiah 43:6 I'll say to the north, 'Give them up'! and to the south, 'Don't keep them back!' Bring my sons from far away and my daughters from the ***ends of the earth***—

Daniel 4:
10 Thus were the visions of mine head in my bed; I saw, and behold a tree in the midst of the earth, and ***the height thereof was great***.
11 The tree grew, and was strong, and ***the height thereof reached unto heaven, and the sight thereof to the end of all the earth***:

Jonah 2:6 I went down to the bottoms of the mountains; ***the earth with her bars*** was about me for ever: yet hast thou brought up my life from corruption, O Lord my God.

Matthew 4:
8 Again, the devil taketh him ***up into an exceeding high mountain, and sheweth him all the kingdoms of the world***, and the glory of them; 9 And saith unto him, All these things will I give thee, if thou wilt fall down and worship me.

Matthew 24:31 And he shall send his angels with a great sound of a trumpet, and they shall gather together his elect from ***the four winds, from one end of heaven to the other***.

John 17:24 Father, I desire that they also, whom thou hast given me, may be with me where I am, to behold my glory which thou hast given me in thy love for me ***before the foundation of the world***.

Revelation 1:7 Behold, he cometh with clouds; ***and <u>every eye</u> shall see him***, and they also which pierced him: and all kindreds of the earth shall wail because of him. Even so, Amen.

Revelation 7:1 And after these things I saw ***four angels standing on the four corners of the earth, holding the four winds of the earth***, that the wind should not blow on the earth, nor on the sea, nor on any tree.

Revelation 20:8 He will go out to deceive Gog and Magog, the nations at ***the four corners of the earth***, and gather them for war. They are as numerous as the sands of the seashore.

SCRIPTURES CONCERNING THE NATURE OF THE SUN, MOON AND STARS

Job 38:7 When the ***morning stars sang together***, and all the ***sons of God*** shouted for joy?

Genesis 1:
14 And God said, ***Let there be lights <u>in the firmament</u> of the heaven*** to divide the day from the night; and let them be for signs, and for seasons, and for days, and years
15 And let them be for lights ***<u>in the firmament</u> of the heaven to give light upon the earth:*** and it was so.
16 And God made <u>two great lights</u>; the greater light to rule the day, and the lesser light to rule the night: he made the stars also.
17 And ***God set them <u>in the firmament</u> of the heaven*** to give light upon the earth,
18 And to rule over the day and over the night, and to divide the light from the darkness: and God saw that it was good.

Deuteronomy 4:19 And lest thou lift up thine eyes unto heaven, and ***when thou seest the sun, and the moon, and the stars, even <u>all the host of heaven</u>, shouldest be driven to worship them, and serve them***, which the Lord thy God hath divided unto all nations under the whole heaven.

Joshua 10:
12 Then spake Joshua to the LORD in the day when the LORD delivered up the Amorites before the children of Israel, and he said in the sight of Israel, ***Sun, stand thou still upon Gibeon; and thou, Moon, in the valley of Ajalon***.
13 And ***the sun stood still, and the moon stayed***, until the people had avenged themselves upon their enemies. Is not this written in the book of Jasher? So the sun stood still in the midst of heaven, and hasted not to go down about a whole day.

Judges 5:20 They fought from heaven; ***the stars in their courses fought against Sisera***.

Psalms 19:
1 ***The heavens declare the glory of God; and the firmament sheweth his handywork***.
2 Day unto day uttereth speech, and night unto night sheweth knowledge.
3 There is no speech nor language, where their voice is not heard.
4 Their line is gone out through all the earth, and their words to the end of the world. ***In them hath he set a tabernacle for the sun***,

5 **Which is as a bridegroom coming out of his chamber**, and rejoiceth as a strong man **to run a race**.
6 **His <u>going forth</u> is from the end of the heaven, and <u>his circuit</u> unto the ends of it**: and there is nothing hid from the heat thereof.

Psalm 136:
7 **To him that made great lights**: for his mercy endureth for ever:
8 **The sun** to rule by day: for his mercy endureth for ever:
9 **The moon** and stars to rule by night: for his mercy endureth for ever.

Psalm 147:4 He telleth the number of the **stars**; he calleth them all **by their names**.

Psalm 148:3 Praise ye him, **sun and moon: praise him, all ye stars of light**.

Ecclesiastes 1:5 The sun also ariseth, and the sun goeth down, and hasteth to his place where he arose.

Isaiah 13:
9 Behold, the day of the LORD cometh, cruel both with wrath and fierce anger, to lay the land desolate: and he shall destroy the sinners thereof out of it.
10 For **the stars of heaven and the constellations thereof shall not give their light: the sun shall be darkened in his going forth, and the moon shall not <u>cause</u> her light to shine**.

Isaiah 34:4 (KJV) And **<u>all the host of heaven</u> shall be dissolved, and the heavens shall be rolled together as a scroll: and <u>all their host shall fall down</u>**, as the leaf falleth off from the vine, and as a falling fig from the fig tree.

Isaiah 34:4 (NIV) **<u>All the stars in the sky</u> will be dissolved and the heavens rolled up like a scroll; <u>all the starry host will fall</u>** like withered leaves from the vine, like shriveled figs from the fig tree.

Isaiah 34:4 (ISV) ...**<u>all the stars in the heavens</u> will fall down, and the skies will be rolled up like a scroll. <u>All their starry host will fade away</u>** like leaves withering on a vine, or fruit withering on a fig tree.

Isaiah 38:8 Behold, I will bring again the shadow of the degrees, which is gone down in the sun dial of Ahaz, **ten degrees backward**. So **the sun returned ten degrees**, by which degrees it was gone down.

Ezekiel 32:
7 And when I shall put thee out, I will cover the heaven, and **make the stars thereof dark; I will cover the sun with a cloud, and the moon shall not <u>give</u> her light**.
8 **All the bright lights of heaven will I make dark** over thee, and set darkness upon thy land, saith the Lord God.

Daniel 8:10 And it waxed great, ***even to the <u>host of heaven</u>***; and it <u>***cast down some of the host and of the stars to the ground***</u>, and stamped upon them.

Joel 2:10 The earth shall quake before them; the heavens shall tremble: ***the sun and the moon shall be dark, and the stars shall withdraw their shining***:

Joel 3:15 The sun and the moon shall be darkened, and the stars shall withdraw their shining.

Amos 5:26 But ye have borne the tabernacle of your Moloch and Chiun your images, ***the star of your god***, which ye made to yourselves.

Habakkuk 3:11 ***The sun and moon stood still in their habitation***: at the light of thine arrows they went, and at the shining of thy glittering spear.

Matthew 24:29 Immediately after the tribulation of those days shall ***the sun be darkened, and the moon shall not <u>give</u> her light, and <u>the stars shall fall from heaven</u>***, and the powers of the heavens shall be shaken:

Acts 7:43 Yea, ye took up the tabernacle of Moloch, and ***the star of your god Remphan***, figures which ye made to worship them: and I will carry you away beyond Babylon.

1 Corinthians 15:41 There is one glory of the sun, and another glory of the moon, and another glory of the stars: for one star differeth from another star in glory.

2 Peter 3:10 But the day of the Lord will come as a thief in the night; ***in the which the heavens shall pass away with a great noise, and the elements shall melt with fervent heat,*** the earth also and the works that are therein shall be burned up.

Revelation 1:20 The mystery of the seven stars which thou sawest in my right hand, and the seven golden candlesticks. ***The seven stars are the angels*** of the seven churches: and the seven candlesticks which thou sawest are the seven churches.

Revelation 6:13 And <u>***the stars of heaven fell unto the earth***</u>, even as a fig tree casteth her untimely figs, when she is shaken of a mighty wind.

Revelation 8:
10 And the third angel sounded, and there fell ***a great star from heaven***, burning as it were a lamp, and it fell upon the third part of the rivers, and upon the fountains of waters;
11 And ***the name of the star is called Wormwood***: and the third part of the

waters became wormwood; and many men died of the waters, because they were made bitter.

12 And the fourth angel sounded, and **the third part of the sun was smitten, and the third part of the moon, and the third part of the stars; so as the third part of them was darkened**, and the day shone not for a third part of it, and the night likewise.

Revelation 9:1 And the fifth angel sounded, and **I saw a star fall from heaven unto the earth: and to <u>him</u>** was given the key of the bottomless pit.

Revelation 12:4 And **his tail drew the third part of the stars of heaven, and did cast them to the earth**: and the dragon stood before the woman which was ready to be delivered, for to devour her child as soon as it was born.

Again, applying no preconceived notions upon the text, how do you imagine a newcomer to the Scriptures would view the heavens, earth, sun, moon and stars just based on what is presented here? Would he see a spinning, heliocentric, globular Earth in an ever expanding universe? Or would he see something vastly different? I believe—without a doubt—he would see something completely different from what we've all been taught to believe. In fact, as I read these Scriptures, doing my best not to apply my own biases upon the text, I was seeing something more along the lines of an enclosed world, surrounded by water. Essentially, something like this:[10]

YHWH'S TERRARIUM
by Rob Skiba

---

10 **NOTE**: The above represents a cutaway, which leaves out the surrounding watery, thick darkness (Job 38:9) and what is above the firmament. To see the more complete artistic concept model I've created, go to: http://www.testingtheglobe.com/3dmodel.html .

But wait! You may argue—like many a "theologian" does these days—that the Bible is written in "poetic language" and it is just using simile and metaphor. It's *not* meant to be taken literally. It's aim is "theological messaging" not attempting to explain science.

While I can agree that the overall theme of the Bible is to convey YHWH's plan for mankind, I cannot agree with the notion that where it speaks in terms of cosmology it is any less trustworthy... or literal. If the Creator can't even get the description of His own Creation right, what possible reason do we have for trusting any of the rest of His "theological message"? And even if we were to accept that the Scripture uses "poetic language," does this make it any less accurate in terms of what it is describing?

We say *"Roses are red - violets are blue..."* because they are! We don't say, *"Roses are plaid - violets are black..."* because these flowers neither grow in those shades nor are they known by anyone to be of such natures. Likewise, when an author uses simile, metaphor and poetry, he's still using language that would paint a picture in the mind of the listener/reader of things that should at least be *remotely similar* to whatever it is he's trying to convey. Otherwise the "poetry," "metaphor" and "simile" are lost on the audience.

When Isaiah said that the heavens are "stretched out as a tent," his audience immediately had an image in their mind of a dwelling place stretched out over a flat surface, which was something *everyone* would have easily understood. King David had previously described the glory of the firmament, calling it the "chamber" within which the sun runs his "race" on a "circuit."

Psalms 19:
1 *The heavens declare the glory of God; and the firmament sheweth his handywork*.
2 Day unto day uttereth speech, and night unto night sheweth knowledge.
3 There is no speech nor language, where their voice is not heard.
4 Their line is gone out through all the earth, and their words to the end of the world. *In them hath he set a <u>tabernacle</u> for the sun*,
5 *Which is as a bridegroom coming out of his <u>chamber</u>*, and rejoiceth as a strong man *to run a race*.
6 *His <u>going forth</u> is from the end of the heaven, and <u>his circuit</u> unto the ends of it*: and there is nothing hid from the heat thereof.

And then—as if to do away with all speculation—there's the book of Enoch, which comes right out and tells us point-blank the nature of the stretched out, chamber-enclosed cosmology. In a vision concerning the coming Flood of Noah, we read...

1 Enoch 89:

2 And again I raised mine eyes towards heaven and saw *a lofty roof*, with seven water torrents thereon, and those torrents flowed with much water *into an enclosure*.

3 And I saw again, and behold fountains were opened on the surface of *that great enclosure*, and that water began to swell and rise upon the surface, and I saw *that enclosure* till all its surface was covered with water.

4 And the water, the darkness, and mist increased upon it; and as I looked at the height of that water, that water had risen above the height of *that enclosure*, and was streaming over *that enclosure*, and it stood upon the earth.

5 And all the cattle of *that enclosure* were gathered together until I saw how they sank and were swallowed up and perished in that water.

In confirmation of this concept of our world as an *enclosure*, we find the phrase "**in** the Earth" used *76 times* in the King James Bible. Oddly enough, the first time the phase shows up is in reference to the birds, wherein they are commanded to "multiply *in* the earth" (Genesis 1:22).

◄ Genesis 1:22 ►

Text Analysis

Sb	Translit	Hebrew	English	Morph
1288 [e]	way-bā-reḵ	וַיְבָ֧רֶךְ	and blessed	Verb
853 [e]	'ō-ṯām	אֹתָ֛ם	them	Acc
430 [e]	'ĕ-lō-hîm	אֱלֹהִ֖ים	God	Noun
559 [e]	lê-mōr;	לֵאמֹ֑ר	saying	Verb
6509 [e]	pə-rū	פְּר֣וּ	Be fruitful	Verb
7235 [e]	ū-rə-ḇū,	וּרְב֗וּ	and multiply	Verb
4390 [e]	ū-mil-'ū	וּמִלְא֤וּ	and fill	Verb
853 [e]	'eṯ-	אֶת-	-	Acc
4325 [e]	ham-ma-yim	הַמַּ֙יִם֙	the waters	Noun
3220 [e]	bay-yam-mîm,	בַּיַּמִּ֔ים	in the seas	Noun
5775 [e]	wə-hā-'ō-wp̄	וְהָע֖וֹף	and the birds	Noun
7235 [e]	yi-reḇ	יִ֥רֶב	let multiply	Verb
776 [e]	bā-'ā-reṣ.	בָּאָֽרֶץ׃	in the earth	Noun

So, are we talking about troglodyte birds here? This makes no sense if the Earth is a globe. Yet, it makes perfect sense if the Earth is an enclosed world system. And you cannot get around the wording used here. When the letter *bet* precedes a Hebrew word, it serves the function of meaning "in/inside" not "on/above" as should be the case if the text meant to describe birds multiplying *on* a spherical Earth (more on this shortly).

Oddly enough, Dr. Robert Sungenis seemed to have difficulty comprehending the function of the letter *bet* both here and in reference to the sun, moon and stars, which are also stated to be *in* the firmament. In his book, *Flat Earth/Flat Wrong: An Historical, Biblical & Scientific Analysis*, on pages 263 and 264 he writes:

We read in Genesis 1:6-9 that:

1. the firmament is synonymous with the heavens (Gn 1:8: "and God called the firmament heaven");

2. that the sun, moon and stars are placed "in" the firmament; and

3. that birds fly "in" the firmament.

The only way for these three criteria to be fulfilled is to understand that the firmament is simply the constitution of space. We look up and see that the heavens are filled with a lot of space. We see that the celestial bodies reside in that space. Lower, towards the earth, we see the birds flying in the same space. There is nothing but space. As it stands, we do not see birds flying "in" a dome and we do not see celestial bodies "in" a dome. If one wants to use "dome" as the translation for the Hebrew *raqiya*, he can only say that birds and stars exist *underneath* a dome, but they are not, as the text of Genesis 1 specifies, "in" the *raqiya* (a very important point we will address later).

If one then argues that the *raqiya* also includes all the spatial area from the surface of the Earth to the outside layer of a dome a few thousand miles above the Earth, he has created two opposing definitions for the *raqiya*: (1) the *raqiya* is a hard and thin semispherical <u>dome</u> a few thousand miles above the Earth, yet (2) the *raqiya* is also the few thousand miles of <u>space</u> between Earth and the dome. This is a contradiction, and when there is a contradiction then at least one of the two premises is wrong. Either the *raqiya* is space or it is a dome, but it cannot be both.

First, let me say that I have a great deal of respect for Dr. Robert Sungenis. Because, unlike *most* (in fact the vast majority), he at least did *some* research into the topic before coming out against it. That said, he still gets a *lot* wrong in his book, which shall likely be the subject for another book I may write at some point in the future in order to address his *many* errors (especially as it pertains to his eisegetical approach to Scripture). Second, his big problem as it pertains to the issues of the heavenly luminaries and birds being *in* the firmament is his gross misunderstanding of the Hebrew letter *bet* when used as a prefix.

Later in his book, Sungenis rightly points out that there are two ways to look at the word *in*. It can mean the peppermint is *in the candy* as in part of its makeup. Or it can mean, *I am sitting in my room,* as in I am within the walls of this room. The latter definition (meaning *inside*) is where his primary struggle appears to be, because he doesn't want to accept it.

His world view necessitates this because he clearly has a need to hold on to the vast, ever-expanding void of *Star Trek* style space. He writes on page 287:

> We only see space extending in all directions whose boundaries, from our vantage point on the surface of the Earth, appear to be hemispherical, but from outer space are spherical. Thus, as the text of Genesis 1 specifies, we see birds flying "in" and we see the sun, moon and stars revolving "in" the *raqiya*. Logically, this should tell us that the primary definition for *raqiya* is space.

No. The primary definition of the Hebrew word *raqiya* is given for us in numerous on-line resources, rendering Strong's #7549 as:

Brown-Driver-Briggs

רָקִיעַ **noun masculine**^Genesis 1:6 **extended surface**, (solid) **expanse** (as if *beaten out*, compare Job 37:18); — absolute רָ Ezekiel 1:22 +, construct רְ Genesis 1:14 +; — ᵐ5 στερέωμα, ᵐ9 *firmamentum*, compare Syriac below √above; —

1 (flat) *expanse* (as if of ice, compare כְּעֵין הַקֶּרַח), as base, support (Wkl^Altor. Forsch. iv. 347) Ezekiel 1:22,23,25(gloss ? compare Co Toy), Ezekiel 1:26 (supporting ᵛ's throne). Hence (Co^Ezekiel 1:22)

2 the vault of heaven, or 'firmament,' regarded by Hebrews as solid, and supporting 'waters' above it, Genesis 1:6,7 (3 t. in verse); Genesis 1:8 (called שָׁמַיִם; all P), Psalm 19:2 ("" הַשָּׁמַיִם, יַזְהִר, הַר Daniel 12:3; also רְ הַשָּׁמַיִם Genesis 1:14,15,17, יְהֵשׁ עַלמְנֵי ר Genesis 1:20 (all P). רְקִיעַ עֻזּוֹ'' Psalm 150:1 (suffix reference to ᵛ).

You can look on virtually any Bible study website such as BibleHub.com (above) or BlueLetterBible.org (right) for the definition of the word *raqiya* and consistently find that it means a hard, solid, firm structure. In fact, when the Hebrew translators of the Greek Septuagint came to the text, they chose the Greek word *stereoma*, which means "solid," and is used with reference to hardness, solidity, three-dimensionality in the formation of compound words. Thus, when Jerome took a stab at it in Latin, he chose the word *firmamentum*, which again coveys the same meaning as that of the Hebrew and Greek, and from which we get the English word *firmament*.

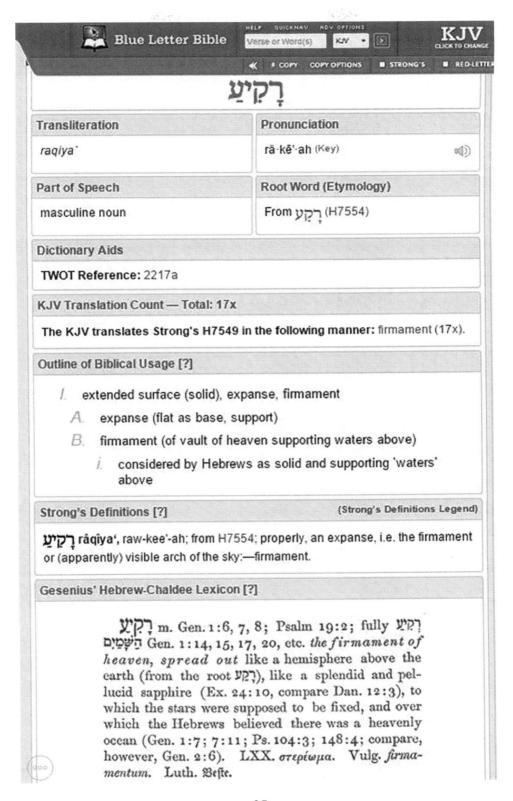

25

So, Dr. Sungenis is clearly choosing to remain willfully ignorant on this topic. Sadly, he's not alone. Dr. Danny Faulkner of *Answers in Genesis* at least admits the proper definitions, but then still justifies dismissing what the Bible says. On page 96 of his book, *Universe by Design* he writes:

> [T]he translators of the Greek Septuagint (LXX) rendered the Hebrew word *raqia* as *stereoma*, which Jerome followed as *firmamentum* in the Latin Vulgate, which in the AV (authorized King James Version) was transliterated as *firmament*. This is a terrible translation, and many modern translations break from this to render *raqia* as expanse.
>
> The word *stereoma*, conveys the meaning of something hard, such as the crystalline spheres of ancient Greek cosmology upon which the stars were implanted. Thus, the translators of the LXX incorporated the current cosmology of their day into their own translation. This is very similar to those who wed the big bang to the Genesis creation account today.

I'm sorry, but this is outrageously unacceptable nonsense! All the more so when one takes the time to look into the history of the Septuagint (LXX). Seventy-two Jewish scholars were asked by the Greek King of Egypt, Ptolemy II Philadelphus to translate the Torah from Biblical Hebrew into Greek, for inclusion in the Library of Alexandria.[11]

The translation of the Torah began in the 3rd century BC and the following narrative is found in the pseudepigraphic Letter of Aristeas to his brother Philocrates,[12] and is repeated by Philo of Alexandria, Josephus[13] and by various later sources, including St. Augustine.[14] The story is also found in the Tractate Megillah of the Babylonian Talmud and is generally told as follows:

> *King Ptolemy once gathered 72 Elders. He placed them in 72 chambers, each of them in a separate one, without revealing to them why they were summoned. He entered each one's room and said: "Write for me the Torah of Moshe, your teacher". God put it in the heart of each one to translate identically as all the others did.*

Philo of Alexandria, who relied extensively on the Septuagint, says that the number of scholars was chosen by selecting six scholars from each of the twelve tribes of Israel. If these accounts are true, do you really think Hebrew scholars, who were so incredibly dedicated to the preservation of their Hebrew Torah, would simply *change it* to reflect Greek cosmology—in direct violation of Deuteronomy 4:2, which says:

---

11 Jennifer M. Dines, *The Septuagint*, Michael A. Knibb, Ed., London: T&T Clark, 2004.
12 Davila, J (2008). *"Aristeas to Philocrates"*. Summary of lecture by Davila, February 11, 1999. University of St. Andrews, School of Divinity. Retrieved 19 June 2011.
13 http://www.setterfield.org/Septuagint_History.html
14 Augustine of Hippo, *The City of God* 18.42.

Ye shall not add unto the word which I command you, *neither shall ye diminish ought from it*, that ye may keep the commandments of the Lord your God which I command you.

This seems especially unlikely when we consider (according to the story) these scholars were separated and working *independently* from one another and yet all still came to translate it "identically as all the others did." Sorry Danny. Not buying your argument. Faulkner, just like Sungenis and many others are simply desperate to do away with the firmament as it has always been historically understood in order to hold on to their own biases and space fantasies. Thus, it is Dr. Danny Faulkner who ironically is the one guilty of "incorporating the current cosmology of [our] day into [his] own translation."

Whereas, anyone who is being intellectually honest with the text will come to the inescapable conclusion that the firmament does *not* mean air, gas and the vacuum of space. Rather, the text quite clearly describes a hard, firm structure, which according to Amos 9:6 is *attached* to the Earth. However, this is easy to miss in the King James:

Amos 9:6 (KJV) It is he that *buildeth his stories in the heaven*, and hath *founded his troop in the earth*; he that calleth for the waters of the sea, and poureth them out upon the face of the earth: The LORD is his name.

Most other translations render it along the lines of the following...

Amos 9:6 (ASV) it is he that buildeth *his chambers in the heavens, and hath founded his <u>vault</u> upon the earth*; he that calleth for the waters of the sea, and poureth them out upon the face of the earth; Jehovah is his name.

Amos 9:6 (ESV) it is he that *buildeth his chambers in the heaven, and hath founded his <u>vault</u> upon the earth*; he that calleth for the waters of the sea and poureth them out upon the face of the earth; the LORD is his name.

Amos 9:6 (Darby) It is he that *buildeth his <u>upper chambers</u> in the heavens, and hath founded his <u>vault</u> upon the earth*; he that calleth for the waters of the sea, and poureth them out upon the face of the earth: Jehovah is his name.

Amos 9:6 (NASB) The One who builds *His <u>upper chambers</u> in the heavens And has founded His <u>vaulted dome</u> over the earth*, He who calls for the waters of the sea and pours them out on the face of the earth, The Lord is His name.

The word translated as "troop" by the KJV and "vault" or "vaulted dome" in the other translations is the Hebrew word *aguddah*,[15] which is a word that conveys the meaning of a tightly knit unit bound together.[16]

---

15 The definition pictured on the next page is from BibleHub.com
16 For more on this see also my YouTube video: *Was Israel's Wilderness Tabernacle a Miniature Flat Earth Model?* https://youtu.be/ok9dUaG7peM

◀ 92. aguddah ▶

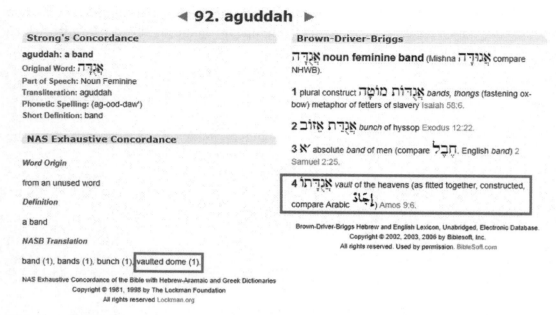

Strong's Concordance

aguddah: a band

Original Word: אֲגֻדָּה
Part of Speech: Noun Feminine
Transliteration: aguddah
Phonetic Spelling: (ag-ood-daw')
Short Definition: band

NAS Exhaustive Concordance

Word Origin

from an unused word

Definition

a band

NASB Translation

band (1), bands (1), bunch (1), vaulted dome (1).

NAS Exhaustive Concordance of the Bible with Hebrew-Aramaic and Greek Dictionaries
Copyright © 1981, 1998 by The Lockman Foundation
All rights reserved Lockman.org

Brown-Driver-Briggs

אֲגֻדָּה noun feminine band (Mishna אֲגוּדָּה compare NHWB).

1 plural construct אֲגֻדּוֹת מוֹטָה *bands, thongs* (fastening ox-bow) metaphor of fetters of slavery Isaiah 58:6.

2 אֲגֻדַּת אֵזוֹב *bunch* of hyssop Exodus 12:22.

3 אֲ absolute *band* of men (compare חֶבֶל. English *band*) 2 Samuel 2:25.

4 אֲגֻדָּתוֹ *vault* of the heavens (as fitted together, constructed, compare Arabic اجاد) Amos 9:6.

Brown-Driver-Briggs Hebrew and English Lexicon, Unabridged, Electronic Database.
Copyright © 2002, 2003, 2006 by Biblesoft, Inc.
All rights reserved. Used by permission. BibleSoft.com

This is why Isaiah described it as a tent, which is a structure stretched out over and *attached to* a flat surface.

> **Isaiah 40:22 (KJV)** It is he that sitteth upon the circle of the earth, and the inhabitants thereof are as grasshoppers; that ***stretcheth out the heavens as a curtain, and spreadeth them out as a tent to dwell in***:

While the above text does appear to convey some measure of "flexibility" in that it was *stretched out*, we are still left with the concept of something solid—a tent, or as King David puts it in Psalm 19, a *tabernacle* for us to dwell in. So now we come back around to Dr. Sungenis' dilemma. On page 268 of *Flat Earth/Flat Wrong*, he writes:

> Translations that choose "dome" or "solid arch" as the meaning of *raqiya* seek to emphasize the hardness and firmness concepts, but fail to include the flexible and ethereal characteristics that allow the birds and celestial bodies to move freely in the *raqiya*. They are then forced to modify "*in* the firmament" to "*inside* the firmament" so that the firmament becomes a hard boundary that encases an ethereal firmament inside the boundary, thus making *raqiya* into two separate entities, one a hard dome and the other ethereal space.

What is Dr. Sungenis' solution to the fact that the Hebrew word *raqiya* is describing something solid and that it comes from the root word *raqa* (Strong's #7554)[17] which means to beat, stamp, pound (as a sign of passion), beat out, spread out, stretch and/or to expand by hammering? On page 285, he writes:

---

17 https://biblehub.com/hebrew/7554.htm

Skiba neglects to see that the firmament is the *result* of a solid substance being beaten down and spread out, which *result* allows the firmament to retain a solid quality but also obtain another quality, one, perhaps, that it didn't have before it was beaten out. Scripture insists that this second quality is its flexibility and ethereal form (*e.g.*, Basil's "smoke"), since the birds must be able to fly in it and the sun, moon, and stars to move in it. Hence Skiba's questions, "how do you beat out air?" and "how do you beat out the vacuum of space" are misplaced, since space, both inner and outer, is the *result* of God beating out the firmament so that the celestial bodies could be placed in it on the Fourth Day. Hence one can't beat down the vacuum of space because it has already been beaten down to its finest and most discrete level that nature will allow.

Thus, according to Sungenis, the firmament once was a solid structure, but it has since been beaten out into thin air and the vacuum of space so that the birds and heavenly luminaries and are now free to move about within it. He also continues to claim I have created a "problem" for myself, stating on page 286...

> ...the firmament is not metal since obviously birds can't fly in metal (which relates to the basic problem Skiba created for himself earlier by conflating a hard dome firmament with a spatial firmament in which the birds fly).

I have created no problem for myself nor anyone else. All of this is easily resolved for Sungenis if he would just go and do a little more study on the Hebrew letter *bet*. If he were to do this, he'd see that no one is being "forced to modify" anything. This is because the letter *bet* **does** serve the function of meaning *inside*. He has a section in his book called **"In" or "Inside" the Firmament?** wherein he telegraphs his lack of understanding on this point. On pages 307-309, he says:

> To place something "in" a hard dome would mean that it is actually encased in the substance of the hard dome, which would essentially make it part of the hard dome. If so, then the moon, sun and stars could not move in the firmament since a dome would be inflexible. The celestial bodies can only move "in" the firmament if the firmament itself is so flexible that it doesn't cause any friction or curtail in any way their independent movement. Similarly, Genesis 1 says that the birds fly "in" the firmament. They could not do so if the firmament was a hard, inflexible substance. It is obvious, then, the firmament cannot refer to a hard dome.

Flat-earthers try to get around this problem by claiming that "in the firmament" really means *inside* or *underneath* the firmament. In this sense, the firmament is like a wall with objects placed next to its wall, but not "in" the wall. Although such an interplay between "in" and "inside" is linguistically possible, it does not do justice to the distinction when "in" does not mean "inside." If we use "in," it always refers to a smaller object being put into or being surrounded by a bigger object, whether we say "John is in the house" or "peppermint is in the candy." Although we can also say "John is inside the house" which includes John and the house as one collective unit, all other cases show that "inside" separates the smaller object from the larger object. Such is the case when a flat-earther says, "the stars are inside the firmament." He means that the stars are separate from the firmament and are not in the substance of the firmament. But is this the meaning and intent of Genesis 1? Hardly.

First, the Hebrew language, although it didn't have the most comprehensive vocabulary, did, indeed, have different words for "in" and "inside." As noted by Skiba himself, "in" is usually denoted by putting the letter *bet* (ב) before the noun. We find this formation, for example, in the first phrase of Genesis 1:1, "In the beginning…" (בראשית), or the phrase "in the firmament" (ברקיע) in which ב the begins the word (reading right to left in Hebrew).

But when Hebrew wants to say "inside," it does not use a ב before the noun; rather, it uses a different letter, the letter *mem* (מ). For example, in Gn 6:14 it says, "and cover it *inside* and out with pitch," from the word *mabit* (מבית). The same occurs in Lv 14:41: "and he shall cause the *inside* (מבית) of the house to be scraped round about," or 1Kg 6:15: "He lined the walls of the house on the *inside* (מביתה) with boards of cedar," or 2Ch 3:4: "He overlaid it on the *inside* (מפנימה) with pure gold."

The purpose of using the Hebrew prefix *mem* (מ) for "inside" (as opposed to ב for "in") is that whatever item is put on the "inside" is separate from the overarching structure that lies next to it. On the ark, the pitch was put on the surface of the wood, but the pitch was not put in the wood itself. Likewise, cedar was put on the walls of the temple, but cedar was not mixed with the wall; and the temple was not made of gold; rather, gold was put on the temple walls, on the inside of the wall, not in the wall itself.

This grammatical issue becomes quite relevant for our discussion since in Genesis 1 there is no appearance of the Hebrew word "inside" when it speaks of the firmament. While the Hebrew prefix for "inside" (מ) is never used, the prefix for "in" (ב) is always used. For example, Gn 1:14,15, 17 says, "<u>in</u> the firmament (ברקיע: pronounced: bir-ee-kee-yah) of the heavens." If the text said, "Let there be lights inside the firmament of the heavens," with the intent of saying that the lights were underneath the firmament, the phrase would be מרקיע (pronounced: mir-ee-kee-yah).

The only exception to the use of "in the firmament (בְרָקִיעַ) of the heavens" appears in Gn 1:20 regarding the realm of the birds. Here the translation is: "let birds fly above the earth *across the firmament of the heavens*" (RSV). The phrase "across the firmament" is עַל־פְּנֵי רְקִיעַ, which literally means "on the face of the firmament." The "face" is the front of the firmament (as our face is the front of our head), which means that the portion of the firmament in which the birds cannot fly is the "back" of the firmament, that is, outer space. The "face" of the firmament is that portion which, for lack of a better term, "faces" the Earth, or is closest to the Earth, which is just above the Earth's surface. Hence the birds fly in the front part of the firmament as opposed to the back of the firmament where the moon, sun and stars move.

There are a number of on-line courses you can check out in order to learn basic Hebrew, and specifically the ancient letter meanings. Jeff A. Benner is considered by many to be an expert in this field. On his website for the *Ancient Hebrew Research Center*, he has a section on *The Ancient Hebrew Alphabet*. There he says concerning the letter *bet*:[18]

Beyt

Early Hebrew	Middle Hebrew	Late Hebrew	Modern Hebrew
ʊ	פ	ב	ב

Pictograph: Floorplan of a Tent
Meanings: Family, House, In
Sound: B, Bh (v)

History & Reconstruction

Several variations were used for the original pictograph including ⬜, ⬜, ⬜ and ʊ. Each of these pictographs is representative of a house or tent. The pictograph ʊ is chosen as it best represents the nomadic tents of the Hebrews. The tent was divided into two sections, men's and women's, with the entrance at the front of the tent in the men's section and an entrance from the men's to the women's section.

The Hebrew word (*beyt*), the name of this letter, means house or tent as well as family. A common designation for a family is to identify the "house" of the family patriarch such as in "The house of Jacob."

The meanings of this letter are house, tent, and family as well as in, with, inside or within as the family resides within the house or tent.

In the last paragraph of the above screen capture from his website, you can see how Benner *clearly* states the meanings of this letter include "in, with, ___inside___ or ___within___."

18 http://www.ancient-hebrew.org/alphabet_letters_beyt.html

In a YouTube video titled *BET - Secrets of the Hebrew Letters*,[19] Rabbi Avraham Arieh Trugman[20] likewise confirms the meaning of *bet* as being that of a house; something that is to be "indwelt." Obviously to indwell something is to be *inside* of it.

In his teaching titled, *Jim Staley - Hebrew Alphabet (Part 1) - Aleph, Bet*,[21] beginning at about 40 minutes 24 seconds into this YouTube video, Staley likewise confirms this meaning of *bet* as a tent/house to be indwelt.

But Dr. Sungenis wants you to believe that the letter *mem*, when serving as a prefix to a word means "inside". Yet, in virtually any Hebrew resource you look at, you will find when *mem* precedes a word as a prefix, it means "from" or "out of" such as depicted here in this screen capture from the website Hebrew4Christians.com:[22]

עִבְרִית לַנּוֹצְרִים   בס"ד

7.4 The Preposition Min

Section Vocabulary

from, out of (prefix) .... מִ מֵ	from, out of (preposition) .... מִן
wine (m) .... יַיִן	sword, knife (f) .... חֶרֶב
gold (m) .... זָהָב	altar........................... מִזְבֵּחַ
fruit (m) .... פְּרִי	vine (m) .... גֶּפֶן

The Preposition Min

The preposition *min* ("from," "out of") is perhaps the most versatile of the Hebrew prepositions, appearing both as an independent preposition and as an inseparable preposition. In addition, *min* is used to form comparative, superlative, and "partitive" grammatical constructions.

As an Independent Preposition

In Unit 7.2 you learned that the preposition *min* can stand alone as an independent (or maqqef) preposition in a prepositional phrase. For example:

He walked from the city. .... הָלַךְ מִן־הָעִיר

In this case, *min* occurs directly before its object and is simply translated "off the page" as "from," or "out of" (note that before definite nouns, *min* is usually joined to its object with a maqqef).

---

19 https://youtu.be/12Mgsjsc6bY
20 He also gets into some of the more esoteric, Kabbalahistic meanings. I am not endorsing this. Rather, I am simply attempting to show the Jewish understanding of the letter.
21 https://youtu.be/cPYEAuIgRIo?t=40m24s
22 The letter *mem* is used as a standalone prefix or with the letter *nun* added to it to become a preposition. For more, see: https://www.hebrew4christians.com/Grammar/Unit_Seven/The_Preposition_Min/the_preposition_min.html .

Again on Hebrew4Christians, under the topic of Inseparable Prepositions[23] we see the letter *bet* serving as a prefix with the function of meaning *inside* of something:

in a place	בְּמָקוֹם	=	מָקוֹם	+ בְּ
in a field	בְּשָׂדֶה	=	שָׂדֶה	+ בְּ

and

in a house	בְּבַיִת	=	בַּיִת	+ בְּ

On the website JewFaq.org under Hebrew Root Words, we find this chart of prefix meanings:

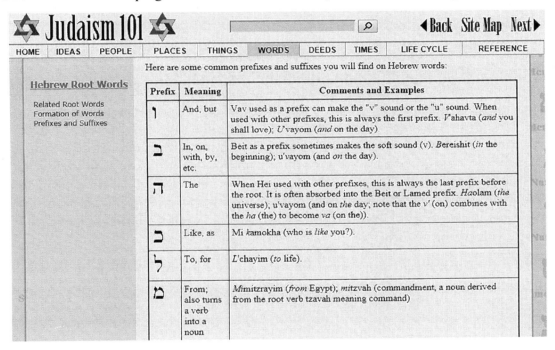

Over and over again, this is the case. So, I don't know where Dr. Sungenis learned Hebrew, but he may want to go back for a refresher course in letter meanings and the use of prefixes. He may also want to look a little harder for Scripture references where the letter *bet,* when used as a prefix to a word, serves the function of describing something being *inside* of something else, such as:

Genesis 18:9 And they said unto him, Where is Sarah thy wife? And he said, Behold, ***in the tent*** [meaning she is *inside* the tent: בָּאֹהֶל].

Genesis 31:34 Now Rachel had taken the images, and put them **in the camel's furniture,** [i.e. *inside* the saddlebag: בְּכַר] and sat upon them. And Laban searched all the tent, but found them not.

---

23 https://www.hebrew4christians.com/Grammar/Unit_Seven/Inseparable_Prepositions/inseparable_prepositions.html

Exodus 27:21 *In the tabernacle* [meaning *inside* the tabernacle: באהל] of the congregation without the vail, which is before the testimony, Aaron and his sons shall order it from evening to morning before the LORD: it shall be a statute for ever unto their generations on the behalf of the children of Israel.

Numbers 1:1 And the LORD spake unto Moses ***in the wilderness of Sinai*** [במדבר], ***in the tabernacle*** [meaning *inside* the tabernacle: באהל] of the congregation, on the first day of the second month, in the second year after they were come out of the land of Egypt, saying,

Numbers 17:7 And Moses laid up the rods before the LORD ***in the tabernacle*** [meaning *inside* the tabernacle: באהל] of witness.

Numbers 19:14 This is the law, when a man dieth ***in a tent*** [meaning *inside* the tent: באהל]: all that come into the tent, and all that is in the tent, shall be unclean seven days.

Sungenis is being somewhat crafty in the choice of Scriptures he used. For instance in the 2 Chronicles 3:4 passage, the *mem* serves the function of "from" (as we have learned from numerous Hebrew learning resources) and the word it is attached to is *penimah*, which means "within"—hence the word literally means *from within* or as in some English translations, simply stated as "inside." The same concept is true of the other passages he used. They are each talking about things being done or applied to from [*mem*] the inside of something else (*e.g.* 1 Kings 6:15 where "he built the walls of the house [from] within [מביתה] with boards of cedar.").

Going a bit deeper, I will also now cite the work of Dr. Frank T. Seekins as he sums up quite nicely what you would learn concerning the letter *bet* elsewhere. He has published a very helpful book on understanding Hebrew "word pictures" through an in-depth look at the letters and their inherent meanings. The book is called, *Hebrew Word Pictures: How Does The Hebrew Alphabet Reveal Prophetic Truths?* Regarding the latter *bet*, on page 16, Dr. Seekins says:

> The second letter of the Hebrew Alef-Bet is *Bet*. The ancient way this letter was drawn agrees with the meaning of the name of the letter. *Bet* in ancient Hebrew means *tent* or a *house*.

From this definition, it is quite easy to immediately understand the meaning of "in the firmament" from Genesis. The heavenly luminaries and the birds move about in/inside this tent/chamber, just as people move about in/inside a house. In short, it's not rocket science we're dealing with here. And frankly, I'm surprised I actually need to explain this to someone like Sungenis—a man with a Ph.D.. I can only conclude it is either a case of willful ignorance or severe cognitive dissonance, which prevents someone so smart from seeing something so simple.

On page 16, Dr. Seekins also says that even the ancient symbols for the letter *bet* represent a house or a tent. Interestingly enough if you rotate the first image 90° counter-clockwise you get what looks a lot like our capital letter "B" in English and if you rotate the image to the right of it 90° clockwise, you get something like our lower-case "b":

בַּיִת **Ba-yeet** - *a tent, a house or a family*

בְּ **B' -** added to the front of a Hebrew word the letter *Bet* is used to mean *in, inside* or *into*.

On page 18, Dr. Seekins shows how the letter *bet* is used as a preposition for:

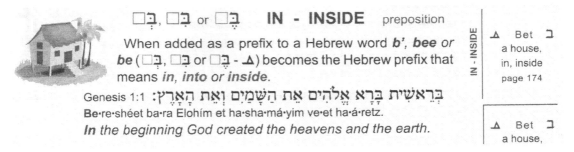

On page 19, he shows how in Hebrew, each of the verses in the second stanza of Psalm 119 starts with the letter *bet* and says:

> The letter *Bet* means *house* or what is *inside* and these eight verses tell us that it is what is inside the person or the family that matters. To live these verses we must seek God with our whole heart.

Indeed, verse 11 alone serves the function of illustrating the point I'm making here:

Psalm 119:11 Thy word have I hid *in* mine heart, that I might not sin against thee.

The word for heart (leb) has the prefix of the letter *bet*, making it bə-lib-bî. Thus, David is hiding the Word of YHWH *in* his heart the same way the heavenly luminaries and the birds move about "in the firmament" and I'm sitting *in* a room typing this.

The scan on the next page is from Dr. Frank T. Seekins' Reference Guide section, once again defining the letter *bet* by the "word picture" association of a house. He also illustrates a variety of other languages that agree with this concept for their equivalent to the Hebrew letter *bet*.

House ᐃᒍᚷ *Bayit - Beyt* בַּיִת בֵּית

Inside the Covenant

In the Middle East the house was a crucial place of relationship. Anyone inside the house (family, guest etc.) was considered protected by covenant.

Note: This word is pronounced בַּיִת *Bayit* by itself and בֵּית *Beyt* when used with another word such as בֵּית־אָב Beyt-av (בֵּית *house of* the אָב father) or *family*. The spelling and pronunciation of בֵּית *Bet the house of* and בֵּית *Bet* the letter is the same.

adj.	ᐃ Bet ב - house, inside
adv.	ᒍ Yood י - hand, possessive (mine, of)
noun	ᚷ Tav ת - sign, covenant

S# 1004	B# 198b	C# 72c
DT# 167 בֵּית	E# 214	G# 115 בֵּית, בַּיִת
K# 1074	W# 33 bayeet	
מֵמ# 132, ב בֵּית 160		B-Y# 25 בֵּית, בַּיִת

Gesenius says on page 115:

The word בַּיִת *Bayit* may have come from the root בּוּת *boot* which means *to pass the night, to remain*. The other option is that it came from בֶּנֶת *bant* or from the root בָּנָה *bootanah* which means *to build* (see daughter).

בֵּית *Byet* means *the house of* and בַּיִת *Bayit* mean a *house, family* or *what is inside the covenant*. These represent foundational precepts in both the ancient Hebrew culture and in the Bible.

Related languages that agree with the Hebrew use of בֵּית **Bet** as the letter for ב, as a **house** or to mean **in** or **inside**:

ᚼᚲᚲᚲ Akkadian *bitu, house*- *betanu inside*·

ᚷ Ugaritic *Ba* ᚷ— *bt, house* (compare ᚷ with 𐤟)

ᚠ Sabean *Ba*

ᚡ Amharic *Beh* ቤት *bayt - house,* ᚡ *in*

ܒ Syriac *Bet* ܒܰܝܬܐ *bayta; house;* ܒ *in*

ب Arabic *Ba* بَيْت *bayt, house;* ب *in.*

𐤟 Proto-Semitic 𐤟𐤟𐤟 *bayt letter, house;* 𐤟 *in*

Further complicating the problem for those who refuse to accept what the Bible has to say concerning the shape and nature of our world, is the fact that the phrase "face of the earth" is used 29 times in the King James Bible. While theologians try to argue that a "circle doesn't exist in reality" as they cite geometry, they conveniently ignore the fact that you can not have a "face" on a sphere. As one geometry website[24] puts it:

Solid Shapes with Faces

Solid shapes in math mean any object that is three-dimensional with a width, height, and depth. To get the face of a solid shape, you would need to trace the flat side of the solid shape. All plane shapes have faces, but not all solid shapes have a face. Actually, some solid shapes have more than one face, or don't even have a face at all.

Look at the picture below:

As you can see with the picture:

A pyramid has four triangle faces and one square face.

A **sphere** (or a ball shape) has no faces.

In Genesis 1:2, we see the Spirit of YHWH "moved upon the face of the waters." So clearly there was some flat surface over which the Spirit moved. Long before Isaiah wrote the twenty-second verse of his fortieth chapter, Job records YHWH saying:

> **Job 26:10** He hath **compassed the waters with bounds**, until the day and night come to an end.

The Darby Bible translation says "He hath **traced a fixed circle** over the waters..." and the ESV renders it as "He **inscribed a circle** on the face of the waters..." all of which appears to be confirmed by King Solomon in Proverbs 8:27:

> **Proverbs 8: (KJV)**
> 27 When he prepared the heavens, I was there: when **he set** {Hebrew: "chaqaq"} **a compass** {Hebrew: "chug"} **upon the face of the depth**:
> 28 When he established the clouds above: when he **strengthened the fountains of the deep**:
> 29 When **he gave to the sea his decree, that the waters should not pass his commandment**: when he appointed **the foundations of the earth**:

> **Proverbs 8: (NASB)**
> 27 When He established the heavens, I was there, When **He inscribed a circle** on the face of the deep.
> 28 when he **made firm the skies above**, When **the springs of the deep became fixed**,
> 29 When He **set for the sea its boundary** So that the water would not transgress His command, When He **marked out the foundations of the earth**;

---

24 For instance: https://study.com/academy/lesson/what-is-a-face-in-math.html

The NASB is a far more accurate translation here as the Hebrew word translated merely as "set" in the KJV is *chaqaq*, which actually means ***inscribed***:

◄ 2710. chaqaq ►

Strong's Concordance

chaqaq: to cut in, inscribe, decree
Original Word: חָקַק
Part of Speech: Verb
Transliteration: chaqaq
Phonetic Spelling: (khaw-kak')
Short Definition: inscribed

NAS Exhaustive Concordance

Word Origin

a prim. root

Definition

to cut in, inscribe, decree

NASB Translation

carve (1), commanders (2), decree (1), decreed (1), enact (1), inscribe (2), inscribed (3), lawgiver (1), marked (1), portrayed (1), ruler's (1), ruler's staff (1), scepter (3).

NAS Exhaustive Concordance of the Bible with Hebrew-Aramaic and Greek Dictionaries
Copyright © 1981, 1998 by The Lockman Foundation
All rights reserved Lockman.org

Brown-Driver-Briggs

[חָקַק] **verb cut in, inscribe, decree** (Late Hebrew *id.*, Aramaic חֲקַק, Zinjirli חקק; Phoenician *id. Participle* Hiph`il; Arabic be just, right, obligatory, also *make* or *decide to be just*, etc.; justness, truth, necessity, obligation; Ethiopic adjective *moderate, sufficient*; compare also חקה) —

Qal וְחַקּוֹתָ Ezekiel 4:1; suffix חַקֹּתִיךְ Isaiah 49:16; *Infinitive* suffix בְּחֻקוֹ Proverbs 8:27; בְּחוּקוֹ Proverbs 8:29 (assimilated to חָקְקָ ; בְּשׁוּמוֹ Isaiah 30:8; *Participle* חֹקְקִי Isaiah 22:16 (archaic case ending Ges§ 90. 3 a); plural חֹקְקִים Isaiah 10:1; construct חוֹקְקֵי Judges 5:9 (possibly Po`el = מְחוֹקְקִי with מְ omitted, see Ges§ 52 (2), note 6); *Participle Pass.* plural מְחֻקָּקִים Ezekiel 23:14 (Co מְחֻקִּים); —

1 *cut in*, with בְּ, Isaiah 22:16, of a dwelling-place = tomb, in a rock.

2 *cut in* or *on, upon, engrave, inscribe*, with עַל on roll of a book Isaiah 30:8; representation of city on brick (as in Babylonia) Ezekiel 4:1; images on a wall Ezekiel 23:14; figurative of Zion's walls on palms of ⅄ Isaiah 49:16.

3 *trace, mark out*, a circle, with עַל over the face of deep Proverbs 8:27; with accusative, foundations of earth Proverbs 8:29.

4 of a law, *engrave, inscribe* (on a tablet), figurative for *enact, decree* חֹקְקִים אוֹן חֹקְקִי Isaiah 10:1 (= חוֹקְקֵי יִשְׂרָאֵל עַמִּי כָּתַב poetic = *commanders* (see **Po`el**) Judges 5:9

Thus we find that Isaiah was not writing in a void. Both Job and Solomon had previously laid the foundation of understanding upon which he would *much* later describe the Earth as a circle.[25] Since the circle was ***inscribed*** into something else that had a "face" and was thus flat, it therefore stands to reason the inscribed circle would also be flat—albeit with texture (as in mountains, hills, valleys, etc.). Hence, the Earth is described by Job as:

Job 38:14 It is ***turned as clay to the seal***; and they stand as a garment.

Dr. Robert Schneider, of Berea College, weighs in on this discussion in an on-line article[26] he wrote for *American Scientific Affiliation...*

> **A circle is no more a sphere in Scripture than it is in geometry.**
>
> Looking at these usages together, I am hard put to see how anyone could justify rendering *chûgh* in Isa. 40:22a as "sphericity." The earliest translations of these Scriptures bear this out. In the Septuagint (LXX), the translators render the nominal and verbal forms of *chûgh* in every case with the Greek *gýros* (noun), "circle" or "ring," which they use in Isa. 40:22a, or *gyróo* (verb), "to make or inscribe a circle." *Gýros* does not mean "sphere," and in fact nowhere in any Greek recension of the Hebrew Scriptures will one find the proper word *sphaíra* used in this context at all. The history of the formation of the LXX is largely lost, and we do not know if the Prophets were translated in Alexandria as the Torah was in the third century BC. But if they were and if the translators were familiar with the concept of a spherical earth taught at the Museon of Alexandria, then the center of Greek science, they give no hint of it in their translation of *chûgh*.
>
> — Dr. Robert J. Schneider

Here Dr. Schneider also refutes Dr. Faulkner's notion that the translators of the Septuagint were borrowing from and thus inserting pagan cosmology into their Greek translation of the Hebrew Scriptures. They didn't do it with Isaiah, nor did they do it with Genesis.

Dr. Schneider continues...

> Greek *gýros* turns up in its transliterated form *gyrus*--present in Roman literature as early as Lucretius (mid-first century BC)--in the Latin versions of the Bible as well. St. Jerome (c. 340-420), the early Latin Church's master linguist and Bible translator, began his work on the Old Testament by creating a standard version from the several unreliable Old Latin recensions then in existence, using as a valuable aid Origen's fair copy of the Hexapla which he consulted in the library at Caesarea around 386 AD.28 The Old Latin recensions were based on the LXX and commonly rendered this same portion of Isa. 40:22a as *"qui tenet gyrum terrae."*

---

25 Isaiah 40:22.
26 https://www.asa3.org/ASA/PSCF/2001/PSCF9-01Schneider.html

Later, when he prepared a new version from the Hebrew that would become part of the Vulgate, he kept the Old Latin reading, changing only the verb *tenet*, "dwells," to *sedet*, "sits." And in his Commentary on Isaiah, Jerome, who is regarded by critics today as a competent and careful scholar, specifically rejected the notion that in this verse the prophet is referring to a spherical earth.[27]

Dr. Schneider actually covers the issue of Isaiah 40:22 quite well; more than adequately confirming what I'm saying here when he ridicules modern scholars for torturing the text, grossly manipulating it to mean things it most certainly does not:

> A number of young-earth creationists purport to find in Isa. 40:22 and Job 26:7 evidence that the Bible teaches that the earth is spherical. A detailed analysis of key Hebrew words and their translations in ancient and modern versions shows that there is no substantive evidence and thus no warrant for this claim.

Like Dr. Michael Heiser and his affiliated scholars over at Logos Bible Software,[28] Dr. Schneider is being intellectually honest with the text when he states in no uncertain terms that the Holy Spirit inspired authors of Scripture did *not* have the same cosmological world view we have today. Likewise speaking against modern Creationists, Schneider writes:

> While the writers assert that the Hebrew *khug*--I shall use *chûgh*--of Isa. 40:22a means "sphericity," they provide no lexicological support. They also assume that Job 26:7 refers to "empty space," that is, the modern concept of physical, astronomical space. Some proponents are primarily concerned with refuting the "canard" (Sarfati) that the Bible teaches a flat earth. They inform their readers that the notion of a spherical earth was common among early and medieval Christian thinkers. Yet they do not make the case that these thinkers took the notion of a spherical earth from the Bible. In supporting their interpretations, they also appeal to the extraterrestrial perspectives of an astronaut (Sarfati) or God (Eastman).
>
> While I find these arguments either unsubstantiated or irrelevant (*e.g.*, it is what Isaiah saw, not Armstrong, that counts), as a teacher, I take them seriously.[29]

Addressing also the issue of the Hebrew word *raqa*, which is the root of *raqiya* (firmament), Dr. Schneider writes:

> The prophet who uttered the words of 40:22 is the same prophet who proclaimed that Yahweh is the Creator who "spread out the earth" (42:5; 44:24). The Hebrew verb in both passages is *raqa'*, which means "to stretch out, spread out or abroad,

---

27 Ibid.

28 See Michael Heiser's on-line presentation: *Genesis & Creation - Class 3 of 4 - September 29, 2010:* https://vimeo.com/16031751 and his follow-up blog *Interpreting Genesis 1: Who's the Literalist Now?* at: http://drmsh.com/interpreting-genesis-1-literalist . Compare also the Logos Bible Software entry for *Ancient Hebrew Conception of the Universe*.

29 https://www.asa3.org/ASA/PSCF/2001/PSCF9-01Schneider.html

cover over" and, according to Theodore Gaster, "to flatten out." Among his people in the exile community in Babylon, looking out over the enormous desert expanse that reached from horizon to horizon, it is not surprising that this prophet would describe God as "flattening out" the land. These other expressions also militate against the notion that the prophet was implying a spherical earth in 40:22a, and they act as a check against focusing upon one verse and reading it outside the larger context of this prophet's other inspired oracles of creation and salvation.[30]

Simply put, I like to word it this way:

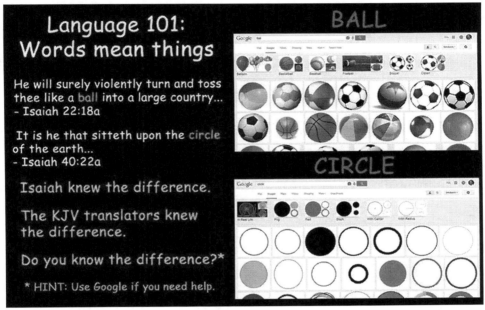

Over this *circle* is a hard structure known as the firmament, within which are the sun, moon and stars... and below them birds flying in the "open face of the firmament." But Dr. Sungenis seems to get tripped up by this phrase. As a devout Roman Catholic, perhaps he should just read his Douay-Rheims Bible, which renders it:

> **Genesis 1:20** God also said: Let the waters bring forth the creeping creature having life, and the fowl that may fly over the earth **<u>under</u> the firmament** of heaven.

The KJV and many others render it as "in the open firmament of heaven" (or something similar) because the Hebrew word used here is *paneh* (face), which is preceded by the preposition *al* (across). The word *paneh* is first used in Genesis 1:2 when "darkness was upon the *face* of the deep." The second time it is used is in the same verse where "the Spirit of God moved upon the *face* of the waters." In verse 20, we have the third occurrence of the word. But here, for some reason, it is translated as "open" referring to the firmament. With the precedence of the other two occurrences of this same word

---

30 Ibid.

in place however, it seems to me it should have been more consistently translated as the birds moving "across the face of the firmament" or in other words, contextually speaking, simply *in front of* it, which from the Earth-facing side of the firmament would naturally have to be considered *below*[31] or *under* it just as the Douay-Rheims has rendered this verse. But what Dr. Sungenis seems to miss is that the sun, moon and stars are *also* on this side of the structure, not somewhere at the "back of the firmament" as he suggests.[32]

In the NASB, the concordance has *paneh* listed as being translated "before" 868 times, as "face" 259 times, as "presence" 131 times, and as "front" 86 times.[33] Considering the context of the preceding events (*i.e.* the establishment of the firmament on Day 2, which was made to separate the waters above from the waters below, and within which the sun, moon and stars were placed on Day 4) it therefore only seems logical to consider the birds to likewise be flying *within*—thus, before/in the face/presence/front of—this hard, solid structure. Indeed, with such a "vaulted dome" overhead, and attached to the Earth,[34] this would be the only way the birds *could* fly. As soon as they left the ground, the *only* direction they could go in would be *toward* the firmament.

This understanding is also consistent with another passage where we have both *al* and *paneh* together meaning *toward* the direction of something. The KJV has the account of Abraham observing the aftermath of the destruction of Sodom and Gomorrah rendered as:

> **Genesis 19:28** And he looked **toward** Sodom and Gomorrah, and **toward** all the land of the plain, and beheld, and, lo, the smoke of the country went up as the smoke of a furnace.

But Young's Literal Translation follows... well, the more *literal* interpretation, stating that Abraham "looketh **on the face of** Sodom and Gomorrah, and **on all the face of** the land" as seen in the Interlinear on BibleHub.com:

3603 [e]	776 [e]	6440 [e]	3605 [e]	5921 [e]	6017 [e]	5467 [e]	6440 [e]	5921 [e]	8259 [e]
ak·kik·kār;	'e·reṣ	pa·nê	kāl-	wə·'al-	wa·'ă·mō·rāh,	sə·ḏōm	pa·nê	'al-	way·yaš·qêp̄,
הַכִּכָּר	אֶרֶץ	פְּנֵי	כָּל־	וְעַל־	וַעֲמֹרָה	סְדֹם	פְּנֵי	עַל־	וַיַּשְׁקֵף 28
of the plain	the land		all	and toward	and Gomorrah	Sodom	the face-of	toward	And he looked
Art | N-fs	N-fsc	N-cpc	N-msc	Conj-w | Prep	Conj-w | N-proper-fs	N-proper-fs	N-cpc	Prep	Conj-w | V-Hifil-ConsecImperf-3ms

But in case you still want to argue along with Dr. Robert Sungenis, Dr. Danny Faulkner, Dr. Kent Hovind, Dr. Douglas Hamp and a host of other modern "scholars" who would rather think of the firmament in terms of air, gas and the vacuum of space, describing it merely as an "expanse," the Holy Spirit saw fit to give us two witnesses from Scripture to refute this notion. Once again, I present the words of Job and Solomon:

---

31 The Greek reads, *kai peteina petomena epi ts gs kata to stereoma tou ouranou*, which means "and winged creatures flying upon the earth **below** the firmament of the heavens!" See the comparative entry for Gen. 1:20 here: http://www.bayithamashiyach.com/Genesis_1.pdf .

32 See again the Sungenis quote I gave in the paragraph at the top of page 31.

33 https://biblehub.com/hebrew/6440.htm

34 Amos 9:6.

Job 37:18 (KJV) Hast thou with him *spread out the sky, which is strong, and as a molten looking glass*?

Job 37:18 (ESV) Can you, like him, *spread out the skies, <u>hard</u> as a cast metal mirror*?

Proverbs 8: (KJV)
28 When he *established the clouds above*: when he strengthened the fountains of the deep:

Proverbs 8: (ESV)
28 when he *<u>made firm</u> the skies above*, when he established the fountains of the deep,

The Hebrew word translated by the ESV as "made firm" is *amets*, Strong's #553, which means *"confirm, be courageous, of good courage, steadfastly minded, strong, stronger; to establish, fortify, make firm, harden."* The Greek word used here is ἰσχυρὰ which likewise means *"strong."* Although the KJV curiously renders Proverbs 8:28 as "When he *established the <u>clouds</u>* above...," it translated the same Hebrew word *shachaq* (used here as "clouds") as "sky" in Job 37:18 (and elsewhere). In fact, both Strong's and the NAS Exhaustive Concordance have *shachaq* as "skies" for many of the 21 times it is translated.[35] The KJV even translates it as "heaven" twice.[36] Thus, we have a direct correlation between these two passages, wherein the firmament/sky/heaven above is described as being hard/strong/firm. Therefor, you can **not** say the firmament equates to air/gas/vacuum of space!

Honestly, the firmament is what sealed the deal (pardon the pun) for me. Unquestionably, the structure was considered to be hard (Job 37:18), firm (Proverbs 8:28), supporting the waters above (Genesis 1:6-8; Psalm 148:4), attached to the Earth (Amos 9:6), within which YHWH placed the sun, moon and stars (Genesis 1:14-19; Psalm 19:1-6) and upon which His throne sits (Ezekiel 1:26; Isaiah 66:1). Clearly, this is a *very* important issue to YHWH (Psalm 19:1) and therefore it should be for us as well.

Once you come to this conclusion, frankly, the only model that accommodates every aspect of the firmament is the circular, enclosed world model. The only way around this is to grossly misrepresent the Scriptures, yanking the true meanings of the words used out of context, while fantasizing about definitions for those words, which are not even remotely supported by the text (or the historical contexts in which the Scriptures were written).

One thing is certain: whether we're talking about the pre-Flood world known to Enoch, or the post-Flood world of the Old and New Testaments, *no one* in Biblical times imagined a spinning, globular Earth, whirling around a fireball, which is itself hurling through the vacuum of space at a half-million miles per hour. There's *nothing whatsoever* in the "poetic language" employed by the use of simile that could ever paint such a picture in

---

35 https://biblehub.com/hebrew/7834.htm
36 See Palm 89:6 and 89:37.

anyone's mind... until today. This is because we are placing our own personal bias unto the text. But as professor John Walton of Wheaton College once said...

> *"We can't do that. We have to read it the way the Israelites meant it. You cannot read the text more seriously - more literally - than to read it according to what that ancient author meant to say."*
>
> * * *
>
> *"We're not free to read new meanings into those text. On what authority would we do that?"*[37]

The answer is simple: we have *no* authority to do that. The Holy Spirit inspired authors of Scripture wrote what they wrote. We must either choose to accept or reject it. I have chosen to simply accept what it says. There is a great deal more I'd like to write about concerning the numerous verses of Scripture, which describe the shape and nature of this Earth and its place in the cosmos, but that will have to wait for another publication (this Introduction has already grown longer than originally intended). For now, the following summary will have to suffice.

From Genesis to Revelation, the Earth is consistently described by Holy Spirit inspired authors as:

- Fixed and not moving (spinning, orbiting, etc)
- Circular, with edges/corners/pillars/foundations, etc.
- Under a dome, within which the sun, moon and stars were placed on Day 4

We live in a self-contained, three-tiered system consisting of Heaven, Earth, and an Underworld according to: Job 1:7-8; 2:2-3; 37:12; 38:30-34; Gen. 28:12-17; Ex. 20:4; Num. 16:31-33; Deut. 5:8; 1 Sam. 28:13-14; 1 Chron. 29:11; 2 Chron. 6:4; Psa. 46:8-10; 113:6; 119:19; Isa. 14:9-11; 51:13-14; Joel 2:30; Amos 9:2; Luke 10:15; 16:19-31; Acts 2:19; Phil. 2:10; 1 Pet. 3:18-20; 2 Pet. 2:4-5; Jude 6; Rev. 5:3, 13; 9:1-11; 20:14 (see also: 2 Esdr. 4:7,8; 1 Enoch 89; Pesachim 94b).

There is a solid firmament (dome/vault) over us according to: Job 22:14; 37:18; Gen. 1:6-8, 20; Ex. 24:10; Psa. 104:2; Prov. 8:27-28; Isa. 40:21-22; 45:12; 66:1; Jer. 10:12; 51:15; Ezek. 1:22-26; Amos 9:6 (see also: 2 Apoc. Baruch 21:4; Gen. Rabbah 4.5.2; Josephus Antiquities 1:30).

YHWH's throne sits above the firmament (and waters) according to: Job 9:8; 22:14; 37:18; Deut. 26:15; Psa. 11:4; 29:3, 10; 33:13; 103:19; 104:2-3; 148:4; Isa. 40:21-22; 66:1; Jer. 10:12-13; Ezek 1:22-28; 28:2; Amos 9:6 (see also: 2 Esdr. 4:7-8).

There are "floodgates" and "windows" in the firmament according to: Gen. 7:11; 8:2; 2 Kings 7:2-19; Mal. 3:10; (see also: 1 Enoch 89).

---

37 See my commentary on pages 320-321 for more on Dr. John Walton and how we should read the Bible.

The sun, moon and stars are in the firmament (and all the stars are going to fall to Earth) according to: Gen. 1:14-18; Psa. 19:4-6; Isa. 34:4; Dan. 8:10; Matt. 24:29; Mark 13:25; 2 Peter 3:10; Rev. 6:13-14; 9:1; 12:4.

The Bible says the Earth is inscribed in a circular (flat) fashion into something with four corners and surrounded by water according to the following Scriptures: Job 11:9; 26:10-11; 37:3; 38:12-18; Gen. 1:1-9; 49:25; Psa. 24:1-2; 72:8; 136:6; Prov. 8:27-29; Isa. 11:12; 13:5; 40:22; 41:8-9; 44:24; Ezek. 7:2; Dan. 4:10-11, Zech. 9:10; Matt. 4:8; 24:31; Rev. 7:1; 20:8.

According to the following, the Earth is a geocentric, stationary world set on pillars: Job 26:11; 38:4-6; Josh. 10:13; Psa. 19:4-6; 75:3; 104:5; Prov. 8:29; Ecc. 1:5; 1 Sam. 2:8; 2 Sam. 22:8; Joel 2:10; Zech. 12:1 (see also: Targum Job 26:7).

There are probably a lot of other references. The more I look into this subject from a Biblical perspective, the more I continue to find. And I'm sorry, but the weight of this Scriptural evidence far outweighs the *two* verses[38] others attempt to use in a lame defense of the globe. When I finally came to this realization, I could do nothing more than finally yield to the authority of Scripture and say, *"Let God be true and every man a liar."*

What inspires me about the authors in this compilation work is that they did too. And long before you and I even thought about looking into any of this, these authors were taking a stand against the "science" of their day. This science—*falsely so called*—was based on the relatively new ideas of people like Lyell, Darwin, Huxley and others who were formulating their theories based on bogus assumptions of extreme durations of time, random chance and just about everything antithetical to Scripture that can be imagined since the days of Copernicus (or Pythagoras for that matter).

HOW I FIRST LEARNED ABOUT THESE AUTHORS

Shortly after my encounter with Mark Sargent, I stumbled upon various YouTube videos by a modern flat Earth pioneer named Eric Dubay,[39] along with the few others who were producing content at that time. Now, let me just pause here a moment and say that I do *not* agree with everything these guys say or believe. I'm very much a *"chew the meat and toss the bones"* kind of guy when it comes to receiving information from people. So, please don't imagine that I'm in lockstep agreement with anyone I mention here— especially as it pertains to issues of faith and doctrine. But when it comes to the issue of flat Earth, I found several people to be quite interesting to listen to, and Eric was the most articulate of all of them on this subject.

I soon realized he was quoting from a variety of texts, including the ones presented here in this volume. I was immediately intrigued and decided to look up the names he was

---

38 Isaiah 40:22 and Job 26:7.
39 https://www.youtube.com/c/ericdubay

mentioning, order the books and begin reading their writings for myself. Now, I'd like to present them here for your consideration as well.

So, who are these people and why should we listen to them?

Samuel Birley Rowbotham (1816–1884) was an English inventor and author who wrote *Zetetic Astronomy: Earth Not a Globe* under the pseudonym "Parallax".[40] His work was based on his decade-long studies of Earth and it was originally published as a 16-page pamphlet (1849), which he later expanded into a 430-page book (1881).

Rowbotham's method, which he called *Zetetic Astronomy*, models the Earth as an enclosed plane centered at the North Pole and bounded along its perimeter by a wall of ice, with the Sun, Moon, planets, and stars moving only several hundred miles above the surface of Earth.

He was a very gifted and passionate public speaker and a man on a mission. In chapter two of her book, *Flat Earth: History of an Infamous Idea*, Christine Garwood describes how and why he took on the pseudonym "Parallax."

> His methodology was an intellectually and morally improving pastime, the zetetics were free men and women, unrestrained by dogma and willing to be guided first and foremost by facts. They were the true objective investigators, the ideal practitioners of science whose work would lead to the salvation and redemption of mankind. For this reason, Parallax declared, 'Bigots may howl; tyrants may frown; hypocrites may sneer; the coward may quail; the indifferent may marvel but the champion of truth, armed in honesty of purpose, pursues the festal path, invulnerable and victorious.' This mythological image of the zetetic 'truth-seeker,' the alternative hero of Baconian science, was to become central to Parallax's work. With such laudable sentiments underpinning his philosophy, he decided he needed a new identity to reflect his alternative perspective on knowledge and the shape of the earth. To be truly memorable, the pseudonym should also relate to astronomy, and for this reason Samuel Birley Rowbotham decided that he would present himself to the world as 'Parallax' (meaning the apparent change in the position of an object when viewed from two different points). The public phase of his campaign was about to begin.[41]

---

40 Rowbotham went by a number of pseudonyms, including "Dr. Birley" (his middle name) and "Dr. Samuel B. Rowbotham. Apparently, according to *Earth Not A Globe Review No. 4*, October 1893, p. 14, [as cited in a footnote by Garwood on p. 385 of *Flat Earth*], on New Years Eve 1884, he was laid to rest as "Samuel Birley Rowbotham M.D., Ph.D.," but I have yet to see any information detailing where he went to school or what qualified him to legitimately have those credentialed letters after his name.

41 Christine Garwood, Flat Earth: History of an Infamous Idea, ©2007 Pan Macmillian p. 43.

And what a public campaign it was! From what I've read, it would seem "Parallax" took a fair part of the United Kingdom by storm during the mid-to-late 19th century. And he did so at a time when the authority of the Bible was being seriously undermined by the "science" (falsely so called) of his day. Again, this was at a time when the works of Charles Lyell and Charles Darwin were essentially relegating the formerly held, literal interpretation of authoritative Scripture to the realms of poetic allegory at best or fairy tales at worst. I can only imagine what he would think/do if were he alive in our day.

In the United States, Rowbotham's ideas were taken up by the Christian Catholic Apostolic Church[42] and promoted widely on their radio station. His work was also continued in the United States by a man named, William Carpenter.

William M. Carpenter (1830–1896) was a printer and stenographer originally from Greenwich, England. As a supporter of Rowbotham, he published *Theoretical Astronomy Examined and Exposed — Proving the Earth not a Globe* in eight parts from 1864 under the name *Common Sense*. He later emigrated to Baltimore where he published *100 Proofs That The Earth Is Not A Globe* in 1885 (which I've included in this work), within which it appears his primary opponent, was Richard Anthony Proctor, a very prominent 19th century English astronomer.

In *Testing the Globe: A Zetetic Investigation Volume II*, we will look at the works of David Wardlaw Scott, Frederick Emil Pasche and Gerrard Hickson. I initially wanted to include them with this volume, but the page count grew far too large. It was beginning to look like we were publishing an unabridged dictionary or the phone book for a major metropolitan area. I didn't want to intimidate people, so we made the decision to move their works into a second volume.

No doubt, as you look into the biographies of each of these men, some of you may begin wondering what possible credentials do *any* of them have for so boldly challenging the *status quo* of well established and accepted science? In what fields of science were they experts? What sort of academic degrees did they hold? As far as I can tell, none of these men held any formal degrees in science. But is this a handicap or a benefit? The reader will have to decide for themselves. Perhaps in consideration of this, it is best we start by looking at how Webster defines a "scientist":

---

42 Christ Community Church in Zion, Illinois, formerly the Christian Catholic Church or Christian Catholic Apostolic Church, is an evangelical non-denominational church founded in 1896 by John Alexander Dowie. The city of Zion was founded by Dowie as a religious community to establish a society on the principles of the Kingdom of God. For more, see: https://en.wikipedia.org/wiki/Christ_Community_Church

scientist noun

sci·en·tist | \ˈsī-ən-tist 🔊 \

Definition of *Scientist*

1   : a person learned in <u>science</u> and especially natural science : a <u>scientific</u> investigator

I see nothing in the definition of a "scientist" that demands a formal education, nor any degrees from formal academic institutions. I see merely the attributes of a person who learns through investigation. Now what exactly is science? Again, Webster comes to our aid with the following definition:

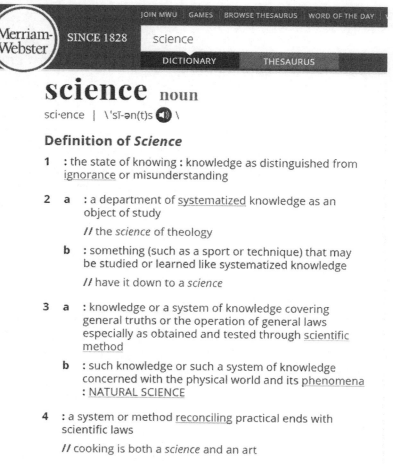

science noun

sci·ence | \ˈsī-ən(t)s 🔊 \

Definition of *Science*

1   : the state of knowing : knowledge as distinguished from <u>ignorance</u> or misunderstanding

2   a   : a department of <u>systematized</u> knowledge as an object of study

   // the *science* of theology

    b   : something (such as a sport or technique) that may be studied or learned like systematized knowledge

   // have it down to a *science*

3   a   : knowledge or a system of knowledge covering general truths or the operation of general laws especially as obtained and tested through <u>scientific method</u>

    b   : such knowledge or such a system of knowledge concerned with the physical world and its <u>phenomena</u> : <u>NATURAL SCIENCE</u>

4   : a system or method <u>reconciling</u> practical ends with scientific laws

   // cooking is both a *science* and an art

The "Scientific Method" is defined as "principles and procedures for the systematic pursuit of knowledge involving the recognition and formulation of a problem, the collection of data through observation and experiment, and the formulation and testing of hypothesis."[43] This concept is a more developed form of inquiry based on a system often credited to Francis Bacon known as the "Baconian Method", which is defined by the Encyclopedia Britannica as:

> **Baconian method**, methodical observation of facts as a means of studying and interpreting natural phenomena. This essentially empirical method was formulated early in the 17th century by Francis Bacon, an English philosopher, as a scientific substitute for the prevailing systems of thought, which, to his mind, **<u>relied all to often on fanciful guessing and the mere citing of authorities to establish truths of science.</u>** After first dismissing all prejudices and preconceptions, Bacon's method, as explained in *Novum Organum* (1620; *"New Instrument"*), consisted of three main steps:
>
> - First, a description of facts;
> - Second, a tabulation, or classification, of those facts into three categories—instances of the presence of the characteristic under investigation, instances of its absence, or instances of its presence in varying degrees;
> - Third, the rejection of whatever appears, in the light of these tables, not to be connected with the phenomenon under investigation and the determination of what is connected with it.
>
> Bacon may be credited with recognizing, in their essence, the method of agreement, the joint method, and the method of concomitant variations. His emphasis on the exhaustive cataloguing of facts, however, has since been replaced as a scientific method, for it provided no means of bringing investigation to an end or of insightful delimitation of the problem by creative use of hypotheses.[44]

I added the bold, underline to the definition above in order to highlight what has become an epidemic in our day, wherein "science" has truly been replaced by "scientism," which at its core is no different than a religious belief system. This is perhaps best illustrated in the documentary *Expelled: No Intelligence Allowed* hosted by Ben Stein (pictured right). The film shows how real science is often pushed under the carpet and people who buck the *status quo* (Darwinian) narrative are marginalized, fired, and persecuted in various ways—even when they do legitimate science, finding legitimate answers

43 https://www.merriam-webster.com/dictionary/scientific%20method
44 https://www.britannica.com/science/Baconian-method

to legitimate questions. If those answers contradict the prevailing belief system, said scientists are "expelled." This, therefor, is not science. It is an agenda-based religious belief system.

The Encyclopedia Britannica defines the Scientific Method as:

> **Scientific method**, mathematical and experimental technique employed in the sciences; more specifically, technique used in the construction and testing of a scientific hypothesis[45].

> The scientific method is critical to the development of scientific theories, which explain empirical (experiential) laws in a scientifically rational manner. In a typical application of the scientific method, a researcher develops a hypothesis, tests it through various means, and then modifies the hypothesis on the basis of the outcome of the tests and experiments. The modified hypothesis is then retested, further modified, and tested again, until it becomes consistent with observed phenomena and testing outcomes. In this way, hypotheses serve as tools by which scientists gather data. From that data and the many different scientific investigations undertaken to explore hypotheses, scientists are able to develop broad general explanations, or scientific theories.

Scientific theories are described by the Encyclopedia Britannica as:

> **Scientific theory,** systematic ideational structure of broad scope, conceived by the human imagination, that encompasses a family of empirical (experiential) laws regarding regularities existing in objects and events, both observed and posited. A scientific theory is a structure suggested by these laws and is devised to explain them in a scientifically rational manner.

> In attempting to explain objects and events, the scientist employs (1) careful observation or experiments, (2) reports of regularities, and (3) systematic explanatory schemes (theories). The statements of regularities, if accurate, may be taken as empirical laws expressing continuing relationships among the objects or characteristics observed. Thus, when empirical laws are able to satisfy curiosity by uncovering an orderliness in the behaviour of objects or events, the scientist may advance a systematic scheme, or scientific theory, to provide an accepted explanation of why these laws obtain.

> Empirical laws and scientific theories differ in several ways. In a law, reasonably clear observational rules are available for determining the meaning of each of its terms; thus, a law can be tested by carefully observing the objects and properties referred to by these terms. Indeed, they are initially formulated by generalizing

---

45 See: https://www.britannica.com/science/scientific-hypothesis

or schematizing from observed relationships. In the case of scientific theories, however, some of the terms commonly refer to objects or events that are not observed. Thus, it is evident that **theories are imaginative constructions of the human mind**—the results of philosophical and aesthetic judgments as well as of observation—for they are only suggested by observational information rather than inductively generalized from it. Moreover, **theories cannot ordinarily be tested and accepted on the same grounds as laws.** Thus, whereas an empirical law expresses a unifying relationship among a small selection of observables, scientific theories have much greater scope, explaining a variety of such laws and predicting others as yet undiscovered. [bold emphasis mine]

A theory may be characterized as a postulational system (a set of premises) from which empirical laws are deducible as theorems. Thus, it can have an abstract logical form, with axioms, formation rules, and rules for drawing deductions from the axioms as well as definitions for empirically interpreting its symbols. In practice, however, theories are seldom structured so carefully.

Nikola Tesla was a contemporary of Rowbotham, Carpenter, Scott, Pasche and Hickson. Whatever his views were regarding the shape and nature of the Earth and its place in the cosmos, as the years progressed toward the mid-twentieth century, it is clear he shared similar views with them concerning the problems manifesting in the "science" of their day, which eventually prompted him to say:

> *"Today's scientists have substituted mathematics for experiments, and they wander off through equation after equation, and eventually build a structure which has no relation to reality."*

Today, especially in the field of cosmology, "science" has turned into a hodge-podge of *ad hoc* theories and mathematical equations used to justify nearly anything a "theoretical physicist" wants to promote. In short, real science, which used to be done in the field or in a laboratory, with practical experimentation, that was both observable and repeatable is now largely being replaced by scribbled equations on chalk boards and computer monitors.

The men whose works are featured in this book preferred more of a "zetetic" form of science, which means to proceed by inquiry, generally accompanied by hands-on observation and experimentation. But some argue that "the term refers to flipping the scientific method on its head and deriving one's observations from testing, with no regards to any hypothesis"[46] as if that's a bad thing. From what I've read, I don't see the authors presented here as believing there is anything wrong with coming up with hypotheses first. That said, they were not content to just come up with interesting ideas, justified by mathematical equations. Rather, they were eager to get out and test what they observed through actual experimentation in order to arrive at their conclusions.

---

46 https://rationalwiki.org/wiki/Zetetic

Circling back around to the definitions of a scientist doing real science, I find more "credibility" in the likes of Rowbotham, Carpenter, Scott, Pasche and Hickson than I do with the likes of Einstein, Sagan, Tyson, Kraus and Kaku who seem to do the bulk of their work on chalkboards and computer screens. Oh, but the scientist of today has that expensive, pretty piece of paper hanging on their "I love me wall" and they have letters after their name. So, we should listen to them, right? Since when is this a measure of "credibility"? And why is it that we are so prone to not pay any attention to those who lack the letters and pretty pieces of expensive paper? Is a college degree and the words "doctor" or "professor" before one's name really necessary? Webster's Dictionary does not indicate this is so. Nor does history. In fact, here is a very short list of famous, notable people who dropped out of school at early ages:

- **George Washington** was not just the first U.S. president, but he is regarded by many as one of the greatest. He was also a respected military general and yet he didn't even have a bachelor's degree in college (though he did earn a surveyor's license from the College of William & Mary in Virginia).

- **Benjamin Franklin** dropped out of school at age ten, yet he became a very noteworthy politician, diplomat, published author, printer, scientist, inventor and one of the founding fathers of our nation, cosigning the Declaration of Independence.

- **Andrew Jackson** had no formal education, yet he went on to become a successful judge, attorney, military general, congressman and U.S. president.

- **Abraham Lincoln** left school at age 12, yet he managed to teach himself trigonometry and how to become a lawyer. He eventually became one of our most famous U.S. presidents.

- **Thomas Edison** is probably the most famous and productive inventor of all time, with more than 1,000 patents in his name. He became a multimillionaire and won a Congressional Gold Medal.

- **John D. Rockefeller** dropped out of high school two months before graduation. Yet he went on to found Standard Oil Company and became history's first recorded billionaire.

- **George Eastman** dropped out of high school and went on to become the multimillionaire inventor and founder of Kodak.

- **Albert Einstein** originally dropped out of high school at age 15, but eventually got his diploma after failing his entrance exam the first time. Yet somehow he managed to be recognized all over the world as a Nobel Prize-winning physicist, whose name has become synonymous with extreme intelligence.

- **Walt Disney** dropped out of high school at age 16, yet somehow managed to build an empire, with his own "kingdom" and received the Presidential Medal of Freedom.

- **Henry Ford** never attended college, but at age 16 he apprenticed as a machinist and later his first success came with the Model T car, which led to him becoming the billionaire founder of Ford Motor Company.

- **Bill Gates** dropped out of Harvard his junior year to co-found Microsoft and become one of the wealthiest people in the world.

- **Steve Jobs** only attended one semester of college before dropping out and later co-founding Apple Computers (with **Steve Wozniak** who also did not complete college), which has become known as one of the most innovative companies in the world. He was also the co-founder and CEO of Pixar and in 2007 was recognized by Fortune Magazine as the "most powerful businessman."

- **Michael Dell** dropped out of college his freshman year at age 19, but went on to found Dell Technologies and is now a multi-billionaire.

- **Sir Richard Branson** suffers from dyslexia and dropped out of school at age 16, yet managed to become a self-made billionaire businessman, having founded Virgin Atlantic Airways, Virgin Records, Virgin Mobile and more.

There are of course many, many others[47]—some famous and some no one has ever heard of before. Granted, looking at the above list of characters, we may see a wide variety of reasons for why they "dropped out of school." We may also see other contributing factors to their success (like belonging to secret societies for instance). This is not to say formal education is all bad. However, clearly, history has shown it is *not* required as a means of determining success or even intellect. A person can still be an absolutely brilliant "drop out." In fact, often, someone with a very high IQ is simply too bored to continue subjecting themselves to the torture of the modern education system. They have no need of expensive, pretty pieces of paper and letters after their name. They know they're smart and have no need to impress others. They'd rather just get out and do stuff that will change the world. In this regard, perhaps it is best summed up by a quote from a very successful teenage entrepreneur:

"No one has ever changed the world by doing what the world has told them to do."
— Eddy Zhong[48]

---

[47] See for instance: https://moneysmartfamily.com/blog/successful-college-drop-outs/ or https://www.thefamouspeople.com/school-dropouts.php among other similar websites.

[48] Eddy Zhong is an aspiring young, technology entrepreneur and the founder of Blanc, a smart-watch company based in Cambridge, Massachusetts. His ideas have been featured in numerous publications and he is passionate about empowering youth to think differently. Eddy is the founder of Leangap, a summer program that helps high school students start their own companies. He started his first very successful technology company at age 16. See *How School Makes Kids Less Intelligent*: https://youtu.be/2Yt6raj-S1M

CONSIDER ALSO THE FOLLOWING VIDEOS:

10 SUCCESSFUL People Who Dropped OUT of School

The Most Successful People Explain Why a College Degree is USELESS

I JUST SUED THE SCHOOL SYSTEM!

I am therefor, in no way deterred by any *perceived* lack of academic "credentials" in people like Rowbotham, Carpenter and the others which will be featured in this series. True wisdom comes from above (*cf.* Proverbs 8; James 3:17). The fact they take Scripture literally and were willing to take a stand on what it says, while also backing up their views with actual investigation and experimentation speaks volumes to me. I hope as you read this book, it will for you as well.

Christine Garwood has written a very well-researched book (which I mentioned earlier) titled, *"Flat Earth: The History of an Infamous Idea"*.[49] While it seems quite clear that she does *not* believe the Earth is flat herself, her book stands out as a reasonably fair representation of those who do. As such, I consider it to be part of the required reading for anyone seeking to understand this topic and the players involved—particularly in the 19th and 20th centuries. I confess, as I have just recently purchased the book, I have only read through the first few chapters and have skimmed the rest, pausing numerous times to read and highlight a number of pages and taking time to read the End Notes. I fully intend to finish reading it in its entirety though because coming in at 396 pages worth of content (plus End Notes, Bibliography and an Index extending the page count to 436), it is abundantly clear that she has done a considerable amount of research. Thus, I feel she more than deserves a spot in this discussion.

In her Prologue, she writes about what she calls, "The Columbus Blunder" and goes on to detail how writers like Francesco Petrarch, Washington Irving, John William Draper, Andrew Dickson White, Emma Miller Bolenius and many others have created and perpetuated the "myth" that Columbus successfully argued against those who (according to the popular tale) firmly believed the Earth was flat. Thus she says, "the Columbus story invented by Washington Irving was translated into hard 'fact'. In educational terms the damage was done." She then shows us how pop-culture recycled the myth in a wide variety of publications and other mediums until it has become embedded in our collective consciousness as truth. She concludes her Prologue (on page 14) with:

> Interlinked with images of warfare and the 'Dark Ages', such stories are a hall of mirrors, a series of grotesque and distorted reflections of the not-so-distant past. Yet, like so many illusions, the image of dark days when superstitious people believed the earth was flat is intriguing, and this is one of the reasons why it remains a lingering assumption in the popular mind. The myth is all too convenient: the flat-earth idea has become shorthand for 'Dark Age' stupidity, a handy one-liner to capture the days of yore before the Enlightenment era of progress and science. For the purpose of history, this is a straight-forward narrative, one-dimensional and over-simplified but easy to digest, and the idea has more human appeal as a way of conceptualizing science and its role in historical advance. While the earth is flat for medieval people, we can assume a sense of superiority and security in our progress from an ignorant and deluded age. Just as we know our true position

---

49 *Flat Earth: The History of an Infamous Idea* by Christine Garwood, © 2007, Pan Macmillan.

on the surface of the world, we know our true place in the history of knowledge. From religion to reason, superstition to science, these are deep waters, yet they run through the assumption that flat-earth belief was commonplace before Columbus successfully avoided sailing off the edge of the world. Under these circumstances, it is somewhat ironic that, beneath these false images of science and history, flat-earth belief has a chronology far stranger than all the inventions.

And this brings us to *Zetetic Astronomy* by Dr. Samuel B. Rowbotham. There may have been others before him and/or contemporary with him, but his work truly stands out as the foundation for the modern flat Earth movement. So it seems fitting to start here. But before we dive into his book, I wish to address once again the issue of "credibility" and academic credentials. Did he really have a doctorate degree? I have yet to find evidence that he did. From what I've read, he simply started referring to himself by his middle name and attaching the title of "Dr." before it, thus becoming Dr. Birley. As such, he apparently started marketing and administering various tonics, promising to cure or in some way aid in the relief of a wide variety of ailments.[50] So, was he just some sort of scam artist or what?

In Chapter Two of her book, Garwood gives us a hint as to the possible motivations Parallax may have had for doing what he did:

> Meanwhile, a flat-earth campaign had another more obvious appeal. Ideas about the earth were changing rapidly, and the apparent divergence between a literal interpretation of Genesis and scientific findings, especially from the new field of geology, was contentious. This was especially the case in the wake of Lyell's *Principles of Geology* (1833) and Edinburgh's publisher Robert Chamber's widely read Ve*stiges of the Natural History of Creation*, which he published anonymously in 1844. Influenced by phrenology, Chambers argued for the progressive 'development' (evolution) of species including humankind, although he was careful to distance himself from the radical French evolutionary thinker Jean-Baptiste Lamarck by emphasizing that this process was divinely guided by laws that God had deliberately built into nature. Nevertheless, the 'development' thesis posed problems for those who interpreted Genesis literally: one churchman went so far as to lambast *Vestiges* as a 'filthy abortion' capable of corrupting the nation's 'glorious maidens and matrons'.[51] Within this context, one suspects that Parallax saw the potential to feed off controversies about science and the Bible and to exploit popular scientific culture in a single campaign. By teaching that the earth was flat, and emphasizing the scriptural basis of the idea, he could confirm the Bible as the ultimate authority on the earth and its creation, a critical and controversial point. By claiming to defend the Bible against science, and by

---

50 For instance, in *Flat Earth: The History of an Infamous Idea*, Christine Garwood cites a number of sources, which claim Rowbotham was essentially just a con-man, selling snake oil-style "remedies" and doing anything for a buck.
51 Garwood endnote # 12 of Chapter Two says: "See J. Secord, *A Victorian Sensation*".

setting the two in irresolvable conflict, he was bound to attract an audience willing to pay to hear such ideas. In addition, his emphasis on democratic fact-finding could potentially attract self-educated working men, while experimental proofs would gain authority and credibility for his cause. So, under a banner of power to the people and to the Bible, Parallax sought to mobilize public support.[52]

In the next paragraph however, she throws doubt on this, stating, "Questions remain about whether Parallax truly believed his own theory..." and she goes on to say that "it appeared that he had found his niche: the use of arch-debating skills developed in the most intimidating circumstances to test the boundaries of science and popular belief."

Was Samuel "Parallax" Rowbotham just a gifted, manipulative charlatan who did not really believe what he was saying and who was only "doing it for the money?" as some suspect? What's funny about this is I have often received the same criticism. In this regard, let me just say, you would have to be *quite insane* to even remotely entertain the notion that flat Earth is the topic to get into for fame and fortune. Quite the contrary. This topic will ruin your life. The only "fame" you will get for endorsing this topic is the growing number of people making fun of you, ridiculing, mocking and calling you names (and often on a very public scale too). You immediately become the butt of jokes and your "credibility" goes out the window. As such, how much money do you really think you are going to make? Sorry. No. There are ***far better*** ways to gain fame and fortune if that is your goal. As for me, endorsing this subject nearly put my family into bankruptcy. And I can tell you for a fact, having hundreds or even thousands of people ridicule you every day is no fun. Indeed, it's quite depressing. To the point where just waking up again each morning no longer has much appeal. The only saving grace I have found in this journey was in experiencing the favor of YHWH like never before. The best way I can describe it is that I can almost feel his smile. And on my worst days, He has always shown Himself faithful in picking me back up again and sustaining us through the blessings of countless testimonies and the occasional, well-timed donation sent with a letter often telling me *"You can't give up. Don't quit. You are changing lives and I am one of them."* Interestingly enough, many such letters have come from now former atheists. It is *only* YHWH's supernatural provision that has sustained my wife and I through this season. And for this I will be forever grateful—both to YHWH and to those who, through sensitivity to the prompting of the Holy Spirit, have seen fit to support us along the way.

But rather than engage in slanderous speculation based on hearsay, largely put forward by his opposition as *ad hominem* attacks, and/or by those who simply refuse to believe the claims Parallax was making were true, why don't we let his work speak for itself? Before we do this though, I'd like to present for your consideration a collection of quotes from various newspapers and articles written about him regarding his lectures. For in them, we may see that even his critics respected his intellect and ability to present the information you are about to read.

---

52 Ibid pp. 44-45.

"PARALLAX" AND HIS TEACHINGS OPINIONS OF THE PRESS

"TROWBRIDGE MECHANICS' INSTITUTION.--On Monday and Tuesday evenings last two lectures were delivered by a gentleman adopting the name of 'Parallax,' to prove modern astronomy unreasonable and contradictory: that the earth is a plane or disc and not a globe, the sun, moon, and stars, self-luminous, &c., &c. The lectures were well attended, and were delivered with great skill, the lecturer proving himself thoroughly acquainted with the subject in all its bearings."--*Wilts Independent*, January 18th, 1849.

[Although "Parallax" had been delivering lectures for several years previously, in various parts of England, the above was the first notice which ever appeared in any newspaper.]

"ZETETIC ASTRONOMY [after details].--The lecturer is not a theorist, and the matter is sufficiently important to claim the attention of the scientific world." --*Liverpool Mercury*, January 25th, 1850.

"ZETETIC ASTRONOMY.--'Parallax' repeated his lectures on this subject (by permission of the High Sheriff of the county) in the Court House here, to large and respectable auditories of our townspeople. The nature of these lectures is extraordinary, explaining that the earth is not a globe, but a fixed circular plane--that the sun moves in the firmament-- and that, in fact, our present astronomical knowledge is altogether fallacious and inconsistent with natural phenomena. . . . The audience listened with the deepest attention, and appeared astonished at the revelations of the lecturer. At the close of each lecture several gentlemen entered the lists with 'Parallax,' and a lively and interesting discussion ensued. 'Parallax,' however, maintained his principles with infinite tact and ability, and answered his opponents in a masterly manner. The audiences left strongly impressed with the startling facts to which they had been listening--the most sceptical, at least, philosophising after the manner of Hamlet:--

> 'There are more things in heaven and earth, Horatio, Than are dreamt of in our philosophy.'

As to 'Parallax' himself, we must say that we seldom listened to a more clear, perspicuous, and convincing lecturer. He is evidently a man of gifted intellect, and deep scientific attainments. "--*Athlone Sentinel*, May 21st, 1851.

"ZETETIC ASTRONOMY.--'Parallax' has just concluded a second course of four very interesting lectures, to large and respectable audiences, in the Court House here [details follow]. At the close of each lecture a very animated discussion took place; and although some very strong arguments were brought forward, 'Parallax' maintained his ground. We have seldom met with a lecturer endowed with such strong argumentative powers who, in language so simple, could present so quickly and clearly to the mind the ideas he wished to impart. The simple manner in which he endeavoured to elucidate his subject, and bring it within the comprehension of his hearers, as well as the good temper and forbearance displayed during a lengthened discussion with some very able disputants, called forth a vote of thanks at the conclusion, which was acceded to without a dissentient voice."--*Westmeath Independent*, May 24th, 1851.

"During the past week 'Parallax' has visited Preston, and lectured at the Institution to numerous and respectable audiences. The first was con- fined to a marshalling of his experiments [here lengthy details follow]. His lectures were delivered in a simple, unassuming style, and his illustrations and language were of a character to suit the comprehension of all. He appears to have studied well his subject, to have made himself master of it in all its details, and to be armed at all points against those who may enter with him into the lists of controversy."--*Preston Guardian*, August 7th, 1852.

"A gentleman adopting the name of 'Parallax' has been delivering lectures at the Hall on Zetetic Astronomy. The principle he proceeds upon is to admit of no theories, and to take nothing for granted. He holds that the earth is not a revolving globe but a fixed plane, and that the sun moves in the firmament. The lecturer is evidently a gentleman of deep learning, and is thoroughly in earnest. We understand that the lectures are about to be re-delivered, and that then the system will be fully developed."--*Leicester Chronicle*, June3rd, 1854.

"We invite the attention of all who feel an interest in subjects of this kind to these lectures, as, if the statements made by the lecturer in reference to the heights of distant objects be incontrovertible, they would seem very seriously to invalidate some of the most important conclusions of modern astronomy."--*Leicester Advertiser*, June 3rd, 1854.

"In another part of today's Herald we publish a synopsis of the lecture on 'Zetetic Astronomy.' We have taken some pains to give the lecturer's definitions of his philosophy, and mode of illustrating it. But, inasmuch as the system of the lecturer differs in every point of view from our own study of astronomy, and from all previous teachings on the subject, there must be a great error on one side or the other. 'Parallax,' as a lecturer, as a sound logician, clear, lucid reasoner, calm and self-possessed, we have never seen surpassed."--*Norfolk Herald*, November 1st, 1856.

"'PARALLAX' --The closing lectures of the series were delivered on Monday and Wednesday last, and we do not know when we have heard such striking lessons on the art of reasoning as were afforded by these lectures. As a reasoner we much question if 'Parallax' can be surpassed; and the gentlemanly manner in which the discussions were conducted brought out that power to a very high degree."--*Yarmouth Free Press*, November 22nd, 1856.

"ZETETIC ASTRONOMY---THE EARTH NOT A GLOBE--'Parallax' has lectured to respectable and critical audiences in the new room, Corn Exchange. No one could fail to admire his power as a disputant. After the lectures he met the questions put to him by the most enlightened and scientific citizens with a readiness of reply which astonished his hearers; and he challenged to meet any of them on the points raised, and would stand or fall by the issue depending on facts; but no one accepted his challenge. Report states that he will visit Ely again, when no doubt there will be a full room. Lecturers on the Newtonian system, with their apparatus, orreries, &c., completely fail to interest the people here. 'Parallax' has the ability to do this; he met even the 'sledge-hammer' of Mr. Burns with only a gentlemanly retort."--*Cambridge Chronicle*, December 27th, 1856.

"ZETETIC ASTRONOMY.--Three lectures were delivered on Tuesday, Wednesday, and Thursday evenings last, at the Lecture Hall in this town, by a gentleman adopting the name of 'Parallax,' to prove modern astronomy unreasonable and contradictory--that the earth is a plane, or a disc, and not a globe--the sun, moon, and stars, self-luminous, &c., &c. The lectures were delivered in a manner which could not fail to be comprehended, and which left no doubt that the lecturer was thoroughly acquainted with the subject he was discussing. We have seldom heard a man with stronger argumentative powers, sounder logic, or more convincive reasoning. The revelations of the lecturer appeared to completely astound his audiences, who, for the greater part, left with a strong impression that the previous teachers of astronomy must have been greatly in error. 'Parallax' is undoubtedly a gentleman of no mean intellect, and must have studied deeply to have reached such scientific attainments."--*Croydon Chronicle,* January 24th, 1857.

[After report.] "The unquestionable ability with which 'Parallax' has met his opponents has drawn forth much applause."--*Leicestershire Mercury*, August 14th, 1858.

"ZETETIC ASTRONOMY.--No doubt many of our readers have been mystified and surprised within the last week by the announcement that, in three lectures, at the Northampton Mechanics' Institute, a gentleman who calls himself 'Parallax,' would undertake to prove the earth not a globe, &c., &c. . . . We were highly gratified by the manner in which this important subject was handled by 'Parallax'--a pseudonym which the lecturer informed his audience he had adopted in order to avert the effect of an insinuation that his startling announcement is but the morbid desire of an individual to be known as the propounder of a philosophy boldly at variance with that of the great astronomers of the past and present. His subject was handled in a plain and easy manner, his language and allusions proving him a man of education and thought, and certainly not a pedant. The experiments mentioned, divested of technicality in their recital, and understandable by all, were of such a nature as to cause a start of surprise at their simplicity and truthfulness. . . . It is not for us to pronounce a verdict upon so important an issue; 'Parallax' may be in error, but as far as his reasonings from fact and experiment go, there is much to set scientific men thinking. His arguments consist of facts, and such as are patent to all degrees of mental capacity. . . . In the discussions which followed, 'Parallax' certainly lost no ground, either in answer to questions or to some broad assertions quoted from learned authorities."--*South Mid-land Free Press*, August 14th, 1858.

"While Lord Brougham, Professor Owen, and Dr. Whewell, have been assisting at the inauguration of the statue of Sir Isaac Newton, at Grantham, 'Parallax' has been startling the good people of Coventry by blotting the face of fair Mother Earth, declaring her long respected rotundity a modern fable. . . . This is not the age for intolerance and bigotry with respect to science; new discoveries and new lights are treated with respect from whatever quarter they may emanate, and if 'Parallax' can make good his pretensions, his name will be immortalised by posterity. . . . We thank 'Parallax' for exciting an interest in the subject of astronomy which perhaps lecturers, according to the received hypothesis, would have failed to create."--*Coventry Herald*, October 1st, 1858.

"ZETETIC ASTRONOMY.--In this glorious nineteenth century, the boasted age of progress and reform, in which the strides of intellect are so rapidly approaching perfection, we cannot be surprised that such a beautiful system of Zetetic Astronomy as that expounded by 'Parallax' should entirely supersede the doctrine taught by Newton, and more especially when we are told that this Zetetic system is the only one which is consistent with common sense, and agreeable with the records contained in the Holy Scriptures. Now if this statement be true, all the readers of the 'Free Press' will agree in giving this philosophy a hearty welcome."--*Coventry Free Press*, October 1st, 1858.

"ZETETIC PHILOSOPHY.--During the past week four lectures have been delivered at our Institution, Royal Hill, which are to be continued on four evenings next week. To say that these lectures are extraordinary in their character is but saying the least that can possibly be said concerning them. The exceedingly gifted lecturer, who apparently prefers to be known as 'Parallax,' demonstrates the Newtonian theory of astronomy to be in opposition to facts; and in so doing demonstrates that the Bible is literally true in its philosophical teachings. From this, the groundwork of his philosophy, spring teachings and doctrines which cause us to hold our breath in the contemplation of them, and compel us, as public journalists, to withhold our opinion on subjects so vast, so important to man, and so utterly at variance with the commonly received notions of the day. Is it for us to say that a greater than a Newton shall not arise? No! we wait the issue. If 'Parallax' be wrong there can be nothing easier than for our savans of Greenwich to overthrow his doctrines; but if our readers think they would have an easy task so to do, we can only say be present at his concluding lectures, and judge for yourselves. . . . It is urged that this 'somebody or other' who has the audacity to come right into Greenwich, above all places in the enlightened world, is very strong- -strong in his facts, strong in his arguments, and appears after all to get on the right side of his audiences. This much we do know, that there are thinking men in our town who have been compelled to bend to the overpowering weight of evidence against our modern ideas. If it be true that some have tried to overthrow him and yet failed, let them go again, and still again, and nip this growth in the bud, ere a giant oak arises which will scorn their science and defy their teachings."--*Greenwich Free Press*, May 11th 1861.

"'PARALLAX' AT THE LECTURE HALL.--This talented lecturer is again in Greenwich, rivetting the attention of his audiences, and compelling them to submit to the facts which he brings before them--we say submit, for this they do; it seems impossible for any one to battle with him, so powerful are the weapons he uses. Mathematicians argue with him at the conclusion of his lectures, but it would seem as though they held their weapons by the blade and fought with the handle, for sure enough they put the handle straight into the lecturer's hand, to their own utter discomfiture and chagrin. It remains yet to be seen whether any of our Royal Astronomers will have courage enough to meet him in discussion, or whether they will quietly allow him to give the death-blow to the Newtonian theory, and make converts of our townspeople to his own Zetetic philosophy. If 'Parallax' be wrong, for Heaven's sake let some of our Greenwich stars twinkle at the Hall, and dazzle, confound, or eclipse altogether this wandering one, who is turning men, all over England, out of the Newtonian path. 'Parallax' is making his hearers disgusted with the Newtonian and every other theory, and turning them to a consideration of facts and first principles, from which they know not how to escape. Again we beg and trust that some of our Royal Observatory gentlemen will try to save us, and prevent anything like a Zetetic epidemic prevailing amongst us." --*Greenwich Free Press*, May 19th, 1862.

"EARTH NOT A GLOBE.--On Wednesday, Thursday, and Friday, 'Parallax' delivered his lectures at the Chatham Lecture Hall. The science he sets forth he denominates 'Zetetic Astronomy.' Whatever his hearers may think of his philosophy, they must admit that his lectures show him to have read and thought much. His discourses are very pleasing and interesting, and he expounds his doctrines in a way that ought to offend none. The variety of questions which a number of gentlemen asked the lecturer were readily and courteously answered, and in a way which appeared to satisfy most of the questioners. The audiences got so interested in these discussions that it was midnight before all the arguers left. They evidently took the deepest interest in the subjects presented to them. Next week 'Parallax' is to give more lectures, as announced in our advertising columns."--*Chatham News*, June 6th, 1863.

"ZETETIC ASTRONOMY.--It will be seen, on reference to our advertising columns, that 'Parallax' will repeat his course of three lectures. He has deeply interested the public, and has had full audiences. We defer giving our opinion until the whole series of lectures have been given. Certainly Parallax' is a man of strong argumentative powers, sound logic, and convincing reasoning."--*Rochester and Chatham Journal*, June 6th, 1863.

"There is a startling novelty in store for the scientific men of London. One who calls himself 'Parallax' wields a battle-axe against the present astronomical theories, giving lectures to the effect that the earth is not a globe but a fixed circular plane [particulars follow]. 'Parallax' has moved in the best provincial circles, but his orbit has hitherto been distant from London."--*Court Journal*, April 9th, 1864.

"THE EARTH NOT A GLOBE.--We beg to direct attention to the second course of lectures now being delivered by 'Parallax' at the Society's Hall. Those who take an interest in this scientific subject would be much enlightened by hearing the views of the lecturer, which are given in a clear and logical manner, and carry conviction with them."--*Portsmouth Guardian*, April 21st, 1864.

"THE WORLD WE LIVE IN.--We invite the attention of our readers to the remarkable lectures being delivered by a gentleman adopting the name of 'Parallax,' with illustrations, explaining that the earth is not a globe but a fixed circular plane, and that the sun actually moves in the firmament. These lectures contain a vast amount of deep scientific research, and proclaim 'Parallax' a man of varied and solid attainments. He has well and completely concatenated his subject, and appears master of his position." --*Weekly Mail*,May 23rd, 1864.

"'PARALLAX' AND HIS TEACHINGS.--No one can doubt that 'Parallax' has made a hit at Gosport, and has created quite a sensation. The Zetetic philosopher is an able reasoner; concede but his first point, skilfully put, and you stand no chance against his fifteen years' platform experience. For three nights [details follow]. During these discussions 'Parallax' has not always had fair play; as may well be supposed there is a degree of prejudice against his teachings, and hot words have ensued. On Wednesday the arguments lasted until after midnight."--*Gosport Free Press*, May 14th, 1864.

"EARTH NOT A GLOBE.--Last evening the gentleman bearing the nom de plume of 'Parallax' delivered at the Athenæum the first of a series of lectures to prove the fallacy of the Newtonian principles regarding the rotundity of the earth. There was a very large attendance, every seat in the place being occupied, and many who could not obtain sitting room stood, filling up the whole of the available space in the hall. A chairman was elected, as it was expected there would be a hot discussion on so striking a subject. The lecturer commenced his discourse by [here lengthy details follow]. At the conclusion of the lecture a very animated discussion ensued between many gentlemen of the town and the lecturer, and we must say that he was a good match for his opponents." -- *Western Daily Mercury*, September 27th, 1864.

"The second lecture of this series was delivered last evening. The hall was crammed to excess--in fact, many were unable to obtain admission. The lecturer briefly recapitulated a portion of his previous lecture. He went through the whole of the syllabus, amidst constant interruption, with the best possible temper, making his subject extremely interesting, and handling it in such an able manner as to elicit loud and frequent applause. Before the lecture was concluded it was quite evident, judging from the feelings exhibited by the majority of the audience, that 'Parallax' had impressed many of them with the truth of his ideas. It cannot be denied that he treats his subject in a very clever and ingenuous manner, and succeeds in drawing many over to agree with him." -- *Western Daily Mercury*, September 28th, 1864.

"The third of the above series of lectures was delivered last evening. The subject underwent a long and warm discussion, and the questions which were put to the lecturer were answered with a great degree of ingenuity. Upon the suggestion of a gentleman present, the lecturer said that, in conjunction with other gentlemen, he would be happy to make any experiments to ascertain the truth or fallacy of his teachings. This, we believe, will be acted upon, it being purposed to visit the Breakwater and the Eddystone Lighthouse, and there make the necessary observations, which no doubt will prove very interesting."--*Western Daily Mercury,* September 30th, 1864.

"'PARALLAX' ON ZETETIC ASTRONOMY.--Last evening the lecturer who has adopted this nom de plume gave his first lecture at the Athenæum. . . . The hall was crowded by a respectable audience. He laid before his hearers an entertaining, instructing, and very plausible collection of facts, upon which he based the deduction that the world was not an oblate spheroid, but a plane. The details were illustrated by diagrams, that were interestingly explained, in aid of his arguments; and when, in response to invitation, several gentlemen of experience, as nautical men and in the survey of land, questioned his opinions, and advanced strong antagonistic reasons, the replies were both clever and courteous. It was much regretted that very warm feeling was manifested by some of the auditors. . . . The lecturer was frequently applauded. He lectures again this evening, and there can be no doubt that the audience will be a numerous one, for in his lectures much unquestioned but valuable information is incidentally introduced, and much argument that is singularly difficult of controversion."--*Western Daily News*, September 27th, 1864.

"ZETETIC ASTRONOMY.--During the current week three lectures have been delivered at the Athenæum, Plymouth, which have excited not a little commotion among the learned of our fellow-citizens. The lecturer, who has adopted 'Parallax' as the name by which he would be known among the scientific, commenced his course of lectures on Monday last, the building being crowded with an attentive and, we may add, a critical audience. The subject which was introduced that evening, 'Earth not a Globe,' was one calculated to excite attention in the minds of the philosophers or deep-thinkers of the present day, and as such the lecturer was evidently prepared to meet with opposition [details]. We are bound to admit that he handled his subject with consummate skill; and, whether he is right or wrong, we must do him the justice to acknowledge that he possesses all the great qualities which characterise a lecturer and a debater--consistently maintaining those principles which he holds to be correct, founded, as he proves them to be, upon the great Word of Truth, as established ere time began its course among men. We cannot attempt even an outline of the lectures: we have simply to record the facts that each lecture drew a very crowded assembly; that after each lecture an animated discussion took place, in which many gentlemen bore part; and we are free to express our conviction, without committing ourselves to an absolute belief in the doctrines enunciated, that 'Parallax' proved himself to be equal to the contest on which he had entered. All must admit the lecturer to have shown that his studies and his researches have been deep, powerful, and enduring."--*Plymouth Herald and United Service Journal*, October 6th, 1864.

"'PARALLAX' AT DEVONPORT.--On Wednesday evening last the gentleman adopting this cognomen, and who has been creating a great deal of interest in this locality during the last few weeks, commenced a series of lectures at the Devonport Mechanics' Institute. The reasoning of 'Parallax,' which he has termed Zetetic, is so astounding and diametrically opposed to the great Newtonian theory which has obtained in the world for hundreds of years, that he has often been ridiculed as a crude experimentalist, abused as a false teacher, and even accused of mendacity. He has borne these harsh expressions and ungentlemanly imputations calmly and patiently; and it is but just to say that, in his lectures, he has always courted the fullest inquiry--stating that his only object is the elucidation of truth, no matter what it may be or what it may lead to; and that in his discussions he is courteous in hearing and candid in expression. That he is a clever man, and that he has studied his subject deeply, there can be no possible doubt; and it is certainly the case, whether he is right or wrong, that his arguments are exceedingly plausible, and that he has much the better of his opponents in discussion. Unfortunately those who have entered into discussion with him have in nine cases out of ten become excited and lost their command, while 'Parallax,' remaining cool and calculating, has thus, apart from his demonstrations, been enabled to gain an advantage over them in reasoning. On this occasion the discussion became very warm, and ungracious imputations were made, which 'Parallax' said resulted from a fear to face the consequences resulting from new and true ideas. The demeanour, respectful bearing, and candour of 'Parallax' bear out his assertions that his object is the elucidation of truth; and he appeals to his audience to disprove his statements, while he undertakes to prove them to be true. He is fair in every way, and it is unjust, nay, it is something worse, to treat with disrespect a lecturer of this character."

"The lectures will be repeated next week, and as public discussion is invited at the end of each lecture, we hope it will be conducted temperately and with proper spirit.

Meanwhile we claim, in justice to 'Parallax,' that no unjust erroneous prejudicial notions be formed of him without a hearing."--*Devonport Independent*, October 15th, 1864.

"ZETETIC ASTRONOMY.--[After details.] We can tell our readers that 'Parallax' is a practised lecturer, a good speaker, a clever debater, and a courteous opponent. He has a plausible manner, and is thoroughly 'posted' in the standard philosophy as well as the system which he teaches, and is therefore no mean antagonist. Students of science may break a lance with him, but judging from his meetings at Gloucester and Stroud, we should say that an ordinary man is no match for him."-- *Stroud Journal*, October 28th, 1865.

"A conclave of scientific gentlemen sat to get up a reply, and just one of the number was able to state the answer: even that answer, scientific as it was, had a fallacy in it." --*Spectator*, April 12th, 1856.

"The lecturer gained great praise for his ingenuity in proving that the earth is a plane surrounded by ice. . . The evidence that the earth is round is but cumulative and circumstantial."--*Professor de Morgan, Cambridge University*.

"'PARALLAX' ON ZETETIC ASTRONOMY.--The gentleman who has adopted this noon de plume delivered his first lecture on Monday evening last There was a large and highly respectable audience--the hall being crowded. The lecture was a clear and elaborate exposition, &c. [lengthy details follow]. If we may judge by the applause by which some of the lecturer's arguments were confirmed, we should say that many of those present were ready to exclaim: 'Behold, a greater than Newton is here!' A hot discussion followed, in which the Rev. Nixon Porter and other gentlemen took part, but Parallax' maintained his ground."-- *Warrington Guardian*, March 24th, 1866.

"EARTH NOT A GLOBE.--On Monday last a gentleman adopting the nom de plume of 'Parallax'--a very appropriate name, seeing that the basis of his arguments is the relation to each other of parallel lines-- commenced a series of lectures at the Public Hall on 'Zetetic Astronomy,' a system directly opposed to the great Newtonian theory. That he is a clever man, and has studied the matter deeply, and that he is master of his subject, and thoroughly convinced of its truth, is apparent; and his arguments are certainly very plausible. The lecture drew large audiences, and among those present we noticed [here a list is given of many of the leading men and families of the district]. 'Parallax' commenced by explaining the word 'Zetetic,' which had been adopted, because they did not sit in their closets and endeavour to frame a theory to explain certain phenomena, but went abroad into the world, and thoroughly investigated the subject [here follows a long report of the three lectures]. Lengthy and animated discussions ensued; votes of thanks were passed to the lecturer and the chairman--the Rev. Nixon Porter, who declared that he was much struck with the simplicity and candour with which the lecturer had stated his views; and, after a promise by 'Parallax' that he would pay another visit to Warrington, the audience dispersed."-- *Warrington Advertiser*, March 24th, 1866.

"THE EARTH NOT A GLOBE.--Lectures on the above subject were de- livered this week in the Royal Assembly Room, Great George-street, Liverpool, by 'Parallax,' a gentleman known to the literary world by a work on 'Zetetic Astronomy,' and who came somewhat prominently before the Liverpool public fourteen or fifteen years ago through the columns of the Mercury. The hall was well filled by respectable and critical audiences. He commenced his first lecture by comparing the Newtonian principle of astronomy with the Zetetic (which must prove all and take nothing for granted); and endeavoured to demonstrate in a comprehensive and logical manner that the earth is not a globe but a plane; that, in fact, all theories of the earth's rotundity are fallacious, and that the followers of Newton and other philosophers had been adopting and believing a 'cunningly devised fable.' The lectures were illustrated by numerous diagrams and experiments, and were listened to with the greatest attention by all present. 'Parallax' appears to have studied the peculiarities of his subject thoroughly, and was warmly applauded during the delivery of his lectures."--*Liverpool Mercury*, October 3rd, 1866.

At the end of a detailed report of lectures at the Halifax Mechanics' Hall it is stated:-- "Whatever may be the truth or otherwise of the new system, certain it is that the lectures were well attended, and numbers of the audiences declared themselves converts." --*Halifax Guardian*, April 13th, 1867.

"Coming to the facts of 'Parallax.' They are upon the whole admirably dealt with. . He exhibits an immense number of diagrams, and explains them with great ingenuity." --*Yorkshire Post and Leeds Intelligencer*, May 2nd, 1867.

"The Philosophical Hall last night was crowded with a thoughtful audience attracted by the formidable propositions which the lecturer enunciates and defends [particulars here follow]. These and similar extraordinary statements so utterly at variance with the recognised theories of the day, the lecturer maintains with a perspicuity and mastery of his subject which carries the audience to some extent along with him, and induces them to manifest symptoms of scientific unbelief."--*Leeds Mercury,* May 8th, 1867.

"Without endorsing 'Parallax's' teachings, it must be said that (at the Philosophical Hall, Leeds) he advanced them, supported them, and fought for them with a skill and intelligence, tact, and good temper which were not at all equalled by his opponents." --*Leeds Times*, May 11th, 1867.

"He displays in his lectures a thorough acquaintance with the Newtonian philosophy, and presents his own peculiar views in such a way that they assume great plausibility and astonish his hearers. At the close of each lecture discussion is permitted, in the course of which 'Parallax' exhibits great debating tact and power; his answers to his opponents being frequently loudly applauded." --*Leeds Evening Express*, May 23rd, 1867.

"ZETETIC ASTRONOMY.--His lectures furnish a clear, masterly, and very plausible exposition of his system. At the close of each lecture he invited discussion; and it must be admitted that 'Parallax' evinced varied knowledge, ability, and readiness in replying to objections."--*Bradford Review*, July 6th, 1867.

"'PARALLAX' AT BRADFORD.--So long have astronomers averred the earth's rotundity and its motion round the sun, that when 'Parallax' was announced to lecture we went to see the man who had ventured to controvert facts so long settled by the most recherché students in celestial science. To our surprise every position taken seemed fortified with keen logical reasoning, and an easy explanation was given of many of the tests previously considered absolute proofs of the earth's rotundity. The lecturer contends [particulars are here given]. By many illustrations he disproved this rotundity, and astonished his audiences by showing how little there is to be relied on in what has been hitherto received as demonstration itself. 'Parallax' is unquestionably a very acute reasoner, a paragon of courtesy, good temper, and masterly skill in debate; and, by his frank and ingenuous manner, won largely on the convictions of his audience. Seldom have we seen an assembly so much absorbed in their subject; and the interest was maintained to the close. We feel it due to say that, if the data given are correct, there is no resisting the conclusions arrived at."--*Bradford Advertiser*, July 6th and 13th, 1867.

"The lecturer invited discussion, and a warm controversy took place, but 'Parallax' stood his ground admirably. His delivery is free and unaffected, and the masterly style in which he handled his subject showed that he was a geometrician and mathematician of no ordinary merit."--*Dewsbury Chronicle*, August 5th, 1867.

"'PARALLAX' AT BIRSTAL.--This gentleman delivered his course of lectures in the Public Hall here on Monday, Tuesday, and Wednesday last [particulars here follow]. The lecturer thoroughly understands the subject which he has taken in hand. He is gifted with extraordinary debating power and acumen, and the manner in which he dealt with the subject also proved him to be well versed in all the sciences bearing upon his system of astronomy. His style of delivery, too, is one calculated to win the sympathies of an audience."--*Birstal Record*, August 10th, 1867.

"THE EARTH A PLANE.--[Report of lecture at the Town Hall, Hanley, concludes as follows]:--A contemporary speaks of 'Parallax' as a very acute reasoner, a paragon of courtesy, good temper, and masterly skill in debate, adding that if the data given are correct there is no resisting the conclusions arrived at. Apart from these conclusions, to which he seems to lead most of his hearers in spite of themselves, the lectures are really an intellectual treat."--*Staffordshire Sentinel*, February 8th, 1868.

"'Parallax' has just repeated his lectures in Warrington, which were presided over by the Rev. Nixon Porter, Alderman Holmes, ex-Mayor, and P. Rylands, Esq., M.P. The lecturer was introduced by the first- named gentleman as no stranger to Warrington, having visited them on former occasions, given our scientific men some pretty hard nuts to crack, had made certain statements and drawn certain inferences which, to say the least, were plausible, and demanded fair consideration. Any man should be fairly heard when he stood upon the foundation of truth, and braved the opposition which was invariably incurred when the current modes of thought were attacked and attempted to be controverted. If the lecturer's statements were false, by all means let them be exploded; but, if true, let us thankfully receive them and all their consequences, giving to their zealous expounder the credit to which he is entitled. Questions such as those brought before the meeting should be fully considered and discussed. On introducing the lecturer on the third evening, the chairman (P. Rylands, Esq., M.P.) concluded his address as follows: 'Every philosophical inquiry which challenged contradiction must have a good effect in causing them to think of the various natural phenomena by which they were surrounded, thus improving their minds, increasing the strength of their understandings, and adding to the general intelligence of the people.' The lecturer, on rising, in reply to the oft-repeated question which had been put to him as to the good or use of his particular system of astronomy, even admitting it to be the true one, would say that, at the least, it was of great importance to a large commercial and mercantile nation such as ours, in correcting, improving, and rendering more practical and safe the art of navigation, on which the prosperity of the country so much depended. It was also a most important religious question--one scarcely second to any other religious question of the day. At present there was a great battle going on between religious and scientific men, the former upholding the truth of the Scriptures, and the latter believing in nothing but their own philosophy, which was in direct opposition to Scriptural teachings. Thousands of men at the present day declared the Scriptural astronomical expressions to be false, and regarded science and philosophy as all in all. One or the other must be false; both could not stand. If they were all simply dogs they might 'bow-wow' together, and think nothing more of the matter; but as they were men, endowed with sense and reason, the importance of the subject presented itself to them in all its intensity. If the earth was a globe, and the principles of modern astronomy were true, religious teaching could not be reconciled to such a state of things, and must consequently be false; but if, on the other hand, modern astronomy could be proved to be false, then would the religious philosophy stand

forth as a grand reality, and show itself as the communicated expression of some great master of the universe. He had a few words to say to the so-called 'free-thinkers' of the day; those especially who prided themselves upon having become sceptical in matters of religion. He would have them to take care that the word 'free- thinker' was not misapplied. It was very possible, and not an uncommon thing, for a person to become as great a bigot in this respect as in any other. A free-thinker was not necessarily an atheist or even a sceptic; he might or might not be so, but he might also be a lover of true religion and a good Christian. He alone was a true free-thinker who was prepared to seek out and to hold fast to all the practical truths developed by human experience. He (the lecturer) had the deepest respect for those who could leave the old theoretical 'ruts' of thought, and dare to freely inquire for themselves into every subject, but he could not do other than pity and almost despise all those who profess to be 'truth-seekers' and 'free-thinkers,' and who yet will only use their powers for the promotion of religious scepticism. The man who refused evidence simply because it might lead him back to a recognition of Scriptural philosophy, and to seeing the necessity for a religious or devotional life, was neither wise nor good, but was indeed a bigot in the fullest sense of the term. The lecturer then proceeded to explain" [lengthy details follow].
-- See *Warrington Guardian* of September 36th and 19th, and *Warrington Advertiser and Mail* of September 19th, 1868.

"WESTBOURNE HALL.--By special desire, such was the interest taken in the propositions advanced, 'Parallax' was induced to repeat his three lectures, the first of which was delivered on Thursday evening last to a numerous and appreciative audience. . . . Although we must be understood as not endorsing all, yet he said enough to puzzle the most inveterate Newtonian philosopher present. . . . The lecture was amply illustrated by diagrams, without which it is impossible to do justice to the able remarks of the lecturer. . . . An animated discussion, which at times was rather irregular, took place; some of the gentlemen who entered the arena betraying more animus than ability. The lecturer replied readily to the various objections of his opponents; and, judging by the clamorous approval of the audience, he seemed to have gained the attention of many who were not disposed to look favourably on the claims of what is termed 'Zetetic Astronomy.'"
--*Notting Hill and Bayswater Times*, November 13th, 1869.

"The flat earth floating tremulously on the sea, the sun moving always over it, giving day when near enough, and night when too far off; the self-luminous moon, with a semi-transparent invisible moon created to give her an eclipse now and then; the new law of perspective, by which the vanishing of the hull before the masts, usually thought to prove the earth globular, really proves it flat; all these and other things are well fitted to form exercises in learning the elements of astronomy. 'Parallax,' though confident in the extreme, neither impeaches the honesty of those whose opinions he assails, nor allots them any future inconvenience."-- Augustus De Morgan, Professor of Mathematics in Cambridge University, President of the Royal Astronomical Society, F.R.A.S., &c., &c. --*Athenæum Journal* for October 12, 1872.

Clearly, whether everyone agreed with him or not, Samuel Rowbotham was a respected and educated man, more than capable of giving a "ready defense" for his beliefs. So, it is with great pleasure that I present his writings along with those of the others in this series who were likewise inspired to "carry the torch" in defense of the truths of Scripture, while explaining the results of their "zetetic investigation" of terra firma and its place in the cosmos. I will also give some commentary from time-to-time based on my limited experiences of doing the same for the past three and a half years. My hope is that as you read the works contained in this volume, you will heed the warning the Apostle Paul gave to his disciple Timothy concerning science "falsely so called" and those who have ***erred in their faith*** as a result of believing in it over the words of YHWH.

Rob Skiba
September 30, 2018
The Colony, TX

**Oh Timothy, keep that which is committed to thy trust,
<u>avoiding profane and vain babblings, and oppositions of
science falsely so called: Which some professing
have erred concerning the faith</u>.
Grace be with thee. Amen.
- 1 Timothy 6:20, 21**

ZETETIC ASTRONOMY.

EARTH NOT A GLOBE.

AN EXPERIMENTAL INQUIRY

INTO THE

TRUE FIGURE OF THE EARTH,

PROVING IT A PLANE,

WITHOUT ORBITAL OR AXIAL MOTION,

AND THE

ONLY KNOWN MATERIAL WORLD;

ITS TRUE POSITION IN THE UNIVERSE, COMPARATIVELY RECENT
FORMATION, PRESENT CHEMICAL CONDITION,

AND

APPROACHING DESTRUCTION BY FIRE,

&c., &c., &c.

By "PARALLAX,"

*Author of "Patriarchal Longevity," and other works; and Founder of the
Modern Zetetic Philosophy.*

THE ILLUSTRATIONS BY GEORGE DAVEY, F.Z.S.

Third Edition,—Revised and Enlarged.

LONDON:

1881.

TABLE OF CONTENTS

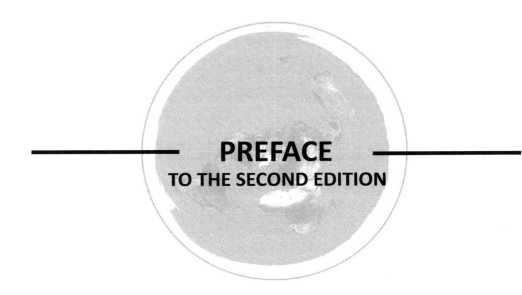

PREFACE
TO THE SECOND EDITION

To the various critics who reviewed unfavourably the first edition of this work, and to those also who wrote and published replies to it, my thanks are due and now respectfully tendered. They pointed out several matters which, on proper examination, were not, as evidence, entirely satisfactory; and as my object is to discover and hold to that only which is true beyond doubt, I have omitted them in the present edition. The true business of a critic is to compare what he reads with known and provable data, to treat impartially the evidence he observes, and point out logical deficiencies and inconsistencies with first principles, but never to obtrude his own opinions. He should, in fact, at all times take the place of Astrea, the Goddess of Justice, and firmly hold the scales, in which the evidence is fairly weighed.

I advise all my readers who have become Zetetic not to be content with anything less than this; and also not to look with disfavour upon the objections of their opponents. Should such objections be well or even plausibly founded, they will only tend to free us from error, and to purify and exalt our Zetetic philosophy. In a word, let us make friends, or, at least, friendly and useful instruments of our enemies; and, if we cannot convert them to the better cause, let us carefully examine their objections, fairly meet them if possible, and always make use of them as beacons for our future guidance.

In all directions there is so much truth in our favour that we can well afford to be dainty in our selection, and magnanimous, charitable, and condescending towards those who simply believe, but cannot prove, that we are wrong. We need not seize upon every crude and ill-developed result which offers, or only seems to offer, the slightest chance of becoming evidence in our favour, as every theorist is obliged to do if he would have his theory clothed and fit to be seen. We can afford to patiently wait, care-fully weigh, and well consider every point advanced, in the full assurance that simple truth, and not the mere opinions of men, is destined, sooner or later, to have ascendancy.

"IN VERITATE VICTORIA."

"PARALLAX."

London, September 24, 1872.

CHAPTER I
ZETETIC AND THEORETIC DEFINED AND COMPARED

THE term Zetetic is derived from the Greek verb *Zeteo*; which means to search, or examine; to proceed only by inquiry; to take nothing for granted, but to trace phenomena to their immediate and demonstrable causes. It is here used in contradistinction from the word "theoretic," the meaning of which is, speculative--imaginary--not tangible,--scheming, but not proving.

None can doubt that by making special experiments, and collecting manifest and undeniable facts, arranging them in logical order, and observing what is naturally and fairly deducible therefrom, the result must be more consistent and satisfactory than the contrary method of framing a theory or system--assuming the existence and operation of causes of which there is no direct and practical evidence, and which is only claimed to be "admitted for the sake of argument," and for the purpose of giving an apparent and plausible, but not necessarily truthful explanation of phenomena. All theories are of this character. "Supposing, instead of inquiring, imagining systems instead of learning from observation and experience the true constitution of things. Speculative men, by the force of genius may invent systems that will perhaps be greatly admired for a time; these, however, are phantoms which the force of truth will sooner or later dispel; and while we are pleased with the deceit, true philosophy with all the arts and improvements that depend upon it, suffers. The real state of things escapes our observation; or, if it presents itself to us, we are apt either to reject it wholly as fiction, or, by new efforts of a vain ingenuity to interweave it with our own conceits, and labour to make it tally with our favourite schemes. Thus, by blending together parts so ill-suited, the whole comes forth an absurd composition of truth and error. * * * These have not done near so much harm as that pride and ambition which has led philosophers to think it beneath them to offer anything less to the world than a complete and finished system of Nature; and, in order to obtain this at once, to take the liberty of inventing certain principles and hypotheses from which they pretend to explain all her mysteries."

"Theories are things of uncertain mode. They depend, in a great measure, upon the humour and caprice of an age, which is sometimes in love with one, and sometimes with another."

The system of Copernicus was admitted by its author to be merely an assumption, temporary and incapable of demonstration. The following are his words:--"It is not necessary that hypotheses should be true, or even probable; it is sufficient that they lead to results of calculation which agree with calculation. * * * Neither let anyone, so far as hypotheses are concerned, expect anything *certain* from astronomy, since that science can afford nothing of the kind, lest, in case he should adopt for truth, things feigned for another purpose, he should leave this science more foolish than he came. * * * The hypothesis of the terrestrial motion was *nothing but an hypothesis*, valuable only so far as it explained phenomena, and not considered with reference to absolute truth or falsehood."

The Newtonian and all other "views" and "systems" have the same general character as the "hypothesis of the terrestrial motion," framed by Copernicus. The foundations or premises are always unproved; no proof is ever attempted; the necessity for it is denied; it is considered sufficient that the assumptions *seem* to explain the phenomena selected. In this way it is that theory supplants theory, and system gives way to system, often in rapid succession, as one failure after another compels opinions to change. Until the practice of theorising is universally relinquished, philosophy will continue to be looked upon by the bulk of mankind as a vain and mumbling pretension, antagonistic to the highest aspirations of humanity. Let there be adopted a true and practical free-thought method, with *sequence* as the only test of truth and consistency, and the philosopher may become the Priest of Science and the real benefactor of his species. "Honesty of thought is to look truth in the face, not in the side face, but in the full front; not merely to look at truth when found, but to seek it till found. There must be no tampering with conviction, no hedging or mental prevarication; no making 'the wish father to the thought;' no fearing to arrive at a particular result. To think honestly, then, is to think freely; freedom and honesty of thought are truly but interchangeable terms. For how can he think honestly, who dreads his being landed in this or that conclusion? Such an one has already predetermined in his heart how he shall think, and what he shall believe. Perfect truth, like perfect love, casteth out fear."

Let the method of simple inquiry--the "Zetetic" process be exclusively adopted--experiments tried and facts collected--not such only as corroborate an already existing state of mind, but of every kind and form bearing on the subject, before a conclusion is drawn, or a conviction affirmed.

"Nature speaks to us in a peculiar language; in the language of phenomena. She answers at all times the questions which are put to her; and such questions are experiments."

"Nature lies before us as a panorama; let us explore and find delight, she puts questions to us, and we may also question her; the answers may ofttimes be hard to spell, but no dreaded sphinx shall interfere when human wisdom falters."

We have an excellent example of a "Zetetic" process in an arithmetical operation, more especially so in what is called the "Golden Rule," or the "Rule of Three." If a hundredweight of any article costs a given sum, what will some other weight, less or more, be worth? The separate figures may be considered as the elements or facts in the inquiry; the placing and working of them as the logical arrangement of the evidence; and the quotient, or answer, as the fair and natural deduction,--the unavoidable or necessitated verdict. Hence, in every arithmetical or "Zetetic" process, the conclusion arrived at is essentially a quotient; which, if the details are correctly worked, must of necessity be true, and beyond the reach or power of contradiction.

We have another example of the "Zetetic" process in our Courts of Justice. A prisoner is placed at the bar; evidence for and against him is demanded: when advanced it is carefully arranged and patiently considered. It is then presented to the Jury for solemn reconsideration, and whatever verdict is given, it is advanced as the unavoidable conclusion necessitated by the whole of the evidence. In trials, for justice, society would not tolerate any other procedure. Assumption of guilt, and prohibition of all evidence to the contrary, is a practice not to be found among any of the civilised nations of the earth--scarcely indeed, among savages and barbarians; and yet assumption of premises, and selection of evidence to corroborate assumptions, is everywhere and upon all subjects the practice of theoretical philosophers!

The "Zetetic" process is also the most natural method of investigation. Nature herself always teaches it; it is her own continual suggestion; children invariably seek information by asking questions, by earnestly inquiring from those around them. Fearlessly, anxiously, and without the slightest regard to consequences, question after question, in rapid and exciting succession, will often proceed from a child, until the most profound in learning and philosophy, will feel puzzled to reply; and often the searching cross-examinations of a mere natural tyro, can only be brought to an end by an order to retire--to bed --to school--to play--to anywhere--rather than that the fiery "Zetetic" ordeal shall be continued.

If then both Nature and justice, as well as the common sense and practical experience of mankind demand, and will not be content with less or other than the "Zetetic" process, why is it ignored and constantly violated by the learned in philosophy? What right have they to begin their disquisitions with fanciful data, and then to demand that, to these all surrounding phenomena be moulded. As private individuals they have, of course, a right to "do as they like with their own;" but as authors and public teachers their unnatural efforts are immeasurably pernicious. Like a poor animal tied to a stake in the centre of a meadow, where it can only feed in a limited circle, the theoretical philosopher is tethered to his premises, enslaved by his own assumptions, and however great his talent, his influence, his opportunities, he can only rob his fellow men of their intellectual freedom and independence, and convert them into slaves like him-self. In this respect astronomical science is especially faulty. It assumes the existence of certain data; it then applies these data to the explanation of certain phenomena. If the solution seems plausible it is considered that the data may be looked upon as proved-- demonstrated by the apparently satisfactory explanation they have afforded. Facts, and explanations of a different character, are put aside as unworthy of regard; since that which is already assumed seems to explain matters, there need be no further concern. Guided by this principle, the secretary of the Royal Astronomical Society (Professor De Morgan, of Trinity College, Cambridge), reviewing a paper by the author, in the Athenæum, for March 25th, 1865, says: "The evidence that the earth is round is but cumulative and circumstantial; scores of phenomena ask, separately and independently, what *other* explanation can be *imagined* except the sphericity of the earth?" It is thus candidly admitted that there is no direct and positive evidence that the earth is round, that it is only "imagined" or assumed to be so in order to afford an explanation of "scores of phenomena." This is precisely the language of Copernicus, of Newton, and of all astronomers who have laboured to prove the rotundity of the earth. It is pitiful in the extreme that after so many ages of almost unopposed indulgence, philosophers instead of beginning to seek, before everything else, the true constitution of the physical world, are still to be seen labouring only to frame hypotheses, and to reconcile phenomena with imaginary and ever-shifting foundations. Their labour is simply to repeat and perpetuate the self-deception of their predecessors. Surely the day is not far distant when the very complications which their numerous theories have created, will startle them into wakefulness, and convince them that for long ages past they have but been idly dreaming! Time wasted, energies thrown away, truth obscured, and falsehood rampant, constitute a charge so grave that coming generations will look upon them as the bitterest enemies of civilisation, the heaviest drags on the wheels of progress, and the most offensive embodiment of frivolity, pride of learning, and canting formality; worse than this--by their position, their standing in the front ranks of learning, they deceive the public. They appear to represent a solid phalanx of truth and wisdom, when in reality they are but as the flimsy ice of an hour's induration--all surface, without substance, or depth, or reliability, or power to save from danger and ultimate destruction.

Let the practice of theorising be abandoned as one oppressive to the reasoning powers, fatal to the full development of truth, and, in every sense, inimical to the solid progress of sound philosophy.

If, to ascertain the true figure and condition of the earth, we adopt the "Zetetic" process, which truly is the only one sufficiently reliable, we shall find that instead of its being a globe- -one of an infinite number of worlds moving on axes and in an orbit round the sun, it is the directly contrary--a Plane, without diurnal or progressive motion, and unaccompanied by anything in the firmament analogous to itself; or, in other words, that it is the *only known material world*.

CHAPTER II

EXPERIMENTS DEMONSTRATING THE TRUE FORM OF STANDING WATER, AND PROVING THE EARTH TO BE A PLANE

INTRODUCTION

IF the earth is a globe, and is 25,000 English statute miles in circumference, the surface of all standing water must have a certain degree of convexity--every part must be an arc of a circle. From the summit of any such arc there will exist a curvature or declination of 8 inches in the first statute mile. In the second mile the fall will be 32 inches; in the third mile, 72 inches, or 6 feet, as shown in the following diagram:

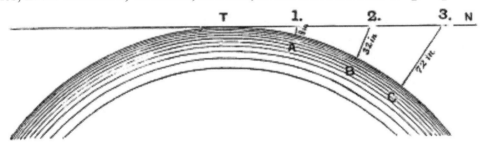

FIG. 1.

Let the distance from T to figure 1 represent 1 mile, and the fall from 1 to A, 8 inches; then the fall from 2 to B will be 32 inches, and from 3 to C, 72 inches. In every mile after the first, the curvature downwards from the point T increases as the square of the distance multiplied by 8 inches. The rule, however, requires to be modified after the first thousand miles.[1] The following table will show at a glance the amount of curvature, in round numbers, in different distances up to 100 miles.

1 Any work on geometry or geodesy will furnish proofs of this declination.

CURVATURE CALCULATION PER STATUTE MILE TABLE[2]

1	mile is	8	inches
2	miles is	32	inches
3	miles is	6	feet
4	miles is	10	feet
5	miles is	16	feet
6	miles is	24	feet
7	miles is	32	feet
8	miles is	42	feet
9	miles is	54	feet
10	miles is	66	feet
20	miles is	266	feet
30	miles is	600	feet
40	miles is	1066	feet
50	miles is	1666	feet
60	miles is	2400	feet
70	miles is	3266	feet
80	miles is	4266	feet
90	miles is	5400	feet
100	miles is	6666	feet

It will be seen by this table that after the first few miles the curvature would be so great that no difficulty could exist in detecting either its actual existence or its proportion. Experiments made on the sea shore have been objected to on account of the constantly changing altitude of the surface of the water, and of the existence of banks and channels which produce a "crowding" of the waters, as well as currents and other irregularities. Standing water has therefore been selected, and many important experiments have been made, the most simple of which are the following:--

In the county of Cambridge there is an artificial river or canal, called the "Old Bedford." It is upwards of twenty miles in length, and (except at the part referred to at page [89]) passes in a straight line through that part of the Fens called the "Bedford Level." The water is nearly stationary--often completely so, and throughout its entire length has no interruption from locks or water-gates of any kind; so that it is, in every respect, well adapted for ascertaining whether any or what amount of convexity really exists.

---

2 To find the curvature in any number of miles not given in the table, simply square the number, multiply that by 8, and divide by 12. The quotient is the curvation required.

EXPERIMENT 1

A boat, with a flag-staff, the top of the flag 5 feet above the surface of the water, was directed to sail from a place called "Welche's Dam" (a well- known ferry passage), to another called "Welney Bridge." These two points are six statute miles apart. The author, with a good telescope, went into the water; and with the eye about 8 inches above the surface, observed the receding boat during the whole period required to sail to Welney Bridge. *The flag and the boat were distinctly visible throughout the whole distance!* There could be no mistake as to the distance passed over, as the man in charge of the boat had instructions to lift one of his oars to the top of the arch the moment he reached the bridge. The experiment commenced about three o'clock in the afternoon of a summer's day, and the sun was shining brightly and nearly behind or against the boat during the whole of its passage. Every necessary condition had been fulfilled, and the result was to the last degree definite and satisfactory. The conclusion was unavoidable that *the surface of the water for a length of six miles did not to any appreciable extent decline or curvate downwards from the line of sight.* But if the earth is a globe, the surface of the six miles length of water would have been 6 feet higher in the centre than at the two extremities, as shown in diagram fig. 2; but as the telescope was only 8 inches above the water, the highest point of the surface would have been at one mile from the place of observation; and below this point the surface of the water at the end of the remaining five miles would have been 16 feet.

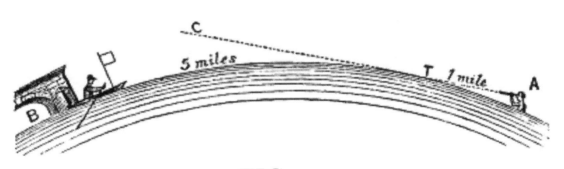

FIG. 2.

Let A B represent the arc of water 6 miles long, and A C the line of sight. The point of contact with the arc would be at T, a distance of one mile from the observer at A. From T to the bridge at B would be 5 miles, and the curvature from T to B would be 16 feet 8 inches. The top of the flag on the boat (which was 5 feet high) would have been 11 feet 8 inches below the horizon T, and altogether out of sight.

85

Such a condition was not observed; but the following diagram, fig. 3, exhibits the true state of the case--A, B, the line of sight, equidistant, from or parallel with the surface of the water throughout the whole distance of 6 milts: From which it is concluded that the surface of standing water is *not convex, but horizontal.*

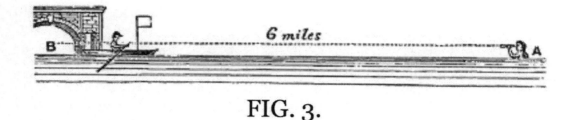

FIG. 3.

EXPERIMENT 2

Along the edge of the water, in the same canal, six flags were placed, one statute mile from each other, and so arranged that the top of each flag was 5 feet above the surface. Close to the last flag in the series a longer staff was fixed, bearing a flag 3 feet square, and the top of which was 8 feet above the surface of the water--the bottom being in a line with the tops of the other and intervening flags, as shown in the following diagram, Fig, 4.

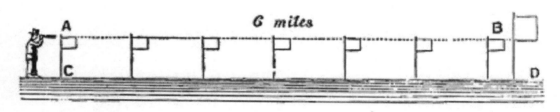

FIG. 4.

On looking with a good telescope over and along the flags, from A to B, the line of sight fell on the lower part of the larger flag at B. The altitude of the point B above the water at D was 5 feet, and the altitude of the telescope at A above the water at C was 5 feet; and each intervening flag had the same altitude. Hence the surface of the water C, D, was equidistant from the line of sight A, B; and as A B was a right line, C, D, being parallel, was also a right line; or, in other words, the surface of the water, C, D, was for six miles *absolutely* horizontal. If the earth is a globe, the series of flags in the last experiment would have had the form and produced the results represented in the diagram, Fig. 5.

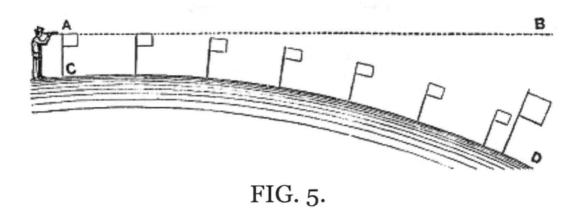

FIG. 5.

The water curvating from C to D, each flag would have been a given amount below the line A, B. The first and second flags would have determined the direction of the line of sight from A to B, and the third flag would have been 8 inches below the second; the fourth flag, 32 inches; the fifth, 6 feet; the sixth, 10 feet 8 inches; and the seventh, 16 feet 8 inches; but the top of the last and largest flag, being 3 feet higher than the smaller ones, would have been 13 feet 8 inches below the line of sight at the point B. The rotundity of the earth would necessitate the above conditions; but as they cannot be found to exist, the doctrine must be pronounced as only a simple theory, having no foundation in fact--a pure invention of misdirected genius; splendid in its comprehensiveness and bearing upon natural phenomena; but, nevertheless, mathematical and logical necessities compel its denunciation as *an absolute falsehood.*

The above-named experiments were first made by the author in the summer of 1838, but in the previous winter season, when the water in the "Old Bedford" Canal was frozen, he had often, when lying on the ice, with a good telescope observed persons skating and sliding at known distances of from four to eight miles. He lived for nine successive months within a hundred yards of the canal, in a temporary wooden building, and had many opportunities of making and repeating observations and experiments, which it would only be tedious to enumerate, as they all involved the same principle, and led to the same conclusions as those already described. It may, however, interest the reader to relate an instance which occurred unexpectedly, and which created such a degree of confusion, that he was repeatedly tempted to destroy the many memoranda he had previously made. Up to this time all his observations had been made in the direction of Welney, the bridge there affording a substantial signal point; but on one occasion, a gentleman who resided within a few miles of the temporary residence already alluded to, and with whom conversations and discussions had been repeatedly held, insisted upon the telescope being directed upon a barge sailing in an opposite direction to that previously selected. Watching the slowly receding vessel for a considerable time, it suddenly disappeared altogether! The gentleman co-observer cried out in a tone of exultation, "Now, sir, are you satisfied that the water declines?" It was almost impossible to say anything in reply. All that could be done was to "gaze in mute astonishment" in the direction of the lost vessel-- compelled to listen to the jeers and taunts of the apparent victor. After thus wonderingly gazing for a considerable time, with still greater astonishment the vessel was seen to suddenly come again into view? Obliged to admit the reappearance of the vessel; neither of us could fairly claim the victory, as both were puzzled and equally in an experimental "fix." This condition of the question at issue lasted for several days, when, one evening conversing with a "gunner" (a shooter of wild fowl), upon the strange appearance referred to, he laughingly undertook to explain the whole affair. He said that at several miles away, beyond the ferry-house, the canal made a sudden bend in the shape of the letter V when lying horizontally, and that the vessel disappeared on account of its entering into one side of the triangle, and reappeared after passing down the other side and entering the usual line of the canal! After a time a large map of the canal was found in a neighbouring town, Wisbeach, and the "gunner's" statement fully verified.

The following diagram will explain this strange, and for a time confounding, phenomenon.

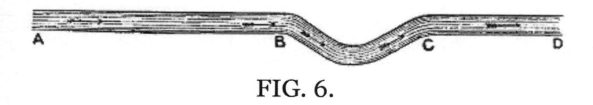

FIG. 6.

A, represents the position of the observer, and the *arrows* the direction of the vessel, which, on arriving at the point B, suddenly entered the "reach" B, C, and disappeared, but which, on arriving at C, became again visible, and remained so after entering and sailing along the canal from C to D. The ferry-house and several trees, which stood on the side of the canal, between the observer and the "bend," had prevented the vessel being seen during the time it was passing from B to C. Thus the "mystery" was cleared away; the author was the real victor; and the gentleman referred to, with many others of the neighbourhood, subsequently avowed their conviction that the water in the "Bedford Level" at least, was horizontal, and they therefore could not see how the earth could possibly be a globe.

EXPERIMENT 3

A good theodolite was placed on the northern bank of the canal, midway between Welney Bridge and the Old Bedford Bridge, which are fully six miles apart, as shown in diagram, fig. 7.

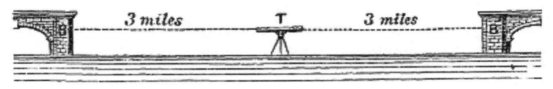

FIG. 7.

The line of sight from the "levelled" theodolite fell upon the points B, B, at an altitude, making allowance for refraction, equal to that of the observer at T. Now the points B, B, being three miles from T, would have been the square of three, or nine times 8 inches, or 6 feet below the line of sight, C, T, C, as seen in the following diagram, fig. 8.

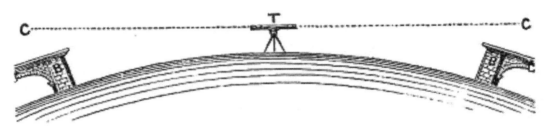

FIG. 8.

EXPERIMENT 4

On several occasions the six miles of water in the old Bedford Canal have been surveyed by the so-called "forward" process of levelling, which consisted in simply taking a sight of, say 20 chains, or 440 yards, noting the point observed, moving the instrument forward to that point, and taking a second observation; again moving the instrument forward, again observing 20 chains in advance, and so on throughout the whole distance. By this process, without making allowance for convexity, the surface of the water was found to be perfectly horizontal. But when the result was made known to several surveyors, it was contended "that when the theodolite is levelled, it is placed at right angles to the earth's radius--the line of sight from it being a tangent; and that when it is removed 20 chains forward, and again 'levelled,' it becomes a second and different tangent; and that indeed every new position is really a fresh tangent--as shown in the diagram, fig. 9, T 1, T 2, and T 3, representing the theodolite levelled at three different positions, and therefore square to the radii 1, 2, 3. Hence, levelling forward in this way, although making no allowance for rotundity, the rotundity or allowance for it is involved in the process."

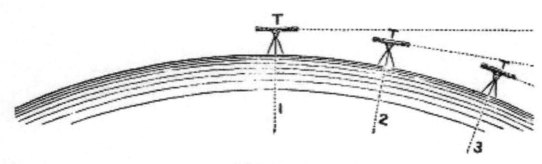

FIG. 9.

This is a very ingenious and plausible argument, by which the visible contradiction between the theory of rotundity and the results of practical levelling is explained; and many excellent mathematicians and geodesists have been deceived by it. Logically, however, it will be seen that it is not a proof of rotundity; it is only an explanation or reconciliation of results with the supposition of rotundity, but does not prove it to exist. The following modification was therefore adopted by the author, in order that convexity, if it existed, might be demonstrated.

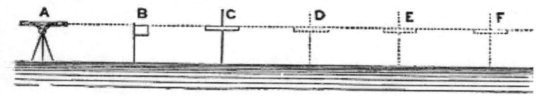

FIG. 10.

A theodolite was placed at the point A, in fig. 10, and levelled; it was then directed over the flag-staff B to the cross-staff C--the instrument A, the flag-staff B, and the cross-staff C, having exactly the same altitude. The theodolite was then advanced to B, the flag-staff to C, and the cross- staff to D, which was thus secured .as a continuation of one and the same line of sight A, B, C, prolonged to D, the altitude of D being the same as that of A, B, and C. The theodolite was again moved forward to the position C, the flag-staff to D, and the cross-staff to the point E--the line of sight to which was thus again secured as a prolongation of A, B, C, D, to E. The process was repeated to F, and onwards by 20 chain lengths to the end of six miles of the canal, and parallel with it. By thus having an object between the theodolite and the cross-staff, which object in its turn becomes a test or guide by which the same line of sight is continued throughout the whole length surveyed, the argument or explanation which is dependent upon the supposition of rotundity, and that each position of the theodolite is a different tangent, is completely destroyed. The result of this peculiar or modified survey, which has been several times repeated, was that the line of sight and the surface of the water ran parallel to each other; and as the. line of sight was, in this instance, a right line, the surface of the water for six miles was demonstrably horizontal.

This mode of forward levelling is so very exact and satisfactory, that the following further illustration may be given with advantage.

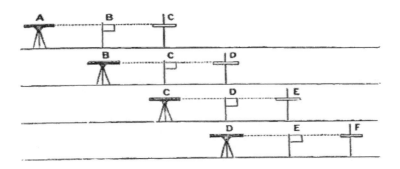

FIG. 11.

In fig. 11, let A, B, C, represent the first position, respectively of the theodolite, flag-staff, and cross-staff; B, C, D, the second position; C, D, E, the third position; and D, E, F, the fourth; similarly repeated throughout the whole distance surveyed.

The remarks thus made in reference to simple "forward" levelling, apply with equal force to what is called by surveyors the "back-and-fore-sight" process, which consists in reading backwards a distance equal to the distance read forwards. This plan is adopted to obviate the necessity for calculating, or allowing for the earth's supposed convexity. It applies, however, just the same in practice, whether the base or datum line is horizontal or convex; but as it has been proved to be the former, it is evident that "back-and-fore-sight" levelling is a waste of time and skill, and altogether unnecessary. Forward levelling over intervening test or guide staves, as explained by the diagram, fig. 11, is far superior to any of the ordinary methods, and has the great advantage of being purely practical and not involving any theoretical considerations. Its adoption along the banks of any canal, or lake, or standing water of any kind, or even along the shore of any open sea, will demonstrate to the fullest satisfaction of any practical surveyor that the surface of all water is horizontal.

EXPERIMENT 5

Although the experiments already described, and many similar ones, have been tried and often repeated, first in 1838, afterwards in 1844, in 1849, in 1856, and in 1862, the author was induced in 1870 to visit the scene of his former labours, and to make some other (one or more) experiment of so simple a character that no error of complicated instrument or process of surveying could possibly be involved. He left London (for Downham Market Station) on Tuesday morning, April 5, 1870, and arrived at the

Old Bedford Sluice Bridge, about two miles from the station, at twelve o'clock. The atmosphere was remarkably clear, and the sun was shining brightly on and against the western face of the bridge. On the right hand side of the arch a large notice-board was affixed (a table of tolls, &c., for navigating the canal). The lowest edge of this board was 6 feet 6 inches above the water, as shown at B, fig. 12.

FIG. 12.

A train of several empty turf boats had just entered the canal from the River Ouse, and was about proceeding to Romsey, in Huntingdonshire. An arrangement was made with the "Captain" to place the shallowest boat the last in the train; on the lowest part of the stern of this boat a good telescope was fixed--the elevation being exactly 18 inches above the water. The sun was shining strongly against the white notice-board, the air was exceedingly still and clear, and the surface of the water "smooth as a molten mirror;" so that everything was extremely favourable for observation. At 1.15, p.m., the train of boats started for Welney. As the boats receded the notice-board was kept in view, and was plainly visible to, the naked eye for several miles; but through the telescope it was distinctly seen throughout the whole distance of six miles. But on reaching Welney Bridge, a very shallow boat was procured, and so fixed that the telescope was brought to within 8 inches of the surface of the water; and still the bottom of the notice-board was clearly visible. The elevation of the telescope being 8 inches, the line of sight would touch the horizon, if convexity exists, at the distance of one statute mile; the square of the remaining five miles, multiplied by 8 inches, gives a curvature of 16 feet 8 inches, so that the bottom of the notice-board--6 feet 6 inches above the water--should have been *10 feet 2 inches below the horizon,* as shown in fig. 13-- B, the notice-board; H, the horizon; and T, the telescope.

FIG. 13.

EXPERIMENT 6

The following important experiment has recently been tried at Brighton, in Sussex. On the new or Western Pier a good theodolite was fixed, at an elevation of 30 feet above the water, and directed to a given point on the pier at Worthing, a distance of at least ten statute miles. Several small yachts and other vessels were sailing about between the two piers, one of which was brought to within a few yards of the Brighton Pier, and directed to sail as nearly as possible in a straight line towards the pier at Worthing; when the top of the mast, which scarcely reached the theodolite, was observed to continue below the line of sight throughout the whole distance, as shown in fig. 14--A, representing the theodolite, and B, the pier at Worthing. From which it is concluded that the surface of the water is horizontal throughout the whole length of ten miles.

FIG. 14.

Whereas, if the earth is a globe, the water between the two piers would be an arc of a circle (as shown in fig. 15), the centre of which would be 16 feet 8 inches higher than the two extremities, and the vessel starting from A, would ascend an inclined plane, rising over 16 feet, to the summit of the arc at C, where the mast-head would stand considerably *above* the line of sight.

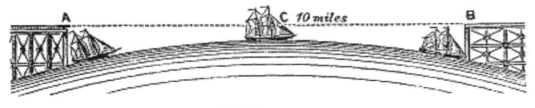

FIG. 15.

From this point the vessel would gradually descend to the point B, at Worthing. As no such behaviour of the vessel was observed, the ten miles of water between the two piers must be horizontal.

EXPERIMENT 7

The sea horizon, to whatever distance it extends to the right and left of an observer on land, always appears as a perfectly straight line, as represented by H, H, in fig. 16.

93

FIG. 16.

Not only does it *appear* to be straight as far as it extends, but it may be proved to be so by the following simple experiment. At any altitude above the sea-level, fix a long board--say from 6 to 12 or more feet in length--edgewise upon tripods, as shown in fig. 17.

FIG. 17.

Let the upper edge be smooth, and perfectly levelled. On placing the eye behind and about the centre of the board B, B, and looking over it towards the sea, the distant horizon will be observed to run perfectly parallel with its upper edge. If the eye be now directed in an angular direction to the left and to the right, there will be no difficulty in observing a length of ten to twenty miles, according to the altitude of the position; and this whole distance of twenty miles of sea horizon will be seen as a perfectly straight line. This would be impossible if the earth were a globe, and the water of the sea convex. Ten miles on each side would give a curvature of 66 feet (10^2 x 8 = 66 feet 8 inches), and instead of the horizon touching the board along its whole length, it would be seen to gradually decline from the centre C, and to be over 66 feet below the two tremities B, B, as shown in fig. 18.

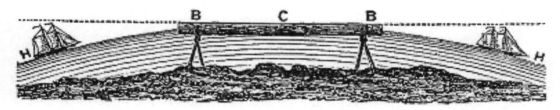

FIG. 18.

Any vessel approaching from the left would be seen to ascend the inclined plane H, B, C, and on passing the centre would descend from C towards the curvating horizon at H. Such a phenomenon is never observed, and it may be fairly concluded that such convexity or curvature does not exist.

EXPERIMENT 8

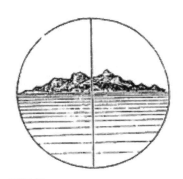

FIG. 19.

A very striking illustration of the true form of the sea horizon may be observed from the high land in the neighbourhood of the head of Portsmouth Harbour. Looking across Spithead to the Isle of Wight, the base or margin of the island, where water and land come together, appears to be a straight line from east to west, a length of twenty-two statute miles. If a good theodolite is directed upon it, the cross-hair will show that the. land and water line is perfectly horizontal, as shown in fig. 19.

If the earth is globular, the two ends east and west of the Isle of Wight would be 80 feet below the centre, and would appear in the field of view of the theodolite as represented in fig. 20. As a proof that such would be the appearance, the same instrument directed upon any object having an upper outline curved in the smallest degree, will detect and plainly show the curvature in relation to the cross-hair *a b*; or the levelled board employed in experiment 7, fig. 18, will prove the same condition to exist; viz., that the margin of the Isle of Wight is, for twenty-two miles, a perfectly straight line; and instead of curvating downwards 80 feet each way from the centre, as it certainly would if convexity existed, it is absolutely horizontal.

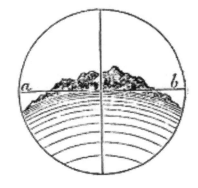

FIG. 20.

From the lighthouse on Bidstone Hill, near Liverpool, the whole length of the Isle of Man, on a clear day and with a good telescope, is distinctly visible, and presents the same horizontal base line as that observed in the Isle of Wight.

From the high land near Douglas harbour, Isle of Man, the whole length of the coast of North Wales is often plainly visible to the naked eye--a distance extending from the point of Ayr, at the mouth of the River Dee, towards Holyhead, not less than fifty miles.

Whatever test has been employed, the line, where the sea and the land appear to join, is always found to be perfectly horizontal, as shown in the following diagram; fig. 21.

FIG. 21.

Whereas, if the earth is spherical, and therefore the surface of all water convex, such an appearance could not exist. It would of necessity appear as shown in fig. 22.

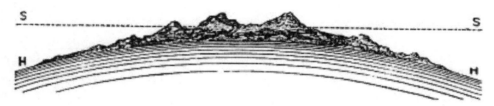

FIG. 22.

A line stretched horizontally before the observer would not only show the various elevations of the land, but would also show the declination of the horizon H, H, below the cross-line S, S. The fifty miles length of the Welsh coast seen along the horizon in Liverpool Bay, would have a declination from the centre of at least 416 feet (25^2 x .8 inches = 416 feet 8 inches). But as such declination, or downward curvature, cannot be detected, the conclusion is logically inevitable that *it has no existence*. Let the reader seriously ask whether any and what reason exists in Nature to prevent the fall of more than 400 feet being visible to the eye, or incapable of detection by any optical or mathematical means whatever. This question is especially important when it is considered that at the same distance, and on the upper outline of the same land, changes of level of only a few yards extent are quickly and unmistakably perceptible.

If he is guided by evidence and reason, and influenced by a love of truth and consistency, he cannot longer maintain that the earth is a globe. He must feel that to do so is to war with the evidence of his senses, to deny that any importance attaches to fact and experiment, to ignore entirely the value of logical process, and to cease to rely upon practical induction.

EXPERIMENT 9

The distance across St. George's Channel, between Holyhead and Kingstown Harbour, near Dublin, is at least 60 statute miles. It is not an uncommon thing for passengers to notice, when in, and for a considerable distance beyond the centre of the Channel, the Light on Holyhead Pier, and the Poolbeg Light in Dublin Bay, as shown in fig. 23.

FIG. 23.

The Lighthouse on Holyhead Pier shows a red light at an elevation of 44 feet above high water; and the Poolbeg Lighthouse exhibits two bright lights at an altitude of 68 feet; so that a vessel in the middle of the Channel would be 30 miles from each light; and allowing the observer to be on deck, and 24 feet above the water, the horizon on a globe would be 6 miles away. Deducting 6 miles from 30, the distance from the horizon to Holyhead, on the one hand, and to Dublin Bay on the other, would be 24 miles. The square of 24, multiplied by 8 inches, shows a declination of 384 feet. The altitude of the lights in Poolbeg Lighthouse is 68 feet; and of the red light on Holyhead Pier, 44 feet. Hence, if the earth were a globe, the former would always be 316 feet and the latter 340 feet below the horizon, as seen in the following diagram, fig. 24.

FIG. 24.

The line of sight H, S, would be a tangent touching the horizon at H, and passing more than 300 feet over the top of each lighthouse.

Many instances could be given of lights being visible at sea for distances which would be utterly impossible upon a globular surface of 25,000 miles in circumference. The following are examples:--

> "The coal fire (which was once used) on the Spurn Point Lighthouse, at the mouth of the Humber, which was constructed on a good principle for burning, has been seen 30 miles off."[3]

---

3 "Lighthouses of the World." Laurie, 53, Fleet Street, London, 1862. Page 9.

Allowing 16 feet for the altitude of the observer (which is more than is considered necessary,[4] 10 feet being the standard; but 6 feet may be added for the height of the eye above the deck), 5 miles must be taken from the 30 miles, as the distance of the horizon. The square of 5 miles, multiplied by 8 inches, gives 416 feet; deducting the altitude of the light, 93 feet, we have 323 feet as the amount this light should be *below the horizon*.

The above calculation is made on the supposition that statute miles are intended, but it is very probable that *nautical* measure is understood; and if so, the light would be depressed fully 600 feet.

> The Egerö Light, on west point of Island, south coast of Norway, is fitted up with the first order of the dioptric lights, is visible 28 statute miles, and the altitude above high water is 154 feet. On making the proper calculation it will be found that this light ought to be sunk below the horizon 230 feet.
>
> The Dunkerque Light, on the south coast of France, is 194 feet high, and is visible 28 statute miles. The ordinary calculation shows that it ought to be 190 feet below the horizon.
>
> The Cordonan Light, on the River Gironde, west coast of France, is visible 31 statute miles, and its altitude is 207 feet, which would give its depression below the horizon as nearly 280 feet.
>
> The Light at Madras, on the Esplanade, is 132 feet high, and is visible 28 statute miles, at which distance it ought to be beneath the horizon more than 250 feet.
>
> The Port Nicholson Light, in New Zealand (erected in 1859), is visible 35 statute miles, the altitude being 420 feet above high water. If the water is convex it ought to be 220 feet below the horizon.
>
> The Light on Cape Bonavista, Newfoundland, is 150 feet above high water, and is visible 35 statute miles. These figures will give, on calculating for the earth's rotundity, 491 feet as the distance it should be sunk below the sea horizon.

The above are but a few cases selected from the work referred to in the note [on the previous page]. Many others could be given equally important, as showing the discrepancies between the theory of the earth's rotundity and the practical experience of nautical men.

The only modification which can be made in the above calculations is the allowance for *refraction*, which is generally considered by surveyors to amount to one-twelfth the altitude of the object observed. If we make this allowance, it will reduce the various

---

4 By all the figures given is meant "The minimum distance to which the light can be seen in clear weather from a height of 10 feet above the sea level." Ibid., p. 32.

quotients so little that the whole will be substantially the same. Take the last case as an instance. The altitude of the light on Cape Bonavista, Newfoundland, is 150 feet, which, divided by 12, gives 13 feet as the amount to be deducted from 491 feet, making instead 478 feet, as the degree of declination.

Many have urged that refraction would account for much of the elevation of objects seen at the distance of several miles. Indeed, attempts have been made to show that the large flag at the end of six miles of the Bedford Canal (Experiment 1, fig. 2) has been brought into the line of sight entirely by refraction. That the line of sight was not a right line, but curved over the convex surface of the water; and the well-known appearance of an object in a basin of water, has been referred to in illustration. A very little reflection, however, will show that the cases are not parallel; for instance, if the object (a shilling or other coin) is placed in a basin *without water* there is *no refraction*. Being surrounded with atmospheric air only, and the observer being in the same medium, there is no bending or refraction of the eye line. Nor would there be any refraction if the object and the observer were both surrounded with water. Refraction can only exist when the medium surrounding the observer is different to that in which the object is placed. As long as the shilling in the basin is surrounded with air, and the observer is in the same air, there is no refraction; but whilst the observer remains in the air, and the shilling is placed in water, refraction exists. This illustration does not apply to the experiments made on the Bedford Canal, because the flag and the boats were in the same medium as the observer--both were in the air. To make the cases parallel, the flag or the boat should have been *in the water*, and the observer *in the air*; as it was not so, the illustration fails. There is no doubt, however, that it is possible for the atmosphere to have different temperature and density at two stations six miles apart; and some degree of refraction would thence result; but on several occasions the following steps were taken to ascertain whether any such differences existed. Two barometers, two thermometers, and two hygrometers, were obtained, each two being of the same make, and reading exactly alike. On a given day, at twelve o'clock, all the instruments were carefully examined, and both of each kind were found to stand at the same point or figure: the two, barometers showed the same density; the two thermometers the same temperature; and the two hygrometers the same degree of moisture in the air. One of each kind was then taken to the opposite station, and at three o'clock each instrument was carefully examined, and the readings recorded, and the observation to the flag, &c., then immediately taken. In a short time afterwards the two sets of observers met each other about midway on the northern bank of the canal, when the notes were compared, and found to be precisely alike--the temperature, density, and moisture of the air *did not differ* at the two stations at the time the experiment with the telescope and flag-staff was made. Hence it was concluded that refraction had not played any part in the observation, and could not be allowed for, nor permitted to influence, in any way whatever, the general result.

In 1851, the author delivered a course of lectures in the Mechanics' Institute, and afterwards at the Rotunda, in Dublin, when great interest was manifested by large audiences; and he was challenged to a repetition of some of his experiments--to be carried out in the neighbourhood. Among others, the following was made, across the Bay of Dublin. On the pier, at Kingstown Harbour, a good theodolite was fixed, at a given altitude, and directed to a flag which, earlier in the day, had been fixed at the base of the Hill of Howth, on the northern side of the bay. An observation was made at a given hour, and arrangements had been made for thermometers, barometers, and hygrometers--two of each--which had been previously compared, to be read simultaneously, one at each station. On the persons in charge of the instruments afterwards meeting, and comparing notes, it was found that the temperature, pressure, and moisture of the air had been alike at the two points, at the time the observation was made from Kingstown Pier. It had also been found by the observers that the point observed on the Hill of Howth had precisely the same altitude as that of the theodolite on the pier, and that, therefore, there was no curvature or convexity in the water across Dublin Bay. It was, of course, inadmissible that the similarity of altitude at the two places was the result of refraction, because there was no difference in the condition of the atmosphere at the moment of observation.

The following remarks from the *Encyclopædia Brittanica*--article, *"Levelling"*--bear on the question:--

> "We suppose the visual ray to be a straight line, whereas on account of the unequal densities of the air at different distances from the earth, the rays of light are incurvated by refraction. The effect of this is to lessen the difference between the true and apparent levels, but in such an extremely variable and uncertain manner that if any constant or fixed allowance is made for it in formula or tables, it will often lead to a greater error than what it was intended to obviate. For though the refraction may at a mean compensate for about one-seventh of the curvature of the earth, it sometimes exceeds one-fifth, and at other times does not amount to one-fifteenth. We have, therefore, made no allowance for refraction in the foregone formulæ."

It will be seen from the above that, in practice, refraction need not be allowed for. It can only exist when the line of sight passes from one medium into another of different density; or where the same medium differs at the point of observation and the point observed. If we allow for the amount of refraction which the ordnance surveyors have adopted, viz., one-twelfth of the altitude of the object observed, and apply it to the various experiments made on the Old Bedford Canal, it will make very little difference in the actual results. In the experiment, fig. 3 for instance, where the top of the flag on the boat should have been 11 feet 8 inches below the horizon, deducting one-twelfth for refraction, would only reduce it to a few inches less than 10 feet.

Others, not being able to deny the fact that the surface of the water in the Old Bedford and other canals is horizontal, have thought that a solution of the difficulty was to be found in supposing the canal to be a kind of "trough" cut into the surface of the earth; and have considered that although the earth is a globe, such a canal or "trough" might exist on its surface as a chord of the arc terminating at each end. This, however, could only be possible if the earth were motionless. But the theory which demands rotundity of the earth also requires rotary motion, and this produces centrifugal force. Therefore the centrifugal action of the revolving earth would, of necessity, throw the waters of the surface away from the centre. This action being equal at equal distances, and being retarded by the attraction of gravitation (which the theory includes), which is also equal at equal distances, the surface of every distinct and entire mass of water must stand equidistant from the earth's centre, and, therefore, must be convex, or an arc of a circle. Equidistant from a centre means, in a scientific sense, "level." Hence the necessity for using the term horizontal to distinguish between "level" and "straight."

EXPERIMENT 10

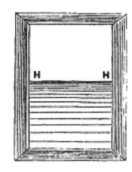

FIG 25

If we stand upon the deck of a ship, or mount to the mast-lead, or ascend above the earth in a balloon and look over the sea, the surface appears as a vast inclined plane rising up from beneath us, until in the distance it reaches the level of the eye, and intercepts the line-of-sight.

If a good plane mirror be held vertically in the opposite direction, the horizon will be reflected as a well defined mark or line across the centre, as represented in fig. 25, H, H, the sea horizon, which rises and falls with the observer, and is always on a level with his eye. If he takes a position where the water surrounds him--as, on the deck or the mast-head of a ship out of sight of land, or on the summit of an island far from the mainland--the surface of the sea appears to rise up on all sides equally, and to surround him like the walls of an immense amphitheatre. He seems to be in the centre of a large concavity--a vast watery basin--the circular edge of which expands or contracts as he takes a higher or lower position. This appearance is so well known to sea- going travellers that nothing more need be said in its support; but the appearance from a balloon is only familiar to a very few observers, and therefore it will be useful to quote the words of some of those who have written upon the subject.

"THE APPARENT CONCAVITY OF THE EARTH AS SEEN FROM A BALLOON.--A perfectly-formed circle encompassed the visibly; planisphere beneath, or rather the concavo-sphere it might now be called, for I had attained a height from which the earth assumed a regularly hollowed or concave appearance--an optical illusion which increases as you recede from it. At the greatest elevation I attained, which was about a mile-and-a-half, the appearance of the world around me assumed a shape or form like that which is made by placing two watch glasses together by their edges, the balloon apparently in the central cavity all the time of its flight at that elevation."-- *Wise's Aëronautics.*

"Another curious effect of the aërial ascent was that the earth, when we were at our greatest altitude, positively appeared concave, looking like a huge dark bowl, rather than the convex sphere such as we naturally expect to see it. . . . The horizon always appears to be on a level with our eye, and seems to rise as we rise, until at length the elevation of the circular boundary line of the sight becomes so marked that the earth assumes the anomalous appearance as we have said of a concave rather than a convex body."--*Mayhew's Great World of London.*

"The chief peculiarity of a view from a balloon at a considerable elevation, was the altitude of the horizon, which remained practically on a level with the eye, at an elevation of two miles, causing the surface of the earth to appear concave instead of convex, and to recede during the rapid ascent, whilst the horizon and the balloon seemed to be stationary."--*London Journal*, July 18th, 1857.

Mr. Elliott, an American aëronaut, in a letter giving an account of his ascension from Baltimore, thus speaks of the appearance of the earth from a balloon:--

"I don't know that I ever hinted heretofore that the aëronaut may well be the most sceptical man about the rotundity of the earth. Philosophy imposes the truth upon us; but the view of the earth from the elevation of a balloon is that of an immense terrestrial basin, the deeper part of which is that directly under one's feet. As we ascend, the earth beneath us seems to recede--actually to sink away--while the horizon gradually and gracefully lifts a diversified slope, stretching away farther and farther to a line that, at the highest elevation, seems to close with the sky. Thus, upon a clear day, the aëronaut feels as if suspended at about an equal distance between the vast blue oceanic concave above and the equally expanded terrestrial basin below."

During the important balloon ascents, recently made for scientific purposes by Mr. Coxwell and Mr. Glaisher, of the Royal Observatory, Greenwich, the same phenomenon was observed.

"The horizon always appeared on a level with the car."--See Mr. Glaisher's Report, in *"Leisure Hour,"* for October 11, 1862.

"The plane of the earth offers another delusion to the traveller in air, to whom it appears as a concave surface, and who surveys the line of the horizon as an unbroken circle, rising up, in relation to the hollow of the concave hemisphere, like the rim of a shallow inverted watch-glass, to the height of the eye of the observer, how high soever he may be--the blue atmosphere above closing over it like the corresponding hemisphere reversed."--Glaisher's Report, in *"Leisure Hour,"* for May 21, 1864.

The appearance referred to in the several foregoing extracts is represented in the following diagram, fig. 26.

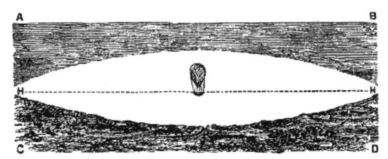

FIG. 26.

The surface of the earth C, D, appears to rise up to the level of the observer in the car of the balloon; and at the same time, the sky A, B, seems to descend and to meet the earth at the horizon H, H.

Nearly 70 years after the above observations were made, Professor Auguste Piccard and his partner Charles Kipfer became the first "aëronauts" to launch themselves over 52,000 feet into the Stratosphere. Their adventure and observations were recorded in Popular Science magazine, wherein Piccard is quoted as saying that the Earth:

"...seemed a flat disc with upturned edge."

The photo on the next page is a screen capture of the story on page 23 of the August, 1931 issue of the magazine (cover pictured right).

Back to earth on Austrian gla-cier, after soaring ten miles above the earth, priceless scientific records are removed from air-tight aluminum ball.

Ten Miles High
in an AIR-TIGHT BALL

A HUGE yellow balloon soared sky-ward, a few weeks ago, from Augsberg, Germany. Instead of a basket, it trailed an air-tight black-and-silver aluminum ball. Within Prof. Auguste Piccard, physicist, and Charles Kipfer aimed to explore the air 50,000 feet up. Seventeen hours later, after being given up for dead, they returned safely from an estimated height of more than 52,000 feet, almost ten miles, shattering every aircraft altitude record. Oxygen tanks kept them alive while they made observations. Records of their instruments are now being checked and interpreted. First to rise safely into the upper layer of the earth's atmosphere, they found the air pressure at ten miles altitude so low — one-tenth of that at sea level—that a man exposed to it would perish much as a deep-sea fish bursts of its own internal pressure when brought to the earth's surface. Piccard and his aid found cosmic rays, mysterious radiations from outer space, far more powerful than at the earth's surface, and gaged their intensity. The explorers trapped samples of the upper air, "blue air," as Piccard reported it to appear, in cylinders. Analysis may prove it exceptionally rich in ozone, the intensely blue gas supposedly

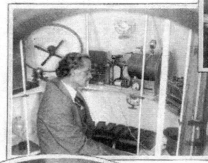

The huge balloon, carrying the big ball in which ride the two scientists, begins its ascent. The metal chamber was designed to save the explorers' lives at altitude never before reached.

responsible for the Heaviside layer or "radio roof." The story of their adventure surpasses fiction. During the ascent, the aluminum ball began to leak. They plugged it desperately with vaseline and cotton waste, stopping the leak. In the first half hour the balloon shot upward nine miles. Through portholes, the observers saw the earth through copper-colored, then bluish, haze. It seemed a flat disk with upturned edge. At the ten-mile level the sky appeared a deep, dark blue. With observations complete, the observers tried to descend, but couldn't. While their oxygen tanks emptied, they floated aimlessly over Germany, Austria, and Italy. Cool evening air contracted the balloon's gas and brought them down on a glacier near Ober-Gurgl, Austria, with one hour's supply of oxygen to spare.

Professor Piccard, center, seated within the ball, studies the instruments before the daring ascent. Above, dismantling balloon on the high glacier.

Two years later, the Russians attempted the same thing and got even higher. At an altitude of 62,304 feet, they looked down and the article printed in the December 1933 issue (cover left) of Popular Science magazine (see screen capture below) recorded the following:

"Looking down, they tried in vain to detect any curvature of the earth's horizon."

THERMOSTAT FOR CARBURETOR

Installed on any car, with only a wrench and pliers for tools, a new thermostatic device automatically adjusts the carburetor mixture to suit the weather and the engine temperature. The thermostatic element, resting on the exhaust manifold, closes an air valve when the motor is cold and opens it, making the mixture leaner, as the motor warms up.

SNOWMOBILE FOR POLAR TRIP

Members of Rear Admiral Richard E. Byrd's second expedition to the Antarctic, which recently started for the South, will whiz over the polar ice and snow in a curious six-wheeled vehicle nicknamed the "snowmobile." Its endless treads provide firm traction, no matter how bad the going, while a pair of ski runners at the front serve to steer the car.

SKY VIOLET IN COLOR AT ELEVEN-MILE ELEVATION

Soaring in their airtight balloon gondola to the record-breaking height of 11.8 miles above the earth, the other day, three Russian aeronauts brought back the first scientific observations ever made at so great an altitude. Above their heads the sky provided a striking spectacle; its color had turned to a soft, deep violet, almost devoid of the light-reflecting haze found at lower levels. Looking down, they tried in vain to detect any curvature of the earth's horizon. Following their successful voyage to the stratosphere, in the gondola illustrated above, still higher ascents are planned.

Six-wheeled snowmobile to be used by Rear Admiral Byrd on his present expedition to the Antarctic

Also of interest, in the above article is the depiction of Admiral Byrd as he prepares for his epic exploration of Antarctica.

EXPERIMENT 11

On the eastern pier at Brighton (Sussex) a large wooden quadrant was fixed on a stand, the upper surface placed square to a plumb line, and directed towards the east, then to the south, and afterwards to the west. On looking over this upper surface the line of sight in each case seemed to meet the horizon, H, H, as shown in fig. 27.

FIG. 27.

The altitude of the quadrant was 34 feet; hence, if the earth is a globe, the water would have curvated downwards from the pier, the horizon would have been more than seven miles away, and 34 feet below the surface immediately beneath the observer; which depression, added to the elevation of the quadrant on the pier, would give 68 feet as the amount the horizon H, H, would have been below the line of sight A, B, as shown in the following diagram, fig. 28.

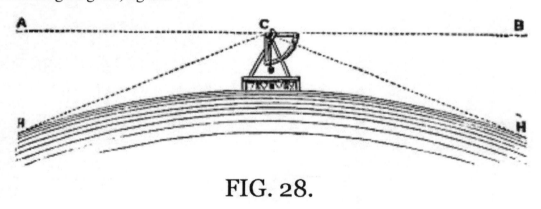

FIG. 28.

To touch the horizon on a convex surface the line of sight, A C, C B, would have to "dip" in the direction C, H; as no such "dip" of the eye line is required, *convexity cannot exist.*

In the case of the balloon at an altitude of two miles, the horizon would have been 127 miles away, and more than 10,000. feet below the summit of the arc of water underneath the balloon, and over 20,000 feet below the line of sight A, B, as shown in fig. 29; and the "dip" C, H, from C, B, to the horizon H, would be so great that the aëronaut could not fail to observe it; instead of which he always sees it "on a level with his eye," "rising as he rises," and "at the highest elevation, seeming to close with the sky."

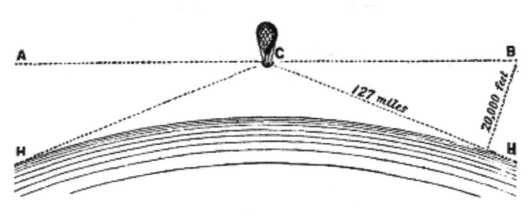

FIG. 29.

The author has seen and tested this apparent rising of the water and the sea horizon to the level of the eye, and to an eye-line at right angles to a plumb-line, from many different places--the high ground near the race- course, at Brighton, in Sussex, from several hills in the Isle of Wight; various places near Plymouth, looking towards the Eddystone Lighthouse; the "Steep Holm," in the Bristol Channel; the Hill of Howth, and "Ireland's Eye," near Dublin; various parts of the Isle of Man, "Arthur's Seat," near Edinburgh; the cliffs at Tynemouth; the rocks at Cromer, in Norfolk; from the top of Nelson's Monument, at Great Yarmouth; and from many other elevated positions. But in Ireland, in Scotland, and in several parts of England, he has been challenged by surveyors to make use of the theodolite, or ordinary "spirit level," to test this appearance of the horizon. It was affirmed that, through this instrument, when "levelled," the horizon always appeared below the cross-hair, as shown in fig. 30--C, C, the cross-hair, and H, H, the horizon.

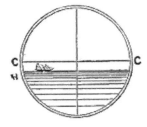

FIG. 30.

FIG. 31.

In every instance when the experiment was tried, this appearance was found to exist; but it was noticed that different instruments gave *different degrees* of horizontal depression below the cross-hair. The author saw at once that this peculiarity depended upon the construction of the instruments. He ascertained that in those of the very best construction, and of the most perfect adjustment, there existed a certain degree of refraction, or, as it is called technically, "collimation," or a slight divergence of the rays of light from the axis of the eye, on passing through the several glasses of the theodolite. He therefore obtained an iron tube, about 18 inches in length; one end was closed, except a very small aperture in the centre; and at the other end cross-hairs were fixed. A spirit level was then attached, and the whole carefully adjusted. On directing it, from a considerable elevation, towards the sea, and looking through the small aperture at one end, the cross-hair at the opposite end was seen to cut or to fall *close to the horizon*, as shown at fig. 31. This has been tried in various places, and at different altitudes, and always with the same result; showing clearly that the horizon visible below the cross-hair of an ordinary levelling instrument is the result of *refraction*, from looking through the various glasses of the telescope; for on looking through an instrument in every respect the same in construction, except being free from lenses, a different result is observed, and one precisely the same as that seen from a balloon, from any promontory, and in the experiment at Brighton, shown in fig. 27.

FIG. 27.

These comparative experiments cannot fail to satisfy any unbiassed observer that in every levelling instrument where lenses are employed, there is, of necessity, more or less divergence of the line of sight from the true or normal axis; and that however small the amount--perhaps inappreciable in short lengths of observation--it is considerable in distances of several miles. Every scientific surveyor of experience is fully aware of this and other peculiarities in all such instruments, and is always ready to make allowances for them in important surveys. As a, still further proof of this behaviour of the telescopic levelling instruments, the following simple experiment may be tried. Select a piece of ground--a terrace, promenade, line of railway, or embankment, which shall be *perfectly horizontal* for, say, five hundred yards. Let a signal staff, 5 feet high, be erected at one end, and a theodolite or spirit level fixed and carefully adjusted to exactly the *same altitude* at the other end. The top of the signal will then be seen a little *below the cross-hair*, although it has the same actual altitude, and stands upon the same *horizontal foundation*. If the positions of the signal staff and the spirit level be then reversed, the same result will follow.

Another proof will be found in the following experiment. Select any promontory, pier, lighthouse gallery, or small island, and, at a considerable altitude, place a smooth block of wood or stone of any magnitude; let this be "levelled." If, then, the observer will place his eye close to the block, and look along its surface towards the sea, he will find that the line of sight will *touch the distant horizon.* Now let any number of spirit levels or theodolites be properly placed, and accurately adjusted; and it will be found that, in every one of them, the same sea horizon will appear in the field of view considerably *below* the cross-hair; thus, proving that telescopic instrumental readings are not the same as those of the naked eye.

In a work entitled "A Treatise on Mathematical Instruments," by J. F. Heather, M.A., of the Royal Military College, Woolwich, published by Weale, High Holborn, London, elaborate directions are given for examining, correcting, and adjusting the collimation, &c.; and at page 103, these directions are concluded by the following words: "The instrument will now be in complete practical adjustment for any distance not exceeding ten chains (220 yards), the maximum error being only 1/1000 of a foot.

At this stage of the enquiry two distinct questions naturally arise: First, if the earth is a plane, why does the sea at all times appear to rise to the axis of the eye? and secondly, would not the same appearance exist if the earth were a globe? It is a simple fact, that two lines running parallel for a considerable distance will, to an observer placed between them at one end, appear to converge or come together at the other end. The top and bottom and sides of a long room, or an equally bored tunnel, will afford a good example of this appearance; but perhaps a still better illustration is given by the two metallic lines of a long portion of any railway.

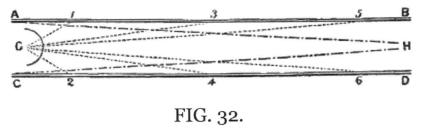

FIG. 32.

In fig. 32, let A, B, and C, D, represent the two lines of a straight portion of horizontal railway. If an observer be placed at G, he will see the two lines apparently meeting each other towards H, from the following cause:--Let G represent the eye looking, first, as far only as figs. 1 and 2, the space between 1 and 2 will then be seen by the eye at G, under the angle 1, G, 2. On looking as far as figs. 3 and 4, the space between 3 and 4 will be seen under the diminished angle 3, G, 4. Again on looking forward to the points 5 and 6, the space between the rails would be represented by the angle 5, G, 6; and, as will at once be seen, the greater the distance observed, the more acute the angle at the eye, and therefore the nearer together will the rails appear. Now if one of these rails should be an arc of a circle and diverge from the other, as in the diagram fig. 33, it is evident that the effect upon the eye at G, would be different to that shown by the diagram fig. 32.

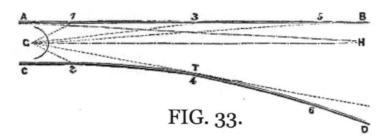

FIG. 33.

The line G, 4, would become a tangent to the arc C, D, and could never approach the line G, H, nearer than the point T. The same may be said of lines drawn to 6, opposite 5, and to all greater distances--none could rise higher than the tangent point T. Hence allowing A, B, to represent the sky, and C, D, the surface of the water of a globe, it is evident that A, B, could appear to decline or come down to the point H, *practically* to a level with the eye at G; but that C, D, could never, by the operation of any known law of optics, rise to the line G, H, and therefore any observation made upon a globular surface, could not possibly produce the effect observed from a balloon, or in any experiment like that represented in.

From the foregoing details the following arguments may be constructed:- -

- Right lines, running parallel with each other, appear to approach in the distance.
- The eye-line, and the surface of the earth and sky, run parallel with each other;
- *Ergo*, the earth and sky appear to approach in the distance. Lines which appear to approach in the distance are parallel lines. The surface of the earth appears to approach the eye-line;
- *Ergo*, the surface of the earth is parallel with the eye-line.
- The eye-line is a right line.
- The surface of the earth is parallel or equidistant;
- *Ergo*, the surface of the earth is *a right line*--a plane.

EXPERIMENT 12

On the shore near Waterloo, a few miles to the north of Liverpool, a good telescope was fixed, at an elevation of 6 feet above the water. It was directed to a large steamer, just leaving the River Mersey, and sailing out to Dublin. Gradually the mast-head of the receding vessel came nearer to the horizon, until, at length, after more than four hours had elapsed, it disappeared. The ordinary rate of sailing of the Dublin steamers was fully eight miles an hour; so that the vessel would be, at least, thirty-two miles distant when the mast-head came to the horizon. The 6 feet of elevation of the telescope would require three miles to be deducted for convexity, which would leave twenty-nine miles, the square of which, multiplied by 8 inches, gives 560 feet; deducting 80 feet for the height of the main-mast, and we find that, according to the doctrine of rotundity, the mast-head of the outward bound steamer should have been 480 feet below the horizon.

Many other experiments of this kind have been made upon sea-going steamers, and always with results entirely incompatible with the theory that the earth is a globe.

EXPERIMENT 13

The following sketch, fig. 34, represents a contracted section of the London and North-Western Railway, from London to Liverpool, through Birmingham.

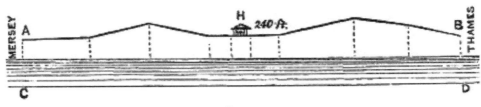

FIG. 34.

The line A, B, is the surface, with its various inclines and altitudes, and C, D, is the *datum* line from which all the elevations are measured; H, is the station at Birmingham, the elevation of which is 240 feet above the datum line C, D, which line is a continuation of the level of the River Thames at D, to the level of the River Mersey, at C. The direct length of this line is 180 miles; and it is a right or absolutely straight line, in a vertical sense, from London to Liverpool. Therefore, the station at Birmingham is 240 feet above the level of the Thames, continued as a right line throughout the whole length of the railway. But if the earth is a globe, the *datum* line will be the *chord* of the arc D, D, D, fig. 35, and the summit of the arc at D, will be 5400 feet above the *chord* at C; added to the altitude of the station H, 240 feet, the Birmingham station, H, would be, if the earth is a globe, 5640 feet above the horizontal *datum* D, D, or vertically above the Trinity high water mark, at London Bridge.

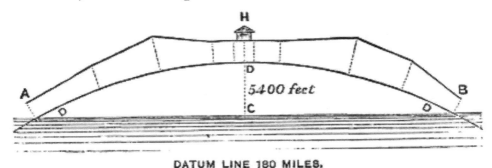

DATUM LINE 180 MILES.

FIG. 35

It is found, practically, and in fact, not to be more than 240 feet; hence the theory of rotundity must be a fallacy. Sections of all other railways will give similar proofs that the earth is in reality a plane.

The tunnel just completed under Mont Fréjus, affords a very striking illustration of the truth that the earth is a plane, and not globular. The elevation above the sea-level of the entrance at Fourneaux, on the French side of the Alps, is 3946 feet, and of the entrance on the Italian side, 4381 feet. The length of the tunnel is 40,000 feet, or nearly eight English statute miles. The gradient or rise, from the entrance on the French side to the summit of the tunnel, is 445 feet; and on the opposite side, 10 feet. It will be seen from the following account, given by M. Kossuth,[5] that the geodetic operations were carried on in connection with a right line, as the axis of the tunnel, and therefore with a horizontal datum which is quite incompatible with the doctrine of rotundity. That the earth is a plane is involved in all the details of the survey, as the following quotation will show:--

> "The observatories placed at the two entrances to the tunnel were used for the necessary observations, and each observatory contained an instrument constructed for the purpose. This instrument was placed on a pedestal of masonry, the top of which was covered with a horizontal slab of marble, having engraved upon its surface two intersecting lines, marking a point which was exactly in the vertical plane containing the axis of the tunnel. The instrument was formed of two supports fixed on a tripod, having a delicate screw adjustment. The telescope was similar to that of a theodolite provided with cross-webs, and strongly illuminated by the light from a lantern, concentrated by a lens and projected upon the cross-webs. In using this instrument in checking the axis of the gallery at the northern entrance, for example; after having proved precisely that the vertical plane, corresponding with the point of intersection of the lines upon the slab, also passed through the centre of the instrument, a visual line was then conveyed to the station at Lochalle (on the mountain), and on the instrument being lowered, the required number of points could be fixed in the axis of the tunnel. In executing such an operation, it was necessary that the tunnel should be free from smoke or vapour. The point of collimation was a plummet, suspended from the roof of the tunnel by means of an iron rectangular frame, in one side of which a number of notches were cut, and the plummet shifted from notch to notch, in accordance with the signals of the operator at the observatory. These signals were given to the man whose business it was to adjust the plummet, by means of a telegraph or a horn. The former was found invaluable throughout all these operations.

---

5 Daily News, September 18, 1871.

"At the Bardonnecchia (Italian) entrance, the instrument employed in setting out the axis of the tunnel was similar to the one already described, with the exception that it was mounted on a little carriage, resting on vertical columns that were erected at distances 500 metres apart in the axis of the tunnel. By the help of the carriage, the theodolite was first placed on the centre line approximately. It was then brought exactly into line by a fine adjustment screw, which moved the eye-piece without shifting the carriage. In order to understand more clearly the method of operating the instrument, the mode of proceeding may be described. In setting out a prolongation of the centre line of the tunnel, the instrument was placed upon the last column but one; a light was stationed upon the last column, and exactly in its centre; and 500 metres ahead a trestle frame was placed across the tunnel. Upon the horizontal bar of this trestle several notches were cut, against which a light was placed, and fixed with proper adjusting screws. The observer standing at the instrument, caused the light to move upon the trestle frame, until it was brought into an exact line with the instrument and the first line; and then the centre of the light was projected with a plummet. In this way the exact centre was found. By a repetition of similar operations the vertical plane containing the axis of the tunnel was laid out by a series of plummet lines. During the intervals that elapsed between consecutive operations with the instrument, the plummets were found to be sufficient for maintaining the direction in making the excavation. To maintain the proper gradients in the tunnel, it was necessary, at intervals, to establish fixed levels, deducing them by direct levelling from standard bench marks, placed at short distances from the entrance. The fixed level marks, in the inside of the tunnel, are made upon stone pillars, placed at intervals of 25 metres, and to these were referred the various points in setting out the gradients."

The theodolite "was placed on a pedestal of masonry, the top of which was covered with a *horizontal* slab of marble, having engraved upon its surface two intersecting lines, marking a point which was exactly in the vertical plane containing the axis of the tunnel." This slab was the starting point--the *datum* which determined the gradients. Its horizontal surface, prolonged through the mountain, passed 445 feet below the summit of the tunnel, and 435 feet below the entrance on the Italian side. This entrance was 4381 feet above the sea, and 435 feet above the horizontal marble slab on the French side. But, if the earth is a globe, the *datum* line from this horizontal slab would be a tangent, from which the sea-level would curvate downwards to the extent of 42 feet; and the summit of the tunnel, instead of being 10 feet above the Italian entrance, would, of necessity, be 52 feet above it. It is not so, and therefore the datum line is not a tangent, but runs parallel to the sea; the sea-level not convex, and the earth not a globe. This will be rendered plain by the following diagram, fig. 36.

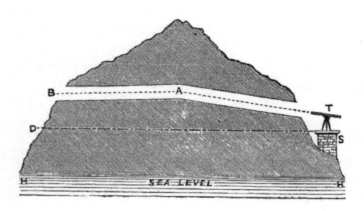

FIG. 36.

Let A represent the summit of the tunnel, and A, T, the axis or centre determined by the theodolite T; S, the marble slab; and D, S, the datum line, running parallel with the sea-level H, H. B, the Italian entrance, at an elevation of 435 feet above D, S, and 4381 feet above the surface of the sea, H, H; A, the summit of the tunnel, 445 feet above the French entrance at T, the same above the datum line D, S; and 4391 feet above the sea-line, H, H. If the earth is a globe, the line, D, S, would be a tangent to the sea at H, S, from which point the sea surface would curvate 52 feet downwards, as shown in diagram, fig. 37. Hence, the elevation of the tunnel at B,would be 52 feet higher above the sea at H, than it is known to be; because taking D, S, as a tangent, and the length of the tunnel being 8 miles--8^2 miles x 8 inches = 52 feet.

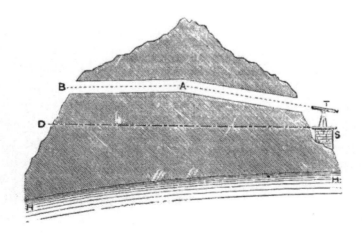

FIG. 37.

Thus, in a length of 8 statute miles of the most skillful engineering operations, carried on by the most accomplished scientific men, there is a difference between theory and practice of 52 feet! Rather than such a reproach should attach to some of the most eminent practical engineers of the day--those especially who have, with such consummate skill and perseverance, completed one of the most gigantic undertakings of modern times--let the false idea of rotundity in the earth be entirely discarded, and the simple truth acknowledged, that the earth is a plane. It is adopted in practice, why should it be denied in the abstract? Why should the education given in our schools and universities include a forced recognition of a theory which, when practically applied, must ever be ignored and contradicted?

The completion of the great ship canal, which connects the Mediterranean Sea with the Gulf of Suez, on the Red Sea, furnishes another instance of entire discrepancy between the theory of the earth's rotundity and the results of practical engineering. The canal is 100 English statute miles in length, and is entirely without locks; so that the water within it is really a continuation of the Mediterranean Sea to the Red Sea. "The average level of the Mediterranean is 6 inches above the Red Sea; but the flood tides in the Red Sea rise 4 feet above the highest, and its ebbs fall nearly 3 feet below the lowest in the Mediterranean." The datum line is 26 feet below the level of the Mediterranean, and is continued horizontally from one sea to the other; and throughout the whole length of the work, the surface of the water runs parallel with this datum, as shown in the following section, fig. 38, published by the authorities.

FIG. 38.

A, A, A, A, is the surface of the canal, passing through several lakes, from one sea to the other; D, D, the bed of the canal, or horizontal datum line to which the various elevations of land, &c., are referred, but parallel to which stands the surface of the water throughout the entire length of the canal; thus proving that the half-tide level of the Red Sea, the 100 miles of water in the canal, and the surface of the Mediterranean Sea, are a continuation of one and the same horizontal line. If the earth is globular, the water in the centre of the canal, being 50 miles from each end, would be the summit of an arc of a circle, and would stand at more than 1600 feet above the Mediterranean and Red Seas (50^2 x 8 inches = 1666 feet 8 inches), as shown in diagram, fig. 39.

FIG. 39.

A, the Mediterranean Sea; B, the Red Sea; and A, C, B, the arc of water connecting them; D, D, the horizontal datum, which, if the earth is globular, would really be the chord of the arc, A, C, B.

The bed of the Atlantic Ocean, from Valencia (western coast of Ireland) to Trinity Bay, Newfoundland, as surveyed for the laying of the cable, is another illustration or proof that the surface of the great waters of the earth is horizontal, and not convex, as will be seen by the following diagram, contracted from the section, published October 8, 1869, by the Admiralty.

FIG. 40.

C, D, is the horizontal datum line, and A, B, the surface of the water, for a distance of 1665 nautical, or 1942 statute miles. At about one-third the distance from A, Newfoundland, the greatest depth is found--2424 fathoms; the next deepest part is 2400 fathoms; at about two-thirds the distance from A, towards B, Ireland, while in the centre, the depth is less than 1600 fathoms; whereas, if the water of the Atlantic is convex, the centre would stand 628,560 feet, or nearly 120 miles, higher than the two stations, Trinity Bay and Valencia; and the greatest depth would be in the centre of the Atlantic Ocean, where it would be 106,310 fathoms, instead of 1550 fathoms, which it is proved to be by actual soundings.

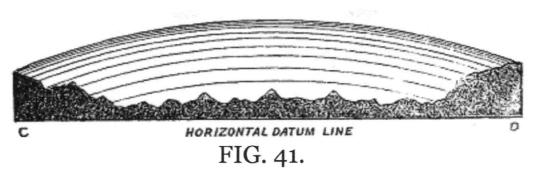

C   *HORIZONTAL DATUM LINE*   D

FIG. 41.

Fig. 41 shows the arc of water which would exist, in relation to the horizontal *datum* line, between Ireland and Newfoundland, if the earth is a globe. Again, if the water in the Atlantic Ocean is convex--a part of a great sphere of 25,000 miles circumference--the *horizontal datum line* would be a chord to the great arc of water above it; and the distance across the bed of the Atlantic would therefore be considerably less than the distance over the surface. The length of the cable which was laid in 1866, notwithstanding the known irregularities of the bed of the Ocean, would be less than the distance sailed by the paying-out vessel, the "Great Eastern;" whereas, according to the published report, the distance run by the steamer was 1665 miles, while the length of cable payed out was 1852 miles.

It is important to bear in mind that all the foregoing remarks and calculations are made in connection with the fact that the *datum* line, to which all elevations and depressions are referred, is *horizontal*, and not an arc of a circle. For many years past, all the great surveys have been made on this principle; but that no doubt may exist in the mind of the reader, the following extract is given from the Standing Orders of the Houses of Lords and Commons on Railway Operations, for the Session of 1862: [6] --

"The section shall be drawn to the same horizontal scale as the plan, and to a vertical scale of not less than one inch to every one hundred feet; and shall show the surface of the ground marked on the plan, the intended level of the proposed work, the height of every embankment, and the depth of every cutting, and a datum horizontal line, which shall be the same throughout the whole length of the work; or any branch thereof respectively; and shall be referred to some fixed point . . . . near either of the termini. (See line D, D; fig. 2.)"

On the page opposite that of the above Standing Order, a section is given to illustrate the meaning of the words of the order--special reference being made to the line D, D, as showing what is intended by the words *"datum horizontal line."* The drawing of the section there given, and which is insisted upon by Government, is precisely the same as the sections recently published of all the great railways, of the Suez Canal, of the bed

---

6 Publishers, Vacher & Sons, 29, Parliament Street, Westminster.

of the Atlantic Ocean, taken for the purposes of laying the Electric Cable, and of many other works connected with railways deep-sea ordnance, and other surveying operations. In all these extensive surveys the doctrine of rotundity is, of necessity, entirely ignored; and the principle that the earth is a plane is practically adopted, and found to be the only one consistent with the results, and agreeing with the plans of the great surveyors and engineers of the day.

EXPERIMENT 14

If a good theodolite is placed on the summit of Shooter's Hill, in Kent, and levelled, the line of sight, on being directed to Hampstead Hill, will cut the cross on St. Paul's Cathedral, and fall upon a part of Hampstead Hill, the altitude of which is the same as that of Shooter's Hill. The altitude of each of these points is 412 feet above the Trinity high water mark, at London Bridge. The distance from Shooter's Hill to St. Paul's Cathedral is 7 statute miles, and from St. Paul's to Hampstead Hill, 5 miles. If the earth is a globe, the line of sight from the "levelled" theodolite would be a tangent, below which St. Paul's cross would be 32 feet, and Hampstead Hill 96 feet. The highest point of Hampstead Hill is 430 feet, which we find, on making the proper calculation, would be 78 feet below the summit of Shooter's Hill; whereas, according to the Ordnance Survey, and as may be proved by experiment, the three points are in the same direct line; again demonstrating that the earth is a plane.

The diagrams, figs. 42 and 43, will show the difference between the theory of rotundity and the results of actual survey. A, represents Hampstead Hill; C, St. Paul's cross; B, Shooter's Hill; and D, D, the datum line--the Trinity high water mark. In fig. 43, A, B, C, and D, D, represent the same points respectively as in fig. 42.

In the account of the trigonometrical operations in France, by M. M. Biot and Arago, it is stated that the light of a powerful lamp, with good reflectors, was placed on a rocky summit, in Spain, called Desierto las Palmas, and was distinctly seen from Camprey, on the Island of Iviza. The elevation of the two points was nearly the same, and the distance between them nearly 100 miles. If the earth is a globe, the light on the rock in Spain would have been more than 6600 feet, or nearly one mile and a quarter, below the line of sight.

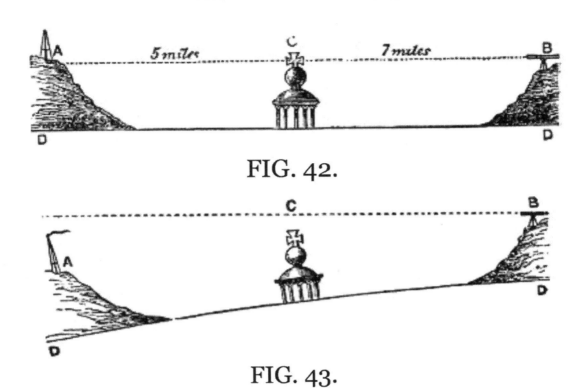

FIG. 42.

FIG. 43.

"The length of some of the sides of the great triangles (in the English survey) is upwards of 100 miles; and many means were employed to render the stations visible from each other at such great distances. The oxy-hydrogen, or Drummond's Light, was employed in some instances; but a heliostat, for reflecting the sun's rays in the direction of the distant observer, was more generally and successfully employed. Lieutenant- Colonel Portlock, R.E., who observed the station on Precelly, a mountain in South Wales, from the station on Kippure, a mountain about 10 miles south-west of Dublin--the distance between the stations being 108 miles- -says: 'For five weeks I watched in vain; when, to my joy, the heliostat blazed out in the early beams of the rising sun, and continued visible as a bright star the whole day.'" [7]

Many other very long "sights" have been taken by surveyors of different countries, which upon a globe of 25,000 miles in circumference, would have been quite impossible; but with the demonstrated fact that the earth is a plane, are practical and consistent.

---

7 Handbook to the Official Catalogue of the Great Exhibition of 1851.

EXPERIMENT 15

From the first floor of the "grand" hotel, opposite the new or western pier, at Brighton, in Sussex, a well-constructed instrument, called a "Clinometer," was "levelled," and directed towards the sea. The water seemed to ascend as an inclined plane, until it intercepted the line of sight at the point H 1, as shown in fig. 44.

FIG. 44.

On taking the instrument to a higher position, again "levelling," and looking over the sea, the surface seemed to ascend a second time, until it met the eye-line at H 2. The instrument was then taken to the highest room, and again directed to the sea, when the uprising surface was again seen to meet the eye-line, as at the point H 3. As already shown, these results are precisely those which an optical or perspective law produces, in connection with a right line, or a plane surface. Upon a globular surface, the appearance would necessarily be as seen in fig. 45.

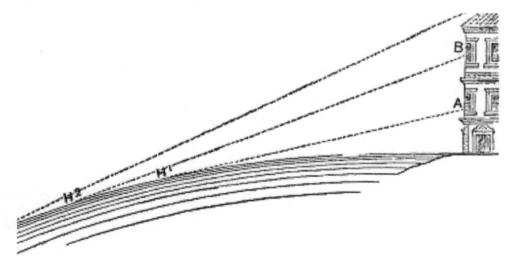

FIG. 45.

From the position A, the horizon would be seen at H 1, and at a considerable angle downwards; from B, the horizon would be at H 2; and from C, at II 3; and the downward angle, or "dip," would increase as the altitude of the observer increased. But as nothing of the kind is anywhere to be seen, and the directly contrary at all times visible, we are compelled by the force of practical evidence to deny the existence of rotundity, and to declare that, "to all intents and purposes," absolutely and logically, beyond doubt, THE EARTH IS A VAST IRREGULAR PLANE.

CHAPTER III
THE EARTH NO AXIAL OR ORBITAL MOTION

IF a ball is allowed to drop from the mast-head of a ship at rest, it will strike the deck at the foot of the mast. If the same experiment is tried with a ship *in motion*, the same result will follow; because, in the latter case, the ball is acted upon simultaneously by two forces at right angles to each other--one, the momentum given to it by the moving ship in the direction of its own motion; and the other, the force of gravity, the direction of which is at right angles to that of the momentum. The ball being acted upon by the two forces together, will not go in the direction of either, but will take a diagonal course, as shown in the following diagram, fig. 46.

FIG. 46.

The ball passing from A to C, by the force of gravity, and having, at the moment of its liberation, received a momentum from the moving ship in the direction A, B, will, by the conjoint action of the two forces A, B, and A, C, take the direction A, D, falling at D, just as it would have fallen at C, had the vessel remained at rest.

123

It is argued by those who hold that the earth is a revolving globe, that if a ball is dropped from the mouth of a deep mine, it reaches the bottom in an apparently vertical direction, the same as it would if the earth were motionless. In the same way, and from the same cause, it is said that a ball allowed to drop from the top of a tower, will fall at the base. Admitting the fact that a ball dropped down a mine, or let fall from a high tower, reaches the bottom in a direction parallel to the side of either, it does not follow therefrom that the earth moves. It only follows that the earth *might* move, and yet allow of such a result. It is certain that such a result would occur on a stationary earth; and it is mathematically demonstrable that it would also occur on a revolving earth; but the question of motion or non-motion--of which is the fact it does not decide. It gives no proof that the ball falls in a vertical or in a diagonal direction. Hence, it is logically valueless. We must begin the enquiry with an experiment which does not involve a supposition or an ambiguity, but which will decide whether motion does actually or actually does not exist. It is certain, then, that the path of a ball, dropped from the mast-head of a *stationary ship* will be *vertical*. It is also certain that, dropped down a deep mine, or from the top of a high tower, upon a *stationary earth*, it would be *vertical*. It is equally certain that, dropped from the mast-head of a moving ship, it would be *diagonal*; so also upon a moving earth it would be diagonal. And as a matter of necessity, that which follows in one case would follow in every other case, if, in each, the conditions were the same. Now let the experiment shown in fig. 46 be modified in the following way:--

Let the ball be thrown *upwards* from the mast-head of a *stationary ship*, and it will fall back to the mast-head, and pass downwards to the foot of the mast. The same result would follow if the ball were thrown upwards from the mouth of a mine, or the top of a tower, on a *stationary earth*. Now put the ship *in motion*, and let the ball be thrown *upwards*. It will, as in the first instance, partake of the two motions--the upward or vertical, A, C, and the horizontal, A, B, as shown in fig. 47; but because the two motions act conjointly, the ball will take the diagonal direction, A, D.

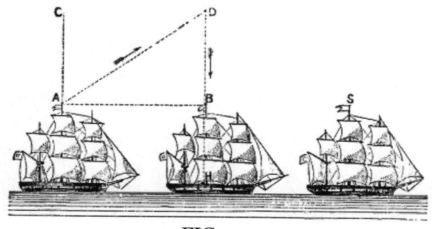

FIG. 47.

By the time the ball has arrived at D, the ship will have reached the position, 13; and now, as the two forces will have been expended, the ball will begin to fall, by the force of gravity alone, in the vertical direction, D, B, H; but during its fall towards H, the ship will have passed on to the position S, leaving the ball at H, a given distance behind it.

The same result will be observed on throwing a ball upwards from a railway carriage, when in rapid motion, as shown in the following diagram, fig. 48. While the carriage or tender passes from A to B, the ball thrown upwards, from A towards (2, will reach the position D; but during the time of its fall from D to B, the carriage will have advanced to S, leaving the ball behind at B, as in the case of the ship in the last experiment.

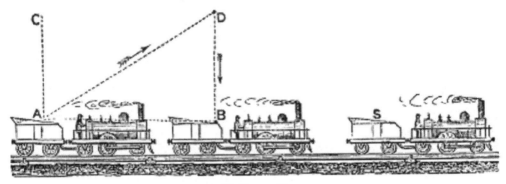

FIG. 48.

The same phenomenon would be observed in a circus, during the performance of a juggler on horseback, were it not that the balls employed are thrown more or less forward, according to the rapidity of the horse's motion. The juggler standing in the ring, on the solid ground, throws his balls as vertically as he can, and they return to his hand; but when on the back of a rapidly-moving horse, he should throw the balls vertically, before they fell back to his hands, the horse would have taken him in advance, and the whole would drop to the ground behind him. It is the same in leaping from the back of a horse in motion. The performer must throw himself to a certain degree forward. If he jumps directly upwards, the horse will go from under him, and he would fall behind.

Thus it is demonstrable that, in all cases where a ball is thrown upwards from an object moving at right angles to its path, that ball will come down to a place behind the point from which it was thrown; and the distance at which it falls behind depends upon the time the ball has been in the air. As this is the result in every instance where the experiment is carefully and specially performed, the same would follow if a ball were discharged from any point upon a revolving earth. The causes or conditions operating being the same, the same effect would necessarily follow.

The experiment shown in fig. 49, demonstrates, however, that these causes, or conditions, or motion in the earth, do not exist.

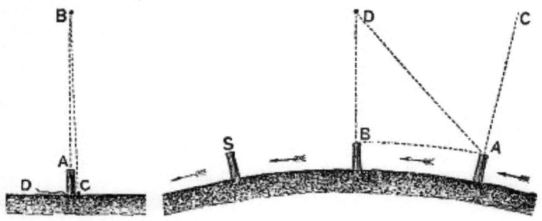

FIG. 49.

A strong cast-iron cannon was placed with the muzzle upwards. The barrel was carefully tested with a plumb line, so that its true vertical direction was secured; and the breech of the gun was firmly embedded in sand up to the touch-hole, against which a piece of slow match was placed. The cannon had been loaded with powder and ball, previous to its position being secured. At a given moment the slow match at D was fired, and the operator retired to a shed. The explosion took place, and the ball was discharged in the direction A, B. In thirty seconds the ball fell back to the earth, from B to C; the point of contact, C, was only 8 inches from the gun, A. This experiment has been many times tried, and several times the ball fell back upon the mouth of the cannon; but the greatest deviation was less than 2 feet, and the average time of absence was 28 seconds; from which it is concluded that the earth on which the gun was placed ***did not move*** from its position during the 28 seconds the ball was in the atmosphere. Had there been motion in the direction from west to east, and at the rate of 600 miles per hour (the supposed velocity in the latitude of England), the result would have been as shown in fig. 49. The ball, thrown by the powder in the direction A, C, and acted on at the same moment by the earth's motion in the direction A, B, would take the direction A, D; meanwhile the earth and the cannon would have reached the position B, opposite to D. On the ball beginning to descend, and during the time of its descent, the gun would have passed on to the position S, and the ball would have dropped at B, a considerable distance behind the point S. As the average time of the ball's absence in the atmosphere was 28 seconds--14 going upwards, and 14 in falling--we have only to multiply the time by the supposed velocity of the earth, and we find that instead of the ball coming down to within a few inches of the muzzle of the gun, it should have fallen behind it a distance of 8400 feet, or more than a mile and a half! Such a result is utterly destructive of the idea of the earth's possible rotation.

The reader is advised not to deceive himself by imagining that the ball would take a parabolic course, like the balls and shells from cannon during a siege or battle. The parabolic curve could only be taken by a ball fired from a cannon inclined more or less from the vertical; when, of course, gravity acting in an angular direction against the force of the gunpowder, the ball would be forced to describe a parabola. But in the experiment just detailed, the gun was fixed in a perfectly vertical direction, so that the ball would be fired in a line the very contrary to the direction of gravity. The force of the powder would drive it directly upwards, and the force of gravity would pull it directly downwards. Hence it could only go up in a right line, and down or back to its starting point; it could not possibly take a path having the slightest degree of curvature. It is therefore demanded that, if the earth has a motion from west to east, a ball, instead of being dropped down a mine, or allowed to fall from the top of a tower, shall be *shot upwards* into the air, and from the moment of its beginning to descend, the surface of the earth shall turn from under its direction, and it would fall behind, or to the west of its line of descent. On making the most exact experiments, however, *no such effect is observed*; and, therefore, the conclusion is in every sense unavoidable, that THE EARTH HAS NO MOTION OF ROTATION.

Not long after the publishing of the first edition of **Zetetic Astronomy** a number of scientific tests were done by others, all of which likewise proved either that the Earth was standing still or that there was an "aether" above us, within which the sun, moon and stars were moving. Among the more famous were:

- **Airy's Failure** (1871)
- **Michelson-Morley Experiment** (1887)
- **Sagnac-Interferometer Experiment** (1913)
- **Michelson-Gale-Pearson Experiment** (1925)

Another on-line researcher[1] summarizes the above:

(A) The Sagnac experiment proved that there WAS an aether which could be used as a reference frame for movements. This demolished Einstein's theories of Relativity.

(B) Using the aether as a frame of reference, the Michelson-Morley experiment showed that we were NOT going round the sun,

(C) Airey's experiment proved that the starlight was already coming into the earth at an angle, being carried along by the rotating aether.

(D) The Michelson-Gale experiment showed that the aether was going round the stationary earth 1 rotation per day. (The alternative that the earth was spinning 1 rotation per day inside a stationary aether is disproven by Airy's experiment).

1 http://mbowden.info/Geocexpl.htm

More recently, a number of scientific tests and observations confirming the central location of the non-rotating Earth can be seen in the documentary, **The Principle**, which can be viewed on-line here:

www.theprinciplemovie.com

NOTE: Neither the filmmakers nor anyone else in the documentary believes the Earth is flat however.

EXPERIMENT 16

When sitting in a rapidly-moving railway carriage, let a spring-gun[8] be fired forward, or in the direction in which the train is moving. Again, let the same gun be fired, but in the opposite direction; and it will be found that the ball or other projectile will always go farther in the first case than in the latter.

If a person leaps backwards from a horse in full gallop, he cannot jump so great a distance as he can by jumping forward. Leaping from a moving sledge, coach, or other object, backwards or forwards, the same results are experienced.

Many other practical cases could be cited to show that any body projected from another body in motion, does not exhibit the same behaviour as it does when projected from a body at rest. Nor are the results the same when projected in the same direction as that in which the body moves, as when projected in the opposite direction; because, in the former case, the projected body receives its momentum from the projectile force, plus that given to it by the moving body; and in the latter case, this momentum, minus that of the moving body. Hence it would be found that if the earth is a globe, and moving rapidly from west to east, a cannon fired in a due easterly direction would send a ball to a greater distance than it would if fired in a due westerly direction. But the most experienced artillerymen--many of whom have had great practice, both at home and abroad, in almost every latitude--have declared that no difference whatever is observable. That in charging and pointing their guns, no, difference in the working is ever required, notwithstanding that the firing is at every point of the compass. Gunners in war ships have noticed a considerable difference in the results of their firing from guns at the bow, when sailing rapidly towards the object fired at, and when firing from guns placed at the stern while sailing away from the object: and in both cases the results are different to those observed when firing from a ship at perfect rest. These details of practical experience are utterly incompatible with the supposition of a revolving earth.

---

8 The barrel containing a spiral spring, so that the projecting force will always be the same, which might not be so with gunpowder.

During the period of the Crimean War, the subject of gunnery, in connection with the earth's rotation, was one which occupied the attention of many philosophers, as well as artillery officers and statesmen. About this time, Lord Palmerston, as Prime Minister, wrote the following letter to Lord Panmure, the Secretary for War:--

"December 20th, 1857.

"My dear Panmure.

"There is an investigation which it would be important and at the same time easy to make, and that is, whether the rotation of the earth on its axis has any effect on the curve of a cannon-ball in its flight. One should suppose that it has, and that while the cannon-ball is flying in the air, impelled by the gunpowder in a straight line from the cannon's mouth, the ball would not follow the rotation of the earth in the same manner which it would do if lying at rest on the earth's surface. If this be so, a ball fired in the meridional direction--that is to say, due south or due north--ought to deviate to the west of the object at which it was aimed, because during the time of flight, that object will have gone to the east somewhat faster than the cannon-ball will have done. In like manner, a ball fired due east, ought to fly less far upon the earth's surface than a ball fired due west, the charges being equal, the elevation the same, and the atmosphere perfectly still. It must be remembered, however, that the ball, even after it has left the cannon's mouth, will retain the motion from west to east which it had before received by the rotation of the earth on whose surface it was; and it is possible, therefore, that, except at very long ranges, the deviations above mentioned may in practice turn out to be very small, and not deserving the attention of an artilleryman. The trial might be easily made in any place in which a free circle of a mile or more radius could be obtained; and a cannon placed in the centre of that circle, and fired alternately north, south, east, and west, with equal charges, would afford the means of ascertaining whether each shot flew the same distance or not.

"Yours sincerely,
"PALMERSTON."

The above letter was published, by Lord Dalhousie's permission, in the "Proceedings of the Royal Artillery Institution for 1867."

It will be observed that Lord Palmerston thought that firing eastwards, or in the direction of the earth's supposed rotation, the ball would "fly less far upon the earth's surface than a ball fired due west." It is evident that his Lordship did not allow for the extra impulse given to the ball by the earth's motion. But the answer given by the advocates of the theory of the earth's motion is the following: Admitting that a ball fired from the earth at rest would go, say two miles, the same ball, fired from the earth in motion, would go, say three miles; but during the time the ball is passing through the air, the earth will advance one mile in the same direction. This one mile deducted from the three miles which the ball actually passes through the air, leaves the two miles which the ball has passed in advance of the cannon; so that practically the distance to which a ball is projected is precisely the same upon a moving earth as it is upon the earth at rest. The following diagram, fig. 50, will illustrate the path of a ball under the conditions above described.

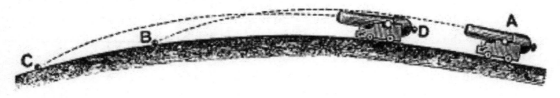

FIG. 50.

Let the curved line A, B, represent the distance a ball would fly from a cannon placed at A, upon the earth, *at rest*. Let A, C, represent the distance the same ball would fly from the conjoint action of the powder in the cannon, A, and the earth's rotation in the direction A, C. During the time the ball would require to traverse the line A, C, the earth and the cannon would arrive at the point D; hence the distance D, C, would be the same as the distance A, B.

The above explanation is very ingenious, and would be perfectly satisfactory if other considerations were not involved in it. For instance, the above explanation does not prove the earth's motion--it merely *supposes* it; but as in all other cases where the result of supposition is explained, it creates a dilemma. It demands that during the time the ball is in the air, the cannon is advancing in the direction of the supposed motion of the earth. But this is granting the conditions required in the experiments represented by figs. 47, 48, and 49. If the cannon can advance in the one case, it must in the other; and as the result in the experiment represented at fig. 49, was that the ball, when fired vertically, essentially returned to the vertical cannon; that cannon could not have advanced, and therefore the earth could not have moved.

EXPERIMENT 17

Take a large grinding stone, and let the whole surface of the rim be well rubbed over with a saturated solution of phosphorus in olive oil; or cover the stone with several folds of coarse woollen cloth or flannel, which saturate with boiling water. If it be now turned rapidly round, by means of a multiplying wheel, the phosphoric vapour, or the steam from the flannel, which surrounds it and which may be called its atmosphere-- analogous to the atmosphere of the earth--will be seen to follow the direction of the revolving surface. Now the surface of the earth is very irregular in its outline, mountains rising several miles above the sea, and ranging for hundreds of miles in every possible direction; rocks, capes, cliffs, gorges, defiles, caverns, immense forests, and every other form of ruggedness and irregularity calculated to adhere to and drag along whatever medium may exist upon it: and if it is a globe revolving on its axis, with the immense velocity at the equator of more than a thousand miles an hour, it is exceedingly difficult if not altogether impossible to conceive of such a mass moving at such a rate, and yet not taking the atmosphere along with it. When it is considered, too, that the medium which it is said surrounds the earth and all the heavenly bodies, and filling all the vast spaces between them, is almost too ethereal and subtle to offer any sensible resistance, it is still more difficult to understand how the atmosphere can be prevented being carried forward with the earth's rapidly revolving surface. Study the details of pneumatics or hydraulics as we may, we cannot suggest an experiment which will show the possibility of such a thing. Hence we are compelled to conclude that if the earth revolves, the atmosphere revolves also, and in the same direction. If the atmosphere rushes forward from west to east continually, we are again obliged to conclude that whatever floats or is suspended in it, at any altitude, must of necessity partake of its eastward motion. A piece of cork, or any other body floating in still water, will be motionless, but let the water be put in motion, in any direction whatever, and the floating bodies will move with it, in the same direction and with the same velocity. Let the experiment be tried in every possible way, and these results will invariable follow. Hence if the earth's atmosphere is in constant motion from west to east, all the different strata which are known to exist in it, and all the various kinds of clouds and vapours which float in it must of mechanical necessity move rapidly eastwards. But what is the fact? If we fix upon any star as a standard or datum outside the visible atmosphere, we may sometimes observe a stratum of clouds going for hours together in a direction the very opposite to that in which the earth is supposed to be moving. See fig. 51, which represents a section of a globe, surrounded with an atmosphere, moving at the rate of 1042 miles an hour at the equator, and in the direction of the arrows 1, 2, 3, while a stream of clouds are moving in the opposite direction, as indicated by the arrows, 4, 5, 6. Not only may a stratum of clouds be seen moving rapidly from east to west, but at the same moment other strata may often be seen moving from north to south, and from south to north. It is a fact well known to aeronauts, that several strata of atmospheric air are often moving in as many different directions at the same time.

Fig. 51.

131

It is a knowledge of this fact which leads an experienced aeronaut, when desiring to rise in a balloon, and to go in a certain direction, not to regard the manner in which the wind is blowing on the immediate surface of the earth, because he knows that at a greater altitude, it may be going at right angles, or even in opposite and in various ways simultaneously. To ascertain whether and at what altitude a current is blowing in the desired direction, small, and so-called "pilot-balloons" are often sent up and carefully observed in their ascent. If during the passage of one of these through the variously moving strata, it is seen to enter a current which is going in the direction desired by the aëronaut, the large balloon is then ballasted in such a manner that it may ascend at once to the altitude of such current, and thus to proceed on its journey.

On almost any moonlight and cloudy night, different strata may be seen not only moving in different directions but, at the same time, moving with different velocities; some floating past the face of the moon rapidly and uniformly, and others passing gently along, sometimes becoming stationary, then starting fitfully into motion, and often standing still for minutes together. Some of those who have ascended in balloons for scientific purposes have recorded that as they have rapidly passed through the atmosphere, they have gone though strata differing in temperature, in density, and in hygrometric, magnetic, electric, and other conditions. These changes have been noticed both in ascending and descending, and in going for miles together at the same altitude.

> "On the 27th November, 1839, the sky being very clear, the planet Venus was seen near the zenith, notwithstanding the brightness of the meridian sun. It enabled us to observe the higher stratum of clouds to be moving in an exactly opposite direction to that of the wind--a circumstance which is frequently recorded in our meteorological journal both in the north-east and south-east trades, and has also often been observed by former voyagers. Captain Basil Hall witnessed it from the summit of the Peak of Teneriffe; and Count Strzelechi, on ascending the volcanic mountain of Kiranea, in Owhyhee, reached at 4000 feet an elevation above that of the trade wind, and experienced the influence of an opposite current of air of a different hygrometric and thermometric condition. . . . Count Strzelechi further informed me of the following seemingly anomalous circumstance--that at the height of 6000 feet he found the current of air blowing at right angles to both the lower strata, also of a different hygrometric and thermometric condition, but warmer than the inter-stratum."[9]

Such a state of the atmosphere is compatible only with the fact which other evidence has demonstrated, that *the earth is at rest*. Were it otherwise-if a spherical mass of eight thousand miles in diameter, with an atmosphere of only fifty miles in depth, or relatively

---

9 "South Sea Voyages," p. 14, vol. i. By Sir James Clarke Ross, R.N.

only as a sheet of note paper pasted upon a globe of one yard in diameter, and lying upon a rugged, adhesive, rapidly revolving surface, there is nothing to prevent such an atmosphere becoming a mingled homogeneous mass of vapour.

Notwithstanding that all practical experience, and all specially instituted experiments are against the possibility of a moving earth, and an independent moving and non-moving atmosphere, many mathematicians have endeavoured to "demonstrate" that with regard to this earth, such was actually the case. The celebrated philosophic divine, Bishop Wilkins, was reasoned by the theorists of his day into this belief; and, in consequence, very naturally suggested a new and easy way of travelling. He proposed that large balloons should be provided with apparatus to work against the varying currents of the air. On ascending to a proper altitude, the balloon was to be kept practically in a state of rest, while the earth revolved underneath it; and when the desired locality came into view, to stop the working of the fans, &c., to let out the gas, and drop down at once to the earth's surface. In this simple way New York would be reached in a few hours, or rather New York would reach the balloon, at the rate, in the latitude of England, of more than 600 miles an hour.

The argument involved in the preceding remarks against the earth's rotation has often been met by the following, at first sight, plausible statement. A ship with a number of passengers going rapidly in one continued direction, like the earth's atmosphere, could nevertheless have upon its deck a number of distinctly and variously moving objects, like the clouds in the atmosphere. The clouds in the atmosphere are compared to the passengers on the deck of a ship; so far the cases are sufficiently parallel, but the passengers are sentient beings, having within themselves the power of distinct and independent motions: the clouds are the reverse; and here the parallelism fails. One case is not illustrative of the other, and the supposition of rotation in the earth remains without a single fact or argument in its favour. Birds in the air, or fish and reptiles in the water, would have offered a parallel and illustrative case, but these, like the passengers on the ship's deck, are sentient and independent beings; clouds and vapours are dependent and non-sentient, and must therefore of necessity move with, and in the direction of, the medium in which they float.

Everything actually observable in Nature; every argument furnished by experiment; every legitimate process of reasoning; and, as it would seem, everything which it is possible for the human mind practically to conceive, combine in evidence against the doctrine of the earth's motion upon axes.

ORBITAL MOTION

The preceding experiments and remarks, logically and mathematically suffice as evidence against the assumed motion of the earth in an orbit round the sun. It is difficult, if not impossible, to understand how the behaviour of the ball thrown from a vertical gun should be other in relation to the earth's forward motion in space, than it is in regard to its motion upon axes. Besides, it is demonstrable that it does not move upon axes, and therefore, the assumption that it moves in an orbit, is utterly useless for theoretical purposes. The explanation of phenomena, for which the theory of orbital and diurnal motion was framed, is no longer possible with a globular world rushing through space in a vast elliptical orbit, but without diurnal rotation. Hence the earth's supposed orbital motion is logically void, and non-available, and there is really no necessity for either formally denying it, or in any way giving it further consideration. But that no point may be taken without direct and practical evidence, let the following experiment be tried.

Take two carefully-bored metallic tubes, not less than six feet in length, and place them one yard asunder, on the opposite sides of a wooden frame, or a solid block of wood or stone: so adjust them that their centres or axes of vision shall be perfectly parallel to each other. The following diagram will show the arrangement.

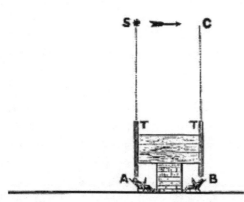

Fig. 52.

Now, direct them to the plane of some notable fixed star, a few seconds previous to its meridian time. Let an observer be stationed at each tube, as at A, B; and the moment the star appears in the tube A, T, let a loud knock or other signal be given, to be repeated by the observer at the tube B, T, when he first sees the same star. A distinct period of time will elapse between the signals given. The signals will follow each other in very rapid succession, but still, the time between is sufficient to show that the same star, S, is not visible at the same moment by two parallel lines of sight A, S, and B, C, when only one yard asunder. A slight inclination of the tube, B, C, towards the first tube A, S, would be required for the star, S, to be seen through both tubes at the same instant. Let the tubes remain in their position for six months; at the end of which time the same observation or experiment will produce the same results--the star, S, will be visible at the same meridian time, without the slightest alteration being required in the direction of the tubes: from which it is concluded that if the earth had moved one single yard in an orbit through space, there would at least be observed the slight inclination of the tube, B, C, which the difference in position of one yard had previously required. But as no such difference in the direction of the tube B, C, is required, the conclusion is unavoidable, that in six months a given meridian upon the earth's surface does not move a single yard, and therefore, that the earth has not the slightest degree of orbital motion.

Copernicus required, in his theory of terrestrial motions, that the earth moved in an extensive elliptical path round the sun, as represented in the following diagram, fig 53, where S is the sun, A, the earth in its place in June, and B, its position in December; when desired to offer some proof of this orbital motion he suggested that a given star should be selected for observation on a given date; and in six months afterwards a second observation of the same star should be made. The first observation A, D, fig. 53, was recorded; and on observing again at the end of six months, when the earth was supposed to have passed to B, the other side of its orbit, to the astonishment of the assembled astronomers, the star was observed in exactly the same position, B, C, as it had been six months previously! It was expected that it would be seen in the direction B, D, and that this difference in the direction of observation would demonstrate the earth's motion from A to B, and also furnish, with the distance A, S, B, the elements necessary for calculating the actual distance of the star D.

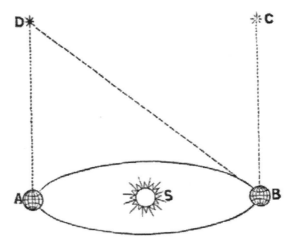

Fig. 53.

The above experiment has many times been tried, and always with the same general result. No difference whatever has been observed in the direction of the lines of sight A, D, and B, C, whereas every known principle of optics and geometry would require, that if the earth had really moved from A to B, *the fixed star* D, should be seen in the direction B, D. The advocates of this hypothesis of orbital motion, instead of being satisfied, from the failure to detect a difference in the angle of observation, that the earth could not possibly have changed its position in the six months, were so regardless of all logical consistency, that instead of admitting, and accepting the consequences, they, or some of them, most unworthily declared that they could not yield up the theory, on account of its apparent value in explaining certain phenomena, but demanded that the star D, was so vastly distant, that, notwithstanding that the earth *must have moved* from A to B, this great change of position would not give a readable difference in the angle of observation at B, or in other words the amount of parallax (" annual parallax," it was called) was inappreciable!

Since the period of the above experiments, many have declared that a very small amount of "annual parallax" has been detected. But the proportion given by different observers has been so various, that nothing definite and satisfactory can yet be decided upon. Tycho Brahe, Kepler, and others, rejected the Copernican theory, principally on account of the failure to detect displacement or parallax of the fixed stars. Dr. Bradley declared that what many had called "parallax," was merely "aberration." But "Dr. Brinkley, in 1810, from his observations with a very fine circle in the Royal Observatory of Dublin, *thought* he had detected a parallax of $1''$ in the bright star Lyra (corresponding to an annual displacement of $2''$). This, however, proved to be illusory; and it was not till the year 1839, that Mr. Henderson, having returned from filling the situation of astronomer royal to the Cape of Good Hope, and discussing as series of observations made there with a large "mural circle," of the bright star, α Centauri, was enabled to announce as a positive fact the existence of a measurable parallax for that star, a result since fully confirmed with a very trifling correction by the observations of his successor, Sir T. Maclear. The parallax thus assigned α Centauri, is so very nearly a whole second in amount ($0''.98$), that we may speak of it as such. It corresponds to a distance from the sun of 18,918,000,000,000 British statute miles.

Professor Bessel made the parallax of a star in the constellation Cygnus to be $0''.35$. Later astronomers, going over the same ground, with more perfect instruments, and improved practice in this very delicate process "of observation, have found a somewhat larger result, stated by one at $0''.57$, and by another at $0''.51$, so that we may take it at $0''.54$, corresponding to somewhat less than twice the distance of a Centauri;"[10] or to nearly 38 billions of miles.

It might seem to a non-scientific mind that the differences above referred to of only a few fractions of a second in the parallax of a star, constitute a very slight amount; but in reality such differences involve differences in the distance of such stars of millions of miles, as will be seen by the following quotation from the *Edinburgh Review* for June, 1850:--

---

10 Sir John F. W. Herschel, Bart., in "Good Words."

"The rod used in measuring a base line is commonly ten feet long; and the astronomer may be said only to apply this very rod to measure the distance of the fixed stars! An error in, placing *a fine dot*, which fixes the length of the rod, amounting to one five-thousandth part of an inch, will amount to an excess, of 70 feet in the earth's diameter; of 316 miles in the sun's distance, and to 65,200,000 miles in that of the nearest fixed star!

"The second point to which we would advert is, that as the astronomer in his observatory has nothing to do with ascertaining length as distances, except by calculation, his whole skill and artifice are exhausted in the measurement of angles. For it is by these alone that spaces inaccessible can be compared. Happily *a ray of light is straight.* Were it not so (in celestial spaces at least) there were an end of our astronomy. It is as inflexible as adamant, which our instruments unfortunately are not. Now an angle of *a second* (3600 to a degree), is a subtle thing, it is an apparent breadth, utterly invisible to the unassisted eye, unless accompanied by so intense a splendour (as in the case of the fixed stars) as actually to raise by its effect on the nerve of sight a spurious image, having a sensible breadth. A silkworm's fibre subtends an angle of one second at 3½ feet distance. A ball 2½ inches in diameter must be removed in order to subtend an angle of one second, to 43,000 feet, or about 8 miles; while it would be utterly invisible to the sharpest sight aided even by a telescope of some power. Yet it is on the measurement of *one single second* that the *ascertainment of a sensible parallax in any fixed star depends*; and an error of one-thousandth of that amount (a quantity still immeasurable by the most perfect of our instruments) would place a fixed star *too far* or *too near* by 200,000,000,000 of miles."

Sir John Herschel says:--

"The observations require to be made with the very best instruments, with the minutest attention to everything which can affect their precision, and with the most rigorous application of an innumerable host of 'corrections,' some large, some small, but of which the smallest, neglected or erroneously applied, would be quite sufficient to overlay and conceal from view the minute quantity we are in search of. To give some idea of the delicacies which have to be attended to in this inquiry, it will suffice to mention that the stability not only of the instruments used and the masonry which supports them, but of the very rock itself on which it is founded, is found to be subject to annual fluctuations capable of seriously affecting the result."

Dr. Lardner, in his "Museum of Science," page 179, makes use of the following words

> "Nothing in the whole range of astronomical research has more baffled the efforts of observers than this question of the parallax. * * * Now, since, in the determination of the exact uranographical position of a star, there are a multitude of disturbing effects to be taken into account and eliminated, such as precession, nutation, aberration, refraction, and others, besides the proper motion of the star; and since, besides the errors of observation, the quantities of these are subject to more or less uncertainty, it will astonish no one to be told that they may entail upon the final result of the calculation, an error of $1''$; and if they do, it is vain to expect to discover such a residual phenomenon as parallax, the entire amount of which is less than one second."

The complication, uncertainty, and unsatisfactory state of the question of annual parallax, and therefore of the earth's motion in an orbit round the sun, as indicated by the several paragraphs above quoted, are at once and for ever annihilated by the simple fact, experimentally demonstrable, that upon a base line of only a single yard, there may be found a parallax, as certain and as great, if not greater, than that which astronomers pretend to find with the diameter of the earth's supposed orbit of many millions of miles as a base line. To place the whole matter, complicated, uncertain, and unsatisfactory as it is, in a concentrated form, it is only necessary to state as an absolute truth the result of actual experiment, that, a given fixed star will, when observed from the two ends of a base line of not more than three feet, give a parallax equal to that which it is said is observed only from the two extremities of the earth's orbit, a distance or base line, of one hundred and eighty millions of miles! So far, then, from the earth having passed in six months over the vast space of nearly two hundred millions of miles, the combined observations of all the astronomers of the whole civilized world have only resulted in the discovery of such elements, or such an amount of annual parallax, or sidereal displacement, as an actual change of position of a few feet will produce. It is useless to say, in explanation, that this very minute displacement, is owing to the almost infinite distance of the fixed stars; because the *very same stars* show an equal degree of parallax from a very minute base line; and, secondly, it will be proved from practical data, in a subsequent chapter, that all the luminaries in the firmament are only a few thousand miles from the surface of the earth.

CHAPTER IV
THE TRUE FORM AND MAGNITUDE OF THE EARTH

THE facts and experiments already advanced render it undeniable, that the surface of all the waters of the earth is horizontal; and that, however irregular the upper outline of the land itself may be, the whole mass, land and water together, constitutes an IMMENSE NON-MOVING CIRCULAR PLANE.

If we travel by land or sea, from any part of the earth in the direction of any meridian line, and towards the northern central star called "Polaris," we come to one and the same place, a region of ice, where the star which has been our guide is directly above us, or vertical to our position. This region is really THE CENTRE OF THE EARTH; and recent observations seem to prove that it is a vast central tidal sea, nearly a thousand miles in diameter, and surrounded by a great wall or barrier of ice, eighty to a hundred miles in breadth. If from this central region we trace the outline of the lands which project or radiate from it, and the surface of which is above the water, we find that the present form of the earth or "dry land," as distinguished from the waters of the "great deep," is an irregular mass of capes, bays, and islands, terminating in great bluffs or headlands, projecting principally towards the south, or, at least, in a direction away from the great northern centre.

If now we sail with our backs continually to this central star, "Polaris," or the centre of the earth's surface, we shall arrive at another region of ice. Upon whatever meridian we sail, keeping the northern centre behind us, we are checked in our progress by vast and lofty cliffs of ice. If we turn to the right or to the left of our meridian, these icy barriers beset us during the whole of our passage. Hence, we have found that there is a great ebbing and flowing sea at the earth's centre; with a boundary wall of ice, nearly a hundred miles in thickness, and three thousand miles in circumference; that springing or projecting from this icy wall, irregular masses of land stretch out towards the south, where a desolate waste of turbulent waters surrounds the continents, and is itself engirdled by vast belts and packs of ice, bounded by immense frozen barriers, the lateral depth and extent of which are utterly unknown.

> *"The storm rampant of nature's sanctuary;*
> *The insuperable boundary raised to guard*
> *Her mysteries from the eye of man profane."*

The earth's surface is represented by the diagram, fig. 54, and a sectional view in fig. 55. N, the central open sea, I, I, the circular wall or barrier of ice, L, L, L, the masses of land tending southwards, W, W, W, the "waters of the great deep," surrounding the land, S, S, S, the southern boundary of ice, and D, D, D, the outer gloom and darkness, in which the material world is lost to human perception.

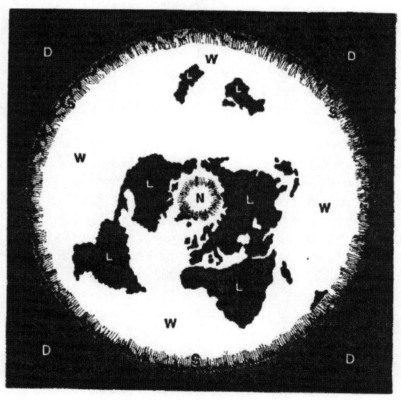

DIAGRAM OF EARTH'S SURFACE.
FIG. 54.

SECTIONAL VIEW OF EARTH'S SURFACE.
FIG. 55.

How far the ice extends; how it terminates; and what exists beyond it, are questions to which no present human experience can reply. All we at present know is, that snow and hail, howling winds, and indescribable storms and hurricanes prevail; and that in every direction "human ingress is barred by unsealed escarpments of perpetual ice," extending farther than eye or telescope can penetrate, and becoming lost in gloom and darkness.

The superficial extent or magnitude of the earth from the northern centre to the southern circumference, can only be stated approximately. For this purpose the following evidence will suffice. In laying the Atlantic Cable from the Great Eastern steamship, in 1866, the distance from Valencia, on the south-western coast of Ireland, to Trinity Bay in Newfoundland, was found to be 1665 miles. The longitude of Valencia is 10° 30´ W.; and of Trinity Bay 53° 30´ W. The difference of longitude between the two places being 43°, and the whole distance round the earth being divided into 360°. Hence if 43° are found to be 1665 nautical, or 1942 statute miles, 360° will be 13,939 nautical, or 16,262 statute miles; then taking the proportion of radius to circumference, we have 2200 nautical, or 2556 statute miles as the actual distance from Valencia, in Ireland, to the polar centre of the earth's surface.

Another and a very beautiful and accurate way of ascertaining the earth's circumference is the following:--

> "The difference of longitude between Heart's Content Station, Newfoundland, and that at Valencia or, in other words, between the extreme points of the Atlantic Cable--has been ascertained by Mr. Gould, coast surveyor to the United States Government, to be 2 hours, 51 minutes, 56.5 seconds."[11]

---

11 Liverpool Mercury, January 8th, 1867.

The sun passes over the earth and returns to the same point in 24 hours. If in 2 hours, 51 minutes, and 56.5 seconds, it passes from the meridian of the Valencia end of the cable to that of its termination at Heart's Content, a distance of 1942 statute miles, how far will it travel in 24 hours? On making the calculation the answer is, 16,265 statute miles. This result is only three miles greater distance than that obtained by the first process.

Again in the *Boston Post*, for Oct. 30th, 1856, Lieut. Maury gives the following as the correct distances, in geographical miles, across the Atlantic by the various routes (circle sailing).

	Nautical Miles.	Statute Miles.
Philadelphia to Liverpool	3000	= 3500
New York "	2880	= 3360
Boston "	2720	= 3173
New York to Southampton	2980	= 3476
" to Glasgow	2800	= 3266
Boston to Galway	2520	= 2940
Newfoundland to Galway	1730	= 2018
Boston to Belfast	2620	= 3056

If we take the distance (given in the above table) between Liverpool and New York as 3360 statute miles, and calculate as in the last case, we find a nearly similar result, making allowance for the detour round the south or north of Ireland.

> "The difference of time between London and New York which the use of the electric cable makes a matter of some consequence, has latterly been ascertained afresh. It is 4 hours, 55 minutes, 18.95 seconds."[12]

---

12 Liverpool Mercury, June 3rd, 1867.

The results of these several methods are so nearly alike that the distance 16,262 statute miles may safely be taken as the approximate circumference of the earth at the latitude of Valencia.

If the distance from Valencia to the Cape of Good Hope, or to Cape Horn, had ever been actually measured, *not calculated*, the circumference of the earth at these points could, of course, be readily ascertained. We cannot admit as evidence the *calculated* length of a degree of latitude, because this is an amount connected with the theory of the earth's rotundity; which has been proved to be false. We must therefore take known distances between places far south of Valencia, where latitude and longitude have also been carefully observed. In the Australian Almanack for 1871, page 126[13], the distance from Auckland (New Zealand), to Sydney, is given as 1315 miles, nautical measure, which is equal to 1534 statute miles. At page 118 of the Australian Almanack for 1859, Captain Stokes, H.M.S. Acheron, communicates the latitude of Auckland as 36° 50′ 05″, S., and longitude 174° 50′ 40″, E.; latitude of Sydney, 33° 51′ 45″, S., and longitude 151° 16′ 15″, E. The difference in longitude, or time distance, is 23° 34′ 25″, calculating as in the case of Valencia to Newfoundland, we find that as 23° 34′ 25″ represents 1534 statute miles, 360° will give 23,400 statute miles as the circumference of the earth at the latitude of Sydney, Auckland, and the Cape of Good Hope. Hence the radius or distance from the centre of the north to the above places is, in round numbers, 3720 statute miles. Calculating in the same way, we find that from Sydney to the Cape of Good Hope is fully 8600 statute miles.

The above calculations receive marked corroboration from the practical experience of mariners. The author has many times been told by captains of vessels navigating the southern region, that from Cape Town to Port Jackson in Australia, the distance is not less than 9000 miles; and from Port Jackson to Cape Horn, 9500 miles; but as many are not willing to give credit to such statements, the following quotation will be useful, and will constitute sufficient evidence of the truth of the foregoing calculations:--

"The Great Britain steamer has arrived, having made one of the best voyages homeward that has yet been effected, viz., 86 days; 72 only of which were employed in steaming; and the remaining 14 days being accounted for by detentions. She left Melbourne on January 6th, and arrived in Simon's Bay on February 10th, or 35 days. She then went round to Cape Town, whence she sailed on the 20th of February; and was afterwards detained for four days at St. Michael's and Vigo. The distance she steamed per log was 14,688 miles; which for the 72 days, gives an average of 204 miles a day."[14]

---

13 Published by Gordon and Gotch, 121, Holborn Hill, London; and 281, George Street, Sydney, and 85, Collins Street West, Melbourne, New South Wales.
14 Australian and New Zealand Gazette, for April 9th, 1853. Published by A. E. Murray, Green Arbour Court, Old Bailey, London. A copy may be seen in the Liverpool Free Library, in "No. 10 Section."

If we multiply the average rate of sailing by the thirty-five days occupied in running between Melbourne and St. Simon's Bay (near Cape of Good Hope), we find that the distance is 7140 nautical miles, From Melbourne to Sydney is 6 degrees of longitude further east, or about S40 nautical miles. Hence 7140 added to 340 give 7480 nautical miles, equal to 8726 statute miles; which is 126 miles in excess of the distance given [previously].

The following extract furnishes additional evidence upon this important point:--

> "EXTRAORDINARY VOYAGE.--Every yachtsman (says the Dublin Express), will share in the pride with which, a correspondent relates a brilliant, and, we believe, unexampled exploit which has just been performed by a small yacht of only 25 tons, which is not a stranger to the waters of Dublin Bay. The gallant little craft set out from Liverpool for the antipodes, and arrived safely in Sydney after a splendid run, performing the entire distance, 16,000 miles, in 130 days. Such an achievement affords grounds for reasonable exultation, not more as a proof of the nautical skill of our amateurs, than of their adventurous spirit, which quite casts in the shade the most daring feats of Alpine climbers."[15]

As the distance from Melbourne to Cape of Good Hope is 7140 nautical miles, as shown by the log of the Great Britain, and as the whole distance from Melbourne to Liverpool was 14,688 nautical miles, it follows that, deducting 7140 from 14,688, that the passage from the Cape of Good Hope to Liverpool was 7548 nautical miles. If we take this distance from the 16,000 miles, which the above mentioned yacht sailed to Sydney, we have as the distance between Cape of Good Hope and Sydney, 8452 nautical, or 9860 statute miles.

In a letter from Adelaide which appeared in the *Leeds Mercury* for April 20th, 1867, speaking of certain commercial difficulties which had existed there, the following incidental passage occurs:--

> "Just as our harvest was being concluded, the first news arrived of anticipated dearth of breadstuffs at home. The times were so hopelessly dull, money was so scarce, and the operation of shipping wheat a distance of 14,000 miles so dangerous, that for a long time the news had no practical effect."

From England to Adelaide is here stated as 14,000 nautical, or 16,333 statute miles; and as the difference of longitude between Adelaide and Sydney is 23 degrees, equal to 1534 statute miles, we find that from England to Sydney the distance is 17,867 statute miles. Taking from this the 7548 nautical, or 8806 statute miles, we have again 9061 statute miles as the distance between the Cape of Good Hope and Sydney.

---

15 Cheltenham Examiner (Supplement), for November 29th, 1865.

From the preceding facts it is evident that the circumference of the earth, at the distance of the Cape of Good Hope from the polar centre, is not less in round numbers than 23,400 miles. Hence the radius or distance in a direct line from the polar centre to Cape Town, to Sydney, to Auckland in New Zealand, and to all the places on the same arc, is about 3720 statute miles. And as the distance from the polar centre to Valencia in Ireland is shown to be 2556 statute miles, the direct distance from Valencia to Cape Town is 1164 statute miles. Should it ever be shown by actual direct measurement to be more than this distance, then the distance from Cape Town to Sydney must be more than 8600 statute miles. It is a subject which must be kept open for rectification. What already been given in the foregoing pages may be considered as the approximate *minimum* distances.

Having seen that the diameter of the earth's surface--taking the distance from Auckland in New Zealand, to Sydney, and thence to the Cape of Good Hope, as a *datum arc*--is 7440 statute miles; we may inquire how far it is from any of the above places to the great belt of ice which surrounds the southern oceans. Although large ice islands and icebergs are often met with a few degrees beyond Cape Horn, what may be called the solid immovable ramparts of ice seem to be as far south as 78 degrees. In a paper read by Mr. Locke before the Royal Dublin Society, on Friday evening, November 19th, 1860, and printed in the Journal of that Society, a map is given representing Antarctic discoveries, on which is traced a "proposed exploration route," by Captain Maury, U.S.N.; and in the third paragraph it is said:

> "I request attention to the diagram No. 1, representing an approximate tracing of the supposed Antarctic continent, and showing the steamer track, about twelve days from Port Philip, the chief naval station of the Austral seas, to some available landing point, bight, or ravine, under shadow of the precipitous coast."

The steamer track is given on this map as a dotted line, curving eastwards from 150 degrees to 180 degrees longitude, and from Port Philip to 78 degrees south latitude. If we take the chord of such an arc, we shall find that the direct distance from Port Philip to 78 degrees south would be about nine days' sail, or ten days from Sydney. No ordinary steamer would sail in such latitudes more than 150 statute miles a day; hence, ten times 150 would be 1500 miles; which added to the previously ascertained radius at Sydney, would make the total radius of the earth, from the northern centre to the farthest known southern circumference, to be 5224 statute miles. Thus from purely practical data, setting all theories aside, it is ascertained that the diameter of the earth, from the Ross Mountains, or from the volcanic mountains of which Mount Erebus is the chief, to the same radius distance on the opposite side of the northern centre, is more than 10,400 miles; and *the circumference, 52,800 statute miles*.

Assuming this circumference is accurate, it would mean the "circle of the Earth" has a radius of **8,403.38 miles**, a diameter of **16,806.76 miles** and an area of **221,849,258 miles²**.

145

By way of comparison, the website Space.com, featuring the fraudulant,[16] 2002 "Blue Marble" [screen capture below] has the equatorial radius of the Earth at 3,963 miles (accounting for the alleged 13 mile "bulge" in the middle), with a polar radius of 3,950 miles. Thus, its equatorial circumference is said to be about 24,901 miles with a meridional circumference of 24,860 miles.[17]

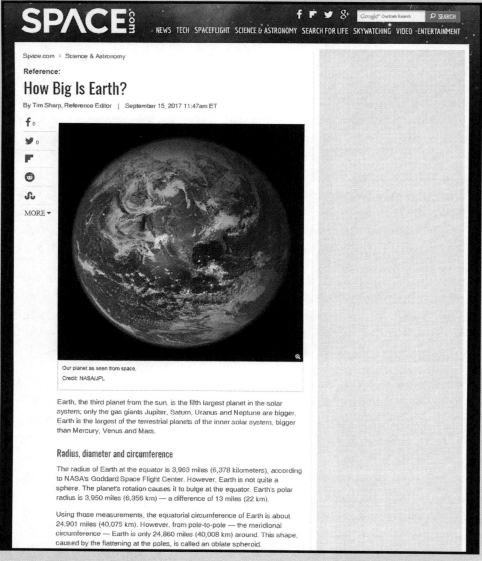

If "Parallax" is correct in his calculations, this means the "circle of the Earth" has a radius/diameter/circumference of more than twice that of the globe.

---

16 Note the caption under the Earth says, "Our planet as seen from space." which simply is not true. It is admitted to be a Photoshop, CGI *representation* of the Earth.

17 Although their math is a bit fuzzy. If you use a website like https://www.omnicalculator.com/math/circumference and punch in a radius of 3,950 miles, you actually get a polar circumference of 24,818.6 miles.

CHAPTER V
THE TRUE DISTANCE OF THE SUN

IT is now demonstrated that the earth is a plane, and therefore the distance of the sun may be readily and most accurately ascertained by the simplest possible process. The operation is one in plane trigonometry, which admits of no uncertainty and requires no modification or allowance for probable influences. The principle involved in the process may be illustrated by the following diagram, fig. 56.

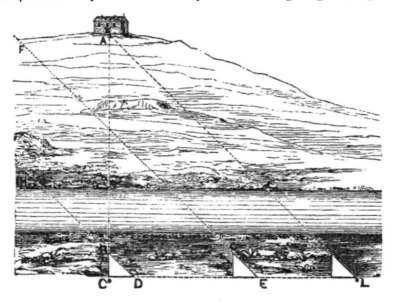

FIG 56.

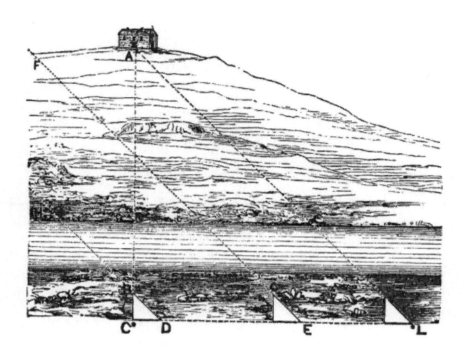

FIG 56.

Let A be an object, the distance of which is desired, on the opposite side of a river. Place a rod vertically at the point C, and take a piece of strong cardboard, in the shape of a right-angled triangle, as B, C, D. It is evident that placing the triangle to the eye, and looking along the side D, B, the line of sight D, B, H, will pass far to the left of the object A. On removing the triangle more to the right, to the position E, the line E, F, will still pass to the left of A; but on removing it again to the right, until the line of sight from L touches or falls upon the object A, it will be seen that L, A, bears the same relation to A, C, L, as D, B, does to B, C, D: in other words, the two sides of the triangle B, C, and C, D, being equal in length, so the two lines C, A, and C, L, are equal. Hence, if the distance from L to C is measured, it will be in reality the same as the desired distance from C to A. It will be obvious that the same process applied vertically is equally certain in its results. On one occasion, in the year 1856, the author having previously delivered a course of lectures in Great Yarmouth, Norfolk, and this subject becoming very interesting to a number of his auditors, an invitation was given to meet him on the seashore; and among other observations and experiments, to measure, by the above process, the altitude of the Nelson's Monument, which stands on the beach near the sea. A piece of thick cardboard was cut in the form of a right-angled triangle, the length of the two sides being about 8 inches. A fine silken thread, with a pebble attached, constituted a plumb line, fixed with a pin to one side of the triangle, as shown at P. The purpose of this plumb line was to enable the observer to keep the triangle in a truly vertical position; just as the object of the rod C, in fig. 56 was to enable the base of the triangle to be kept in one and the same line by looking along from E and L towards C. On looking over the triangle held vertically, and one side parallel with the plumb line P, from the position A, the line of sight fell upon the point B; but on walking gradually backwards, the top of the helmet D, on the head of the figure of Britannia, which surmounts the column, was at length visible from the point C. On prolonging the line D, C, to H, by means of a rod, the distance from H to the centre of the Monument at O, was measured, and the altitude O, D, was affirmed to be the same. But of this no proof existed further than that the principle involved in the triangulation compelled it to be so. Subsequently the altitude was obtained from a work published in Yarmouth, and was found to differ only one inch from the altitude ascertained by the simple operation above described. The foregoing remarks and illustrations are, of course, not necessary to the mathematician; but may be useful to the general reader, showing him that plane trigonometry, carried out on the earth's plane or horizontal surface, permits of operations which are simple and perfect in principle, and in practice fully reliable and satisfactory.

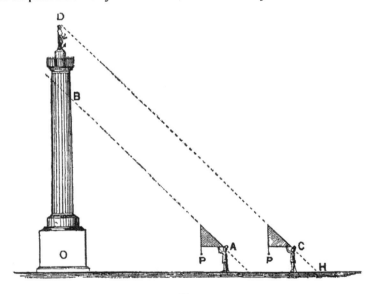

FIG 57.

The illustrations given above have reference to a fixed object; but the sun is not fixed; and therefore a modification of the process, but involving the same principle, must be adopted. Instead of the simple triangle and plumb line, represented in fig. 57, an instrument with a graduated arc must be employed, and two observers, one at each end of a north and south base line, must at the same moment observe the under edge of the sun as it passes the meridian; when, from the difference in the angle observed, and the known length of the base line, the actual distance of the sun may be calculated. The following case will fully illustrate this operation, as well as its results and importance:

The distance from London Bridge to the sea-coast at Brighton, in a straight line, is 50 statute miles. On a given day, at 12 o'clock, the altitude of the sun, from near the water at London Bridge, was found to be 61 degrees of an arc; and at the same moment of time the altitude from the sea-coast at Brighton was observed to be 64 degrees of an arc, as shown in fig. 58. The base-line from L to B, 50 measured statute miles; the angle at L, 61 degrees; and the angle at B, 64 degrees. In addition to the method by calculation, the distance of the under edge of the sun may be ascertained from these elements by the method called "construction."

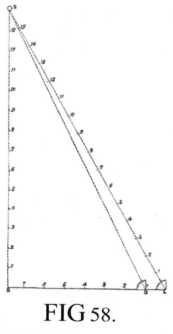

FIG 58.

The diagram, fig. 58, is the above case "constructed;" that is, the base-line from L to B represents 50 statute miles; and the line L, S, is drawn at an angle of 61 degrees, and the line B, S, at an angle of 64 degrees. Both lines are produced until they bisect or cross each other at the point S. Then, with a pair of compasses, measure the length of the base-line B, L, and see how many times the same length may be found in the line L, S, or B, S. It will be found to be sixteen times, or sixteen times 50 miles, equal to 800 statute miles. Then measure in the same way the vertical line D, S, and it will be found to be 700 miles. Hence it is demonstrable that the distance of the sun over that part of the earth to which it is vertical is only 700 statute miles. By the same mode it may be ascertained that the distance from London of that part of the earth where the sun was vertical at the time (July 13th, 1870) the above observations were taken, was only 400 statute miles, as shown by dividing the base-line L, D, by the distance B, L.

If any allowance is to be made for refraction--which, no doubt, exists where the sun's rays have to pass through a medium, the atmosphere, which gradually increases in density as it approaches the earth's surface--it will considerably diminish the above-named distance of the sun; so that it is perfectly safe to affirm that the under edge of the sun is considerably less than 700 statute miles above the earth.

The above method of measuring distances applies equally to the moon and stars; and it is easy to demonstrate, to place it beyond the possibility of error, so long as assumed premises are excluded, that the moon is nearer to the earth than the sun, and that all the visible luminaries in the firmament are contained within a vertical distance of 1000 statute miles. From which it unavoidably follows that the magnitude of the sun, moon, stars, and comets is comparatively small--much smaller than the earth from which they are measured, and to which, therefore, they must of necessity be secondary and subservient. They cannot, indeed, be anything more than "centres of action," throwing down light, and chemical products upon the earth.

CHAPTER VI
THE SUN'S MOTION CONCENTRIC WITH THE POLAR CENTRE

As the earth has been proved to be fixed, the motion of the sun is a visible reality. If it be observed from any latitude a few degrees north of the line called the "Tropic of Cancer," and for any period before or after the time of southing, or passing the meridian, it will be seen to describe an arc of a circle. The following simple experiment will be interesting as demonstrating the fact that the sun's path is concentric with the centre of the earth's surface.

Let the observer take his stand, half-an-hour before sunrise (in the month of June, or any of the summer months will be better than winter, as the results will be more striking), on the head of either the old or the new pier at Brighton, in Sussex. Let him draw a line due north and south; and a second line due east and west, across the first. Now stand with his back to the north. Being thus at his post and ready for observation, let him watch carefully for the sun's first appearance above the horizon; and he will find that the point where the sun is first observed is considerably to the north of east, or the line drawn at right angles to north and south. If he will continue to watch the sun's progress until noon, it will be seen to ascend in a curve southwards until it reaches the meridian; and thence to descend in a westerly curve until it arrives at the horizon, and to set considerably to the north of due west, as shown in the following diagram, fig. 59.

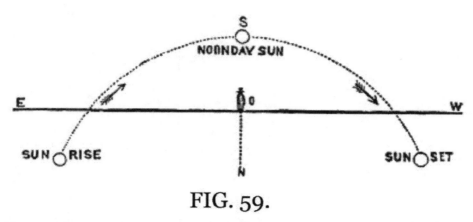

FIG. 59.

An object which moves in an arc of a circle, and returns to a given point in a given time, as the sun does to the meridian, must, of necessity, have completed a circular path in the twenty-four hours which constitute a solar day. To place the matter beyond doubt, the observations of Arctic navigators may be referred to. Captain Parry and several of his officers, on ascending high land near the arctic circle repeatedly saw, for twenty- four hours together, the sun describing a circle upon the southern horizon. Captain Beechy writes:

> "Very few of us had ever seen the sun at midnight; and this night happening to be particularly clear, his broad red disk, curiously distorted by refraction, and sweeping majestically along the northern horizon, was an object of imposing grandeur, which rivetted to the deck some of our crew, who would perhaps have beheld with indifference the less imposing effect of the icebergs. The rays were too oblique to illuminate more than the irregularities of the floes, and falling thus partially on the grotesque shapes either really assumed by the ice, or distorted by the unequal refraction of the atmosphere, so betrayed the imagination, that it required no great exertion of fancy to trace in various directions, architectural edifices, grottos, and caves, here and there, glittering as if with precious metals."

In July, 1865, Mr. Campbell, United States Minister to Norway, with a party of American gentlemen, went far enough north to see the sun at midnight. It was in 69 degrees north latitude, and they ascended a cliff 1000 feet above the arctic sea. The scene is thus described:--

> "It was late, but still sunlight. The arctic ocean stretched away in silent vastness at our feet: the sound of the waves scarcely reached our airy look-out. Away in the north the huge old sun swung low along the horizon, like the slow beat of the tall clock in our grandfather's parlour corner. We all stood silently looking at our watches. When both hands stood together at twelve, midnight, the full round orb hung triumphantly above the wave--a bridge of gold running due north, spangled

the waters between us and him. There he shone in silent majesty which knew no setting. We involuntarily took off our hats--no word was said. Combine the most brilliant sunrise you ever saw, and its beauties will pall before the gorgeous colouring which lit up the ocean, heaven, and mountains. In half an hour the sun had swung up perceptibly on its beat; the colours had changed to those of morning. A fresh breeze had rippled over the florid sea; one songster after another piped out of the grove behind us-- we had slid into another day."[18]

For a 3D model representation of the sun's movements over the flat "circle of the Earth" please see my YouTube video *FEIC 2018 - Day 1 Session 4 (Part 2 of 4): Rob Skiba*:

---

18 "Brighton Examiner," July 1st, 1870.

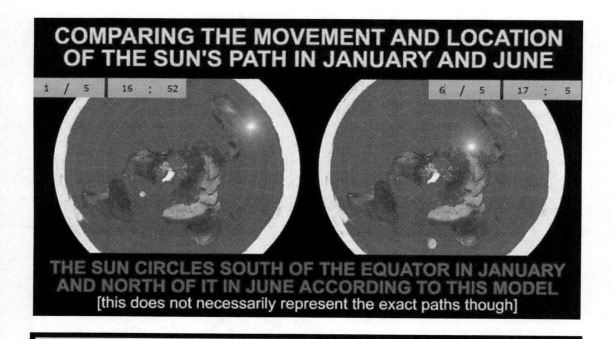

The above is a screen-shot from the same video mentioned on the previous page, showing the expanding and contracting movement of the sun's movements over the flat "circle of the Earth," which creates the four seasons. Please note: I did not make the motion of the sun and moon speed up or slow down. Stellarium (a spinning, heliocentric, globe-based software) did that. Again, if you'd like to see the animation for yourself, use the following QR Code or search for my video titled, *FEIC 2018 - Day 1 Session 4 (Part 2 of 4): Rob Skiba* - this part is at the very end (at about 1 hour 8 minutes into the video):

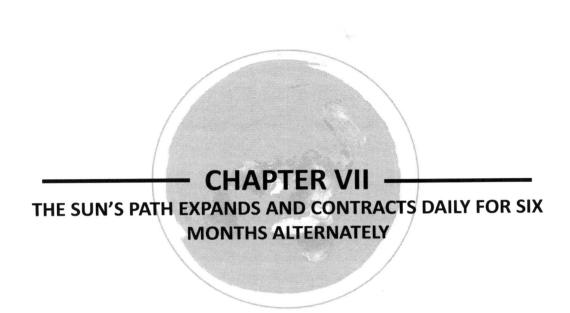

CHAPTER VII

THE SUN'S PATH EXPANDS AND CONTRACTS DAILY FOR SIX MONTHS ALTERNATELY

This is a matter of absolute certainty; proved by what is called, in technical language, the northern and southern declination, which is simply saying that the sun's path is nearest the polar centre in summer, and farthest away from it in winter.

At noon, on the 21st of any December, let a rod be so fixed that on looking along it, the line of sight touches the lower edge of the sun. For several days this line of sight will continue nearly the same, showing that the sun's path for this period is little changed; but on the ninth or tenth day to touch the sun's lower edge, the rod will have to be lifted several degrees towards the zenith. Every day afterwards until the 22nd of June, the rod will have to be raised. On that date there will again be several days without any visible change; after which, day by day, the rod must be lowered until the 21st December. In this simple way it may be demonstrated that the sun's path gets larger every day from December 21st to June 22nd; and smaller every day from June 22nd to December 21st, of every year.

From a number of observations made by the author during the last twenty-five years, it is certain that both the minimum or June path of the sun, and maximum or December path have been gradually getting farther from the northern centre. The amount of expansion is very small, but easily detected; and if it has been going on for centuries, which seems consistent with known phenomena, it explains at once and perfectly, the fact that England as well as more northern latitudes have once been tropical. There is abundant evidence that the conditions and productions now found within the tropics, have once existed in the northern region, which is now so cold and desolate, and inimical to ordinary animal and vegetable life. Hence it is a proper and logical conclusion that the sun's path was once very near to the earth's arctic or polar centre.

The following diagram, fig. 60, will show the sun's peculiar path, N represents the polar centre, A the sun in its path in June; which daily expands like the coils of the mainspring of a watch, until it reaches the outer and larger path B, in December, after which the path gradually and day by day con-tracts until it again becomes the path A, on the 21st of June.

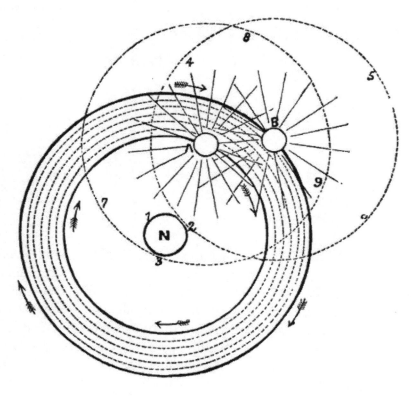

FIG. 60.

That such is the sun's annual course is demonstrable by actual observation; but if it is asked why it traverses such a peculiarly concentric path, no practical answer can be given, and no theory or speculation can be tolerated. At no distant period perhaps, we may have collected sufficient matter-of-fact evidence to enable us to understand it; but until that occurs, the Zetetic process only permits us to say:--

"The peculiar motion is visible to us, but, of the cause, at present we are ignorant."

CHAPTER VIII

CAUSE OF DAY AND NIGHT, WINTER AND SUMMER; AND THE LONG ALTERATIONS OF LIGHT AND DARKNESS AT THE NORTHERN CENTER

IT is a well-established fact that light and heat radiate equally in all directions. When the sun is on the outer circle, B, fig. 60, as it is on the 21st of December, it is known that the light gradually diminishes, until at or about 20 degrees from the northern centre, it shades almost imperceptibly into twilight and darkness. If, then, we take from B (fig. 60), to the arctic circle, 1, 2, 3, as radius, and describe the circle 4, 5, 6, we have represented the whole extent of sun or daylight at a given moment on the shortest day. When, as on the 21st of June, the sun by gradually contracting its path, has arrived at the inner circle, A, the same length of radius will produce the circle 7, 8, 9, which represents the extent of daylight on the longest day. It will be seen by the diagram that, on the shortest day, the light terminates at the arctic circle 1, 2, 3, leaving all beyond in darkness; and as the sun moves forward in the direction of the

arrows, the edge of the circle of light continues during the whole of its course, to fall short at this circle. Hence, although it is daylight all over the rest of the earth in twenty-four hours, the centre, N, is left in continual darkness. But when, in six months afterwards, the sun is on the *inner* circle, A, the light extends *beyond* the arctic circle, 1, 2, 3; and as it moves in its course, the centre, N, is continually illuminated. These changes will be better understood by reference to the diagrams, figs. 61 and 62.

FIG. 61.

In fig. 61, the circle A, A, A, represents the sun's daily path on December 21st, and B, B, B, the same on June 21st; N, the northern centre; S, the sun; and E, the position of Great Britain; the figures, 1, 2, 3, the arctic circle; and 4, 5, 6, the extent of sun-light at noon of that day. The sun, S, describes the circle A, A, A, on the 21st of December in one day, or twenty-four hours. Hence, in that period, mid-day and midnight, and morning and evening twilight, occur to every part of the earth *except within the arctic circle*, 1, 2, 3. There it is more or less in darkness for several months in succession, or until the sun, by gradually coming nearer to the inner circle, throws his light more and more over the centre. The arc of light at 4, is the advancing or morning twilight, and 6, the receding or evening twilight. At every place underneath a line drawn across the circle of the sun's light, 4, 5, 6, through S, to N, it is noonday; and beyond the northern centre, on the same line, it is midnight.

It will now be readily understood that as the sun moves in the direction of the arrows, or from right to left, and completes the circle, A, A, A, in twenty-four hours, it will produce in that period, and where its light reaches, morning, noon, evening,

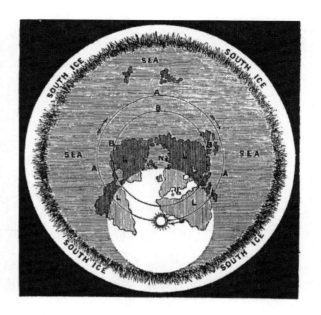

FIG. 61.

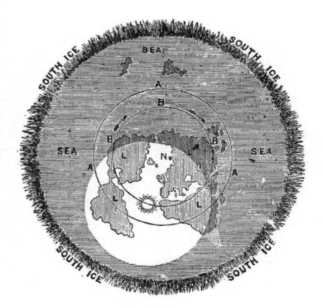

FIG. 62.

and night, on all parts of the earth in succession. As the sun's path now begins to contract every day for six months, or until the 21st of June, when it becomes the circle, B, B, B, it is evident that the same extent of sunlight as that which radiates from the outer circle, A, A, A, will reach over or beyond the northern centre, N, as shown in the diagram, fig. 62; when morning, noon, evening, and night, occur as before; but the light continuing, during the daily motion of the sun, to reach over the northern centre, that centre will, be continually illuminated for several months together, as before it was in constant darkness. It will be seen also by reference to the diagram that when the sun is on the outer path, A, the portion of the disc of light which passes over England is much smaller than when it is on the inner path, B. Hence, the short days and winter season from the first position, and the longer days and summer season from the second. Thus day and night, long and short days and nights, morning and evening twilight, winter and summer, the long periods of alternate light and darkness at the northern or polar centre of the earth, arise from the expansion and contraction of the sun's path, and are all a part of one and the same general phenomenon.

The whole of these explanations have reference only to the region between the sun and the northern centre. It is evident that in the great encircling oceans of the south, and the numerous islands and parts of continents, which exist beyond that part of the earth where the sun is vertical, cannot have their days and nights, seasons, &c., precisely like those in the northern region. The north is a centre, and the south is that centre radiated or thrown out to a vast oceanic circumference, terminating in circular walls of ice, which form an impenetrable frozen barrier. Hence the phenomena referred to as existing in the north must be considerably modified in the south, For instance, the north being central, the light of the sun advancing and receding, gives long periods of alternate light and darkness at the actual centre; but in the far south, the sun, even when moving in his outer path, can only throw its light to a certain distance, beyond which there must be perpetual darkness. No evidence exists of there being long periods of light and darkness regularly alternating, as in the north. In the north, in summer-time, when the sun is moving in its inner path, the light shines continually for months together over the central region, and rapidly develops numerous forms of animal and vegetable life.

> "Beyond the 70th degree of latitude not a tree meets the eye, wearied with the white waste of snow; forests, woods, even shrubs have disappeared, and given place to a few lichens and creeping woody plants, which scantily clothe the indurated soil. Still, in the farthest north, Nature claims her birthright of beauty; and in the brief and rapid summer she brings forth numerous flowers and grasses, to bloom for a few days, to be again blasted by the swiftly-recurring winter."[19]

> "The rapid fervour of an arctic summer had already (June 1st) converted the snowy waste into luxuriant pasture-ground, rich in flowers and grass, with almost the same lively appearance as that of an English meadow."[20]

---

19 "Arctic Explorations." By W. & R. Chambers. Edinburgh.
20 Ibid.

Wrangell tells us that

> "Countless herds of reindeer, elks, black bears, foxes, sables, and grey squirrels, fill the upland forests; stone foxes and wolves roam over the low grounds; enormous flights of swans, geese, and ducks, arrive in spring, and seek deserts where they may moult, and build their nests in safety. Eagles, owls, and gulls, pursue their prey along the sea-coast; ptarmigan run in troops among the bushes; little snipes are busy among the brooks and in the morasses; the social crows seek the neighbourhood of men's habitations; and when the sun shines in spring, one may even sometimes hear the cheerful note of the finch, and in autumn, that of the thrush."

Thus it is a well ascertained fact that the constant sunlight of the north develops, with the utmost rapidity, numerous forms of vegetable life, and furnishes subsistence for millions of living creatures. But in the south, where the sunlight never dwells, or lingers about a central region, but rapidly sweeps over sea and land, to complete in twenty-four hours the great circle of the southern circumference, it has not time to excite and stimulate the surface; and, therefore, even in comparatively low southern latitudes, everything wears an aspect of desolation.

> "On the South Georgias, in same latitude as Yorkshire in the north, Cook did not find a shrub big enough to make a toothpick. Captain Cook describes it as 'savage and horrible. The wild rocks raised their lofty summits till they were lost in the clouds, and the valleys lay covered with everlasting snow. Not a tree was to be seen; not a shrub even big enough to make a toothpick. Who could have thought that an island of no greater extent than this (Isle of Georgia), situated between the latitude of 54 and 55 degrees, should, in the very height of summer, be in a manner wholly covered many fathoms deep with frozen snow? The lands which lie to the south are doomed by Nature to perpetual frigidness--never to feel the warmth of the sun's rays; whose horrible and savage aspect I have not words to describe.' The South Shetlands, occupying a corresponding latitude to their namesakes in the north, present scarcely a vestige of vegetation. Kerguelen, as low as latitude 50 degrees south, boasts eighteen species of plants, of which only one, a peculiar kind of cabbage, has been found useful, in eases of scurvy; while Iceland, 15 degrees nearer to the pole in the north, boasts 870 species. Even marine life is sparse in certain tracts of vast extent, and the sea-bird is seldom observed flying over such lonely wastes. The contrast between the limits of organic life in arctic and antarctic zones is very remarkable and significant. Vegetables and land animals are found at nearly 80 degrees in the north; while, from the parallel of 58 degrees in the south, the lichen, and such like plants only clothe the rocks, and sea-birds and the cetaceous tribes alone are seen upon the desolate beaches." "M'Clintoch describes heads of reindeer--a perfect forest of antlers, moving north in the summer. . . .

The eider duck and the brent goose through the air; the unwieldly family of the cetacea through the waters; the arctic bear upon the ice; the musk ox and reindeer along the land--all wend their way northward at certain seasons. . . . Now these indications are absent from the southern zone, as is also the inhabitation of man. The bones of musk oxen, killed by the Esquimaux, were found north of the 79th parallel; while in the south, man is not found above the 56th parallel of latitude."[21]

These differences in the north and south could not exist if the earth were a globe, turning upon axes underneath a non-moving sun. The two hemispheres would at the same latitudes have the same degree of light and heat, and the same general phenomena, both in kind and degree. The peculiarities which are found in the south as compared with the north, are only such as could exist upon a stationary plane, having a northern centre, concentric with which is the path of the moving sun. The subject may be placed in the following syllogistic form.

The peculiarities observed in the south as compared with the north, could not exist upon a globe. They do exist, *therefore the earth is not a globe*. They are such as could and must exist upon a plane. They do exist, *therefore the earth is a plane*.

It will also be seen by a careful study of the diagram fig. 61, that, as the sun-light has to sweep over the great southern region in the same time, 24 hours, that it takes to pass over the smaller region of the north, the passage of the light must of necessity be proportionably more rapid; and the morning and evening twilight more abrupt. In the north the light on summer evenings seems as it were unwilling to terminate; and at midsummer, for many nights in succession, the sky is scarcely darkened. The twilight continues for hours after visible sunset. In the south, however, the reverse is the case, the day ends suddenly, and the night passes into day in a few seconds. A letter from a correspondent in New Zealand, dated, "Nelson, September 15th, 1857," contains the following passages:

"Even in summer, people here have no notion of going without fires in the evening; but then, though the days are very warm and sunny, the nights are always cold. For seven months last summer, we had not one day that the sun did not shine as brilliantly as it does in England in the finest day in June; and though it has more power here, the heat is not nearly so oppressive. . . But then there is not the twilight which you get in England. Here it is light till about eight o'clock, then, in a few minutes, it becomes too dark to see anything, and the change comes over in almost no time."

In a pamphlet by W. Swainson, Esq., Attorney General for New Zealand, (Smith, Elder, & Co., Cornhill, London, 1856,) among other peculiarities referred to, it is said that at Auckland, "of twilight there is little or none."

21 "Polar Explorations." Read before the Royal Dublin Society.

Captain Basil Hall, RN., F.R.S., in his narration says:

> "Twilight lasts but a short time in so low a latitude as 28 degrees, and no sooner does the sun peep above the horizon, than all the gorgeous parade by which he is preceded is shaken off, and he comes in upon us in the most abrupt and unceremonious way imaginable."

The motion of the sun over the vast southern region, wherein lies Australia and New Zealand, would also give shorter days in the south than in the north, and this is fully corroborated by experience. In the pamphlet above referred to, by Mr. Swainson, the following words occur:

> "The range of temperature is limited, there being no excess of either heat or cold; compared with the climate of England, the summer of New Zealand is but very little warmer though considerably longer. . . . The seasons are the reverse of those in England. Spring commences in September, summer in December, autum in April, and winter in June. . . . The days are an hour shorter at each end of the day in summer, and an hour longer in the winter than in England."

From a work on New Zealand, by Arthur S. Thompson, Esq., M.D., the following sentences are quoted:---

> "The summer mornings, even in the warmest parts of the colony, are sufficiently fresh to exhilarate without chilling; and the seasons glide imperceptibly into each other. The days are an hour shorter at each end of the day in summer, and an hour longer in winter than in England."

In the Cook's Strait Almanack for 1848, it is said:

> "At Wellington, New Zealand, December 21st, sun rises 4 h. 31 m., and sets at 7 h. 29 m., the day being 14 hours 58 minutes. June 21st, sun rises at 7 h. 29 m., and sets at 4 h. 31 m., the day being 9 hours and 2 minutes. In England the longest day is 16 hours 34 minutes, and the shortest day is 7 hours 45 minutes. Thus the longest day in New Zealand is 1 hour and 36 minutes *shorter* than the longest day in England; and the shortest day in New Zealand is 1 hour and 17 minutes *longer* than the shortest day in England."

Another peculiarity is, that though the days are "warm and sunny, the nights are always cold:" showing that although the altitude of the sun is greater, and therefore calculated to give greater heat, its velocity and mid-night distance are much greater than in England, and hence the greater cold of the nights. It is again insisted upon that these various peculiarities could not possibly exist in the southern region, if the earth were a globe and moved upon axes, and in an orbit round the sun. If the sun is fixed, and the earth revolves underneath it, the same phenomena would exist at the same distance on each side of the equator; but such is not the case! What can operate to cause the twilight in New Zealand to be so much more sudden, or the nights so much colder than in England? The southern "hemisphere" cannot revolve more rapidly than the northern! The latitudes are about the same, and the distance round a globe would be the same at 50° south as at 50° north, and as the whole would revolve once in twenty-four hours, the surface at the two places would pass underneath the sun with the same velocity, and the light would approach in the morning, and recede in the evening in exactly the same manner, yet the very contrary is the fact! The differences are altogether incompatible with the doctrine of the earth's rotundity; but "the earth a plane," and they are simple "matters of course." Upon a fixed plane underneath a moving sun, these phenomena are what must naturally and inevitably exist; but upon a globe they are utter impossibilities.

Some have objected to the conclusion here drawn, on the ground that the latitude of New Zealand is considerably less than that of England; but the objection falls before. the fact that the abruptness of twilight and the coldness of the summer nights are observed far out south beyond New Zealand. The author cannot here quote from any recognised work, but he has often been assured that this, is the common experience of navigators, and especially of whaling crews, who often wander over the vast waters beyond the latitude of 50 degrees. A remarkable illustration of this experience occurred some years ago in Liverpool. At the termination of a lecture, in which this subject had been discussed, a sailor requested leave to speak, and gave the following story:--

> "I was once confined on an island in South Tasmania, and had long been very anxious to escape; one morning I saw a whaling vessel in the offing, and being a good swimmer, I dashed into the sea to reach it. Being observed from the ship, a boat was sent out to pick me up. Immediately I got on board, we sailed away directly southwards. There happened to be a scarcity of hands, and I being able-bodied, was at once put to work. In the evening I was ordered aloft, and the captain cried out 'Be quick, Jack, or you'll be in the dark!' Now the sun was shining brightly, and it seemed far from the time of sunset, and I remember well that I looked at the captain, thinking he must be a little the worse for grog. However, I went aloft, and before I had finished the order, which was a very short time, I was in pitch darkness,--the sun seemed all at once to drop behind or below the sea. I noticed this all the time we were in the far south, whenever the sun was visible and the evening fine; and I only mention it now as corroborating the lecturer's statement. Any mariner, who has been a single season in the southern whaling grounds, will tell you the same thing."

The question, "how is it that the earth is not at all times illuminated all over its surface, seeing that the sun is always several hundred miles above it?" may be answered as follows:--

First, if no atmosphere existed, no doubt the light of the sun would diffuse over the whole earth at once, and alternations of light and darkness could not exist.

Secondly, as the earth is covered with an atmosphere of many miles in depth, the density of which gradually increases downwards to the surface, all the rays of light except those which are vertical, as they enter the upper stratum of air are arrested in their course of diffusion, and by refraction bent downwards towards the earth; as this takes place in all directions round the sun--equally where density and other conditions are equal, and *vice versâ*--the effect is a comparatively distinct disc of sun- light.

CHAPTER IX
CAUSE OF SUNRISE AND SUNSET

ALTHOUGH the sun is at all times above the earth's surface, it appears in the morning to ascend from the north-east to the noonday position, and thence to descend and disappear, or set, in the north-west. This phenomenon arises from the operation of a simple and everywhere visible law of perspective. A flock of birds, when passing over a flat or marshy country, always appears to descend is it recedes; and if the flock is extensive, the first bird appears lower or nearer to the horizon than the last, although they are at the same actual altitude above the earth immediately beneath them. When a balloon sails away from an observer, without increasing or decreasing its altitude, it appears to gradually approach the horizon. In a long row of lamps, the second--supposing the observer to stand at the beginning of the series---will appear lower than the first; the third lower than the second; and so on to the end of the row; the farthest away always appearing the lowest, although each one has the same altitude; and if such a straight line of lamps could be continued far enough, the lights would at length descend, apparently, to the horizon, or to a level with the eye of the observer, as shown in the following diagram, fig. 63.

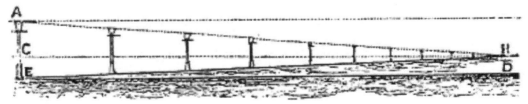

FIG. 63.

Let A, B, represent the altitude throughout of a long row of lamps, standing on the horizontal ground E, D; and C, H, the line of sight of an observer at C. The ordinary principles of perspective will cause an apparent rising of the ground E, D, to the eye-line C, H, meeting it at H; and an apparent descent of each subsequent lamp, from A, to H, towards the same eye-line, also meeting at H. The point H, is the horizon, or the true "vanishing point," at which the last visible lamp, although it has really the altitude D, B, will disappear.

Bearing in mind the above phenomena it will easily be seen how the sun, although always above and parallel to the earth's surface, must appear to *ascend* from the morning horizon to the noonday or meridian position; and thence to *descend* to the evening horizon.

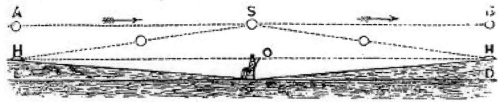

FIG 64.

In the diagram, fig. 64, let the line E, D, represent the surface of the earth; H, H, the morning and evening horizon; and A, S, B, a portion of the true path of the sun. An observer at 0, looking to the east, will first see the sun in the morning, not at A, its *true* position, but in its apparent position, H, just emerging from the "vanishing point," or the morning horizon. At nine o'clock, the sun will have the apparent position, 1, gradually appearing to *ascend* the line H, 1, S; the point S, being the meridian or noonday position. From S, the sun will be seen to gradually *descend* the line S, 2, H, until he reaches the horizon, H, and entering the "vanishing point," disappears, to an observer in England, in the west, beyond the continent of North America, as in the morning he is seen to rise from the direction of Northern Asia. An excellent illustration of this "rising" and "setting" of the sun may be seen in a long tunnel, as shown in diagram, fig. 65.

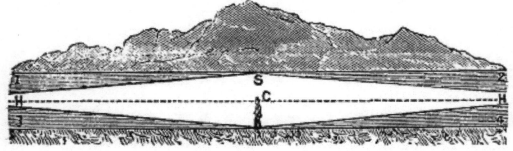

FIG. 65.

The top of the tunnel,1, 2, and, the bottom, 3, 4, although really equi-distant throughout the whole length, would, to an observer in the centre, C, *appear* to approach each other, and converge at the points, H, H; and a lamp, or light of any kind, brought in, and carried along the top, close to the upper surface 1, 2, would, when really going along the line, 1, S, 2, *appear to ascend* the inclined plane H, S, to the centre, S, and after passing the centre, to *descend* the plane S, H; and if the tunnel were sufficiently long, the phenomena of sunrise and of sunset would be perfectly imitated.

A very striking illustration of the convergence of the top and bottom, as well as the sides, of a long tunnel, has been observed in that of Mont Cenis. M. de Porville, when in the centre of the tunnel, noticed that the entrance had apparently become so small that the daylight beyond it seemed like a bright star.

> "Before us, at an apparently prodigious distance, we beheld a small star at the entrance of the gallery. Its vivid light contrasted strangely with the red glare of the lamps. Its brightness increased as the horses dashed on the way. In a short time its proportions were more clearly defined, and its volume increased. The illusion was quickly dispelled as we got over some kilometres. This soft white light is the extremity of the gallery."[22]

We have seen that "sunrise" and "sunset" are phenomena dependent entirely upon the fact that horizontal lines, parallel to each other, appear to approach or converge in the distance The surface of the earth being horizontal, and the line of sight of the observer and the sun's path being over and parallel with it, the rising and setting of the moving sun over the immovable earth are simply phenomena arising necessarily from the laws of perspective.

---

22 "Morning Advertiser," September 16th, 1871.

NOTE: The issues of the sun and moon rising and setting over the flat "circle of the Earth" and why the sun/moon sometimes appear larger (or smaller) when rising and setting are also addressed in my video titled, *FEIC 2018 - Day 1 Session 4 (Part 2 of 4): Rob Skiba* (beginning at about the 59 minute mark):

Perspective is only part of the answer. The atmosphere being quite literally full of moisture (in some places more than others) creates something known as "atmospheric lensing," which can easily cause the lower portion of ships or buildings to disappear at a distance (with no need for curvature), and which can likewise cause the illusion of the sun/moon rising/setting and/or getting bigger or smaller, depending on how much moisture is in the air.

CHAPTER X

CAUSE OF SUN APPEARING LARGER WHEN RISING AND SETTING THAN AT NOONDAY

IT is well known that when a light of any kind shines through a dense medium it appears larger, or rather gives a greater "glare," at a given distance than when it is seen through a lighter medium. This is more remarkable when the medium holds aqueous particles or vapour in solution, as in a damp or foggy atmosphere. Anyone may be satisfied of this by standing within a few yards of an ordinary street lamp, and noticing the size of the flame; on going away to many times the distance, the light or "glare" upon the atmosphere will appear considerably larger. This phenomenon may be noticed, to a greater or less degree, at all times; but when the air is moist and vapoury it is more intense. It is evident that at sunrise, and at sunset, the sun's light must shine through a greater length of atmospheric air than at mid-day; besides which, the air near the earth is both more dense, and holds more watery particles in solution, than the higher strata through which the sun shines at noonday; and hence the light must be dilated or magnified, as well as modified in colour. The following diagram, fig. 66, will show also that, as the sun recedes from the meridian, over a plane surface, the light, as it strikes the atmosphere, must give a larger disc.

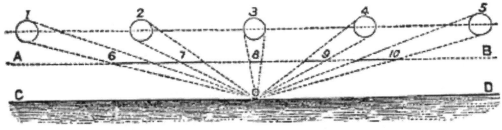

FIG. 66.

Let A, B, represent the upper stratum of the atmosphere; C, D, the surface of the earth; and 1, 2, 3, 4, 5, the sun, in his morning, forenoon, noon, afternoon, and evening positions. It is evident that when he is in the position 1, the disc of light projected upon the atmosphere at 6, is considerably larger than the disc projected from the forenoon position, 2, upon the atmosphere at 7; and the disc at 7 is larger than that formed at 8, when the sun, at 3, is on the meridian; when at 4, the disc at 9 is again larger; and when at 5, or in the evening, the disc at 10 is again as large as at 6, or the morning position. It is evident that the above results are what must of necessity occur if the sun's path, the line of atmosphere, and the earth's surface, are parallel and horizontal lines. That such results do constantly occur is a matter of everyday observation; and we may logically deduce front it a striking argument against the rotundity of the earth, and in favour of the contrary conclusion, that it is horizontal. The atmosphere surrounding a globe would not permit of anything like the same degree of enlargement of the sun when rising and setting, as we daily see in nature.

CHAPTER XI
CAUSE OF SOLAR AND LUNAR ECLIPSES

A solor eclipse is the result simply of the moon passing between the sun and the observer on earth. But that an eclipse of the moon arises from a shadow of the earth, is a statement in every respect, because unproved, unsatisfactory. The earth has been proved to be without orbital or axial motion; and, therefore, it could never come between the sun and the moon. The earth is also proved to be a plane, always underneath the sun and moon; and, therefore, to speak of its intercepting the light of the sun, and thus casting its own shadow on the moon, is to say that which is physically impossible.

Besides the above difficulties or incompatibilities, many cases are on record of the sun and moon being eclipsed when both were above the horizon. The sun, the earth, and the moon, *not in a straight line*, but the earth *below* the sun and moon--out of the reach or direction of both-- and yet a lunar eclipse has occurred! Is it possible that a "shadow" of the earth could be thrown upon the moon, when sun, earth, and moon, were not in the same line? The difficulty has been met by assuming the influence of refraction, as in the following quotations:--

"On some occasions the horizontal refraction amounts to 36 or 37 minutes, and generally to about 33 minutes, which is equal to the diameter of the sun or moon; and, therefore, the whole disc of the sun or moon will appear above the horizon, both at rising and setting, although actually below. This is the reason that the full moon has sometimes been seen above the horizon before the sun was set. A remarkable instance of this kind was observed at Paris, on the 19th of July, 1750,

171

when the moon appeared visibly eclipsed, while the sun was distinctly to be seen above the horizon."[23]

"On the 20th of April, 1837, the moon appeared to rise eclipsed before the sun had set. The same phenomenon was observed on the 20th of September, 1717."[24]

"In the lunar eclipses of July 17th, 1590; November 3rd, 1648; June 16th, 1666; and May 26th, 1668; the moon rose eclipsed whilst the sun was still apparently above the horizon. Those horizontal eclipses were noticed as early as the time of Pliny."[25]

On the 17th of January, 1870, a similar phenomenon occurred; .and again in July of the same year.[26]

The only explanation which has been given of this phenomenon is the refraction caused by the earth's atmosphere. This, at first sight, is a plausible and fairly satisfactory solution; but on carefully examining the subject, it is found to be utterly inadequate; and those who have recourse to it cannot be aware that the refraction of an object and that of a shadow are in opposite directions. An object by refraction is bent upwards; but the *shadow* of any object is bent downwards, as will be seen by the following very simple experiment. Take a plain white shallow basin, and place it ten or twelve inches from a light in such a position that the *shadow* of the *edge* of the basin touches the centre of the bottom. Hold a rod vertically over and on the edge of the shadow, to denote its true position. Now let water be gradually poured into the basin, and the shadow will be seen to *recede or shorten inwards and downwards*; but if a rod or a spoon is allowed to rest, with its upper end towards the light, and the lower end in the bottom of the vessel, it will be seen, as the water is poured in, to bend *upwards*--thus proving that if refraction operated at all, it would do so by elevating the moon above its true position, and throwing the earth's shadow downwards, or directly away from the moon's surface. Hence it is clear that a lunar eclipse by a shadow of the earth is an utter impossibility.

The moon's entire surface, or that portion of it which is presented to the earth, has also been distinctly seen during the whole time of a total lunar eclipse. This also is entirely incompatible with the doctrine that an eclipse of the moon is the result of a shadow of the earth passing over its surface.

Mr. Walker, who observed the lunar eclipse of March 19th, 1848, near Collumpton, says:--

---

23 "Astronomy and Astronomical Instruments," p. 105. By George G. Carey.
24 McCulloch's Geography, p. 85.
25 "Illustrated London Almanack for 1864," the astronomical articles in which are by James Glaisher, Esq., of the Greenwich Royal Observatory.
26 See "Daily Telegraph," July 16th, 1870.

"The appearances were as usual till twenty minutes past nine; at that period, and for the space of the next hour, instead of an eclipse, or the shadow (umbra) of the earth being the cause of the total obscurity of the moon, the whole phase of that body became very quickly and most beautifully *illuminated*, and assumed the appearance of the glowing heat of fire from the furnace, rather tinged with a deep red. . . . The *whole disc* of the moon being as *perfect with light* as if there had been *no eclipse whatever*! . . . . The moon positively gave good light from its disc during the total eclipse."[27]

The following case, although not exactly similar to the last, is worth recording here, as showing that some other cause existed than the earth's shadow to produce a lunar eclipse:--

"EXTRAORDINARY PHENOMENA ATTENDING THE ECLIPSE.--On Saturday evening, February 27th, 1858, at Brussels, the eclipse was seen by several English philosophers who happened to be present. It was attended by a very remarkable appearance, which Dr. Forster said was wholly inexplicable on any laws of natural philosophy with which he was acquainted. The moment before contact a small dusky spot appeared on the moon's surface, and during the whole of the eclipse, a reddish-brown fringe, or penumbra, projected above the shadow of the earth. Another thing still more remarkable was the apparent irregularity of the edge of the shadow. Three persons, one of them an astronomer, were witnesses of these curious phenomena, which no law of refraction can in any way explain."[28]

"LUNAR ECLIPSE OF FEBRUARY 6TH, 1860.--The only remarkable feature in this eclipse was the visibility--it might almost be termed the brilliancy of Aristarchus. Kepler, and other spots, were comparatively lost, or at most, barely discernible, as soon as they became enveloped in the shadow; but not so *Aristarchus*, which evidently *shone* either by *intrinsic or retained illumination*."[29]

"The moon has sometimes shone during a total eclipse with an almost unaccountable distinctness. On December 22nd, 1703, the moon, when totally immersed in the earth's shadow, was visible at Avignon by a ruddy light of such brilliancy that one might have imagined her body to be transparent, and to be enlightened from behind; and on March 19th, 1848, it is stated that so bright was the moon's surface during its total immersion, that many persons could not be persuaded that it was eclipsed. Mr. Forster, of Bruges, states, in an account of that eclipse, that the light and dark places on the moon's surface could be almost as well made out as in an ordinary dull moonlight night.

---

27 "Philosophical Magazine," No. 220, for August, 1848. 6 "Morning Star," of Wednesday, March 3rd, 1858.
28 "Morning Star," of Wednesday, March 3rd, 1858
29 Norman Pogson, Esq., Director of the Hartwell Observatory, in "Monthly Notices of the Royal Astronomical Society," March 9th, 1860.

"Sometimes, in a total lunar eclipse, the moon will appear quite obscure in some parts of its surface, and in other parts will exhibit a high degree of illumination. . . . To a certain extent I witnessed some of these phenomena, during the merely partial eclipse of February 7th, 1860. . . . I prepared, during the afternoon of February 6th, for witnessing the eclipse, without any distinct expectation of seeing much worthy of note. I knew, however, that upwards of eight-tenths of the disc would be covered, and I was anxious to observe with what degree of distinctness the eclipsed portion could be viewed, partly as an interesting fact, and partly with a view of verifying or discovering the weak points of an engraving (in which I am concerned) of a lunar eclipse. After seeing the increasing darkness of the penumbra softly merging into the true shadow, at the commencement of the eclipse (about 1 o'clock a.m., Greenwich time), I proceeded with pencil and paper, dimly lighted by a distant lamp, to note by name the different lunar mountains and plains (the so-called seas), over which the shadow passed. . . . During the first hour and ten minutes I had seen nothing unexpected. . . . I had repeatedly written down my observations of the remarkable clearness with which the moon's eclipsed outline could be seen, both with the naked eye and with the telescope. At 1 hour 58 minutes, however, I suddenly noted the ruddy colour of a portion of the moon. I may as well give my notes in the original words, as copied next day in a more connected form:

> "1 hour 58 minutes, Greenwich time.--I am suddenly struck by the fact that the whole of the western seas of the moon are showing through the shadow with singular sharpness, and that the whole region where they lie has assumed a decidedly reddish tinge, attaining its greatest brightness at a sort of temporary polar region, having 'Endymion' about the position of its imaginary pole. I particularly notice that the 'Lake of Sleep' has disappeared in this brightness, instead of standing out in a darker shade. And I notice that this so-called polar region is not parallel with the rim of the shadow, but rather west of it.

> "2 hours 15 minutes.--Some clouds, though very thin and transparent, now intervene.

> "2 hours 20 minutes.--The sky is now clear. How extra-ordinary is the appearance of the moon! Reddish is not the word to express it; it is red-- red hot! I endeavour to think of various red objects with which to compare it, and nothing seems so like as a red-hot penny--a red-hot penny, with a little white-hot piece at its lower edge, standing out against a dark blue background; only it is evidently not a mere disc, but beautifully rounded by shading. Such is its appearance with the naked eye; with the telescope, its surface varies more in tint than with the naked eye, and is not of quite so bright a red as when thus viewed. The redness continues to be most perceptible at a distance from the shadow's southern edge, and to be greatest about the region of 'Endymion.'

The 'Hercynian Mountains' (north of 'Grimaldus') are, however, of rather a bright red, and 'Grimaldus' shows well. 'Mare Crisium' and the western seas, are wonderfully distinct. Not a trace to be seen of 'Aristarchus' or 'Plato.'

"2 hours 27 minutes.--It is now nearly the middle of the eclipse. The red colour is very brilliant to the naked eye. . . . After this, I noticed a progressive change of tint in the moon.

"2 hours 50 minutes.--The moon does not seem to the naked eye of so bright a red as before; and again I am reminded by its tint, of red-hot copper, which has begun to cool. The whole of 'Grimaldi' is now uncovered. Through the telescope I notice a decided grey shade, at the lower part of the eclipsed portion, and the various small craters give it a stippled effect, like the old aqua-tint engravings. The upper part is reddish; but two graceful blueish curves, like horns, mark the form of the 'Hercynian Mountains,' and the bright region on the other limb of the moon. These are visible also to the naked eye.

"At 3 hours 5 minutes the redness had almost disappeared; a very few minutes afterwards no trace of it remained; and ere long clouds came on. I watched the moon, however, occasionally gaining a glimpse of its disc, till a quarter to 4 o'clock, when, for the last time on that occasion, I saw it faintly appearing through the clouds, nearly a full moon again; and then I took leave of it, feeling amply repaid for my vigil by the beautiful spectacle which I had seen.'"[30]

At the time of totality (the lunar eclipse of June 1st, 1863), the moon presented a soft, woolly appearance, apparently more globular in form than when fully illuminated. Traces of the larger and brighter mountains were visible at the time of totality, and particularly the bright rays proceeding from 'Tycho,' 'Kepler,' and 'Aristarchus.' . . . . At first, when the obscured part was of small dimensions, it was of an iron grey tint, but as it approached totality, the reddish light became so apparent that it was remarked that the moon 'seemed to be on fire;' and when the totality had commenced, it certainly looked like a fire smouldering in its ashes, and almost going out."[31]

In ordinary cases the disc appears, during a total eclipse, of a reddish hue, the colour being, indeed, of the most various degrees of intensity, passing, even when the moon is far removed from the earth into a fiery glowing red. Whilst I was lying at anchor (29th of March, 1801), off the Island of Baru, not far from Cartagena de Indias, and observing a total lunar eclipse, I was exceedingly struck by seeing how

---

30 The Hon. Mrs. Ward, Trimleston House, near Dublin, in "Recreative Science," p. 281.
31 "Illustrated London Almanack for 1864," by Mr. Glaisher, of Royal Observatory, Greenwich. A beautiful tinted engraving is given, representing the moon, with all the light and dark places, the so-called mountains, seas, &c., plainly visable, during the totality of the eclipse.

much brighter the reddened disc of the moon appears in the sky of the tropics than in my northern native land."[32]

"The fiery, coal-glowing colour of the darkened (eclipsed) moon. . . . The change is from black to red, and blueish."[33]

"Great was the confusion created in the camp of Vitellius by the eclipse which took place that night; yet it was not so much the eclipse itself-- although to minds already disturbed this might appear ominous of misfortune--as it was the circumstance of the moon's varying colours-- blood-red, black, and other mournful hues--which filled their souls with uneasy apprehensions."[34]

The several cases above advanced are logically destructive of the notion that an eclipse of the moon arises from a shadow of the earth. As before stated, the earth is proved to be a plane, without motion, and always several hundred miles below the sun and moon, and cannot, by any known possibility come between them. It cannot therefore intercept the light of the sun, and throw its own shadow upon the moon. If such a thing were a natural possibility, how could the moon continue to shine during the whole or any considerable part of the period of its passage through the dark shadow of the earth? Refraction, or what has been called "Earth light," will not aid in the explanation; because the light of the moon is at such times "like the glowing heat of firer tinged with deep red." "*Reddish* is not the word to express it, it was red--*red hot*." "The reddish light made it, seem to be on fire." "It looked like a fire smouldering in its ashes." "Its tint was that of red-hot copper." The sun light is of an entirely different colour to that of the eclipsed moon; and it is contrary to known optical principles to say that light when refracted or reflected, or both simultaneously, is thereby changed in colour. If a light of a given colour is seen through a great depth of a comparatively dense medium, as the sun is often seen in winter through the fog and vapour of the atmosphere, it appears of a different colour, and generally of such as that which the moon so often gives during a total eclipse; but a shadow cannot produce any such effect, as it is, in fact, not an entity at all, but simply the absence of light.

From the facts and phenomena already advanced, we cannot draw any other conclusion than that the moon is obscured by some kind of semi- transparent body passing before it; and through which the luminous surface is visible: the luminosity changed in colour by the density of the intervening object. This conclusion is *forced* upon, us by the evidence; but it involves the admission that the moon shines with light of its own-- that it is not a reflector of the sun's light, but absolutely *self-luminous*. Although this admission is logically compulsory, it will be useful and strictly Zetetic to collect all the evidence possible which bears upon it.

---

32 "Physical Description of the Heavens," p. 356. By Humboldt.
33 Plutarch ("De Facia in Orbe Luna"), T. iv., pp. 780-783.
34 Dion Cassius (lxv., 11; T., iv.; p. 185. Sturz.)

1st. A reflector is a plane or concave surface, which gives off or returns what it receives:--

- If a piece of red hot metal or any other heated object is placed before a plane or concave surface, *heat* is reflected.

- If snow or ice, or any artificial freezing mixture is similarly placed, *cold* will be reflected.

- If light of any given colour is placed in the same way, the same colour of light will be reflected.

- If a given sound is produced, the same tone or pitch will be reflected.

A reflector will not throw off cold when heat is placed before it; nor heat when cold is presented. If a red light is received, red light will be returned, not blue or yellow. If the note C is sounded upon any musical instrument, a reflector will not return the note D or G, but precisely the *same note*, altered only in degree or intensity.

If the moon is a reflector of the sun's light, she could not radiate or throw down upon the earth any other light than such as she first receives from the sun. No difference could exist in the quality or character of the light; and it could not possibly differ in any other respect than that of intensity or quantity. It has been asserted in opposition to the above, that the moon might absorb *some* of the rays of light from the sun and reflect only the remaining rays. To this it is replied that absorption means speedy saturation: a piece of blotting paper, or a lump of hard sugar, or a sponge when brought into contact with any fluid or gaseous substance, would only absorb for a short time; it would quickly become saturated, filled to repletion, and from that moment would cease to absorb, and ever afterwards could only reflect or throw back whatever was projected upon it. So the moon, if an object without light of her own, might at the beginning of her existence absorb the sun's ray's, and, fixing some, might return the others; but as already shown, she could only absorb to saturation, which would occur in a very short time; and from this point of saturation to the present moment she could not have been other than a *reflector*--a reflector, too, of all which she receives.

We have then, in order to know whether the moon is a reflector, merely to ascertain whether the light which we receive from her is, or is not the same, in character as that received from the sun.

- 1st. The sun's light is generally, and in an ordinary state of the atmosphere, of an oppressive, fierce, semi-golden, pyro-phosphorescent character; while that of the moon is pale, silvery and gentle; and when shining most brightly is mild and non-pyrotic.

- 2nd. The sun's light is warm, drying, and preservative, or antiseptic; animal and vegetable substances exposed to it soon dry, coagulate, shrink, and lose their tendency to decompose and become putrid. Hence grapes and other fruits by long exposure to sunlight become solid, and partially candied and preserved; as instanced in raisins, prunes, dates, and ordinary grocers' currants. Hence, too, fish and flesh by similar exposure lose their gaseous and other volatile constituents and by coagulation of their albuminous and other compounds become firm and dry, and less liable to decay; in this way various kinds of fish and flesh well known to travellers are preserved for use.

The light of the moon is damp, cold, and powerfully septic; and animal and nitrogenous vegetable substances. exposed to it soon show symptoms of putrefaction. Even living creatures by long exposure to the moon's rays, become morbidly affected. It is a common thing on board vessels going through tropical regions, for written or printed notices to be issued, prohibiting persons from sleeping on deck exposed to full moonlight, experience having proved that such exposure is often followed by injurious consequences.

"It is said that the moon has a pernicious effect upon those who, in the East, sleep in its beams; and that fish having been exposed to them for only one night, becomes most injurious to those who eat it."[35]

"At Peckham Rye, a boy named Lowry has entirely lost his sight by sleeping in a field in the bright moonlight."[36]

"If we place in an exposed position two pieces of meat, and one of them be subjected to the moon's rays, while the other is protected from them by a screen or a cover, the former will be tainted with putrefaction much sooner than the other."[37]

Professor Tyndall describing his journey to the summit of the Alpine Mountain, Weisshorn, August 21st, 1861, says:--

"I lay with my face towards the moon (which was nearly full), and gazed until my face and eyes became so chilled that I was fain to protect them with a handkerchief."[38]

- 3rd. It is a well known fact, that if the sun is allowed to shine strongly upon a common coal, coke, wood, or charcoal fire, the combustion is greatly diminished; and often the fire is extinguished. It is not an uncommon thing for cooks, housewives, and others to draw down the blinds in summer time to prevent their

35 "Wanderings in the East," p. 367. (Edit. 1854). By Rev. J. Gadsby.
36 Newspaper Paragraph.
37 "Lectures on Astronomy," p. 67. By M. Arago,
38 "Illustrated London News," of September, 7th, 1861

fires being put out by the continued stream of sun-light pouring through the windows. Many philosophers have recently attempted to deny and ridicule this fact, but they are met, not only by the common sense and every-day experience of very practical people, but by the results of specially instituted experiments.

It is not so well known perhaps, but it is an equally decided fact, that when the light of the moon is allowed to play upon a common carbonaceous fire, the action is increased, the fire burns more vividly, and the fuel is more rapidly consumed.

- 4th. In sun-light a thermometer stands higher than a similar thermometer placed in the shade. In the full moon-light, a thermometer stands lower than a similar instrument in the shade.

- 5th. In winter when ice and snow are on the ground, it is patent to every boy seeking amusement by skating or snow-balling, that in the sun light both ice and snow are softer and sooner thaw than that behind a wall, or in the shade. It is equally well known that when, in frosty weather, the night is far advanced, and the full moon has been shining for some hours, the snow and ice exposed to the moon-light are hard and crisp, while in the shade, or behind any object which intercepts the moon's rays it is warmer, and the ice and snow are softer and less compact. Snow will melt sooner in sun-light than in the shade; but sooner in the shade than when exposed to the light of the moon.

- 6th. The light of the sun reflected from the surface of a pool of water, or from the surface of ice, may be collected in a large lens, and thrown to a point or focus, when the heat will be found to be considerable; but neither from the light of the moon reflected in a similar way, nor direct from the moon itself, can a heat-giving focus be obtained.

- 7th. The sun's light, when concentrated by a number of plane or concave mirrors throwing the light to the same point; or by a large burning lens, produces a black or non-luminous focus, in which the heat is so intense that metallic and alkaline substances are quickly fused; earthy and mineral compounds almost immediately vitrified; and all animal and vegetable structures in a few seconds decomposed, burned up and destroyed.

The moon's light concentrated in the above manner produces a focus so brilliant and luminous that it is difficult to look upon it; yet there is no increase of temperature. In the focus of sun-light there is great heat but no light. In that of the moon's light there is great light but no heat. That the light of the moon is without heat, is fully verified by the following quotations:---

"If the most delicate thermometer be exposed to the full light of the moon, shining with its greatest lustre, the mercury is not elevated a hair's breadth; neither would it be if exposed to the focus of her rays concentrated by the most powerful lenses. This has been proved by actual experiment."[39]

"This question has been submitted to the test of direct experiment. . . . The bulb of a thermometer sufficiently sensitive to render apparent a change of temperature amounting to the thousandth part of a degree, was placed in the focus of a concave reflector of vast dimensions, which, being directed to the moon, the lunar rays were collected with great power upon it. Not the slightest change, however, was produced in the thermometric column; proving that a concentration of rays sufficient to fuse gold if they proceeded from the sun, does not produce a change of temperature so great as the thousandth part of a degree when they proceed from the moon."[40]

"The most delicate experiments have failed in detecting in the light of the moon either calorific or chemical properties. Though concentrated in the focus of the largest mirrors, it produces no sensible heating effect. To make this experiment, recourse has been had to a bent tube, the extremities of which terminate in two hollow globes filled with air, the one trans-parent, the other blackened, the middle space being occupied by a coloured fluid. In this instrument, when caloric is absorbed by it, the black ball takes up more than the other, and the air it encloses increasing in elasticity, the liquid is driven out. This instrument is so delicate that it indicates even the millionth part of a degree; and yet, in the experiment alluded to, it gave no result."[41]

"The light of the moon, though concentrated by the most powerful burning-glass, is incapable of raising the temperature of the most delicate thermometer. M. De la Hire collected the rays of the full moon when on the meridian, by means of a burning-glass 35 inches in diameter, and made them fall on the bulb of a delicate air-thermometer. No effect was produced though the lunar rays by this glass were concentrated 300 times. Professor Forbes concentrated the moon's light by a lens 30 inches in diameter, its focal distance being about 41 inches, and having a power of concentration exceeding 6000 times. The image of the moon, which was only 18 hours past full, and less than two hours from the meridian, was brilliantly thrown by this lens on the extremity of a commodious thermopile. Although the observations were made in the most unexceptional manner, and (supposing that half the rays were reflected, dispersed and absorbed), though the light of the moon was concentrated 3000 times, not the slightest thermo effect was produced."[42]

39 "All the Year Round," by Dickens.
40 "Museum of Science," p. 115. By Dr. Lardner. 19 "Lectures on Astronomy," p. 66.
41 "Lectures on Astronomy," p. 66. By M. Arago, (p.108)
42 "Lectures on Astronomy," p. 334.. By Dr. Noad. (p.108)

In the "Lancet" (Medical Journal), for March 14th, 1856, particulars are given of several experiments which proved that the moon's rays when concentrated, actually reduced the temperature upon a thermometer more than eight degrees.

It is the common experience of the world that the light of the sun heats and invigorates all things, and that moon light is cold and depressive. Among the Hindoos, the sun is called "Nidâghakara," which means in Sanscrit "Creator of Heat;" and the moon is called "Sitala Hima," "The Cold," and "Himân'su," "Cold-darting," or "Cold-radiating."

Poets, who but utter in measured words the universal knowledge of mankind, always speak of the "Pale cold moon," and the expression is not only poetically beautiful, but also true philosophically.

> *"The cold chaste moon, the queen of Heaven's bright Isles;*
> *Who makes all beautiful on which she smiles:*
> *That wandering shrine of soft yet icy flame*
> *Which ever is transformed, yet still the same;*
> *And warms not but illumes."*

The facts now placed in contrast make it impossible to conclude otherwise than that the moon does not shine by reflection, but by a light peculiar to herself--that she is in short *self-luminous*. This conclusion is confirmed by the following consideration. The moon is said by the Newtonian philosophers to be a sphere. If so, its surface could not possibly *reflect*; a reflector must be concave or plane, so that the rays of light may have an "angle of incidence." If the surface is convex, every ray of light falls upon it in a line direct with radius, or perpendicular to the surface. Hence there cannot be an angle of *incidence* and therefore none of *reflection*. If the moon's surface were a mass of highly polished silver, it could not reflect from more than a mere point. Let a silvered glass ball of considerable size be held before a lamp or fire of any magnitude, and it will be seen that instead of the whole surface reflecting light there will only be a very small portion illuminated. But during full moon the *whole disc* shines intensely, an effect which from a spherical surface is impossible. If the surface of the moon were opaque and earthy instead of polished like a mirror, it might be seen simply illuminated like a dead wall, or the face of a distant sandstone rock, or chalky cliff, but it could not shine intensely from every part, radiating brilliant light and brightly illuminating the objects around it, as the moon does so beautifully when full and in a clear firmament. If the earth were admitted to be globular, and to move, and to be capable of throwing a shadow by intercepting the sun's light, it would be impossible for a lunar eclipse to occur thereby, unless, at the same time, the moon is proved to be non-luminous, and to shine only by reflection. But this is not proved; it is only assumed as an essential part of a theory. The *contrary* is capable of proof. That **the moon is self-luminous**, or shines with her own light, independently.

The very name and the nature of a reflector demand certain well-defined conditions. The moon does not manifest these necessary conditions, and therefore it must be concluded, of necessity, that she is not a reflector, but a self-luminous body. That she shines with her own light independently of the sun, thus admits of direct demonstration.

As the moon is self-luminous, her surface could not be darkened or "eclipsed" by a shadow of the earth--supposing such a shadow could be thrown upon it. In such a case, the luminosity instead of being diminished, would increase, and would be greater in proportion to the greater density or darkness of the shadow. As the light in a bull's-eye lantern looks brightest in the darkest places, so would the self-shining surface of the moon be most intense in the *umbra* or deepest part of the earth's shadow.

The moon shining brightly during the whole time of eclipse, and with a light of different hue to that of the sun; and the light of the moon having, as previously shown, a different character to that of the sun; the earth not a globe, and not in motion round the sun, but sun and moon always over the earth's plane surface, render the proposition unavoidable as it is clearly undeniable that a lunar eclipse *does not* and *could not* in the nature of things arise from a shadow of the earth, but must of sheer logical necessity be referred to some other cause.

We have seen that, during a lunar eclipse, the moon's self-luminous surface is covered by a semi-transparent something; that this "something" is a definite mass, because it has a distinct and circular outline, as seen during its first and last contact with the moon. As a solar eclipse occurs from the moon passing before the sun, so, from the evidence above collected, it is evident that a lunar eclipse arises from a similar cause--a body semi-transparent and well-defined passing before the moon; or between the moon's surface and the observer on the surface of the earth.

That many such bodies exist in the firmament is almost a matter of certainty; and that one such as that which eclipses the moon exists at no great distance above the earth's surface, is a matter admitted by many of the leading astronomers of the day. In the report of the council of the Royal Astronomical Society, for June 1850, it is said:--

> "We may well doubt whether that body which we call the moon is the only satellite of the earth."

In the report of the Academy of Sciences for October 12th, 1846, and again for August, 1847, the director of one of the French observatories gives a number of observations and calculations which have led him to conclude that,--

> "There is at least one non-luminous body of considerable magnitude which is attached as a satellite to this earth."

Sir John Herschel admits that:--

"Invisible moons exist in the firmament."[43]

Sir John Lubbock is of the same opinion, and gives rules and formulæ for calculating their distances, periods, &c.[44]

At the meeting of the British Association for the Advancement of Science, in 1850, the president stated that,---

"The opinion was gaining ground, that many of the fixed stars were accompanied by companions emitting no light."

"The 'changeable stars' which disappear for a time, or are eclipsed, have been supposed to have very large opaque bodies revolving about or near to them, so as to obscure them when they come in conjunction with us."[45]

"Bessel, the greatest astronomer of our time, in a letter to myself, in July 1844, said, 'I do indeed continue in the belief that Procyon and Sirius are both true double stars, each consisting of one *visible*, and one *invisible* star.' . . A laborious inquiry just completed by Peters at Königsberg; and a similar one by Schubert, the calculator employed on the North American Nautical Almanack, support Bessel."[46]

"The belief in the existence of non-luminous stars was prevalent in Grecian antiquity, and especially in the early times of Christianity. It was assumed that 'among the fiery stars which are nourished by vapours, there move other earthy bodies, which remain invisible tous!' *Origenes.*"[47]

"Stars that are invisible and consequently have no name move in space together with those that are visible." *Diogenes of Appollonica.*[48]

Lambert in his cosmological letters admits the existence of "dark cosmical bodies of great size."[49]

We have now seen that the existence of dark bodies revolving about the luminous objects in the firmament has been admitted by practical observers from the earliest ages; and that in our own day such a mass of evidence has accumulated on the subject,

---

43 "Herschel's Astronomy," pp. 521 and 616.
44 "Philosophical Magazine" for 1848, p. 80.
45 "Encyclopædia Londinensis." Art., "Fixed Stars."
46 "Physical Description of the Heavens." By Humboldt, p. 183, 1867. 25 Ibid., p. 184.
47 Ibid. Notes, p. 184. (p.111).
48 "Comos," p. 122. By Humboldt.
49 Ibid. Notes, p.71. (p. 112).

that astronomers are compelled to admit that not only dark bodies which occasionally obscure the luminous stars when in conjunction, but that cosmical bodies of large size exist, and that "one at least is attached as a satellite to this earth." It is this dark or "non-luminous satellite," which when in conjunction, or in a line with the moon and an observer on earth, IS THE IMMEDIATE CAUSE OF A LUNAR ECLIPSE.

Those who are unacquainted with the methods of calculating eclipses and other phenomena, are prone to look upon the correctness of such calculations as powerful arguments in favour of the doctrine of the earth's rotundity and the Newtonian philosophy, generally. One of the most pitiful manifestations of ignorance of the true nature of theoretical astronomy is the ardent inquiry so often made, "How is it possible for that system to be false, which enables its professors to calculate to a second of time both solar and lunar eclipses for hundreds of years to come?" The supposition that such calculations are an essential part of the Newtonian or any other theory is entirely gratuitous, and exceedingly fallacious and misleading. Whatever theory is adopted, or if all theories are discarded, the same calculations can be made. The tables of the moon's relative positions for any fraction of time are purely practical-- the result of long-continued observations, and may or may not be connected with hypothesis. The necessary data being tabulated, may be mixed up with any, even the most opposite doctrines, or kept distinct from every theory or system, just as the operator may determine.

> "The considered defects of the system of Ptolemy (who lived in the second century of the Christian era), did not prevent him from calculating all the eclipses that were to happen for 600 years to come."[50]

> "The most ancient observations of which we are in possession, that are sufficiently accurate to be employed in astronomical calculations, are those made at Babylon about 719 years before the Christian era, of three eclipses of the moon. Ptolemy, who has transmitted them to us, employed them for determining the period of the moon's mean motion; and therefore had probably none more ancient on which he could depend. The Chaldeans, however, must have made a long series of observations before they could discover their 'Saros,' or lunar period of 6585⅓ days, or about 18 years; at which time, as they had learnt, the place of the moon, her node and apogee return nearly to the same situation with respect to the earth and the sun, and, of course, a series of nearly similar eclipses occur."[51]

> "Thales (B.C. 600) predicted the eclipse which terminated the war between the Medes and the Lydians. Anaxagoras (B.C. 530) predicted an eclipse which happened in the fifth year of the Peloponnesian War."[52]

---

50 Smith's "Rise and Progress of Astronomy.
51 "Lectures on Natural Philosophy," p. 370. By Professor Partington.
52 Professor Barlow, in "Encyclopædia Metropolitana," p. 486.

"Hipparchus (140 B.C.) constructed tables of the motions of the sun and moon; collected accounts of such eclipses as had been made by the Egyptians and Chaldeans, and calculated all that were to happen for 600 years to come."[53]

"The precision of astronomy arises, not from theories, but from prolonged observations, and the regularity of the motions, or the ascertained uniformity of their irregularities."[54]

"No particular theory is required to calculate eclipses; and the calculations may be made with equal accuracy independent of every theory."[55]

"It is not difficult to form some general notion of the process of calculating eclipses. It may be readily conceived that by long-continued observations on the sun and moon, the laws of their revolution may be so well understood that the exact places which they will occupy in the heavens at any future times may be foreseen, and laid down in tables of the sun and moon's motions; that we may thus ascertain by inspecting the tables the instant when these bodies will be together in the heavens, or be in conjunction."[56]

The simplest method of ascertaining any future eclipse is to take the tables which have been formed during hundreds of years of careful observation; or each observer may form his own tables by collecting a number of old almanacks one for each of the last forty years: separate the times of the eclipses in each year, and arrange them in a tabular form. On looking over the various items he will soon discover parallel cases, or "cycles" of eclipses; that is, taking the eclipses in the first year of his table, and examining those of each succeeding year, he will notice peculiarities in each year's phenomena; but on arriving to the items of the nineteenth and twentieth years, he will perceive that some of the eclipses in the earlier part of the table will have been now repeated--that is to say, the times and characters will be alike. If the time which has elapsed between these two parallel or similar eclipses be carefully noted, and called a "cycle," it will then be a very simple and easy matter to predict any future *similar* eclipse, because, at the end of the "cycle," such similar eclipse will be certain to occur; or, at least, because such repetitions of similar phenomena have occurred in every cycle of between eighteen and nineteen years during the last several thousand years, it may be reasonably expected that if the natural world continues to have the same general structure and character, such repetitions may be predicted for all future time. The whole process is neither more nor less--except a little more complicated--than that because an express train had been observed for many years to pass a given point at a given second--say of every eighteenth day, so at a similar moment of every cycle or eighteenth day, for a hundred or more

---

53 "Encyclopædia Londinensis," vol. if., p. 402.
54 "Million of Facts." By Sir Richard Phillips. Page 358.
55 Somerville's "Physical Sciences", p. 46. (p.113).
56 "Mechanism of the Heavens," p. 191. By Professor Olmstead, U.S. Observatory.

years to. come, the same might be predicted and expected. To tell the actual day and second, it is only necessary to ascertain on what day of the week the eighteenth or "cycle day" falls.

Tables of the places of the sun and moon, of eclipses, and of kindred phenomena, have existed for thousands of years, and were formed independently of each other, by the Chaldean, Babylonian, Egyptian, Hindoo, Chinese, and other ancient astronomers. Modern science has had nothing to do with these; farther than rendering them a little more exact, by averaging and reducing the fractional errors which a longer period of observation has detected.

As an instance of the complicated process into which modern theorists have allowed themselves to "drift," the following formula is here introduced:--

"RULES TO FIND ALL PARTICULARS OF A LUNAR ECLIPSE.

"1st.--Find the moon's true hourly motion at the full moon by means.

"TO FIND THE TIME, MAGNITUDE, AND DURATION OF A LUNAR ECLIPSE.

"Let A, B, R, (in the following diagram) be a section of the earth's shadow at the distance of the moon; S, n, the path described by its centre, S, on the ecliptic; M, n, the relative orbit of the moon; M, n, S, n, being considered straight lines. Draw S, o, perpendicular to S, n, and S, m, to M, n; then o, and m, are in the places, with respect to S, of the moon in opposition, and at the middle of the eclipse.

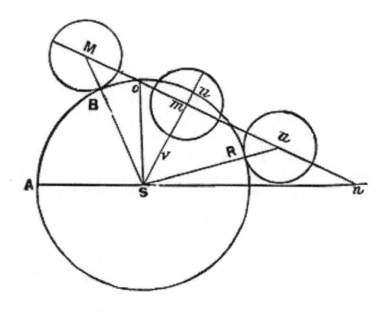

"Let α = S, B = $h + \pi - \sigma$, the radius of the section of the shadow.

λ = S, o, the moon's latitude in opposition.

f = the relative horary motion in longitude of the moon in the relative orbit, M, n.

h = the moon's horary motion in the relative orbit.

g = the moon's horary motion in latitude.

μ = the moon's semi-diameter;

$$\therefore \tan n = \frac{g}{f}, \text{ and } g = h, \sin n.$$

"Let M, and N, be the place of the moon's centre at the time of the first and last contact; therefore

$$SM = SN = a + \mu.$$

"Now S m = λ cos n;

$$\therefore M, m = \sqrt{(a+\mu)^2 - \lambda^2 \cos^2 n} = N, m,$$

and m, o = λ sin n.

"If, therefore, t, and t', be the times from opposition of the first and last contact,

$$t = \frac{M\ m - O\ m}{h,} = \left\{ \sqrt{(a+\mu^2) - \lambda^2 \cos^2 n} - \lambda \sin n \right\} \frac{\sin n.}{g}$$

$$t' = \frac{N\ m + O\ m}{h,} = \left\{ \sqrt{(a+\mu)^2 - \lambda^2 \cos^2 n} + \lambda \sin n \right\} \frac{\sin n.}{g}$$

$$\therefore \text{ the } duration = 2 \sqrt{(+\mu)^2 - \lambda^2 \cos^2 n,} \frac{\sin n.}{g}$$

"The time from opposition, of the middle of the eclipse

$$= \frac{O}{h,} \frac{m}{} = \frac{\lambda \sin^2 n.}{g.}$$

"The *magnitude* of the eclipse, or the part of the moon immersed,

$$= S\,u - S\,v.$$
$$= S\,u - S\,m + m,\,v.$$
$$= a - \lambda \cos n + \mu.$$

"The moon's diameter is generally divided into twelve equal parts, called digits; therefore the digits eclipsed $= 12 :: \alpha - \lambda,\, n + \mu : 2\,\mu$

$$= \frac{6}{\mu}.\ (a - \lambda \cos n, + \mu).$$

"COR. 1.--If $\lambda \cos n$, be greater than $\alpha + \mu$, t and t' are impossible, and no eclipse can take place, as is also evident from the figure.

"COR. 2.--In exactly the same manner it may be proved, if t and t' be the times from opposition, of the centres of the shadow and moon being at any given distance c,

$$t = (\sqrt{c^2 - \lambda^2 \cos^2 n} - \lambda \sin n),\ \frac{\sin n}{g},$$

$$t' = (\sqrt{c^2 - \lambda^2 \cos^2 n} + \lambda \sin n),\ \frac{\sin n}{g}.$$

"COR. 3.--If $c = h + \mu + \sigma + \mu =$ the radius of the penumbra, + the radius of the moon, the times of the moon entering and emerging from the penumbra are obtained.

"The horary motion of the moon is about $32\frac{1}{2}'$, and that of the sun $2\frac{1}{2}'$; therefore the relative horary motion of the moon is $30'$; and as the greatest diameter of the section at the distance of the moon is $1°\ 31'\ 44''$, a lunar eclipse may last more than three hours."[57]

---

[57] "Elements of Astronomy," p. 309, by W. Maddy, M.A., Fellow of St. John's College, Cambridge.

The formulæ quoted are entirely superfluous, because they add nothing to our knowledge of the causes of eclipses, and would not enable us to predict anything which has not hundreds of times already occurred. Hence, all the labour of calculation is truly effort thrown away, and may be altogether dispensed with by adopting and calling that which eclipses the moon the "lunar eclipsor," or the moon's satellite, instead of the "earth's shadow," just as the moon is the sun's eclipsor.

This was one of the toughest things for me to figure out concerning the flat Earth model. Solar eclipses work the same way as in the standard model, but with a fixed flat Earth (not floating in space) and a moon circling overhead, what could possibly be causing the lunar eclipse? Well, as I pointed out in the Introduction, looking at Scripture, we find:

Genesis 1:

14 And God said, ***Let there be lights*** in the firmament of the heaven to divide the day from the night; and let them be for signs, and for seasons, and for days, and years

15 And let them be for lights in the firmament of the heaven ***to give light*** *upon the earth:* and it was so.

16 And God made <u>two great lights</u>; the greater light to rule the day, and the lesser light to rule the night: he made the stars also.

17 And God set them in the firmament of the heaven ***to give light*** upon the earth,

18 And to rule over the day and over the night, and to divide the light from the darkness: and God saw that it was good.

Psalm 136:

7 ***To him that made great lights***: for his mercy endureth for ever:

8 ***The sun*** to rule by day: for his mercy endureth for ever:

9 ***The moon*** and stars to rule by night: for his mercy endureth for ever.

Isaiah 13:

9 Behold, the day of the LORD cometh, cruel both with wrath and fierce anger, to lay the land desolate: and he shall destroy the sinners thereof out of it.

10 For the stars of heaven and the constellations thereof shall not give their light: the sun shall be darkened in his going forth, ***and the moon shall not <u>cause</u> her light to shine***.

Ezekiel 32:

7 And when I shall put thee out, I will cover the heaven, and make the stars thereof dark; I will cover the sun with a cloud, ***and the moon shall not <u>give</u> her light***.

Matthew 24:29 Immediately after the tribulation of those days shall ***the sun be darkened, and the moon shall not <u>give</u> her light,*** and the stars shall fall from heaven, and the powers of the heavens shall be shaken:

So here we have Moses, David, Isaiah, Ezekiel and Yeshua all telling us the moon ***gives*** her own light. There is nothing in Scripture that even remotely suggests "she" is just a rock up there reflecting the light of the sun. And oddly enough, if you go to the Griffith Observatory in Los Angeles, and go to the exhibit made to show how the phases of the moon work, you will see a *self-illuminated* model of the moon going around overhead!

As for the cause of the lunar eclipses, please see my video *Debunking # 2 of the "Top Ten Reasons Why We (allegedly) Know the Earth is Round (as in a globe):*

I find it interesting that even as I am writing this now (Sept. 16, 2018), the Internet is all abuzz with wild speculation about why the Sunspot Solar Observatory in New Mexico mysteriously shut down and was evacuated and why, at the same time, the webcams at a number of other observatories also apparently went blank... shortly after allegedly capturing the moon's (Sept. 9th) transit in front of the sun (moving in two different directions). I personally do not believe most of the various theories being put forth in a lot of the speculative videos[58] currently discussing this topic (a simple Google search will bring up plenty). However, whether or not it was the moon being shown in that footage, there have been lots of other photos and videos of the sun over the years, showing large, spherical objects near it (that are neither the moon, Mercury nor Venus). Some of this is also addressed in the above video. And then there's the issue of what is known as the "selenelion" eclipse (a.k.a. the "impossible eclipse"). There have been at least two that I know of in recent years (12/10/11 and 10/8/14), where a total lunar eclipse occurs while both the sun and moon are still up. "Refraction" they say is the reason. The reader will have to decide whether or not they believe this explanation after looking into it for themselves. I for one do not. Especially after comparing the angles at which the "shadow" tends to come and go over the moon during eclipses. The moon is indeed a very strange object.

---

58 See for instance *Two Objects Eclipse Sun on SDO Satellite on 9th Part 1*: https://youtu.be/FLdHksmAJo4

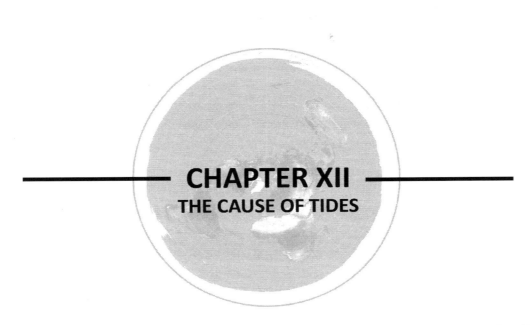

CHAPTER XII
THE CAUSE OF TIDES

IT has been shown that the doctrine of the earth's rotundity is simply a plausible theory, having no practical foundation; all ideas, therefore, of "centre of attraction of gravitation," "mutual mass attraction of earth and moon," &c. &c., as taught in the Newtonian hypothesis must be given up, and the cause of tides in the ocean sought in some other direction. Before commencing such an inquiry, however, it will be useful to point out a few of the difficulties which render the theory contradictory, and therefore false and worthless.

- 1st. The intensity of attraction of bodies on each other is affirmed to be proportional to bulk.

- 2nd. The earth is affirmed to be much larger than the moon ("The mass of the moon according to Lindenau is 1/87 of the mass of the earth"[59]), and therefore to have much the greatest attractive power. How then is it possible for the moon with only one eighty-seventh part of the attractive power of the earth, to lift up the waters of the ocean and draw them towards herself? In other words, how can the lesser power overcome the greater?

- 3rd. It is affirmed that the intensity of attraction increases with proximity, and *vice versâ*.

How, then, when the waters are drawn up by the moon from their bed, and away from the earth's attraction,--which at that greater distance from the centre is considerably

---

59 "Physical Description of the Heavens," p. 352. By Humboldt.

diminished, while that of the moon is proportionately increased--is it possible that all the waters acted on should be prevented leaving the earth and flying away to the moon?

If the moon has power of attraction sufficient to lift the waters of the earth at all, even a single inch from their deepest receptacles, where the earth's attraction is much the greater, there is nothing in the theory of attraction of gravitation to prevent her taking to herself all the waters which come within her influence. Let the smaller body once overcome the power of the larger, and the power of the smaller becomes greater than when it first operated, because the matter acted on is nearer to it. Proximity is greater, and therefore power is greater.

- 4th. The maximum power of the moon is affirmed to operate when on the meridian of any place.

How then can the waters of the ocean immediately underneath the moon flow towards the shores, and so cause a flood tide? Water flows, it is said, through the law of gravity, or attraction of the earth's centre; is it possible then for the moon, having once overcome the power of the earth, to let go her hold upon the waters, through the influence of a power which she has conquered, and which therefore, is less than her own? Again, if the moon really draws the waters of the ocean towards herself, can she take them to her own meridian, and there increase their altitude without depressing or lowering the level of the waters in the places beyond the reach of her influence? Let the following experiments be tried, and then the answer given:--

- 1st. Spread out on a table a sheet of paper of any size, to represent a body of water; place an object or mark at each edge of the paper, to represent the shores. Now draw the paper gently upwards in the centre, and notice the effect upon the objects or marks, and the edge of the paper.

- 2nd. Take a basin of water, and carefully note the level round the edge. Now place the bottom of a small lift-pump upon the surface of the water in the centre of the basin. On making the first stroke of the pump, the water will be slightly elevated in the centre, but it will recede or fall in at the sides.

In both the above experiments it will be seen that the water will be drawn away from the sides representing the shores when it is elevated in the centre. Hence the supposed attraction of the moon upon the waters of the earth could not possibly cause a flood-tide on the shores which are nearest her meridian action, but the very contrary; the waters would recede from the land to supply the pyramid of water formed immediately underneath the moon, and of necessity produce an ebb tide instead of the flood, which the Newtonian theory affirms to be the result.

The above and other difficulties which exist in connection with the explanation of the tides afforded by the Newtonian system, have led many, including Sir Isaac Newton himself, to admit that such explanation is the least satisfactory portion of the "theory of gravitation."

From this point we may proceed to enquire: "What is the real cause of the tides? The process must be purely Zetetic--first to define the leading term, or terms employed; secondly, to collect all the facts we can which bear upon the subject; and thirdly, to arrange the evidence, and see what conclusion necessarily appears.

The tide is either the rising and falling of the water in relation to the land; or the rising and falling of the land in relation to the water; but as it is not at this stage decided which is the case, the following must be the definition of the word tide:

DEFINITION: Tide is the relative change of level between land and water.

FACT 1: There is a constant but variable pressure of the atmosphere upon the surface of the earth and all the waters of the seas and lakes which lie upon and within it, and upon all the oceans which surround it.

PROOF: The workings of an air-pump, and the readings of the barometer wherever experiments have been made. During storms at sea it has been found that the commotion is almost confined to the surface, and seldom extends to a hundred feet below: at which depth the water is always calm, except in the path of currents and local submarine peculiarities.

The following quotations, gathered from casual reading, fully corroborate the above statements:

> "It is amazing how superficial is the most terrible tempest; divers assure us that in the greatest storms calm water is found at the depth of 90 feet.[60]

> "This motion of the surface of the sea is not perceptible to a great depth. In the strongest gale it is supposed not to extend beyond 72 feet below the surface; and at the depth of 90 feet, the sea is perfectly still."[61]

> "The people are under a great mistake who believe that the substance of the water moves to any considerable depth in a storm at sea. It is only the form or shadow which hurries along like a spirit, or like a thought over the countenance of the 'great deep,' at the rate of some forty miles an hour. Even when the 'Flying Dutchman'

---

60 "Chambers' Journal," No. 100, p. 379.
61 "Penny Cyclopœdia," Art. "Sea."

is abroad, the great mass of water continues undisturbed and nearly motionless a few feet below the surface."[62]

"The unabraded appearance of the shells brought up from great depths, and the almost total absence of the mixture of any detritus from the sea, or foreign matter, suggest most forcibly the idea of perfect repose at the bottom of the deep sea."[63]

"The sea may roll and shriek for woe, And kiss the clouds with spray; Yet all is calm and bright below, Down where the fishes play."

FACT 2: Water is (except to a very small degree), incompressible.

PROOF: Globes of metal--of gold and silver, of lead and of iron, the last a large bomb-shell, have been filled with water, and subjected to the force of powerful hydraulic machinery, and in every instance it was found impossible to make them receive any appreciable addition. In some instances, when the hydraulic pressure became very great, the water, instead of exhibiting any signs of compression, was observed to ooze through the pores of the metal, and to appear on the outer surface like a fine dew or perspiration.

FACT 3: The atmospheric air is very elastic and greatly compressible.

PROOF: The condensation of air in the chamber of an air-gun; and numerous experiments with an air-pump, condensing syringe, and similar apparatus.

FACT 4: If a raft, a buoy, a ship, or any other structure which floats on the open sea, is carefully observed, it will be seen to have a gentle and regular fluctuating motion.

PROOF: However calm the water and the atmosphere, this gradual and alternate rising and falling of the floating mass will generally be visible to the naked eye. But a telescope (which magnifies motion as well as bulk) will show its existence invariably.

FACT 5: Floating masses of different sizes and densities, being in the same waters, and acted upon by the same influences, fluctuate with different velocities.

PROOF: Observation with the naked eye and with the telescope.

FACT 6: The largest and heaviest floating masses fluctuate less rapidly than the smallest and lightest.

PROOF: Observation as above. A very striking illustration of the facts 4, 5, and 6, was observed by the author and many friends in Plymouth Bay, in the autumn of 1864. He

---

62 "London Saturday Journal," p. 71, for August 8th, 1840.
63 "Physical Geography of the Sea," p. 265. By Lieut. Maury, U.S .

had previously delivered a course of lectures in the hall of the Athenæum in that town; during which these and other phenomena had been referred to. At the same period the triennial yacht race was advertised, and as many as chose to do so were invited to meet him on the rocks near the bay, early on the morning of the race. There had assembled almost every form and size of vessel, from the smallest yacht to the largest, as well as merchant and war ships. Among the latter was observed laying alongside and within the great Breakwater, the large iron-clad ship, the *Warrior*. The various phenomena were observed by the whole party of ladies and gentlemen, not one of whom expressed a doubt as to their reality.

The *Warrior*, being farthest away, and very large and heavy, was an object of more special scrutiny. With telescopes her long black hull was seen against the grey stone of the breakwater, to slowly fluctuate, and almost with the regularity of a pendulum.

FACT 7: Wherever the general pressure of the atmosphere is greatest or least, so are tides in the ocean less or greater than usual.

PROOF: The records of self-registering barometers in use in various parts of the world.

FACT 8: The velocity of a flood-tide increases as it approaches land.

PROOF: Actual experiment. It is also a fact well known to sailors engaged in coasting service.

FACT 9: If we go out in a boat with an ebb tide, we find the velocity decreasing as we leave the shores and channels, until we reach a certain point where the water is found to merely rise and fall but not to progress.

PROOF: Actual experiment, often tried by, and well known to, pilots and masters of tug steamers.

> "The tide never ebbs and flows beyond 40 miles from land."[64]

> "Tides are great only on coasts and funnel-shaped rivers; in the centres of wide seas, as the Pacific or Atlantic, the tides are trifling, the whole is like water librating in a basin."[65]

> "When a ship is well out at sea, she is not affected by the tide, as it creates no stream in the open sea, the tidal wave sweeping along, but causing no more current than an ordinary billow."[66]

---

64 "Million of Facts," p. 271. By Sir Richard Phillips.
65 Ibid.
66 "Treatise on Navigation," p. 11.

It is recorded, that an ancient philosopher in a small boat allowed himself to be carried to sea by an ebb tide, hoping thereby to discover the source of the tides. After drifting many miles, the boat came to a state of rest; and after a short time he found himself being carried back to the shore. He had only been taken out by the ebb, and brought again to land by the flood. He had discovered nothing, and seeing no hope of doing so by repetitions of such a voyage, he destroyed himself by jumping into the sea.

FACT 10: The times of ebb and flood tide at any given part are not regularly exact, often being from half-an-hour to one hour or more before and after the "Port Establishment time."

The times of ebb and flood and the altitude of the tides all over the known world are very various and irregular. Sometimes running up at one end of a river and down at the other, as in the river Thames. Sometimes the flood tide returning shortly after the usual and expected tide, as in Southampton waters, the St. Lawrence, the Amazon, and other rivers.

PROOF: The hydrographic records of various governments--notably the English and American.

"At Holyhaven, near the mouth of the Thames, the tide is actually falling and running *down* rapidly, when at the *same moment* it is running up rapidly at London Bridge, and still rising. The first steamer that ever hoisted a pennant under the Admiralty, namely the *Echo*, was commissioned under Lieutenant, now Admiral, Frederick Bullock, to survey the river Thames and prove the above fact. Captain George Peacock, second in command, was stationed in one of the ship's boats from 8 o'clock to 3 o'clock, both night and day, on the day before the full moon up to the day after, from June to September, and the same of the new moon of October, 1828, with a tide pole; another assistant being stationed at the same time in the entrance of Holyhaven, with a tide pole; and each having a pocket chronometer to note the exact times of high- water and rise of the tide from low-water mark. The result was that it was found the tide had fallen at Holyhaven six feet, and was running rapidly *down* while at the *same moment* it was, at London Bridge still rising and running rapidly up."

"There are four high waters and three low waters in the river St. Lawrence (North America) at the *same time*; and in the river Amazon (South America) there are no less than six high-waters and five low- waters, at the same time; and in the dry season as many as seven high- waters and six low-waters at the *same time* have been known."[67]

---

67 "Is the World Flat or Round?" A pamphlet, by Captain George Peacock, F.R.G.S. Second Edition. Published by Bellows, Gloucester, 1871.

On many occasions a third tide has flooded the Thames in 24 hours; and some of these extra tides have been higher than the normal tides.

At Southampton there is always a second flood tide two hours after the first.

"The first high water is caused by the eastern current up the Solent and the inset from the English Channel, through St. Helen's and Spithead, meeting near the Brambles. There is a second tide two hours after the first, caused mainly by the stream setting to the westward through the Solent at a rapid rate, assisted by the first quarter's ebb from Chichester, Langston, and Portsmouth harbours, until it meets with a check in the Narrows of Hurst, causing the second rise at Lymington Leap, Southampton, &c. Low water is about 3 hours and 20 minutes after the second high water."[68]

"The tidal water-mark at Portishead (mouth of the Avon), on the 16th of August, 1871, at 7 o'clock in the morning, will be about 50 feet higher relatively, than the tidal mark at London Bridge. At Cape Virgin (the eastern entrance of the Straits of Magellan), at half-past eight the same morning, the tidal mark will be about 51 feet higher than at York Roads, (English Reach) towards the Western end of the Straits. At 2 o'clock of the same afternoon the tidal mark at Panama will be about 21 feet higher than at Colon, on the opposite side of the Isthmus; at Noel Bay, in the Bay of Fundy (North America), at 1 o'clock of the same day, the tidal mark will be about 53 feet higher than at Picton, on the opposite side of the Nova Scotian Isthmus, in the Gulf of St. Lawrence. At 5 o'clock the same evening, at Boisee Island, in the Corea, the tidal mark will be about 49 feet higher than at Hong Kong, and about 42 feet higher than at Cumsingmoon, at the mouth of the Canton river.

"At Christchurch, and at Granville, nearly opposite and across the channel at 7 o'clock on the same morning, the water-mark will be 34 feet higher at the latter part than at the former. At Piel Harbour (Lancashire), at half-past 11 o'clock in the morning of the same date, the water-mark will stand about 40 feet higher than at the same moment at Rathwollen, Lough Swilly, on the N.E. coast of Ireland, nearly opposite. The tide water-mark at Hull at half-past 6 a.m. or a little later p.m. will be about 28 feet higher than at Berwick-on-Tweed, at the same moment (16th or 31st), and about 32 feet higher than at Margate. At Ballycastle Bay, N.E. coast of Ireland, the tide at the highest springs never exceeds 3 feet, whilst at Piel Harbour and Southerness it rises 28 feet, and at Liverpool 26 feet, independent of forced tides by the wind. At Poole it never exceeds 7 feet; whilst at Hastings it rises 24 feet, at Tenby 27 feet, and at Wexford, opposite, only 5 feet; at Ark-low 4 feet, and Waterford 13 feet."[69]

---

68 "Gutch's Southampton Almanack and Tide Tables." Standing note. (p. 124)
69 Captain George Peacock, F.R.G.S., in a Pamphlet referred to at p. 166..

HEIGHT OF TIDES IN VARIOUS PARTS OF GREAT BRITAIN AND IRELAND

Location	Feet
Mouth of Severn	60
Off entrance to Milford Haven	36
At Holyhead	24
Entrance to the Wash	22
Entrance to Solway Frith	21
Off Brighton	21
South-west Coast--Cornwall	19
Mouth of the Thames	19
Location	**Feet**
Mouth of the Humber	18
Portsmouth	17
Mouth of Plymouth Sound	16
Mouth of the Mersey	16
Mouth of the Tyne	15
Entrance of Dublin Bay	12
Yarmouth	7

70

In these extracts abundant proof is given of the irregular character of the tides, both in respect to times and altitudes.

FACT 11: Every ship, raft, or other floating mass, in addition to its visible fluctuation, has a tremulous motion or tremor of the whole body.

PROOF: On the deck of any vessel or other floating body let the most delicate instruments be placed, such as spirit-levels, poised compasses, &c., and the tremulous motion will easily be recognised.

FACT 12: The earth has a tremulous motion more or less at all times.

PROOF: If a delicate spirit-level be firmly fixed on a rock or on the most solid foundation it is possible to construct, and far away from the influence of any railway, or blasting or mining operations, the curious phenomenon will be observed of continual but irregular change in the position of the air bubble. However carefully the level may be adjusted, and the instrument protected from the atmosphere, the "bubble" will not maintain its position long together. A similar effect is noticed in the most favourably situated

---

70 "Liverpool Almanak." (p. 126)

astronomical observatories, where instruments of the very best construction, and placed in the most approved positions, cannot always be relied upon without occasional and systematic readjustment.

The following quotation affords a good illustration of the tremour above described:---

> "MARCH 12TH, 1822, in Adventure Bay, Island of South Georgia, we anchored in seven fathoms water, latitude 54° 2′ 48″ S., longitude 38° 8′ 4″ W. The head of this Bay being surrounded with mountains, I ascended the top of one of them for the purpose of taking the altitude of the sun when at some distance from the meridian; but after planting my artificial horizon, I was surprised to find that although there was not a breath of wind, and everything around perfectly still, yet the mercury had so tremulous a motion that I could not get an observation."[71]

FACT 13: Tides in the extreme south are very small, and in some parts are scarcely perceptible.

PROOF: "The rise and fall of tide in Christmas Harbour, latitude 48° 41′ S, longitude 69° 3′ 35″ E., is remarkably small; not on any occasion amounting to more than 30 inches and the usual spring tides are generally less than two feet. The neap tide varies from four to twelve inches, and the diurnal inequality is, comparatively, very considerable."[72]

> "Auckland Islands, latitude 50° 32′ 30″ S., longitude 166° 12′ 34″ E., high water at full and change of moon took place, at 12 o'clock, and the highest spring tides scarcely exceeded three feet. A remarkable oscillation of the tide when near the time of high-water was observed; after rising to nearly its highest, the tide would fall two or three inches, and then rise again between three and four inches, so as to exceed its former height rather more than an inch. This irregular movement generally occupied rather more than an hour, of which the fall continued about 20 minutes, and the rise again upwards of 50 minutes of the interval."

> "The same was observed at Campbell Island, South Harbour, latitude 52° 33′ 26″ S., longitude 169° 8′ 41″ E."[73]

Along the whole length of southern land discovered by Lieut. Wilkes, near the antarctic circle, and which extended upwards of 1500 miles, very little tide was discovered.

> "During the whole of our stay along the icy coast we found no perceptible current by the reckoning and current log. Tides on such an extent of coast there undoubtedly must be, but of little strength, or we should have perceived them. In many of the

---

71 "Voyage towards the South Pole," p. 52. By Captain James Weddell, F.R.S.E. 2nd Edition, 1827. London: Longman, Rees & Co.
72 "South Sea Voyages." By Capt. Sir Jas. Clarke Ross. Vol. i., p. 96.
73 "South Sea Voyages." By Capt. Sir Jas. Clarke Ross. Vol. i., p. 153.

icy bays we were stationary for a sufficient time to perceive them if they had been of any magnitude, and where the current was repeatedly tried."[74]

FACT 14: The tide generally turns a little earlier below than it does above.

PROOF: Colonel Pasley, when operating on the "Royal George," the war- ship which sunk at Spithead, was the first who observed and recorded this peculiarity, which has also been noticed during diving operations in Liverpool Bay and other places.[75]

FACT 15: Many large inland seas or lakes are entirely without tide, while several wells of only a few feet in diameter have a considerable rise and fall in the water corresponding in times to the tide in a distant tidal sea.

PROOF: Many cases may be found in works on geography and geology.

FACT 16: If, at any hour of the night, a telescope is firmly fixed, securely lashed to any solid object, and turned to the pole-star, it will be found on continuing the observation for some hours that the star "Polaris" does not maintain its position, but seems to slowly rise and fall in the field of view of the telescope. The line-of-sight will be sometimes above it; in about twelve hours it will be below it; and in another twelve hours it will again be above the star.

This peculiar motion of either the star or the earth is represented by the following diagrams

In fig. 67, the line of sight, T, L, is represented as *above* the pole-star, P; and in fig. 68, the same line is below it. That such a peculiar phenomenon exists may be proved by actual experiment on any clear night in winter, when it is dark sufficiently long to observe for twelve hours together.

---

74 Appendix to "Narrative of the United States' Exploring Expedition," p. 366. By Lieut. Charles Wilkes, U.S.N.
75 In "Household Words" for October 18th, 1856, the subject is referred to.

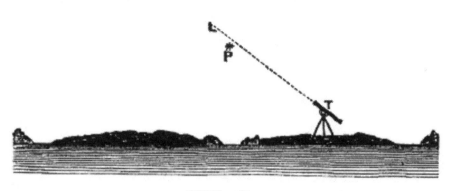

FIG. 67.

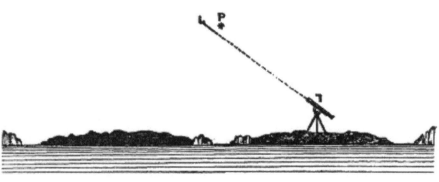

FIG. 68.

Many more facts could be added to the foregoing collection, but already the number is sufficient to enable us to form a definite conclusion as to what is the real cause of the tides.

The facts 1 to 7 fully enable us to establish syllogistically the groundwork of the reply. All bodies floating in an incompressible medium, and exposed to atmospheric pressure, fluctuate, or rise and fall in that medium.

The earth is a vast irregular structure, stretched out upon and standing or floating in the incompressible waters of the "great deep."

Ergo--The earth has, of necessity, a motion of fluctuation.

Hence, when by the pressure of the atmosphere, the earth is depressed or forced slowly down into the "great deep," the waters immediately close in upon the receding bays and headlands, and produce the *flood tide*; and when, by reaction, the earth slowly ascends, the waters recede, and the result is the ebb tide.

Facts 8, 9, 11, 12, and 16, show results that must necessarily follow this fluctuation of the earth. The velocity of the flood is greatest as it approaches land. If the waters were put in motion by the moon, the velocity would be greatest where the altitude was greatest or nearest the moon, and least the farthest from it or nearest the shores. The reverse is the case in nature.

The line of sight being at a given time above the pole-star, as shown in fact 16 (fig. 67), and in twelve hours afterwards below it, as shown in fig. 68, is exactly the result which must follow a slowly rising and falling earth.

Facts 11 and 12 are also consistent with and necessarily attach to a slowly fluctuating elastic mass like the earth.

In fact 10 we see the irregularity of time in flood and ebb, which arises from the irregular form of the bed of the waters. The submarine channels, banks, and depressions which exist in all directions, the action and reaction, mounting and "back-lashing" of the waters, produce the irregular times and altitudes of the tides observed and recorded in the hydrographic offices of different nations.

In fact 13 we see that out of the reach of the great bulk of the fluctuating earth the waters are but little disturbed; but if the waters were lifted up by the moon they would flow towards and flood the southern or antarctic lands as readily and to as great an extent as the land in the equatorial and northern regions.

In fact 14 we have a phenomenon which could not possibly exist if the tides arise from the action of the moon upon the water; for as the action would first be on the surface, that surface would be the first to show change of motion, and the bottom the last.

In fact 15 we see what could not be possible if the moon were the cause of tidal action by lifting the waters underneath her from their normal position. If the moon's attraction operates in one place, what can possibly prevent its action in all other places when and where the relative positions are the same? No direct explanatory answer has yet been given. If, however, the great inland lakes and seas are simply indentations in and upon the land, the water contained in them of course rises and falls *with* the earth on which they lie; there is no change in the relative level of land and water, and therefore *no tide*. Just as the fluctuations of a ship would show rising and falling, or ebb and flood tide outside the hull, any vessel on the deck, filled with water, would rise or fall *with* the ship, and would therefore exhibit no change of level--*no tide*.

Thus we have been carried forward by the sheer force of evidence to the conclusion that the tides of the sea do not arise from the attraction of the moon, but simply from the rising and falling of the floating earth in the waters of the "great deep." That calmness which is found to exist at the bottom of the great seas could not be possible if the waters were alternately raised by the moon and pulled down by the earth. The rising and falling motion would produce such an agitation or "churning" of the water that the "perfect repose," the growth of delicate organic structures, and the accumulation of flocculent matter called "ooze," which has been so generally found when taking soundings for deep-sea cables, could not exist. All would be in a state of confusion, turbidity, and mechanical admixture.

The question: What has the moon to do with the tides? need not entirely be set aside. It is possible that in some at present unknown way this luminary may influence the atmosphere, increasing or diminishing its barometric pressure, and indirectly the rise and fall of the earth in the water; but of this there is not yet sufficient evidence, and therefore the answer remains for the future.

CHAPTER XIII

THE EARTH'S TRUE POSITION IN THE UNIVERSE; COMPARATIVELY RECENT FORMATION; PRESENT CHEMICAL CONDITION; AND APPROACHING DESTRUCTION BY FIRE

IT has been demonstrated that the earth is a plane, the surface-centre of which is immediately underneath the star called "Polaris," and the extremities of which are bounded by a vast region of ice and water and irregular masses of land, which bear evidence of Plutonic or fiery action and origin.

"In the geological structure of extreme northern regions, the sedimentary strata are abundant and of vast extent; while the constitution of Antarctic strata seems, on the contrary, as far as yet examined, entirely igneous."[76]

The whole terminates in fog and darkness, where snow and driving hail, piercing sleet and boisterous winds, howling storms, madly-mounting waves, and clashing icebergs, are almost constant.

"The waves rise like mountains in height; ships are heaved up to the clouds, and apparently precipitated by circling whirlpools to the bed of the ocean. The winds are piercing cold, and so boisterous that the pilot's voice can seldom be heard, whilst a dismal and almost continual darkness adds greatly to the danger."[77]

"The sea quickly rising to a fearful height, breaking over the loftiest bergs. . . . Our ships were involved in an ocean of rolling fragments of ice, hard as floating rocks of granite, which were dashed against them by the waves with so much violence that their masts quivered as if they would fall at every successive

---

76 "Polar Exploration;" p.
77 By W. Locke, of the Royal Dublin Society.

blow. The rudders were destroyed, and nearly torn away from the stern-posts. . . . Hour passed away after hour, without the least mitigation of the awful circumstances in which we were placed. . . . The loud crashing noise of the straining and working of the timbers and decks, as she was driven against some of the heavier pieces, was sufficient to fill the stoutest heart with dismay. . . . Our ships still rolling and groaning amidst the heavy fragments of crushing bergs, over which the ocean rolled its mountainous waves, throwing huge masses one upon another, and then again burying them deep beneath its foaming waters, dashing and grinding them together with fearful violence. The awful grandeur of such a scene can neither be imagined nor described, far less can the feelings of those who witnessed it be understood. . . . The ships were so close together that when the 'Terror' rose to the top of one wave, the 'Erebus' was on the top of that next to leeward of her; the deep chasm between them filled with heavy rolling masses; and as the ships descended into the hollow between the waves, the main-top-sail-yard of each could be seen just level with the crest of the intervening wave from the deck of the other. Night cast its gloomy mantle over the scene, rendering our condition, if possible, more hopeless and helpless than before."[78]

The cold was severe, and every spray that touched the ship was immediately converted into ice. . . . The gale was awful. . . . A seaman, in endeavouring to execute the order to furl, got on the lee yard-arm, remained there some time, and was almost frozen to death. Several of the best seamen were completely exhausted with cold, fatigue, and excitement, and were sent below. . . . All was now still, except the distant roar of the wild storm that was raging behind, before, and above us; the sea was in great agitation, and both officers and men were in the highest degree excited."[79]

So great had been the sufferings of the crew, that the ward-room officers joined the medical officers in petitioning the commander of the expedition not to continue the voyage on account of the "extreme hardships and exposure they had undergone during the last gales of wind."

"The general health of the crew is decidedly affected. . . . We feel ourselves obliged to report that, in our opinion, a few days more of such exposure as they have already undergone would reduce the number of the crew by sickness to such an extent as to hazard the safety of the ship and the lives of all on board."[80]

How far in the gloom and darkness of the south this wilderness of storm and battling elements extends there is at present no evidence. All we can say is that man, with all his

---

78 "Antarctic Voyages." By Sir James Clarke Ross.
79 "Exploring Expedition." By Commander Wilkes, U.S.N.
80 Ibid, p. 142.

mightiest daring and power of endurance, has only succeeded in reaching the threshold of this restless, dark, and forbidding region of the material world.

The earth rests upon and within the waters of the "great deep." It is a vast "floating island," buoyed up by the waters, and held in its place by long "spurs" of land shooting into the icy barriers of the southern circumference. Geological researches demonstrate that it was originally a stratified structure, definite and regular in form and extent, and that all the confused and irregular formations observable in almost every part have resulted from internal convulsions.

Chemical analysis proves to us the important fact that the great bulk of the earth-- meaning thereby the land, as distinct from the waters--is composed of metallic oxides, or metals in combination with oxygen, and also with sulphur, chlorine, carbon, and other elements. When means are taken to remove the oxygen, it is found that many of these metallic bases are highly combustible.. Experiments with electric and other subtle powers of Nature, render it obvious that all the elements of the earth were originally in a state of gaseous solution, or dissolved in the great menstruum of the material world-- electricity. That by a sudden abstraction of this great and universal solvent, the elements were liberated; and owing to the different affinities and relative densities which had been attached to them, combination, precipitation, stratification, crystallization, and concretion, successively occurred, giving rise to all the rocks, minerals, ores, deposits, and strata, which now constitute the material habitable world. That by the action of unconcrete or gaseous unprecipitated elements, and free electric and actinic forces upon pre-existing germs, all the numerous forms of animal and vegetable life were brought into being, and are now maintained.

However great such operations may seem to the mind of present man, all the vast structure of the physical world, and its innumerable myriads of organic beings, were the work of only a few hours. It is easily demonstrable that so rapid and intense were the processes and chemical changes, that a few days--such as we now understand by the word--were ample time to bring out of invisible, imponderable chaos, all the tangible and varied elements which now exist, and to develope every possible form of beauty and elegance, and every condition of happiness and wisdom. All opinions to the contrary which are held by philosophers of the present day, are the result of insufficient perception of the whole subject, which insufficient perception is again the result of self-imposed hypotheses, which bias the judgment and confuse the understanding. No man, however learned and accomplished he may be, is able to understand the simple processes of creative effort unless he is himself a simple and humble observer of phenomena, free from the prejudices of education, and anxious only for a knowledge of the truth as it exists in reality, and not in desire and imagination.

Not only is it readily demonstrable that the material world was brought into being rapidly, perfect in structure, and fully sufficient in all its conditions--but that only a few thousand years have elapsed since it began to change in form and character. Mental and moral confusion, followed by decomposition and chemical and electric action, sufficient to ignite a great portion of the earth, and to reduce it to a molten, incandescent state. Hence, for ages the earth has been on fire. The volatile products of this internal fire being forcibly eliminated, and occasionally accumulating and exploding, have broken up the stratified formations, and produced the irregular confused condition which we now observe. Hence have arisen earthquakes, volcanoes, and other convulsions of Nature. The products of volcanic action enable us to ascertain the character of the internal fire, and what are the elements concerned in the combustion. Some of these products are of a poisonous character, and being thrown out in immense volumes from craters in various parts of the earth, are dispersed by the winds, and diffused through the atmosphere, often in such proportions as to act as deadly poison on both animal and vegetable life. Hence, blight and pestilence in various forms, destroying crops and inferior animals, and affecting numbers of human beings to suffering and death.

That the internal parts of the earth are still on fire is. evident from the following facts:--

> "At the depth of 50 feet from the sea-level, the temperature of the earth is the same winter and summer. . . . At the Killingworth coal mine, the mean annual temperature at 400 yards below the surface is 77 degrees Fahrenheit, and at 300. yards, 70 degrees; while at the surface it is but 48 degrees, being about one degree of increase for every 15 yards. Hence, at 3300 yards, the heat would be equal to boiling water, taking 20 yards to a degree. This explains the origin of hot springs. The heat of the Bath waters is 116 degrees; hence they would appear to rise from a depth of 1320 yards. By experiments made at the Observatory at Paris, for ascertaining the increase of temperature from the surface of the earth towards the interior, 51 feet, or 17 yards, correspond to the increase of one degree Fahrenheit's thermometer. Hence the temperature of boiling water would be at 8212 feet, or about one and a half English miles, under Paris."[81]

> The greatest depth below the surface of the sea that has yet been obtained is probably that of the salt-works of New Salzwerk, near Minden, in Prussia. This was 1993 feet. . . . The temperature of water at the bottom was 90.8 Fahrenheit, giving a mean increase of one degree Fahrenheit for every 53.8 feet."[82]

The coal mine at Rosebridge, near Wigan, is now the deepest in England, having a depth of 808 yards; and it was stated by Mr. Hall, before the Royal Society, in January 1870, that the average temperature at the bottom of the shaft was 93½ degrees.

---

81 "Million of Facts." By Sir Richard Phillips.
82 "Analysis of Newton's Principia," p. 175. By Henry Lord Brougham, F.R.S.

Sir Charles Lyell, in his address to the British Association at Bath, in September, 1864, speaking of hot springs generally, said:

"An increase of heat is always experienced as we descend into the interior of the earth. . . . The estimate deduced by Mr. Hopkins from an accurate series of observations made in the Monkwearmouth shaft, near Durham, and in the Dukenfield shaft, near Manchester, each of them 2000 feet in depth. In these shafts the temperature was found to rise at the rate of 1 degree Fahrenheit for every increase of depth of from 65 to 70 feet."

"The observations made by M. Arago, in 1821, that the deepest Artesian wells are the warmest, threw great light on the origin of thermal springs, and on the establishment of the law that terrestrial heat increases with increasing depth. It is a remarkable fact, which has but recently been noticed, that at the close of the third century, St. Patricius, probably Bishop of Partusa, was led to adopt very correct views regarding the phenomenon of the hot springs at Carthage. On being asked what was the cause of boiling water bursting from the earth, he replied: 'Fire is nourished in the clouds, and in the interior of the earth, as Ætna and other mountains near Naples may teach you. The subterranean waters rise as if through syphons. The cause of hot springs is this: Waters which are more remote from the subterranean fire are colder, whilst those which rise nearer the fire are heated by it, and bring with them to the surface which we inhabit an insupportable degree of heat.'" [83]

Professor Silliman, in the American "Journal of Science," says:--

"In boring the Artesian wells in Paris, the temperature increased at the rate of one degree for every 50 feet downwards; and, reasoning from causes known to exist, the whole of the interior part of the earth, or, at least, a great part of it, is an ocean of melted rock, agitated by violent winds."

"The uppermost strata of the soil share in all the variations of temperature which depend upon the seasons, and this influence is exerted to a depth which, although it varies with the latitude, is never very great. Beyond this point the temperature rises in proportion as we descend to greater depths; and it has been shown by numerous and often-repeated experiments that the increase of temperature is on an average one degree (Fahrenheit) for about every 54.5 feet. Hence it results that, at a depth of about 12 miles from the surface, we shall be on the verge of an incandescent mass."[84]

---

83 Humboldt's "Cosmos," p. 220.
84 "Rambles of a Naturalist." By M. de Quatrefages.

"So great is the heat within the earth, that in Switzerland and other countries where the springs of water are very deep, they bring to the surface the warm mineral waters so much used for baths and medicine for the sick; and it is said that if you were to dig very deep down into the earth, the temperature would increase at the rate of one degree of the thermometer for, every 100 feet; so that at the depth of 7000 feet, or one and a half miles, all the water that you found would be boiling; and at the depth of about 10 miles, all the rocks would be melted.

. . A day will yet come when this earth will be burned up by the fire. There is fire, as you have heard, within it, ready to burst forth at any moment. . . . . This earth, although covered all round with a solid crust, is all on fire within. Its interior is supposed to be a burning mass of melted, glowing metals, fiery gas, and boiling lava. . . . The solid crust which covers this inward fire is supposed not to be much more than from 9 to 12 miles in thickness. Whenever this crust breaks open, or is cleft in any place, there rush out lava, fire, melted rocks, fiery gases, and ashes, sometimes in such floods as to bury whole cities. From time to time we read of the earth quaking, trembling, and sometimes opening, and of mountains and small islands (which are mountains in the sea) being thrown up in a day." [85]

"The conclusion is inevitable that the general distribution all over the earth of volcanic vents, their similarity of action and products, their enormous power and seeming inexhaustibility, their extensiveness of action in their respective sites, the continuance of their energies during countless years, and the incessant burning day and night, from year to year, of such craters as Stromboli; and lastly the apparent inefficiency of external circumstances in controlling their operations, eruptions happening beneath the sea as beneath the land, in the frigid as in the torrid zone--for these and many less striking phenomena, we must seek for some great and general cause, such only as the central heat of the earth affords us."[86]

"It is a fact well ascertained by scientific researches, that the whole inside of the earth is one mass of fire, and what we call terra firma nothing more than a crust or rind by which that mass of fire is inclosed. It is certain that by the action of this central fire the earth's crust is perforated in many places with large conduits, which act as chimneys to the internal furnace. Of these chimneys as many as seven hundred have been actually counted; and out of these three hundred are at this time in active operation, emitting not only smoke and vapour, but at intervals masses of burning liquefied matter. How many more there may be in unexplored regions of the dry land, and how many more beneath the hundred and eleven millions of square miles of water which form the ocean, it is impossible to say.

---

85 "The World's Birthday," p. 42. By Professor Gaussen. Geneva. 11 "Recreative Science," article "Volcanoes."
86 "Recreative Science," article "Volcanoes."

"Besides these regular outlets, the number and condition of which is subject to constant changes--some falling in and ceasing to act, while new ones are forming elsewhere--the action of the central fire manifests itself in the rocking motion imparted from time to time to large portions of the crust, which are tossed up and down, as it were, by the angry billows of the molten sea beneath them. In numerous instances the crust is broken altogether, vast fissures being made in its surface; while at other times large tracts are literally swallowed up by the yawning gulph, the surface closing over them after their disappearance, or submerged by the sea which rushes in to cover the void that has been created."[87]

"The earth contains within it a mass of heated material;, nay, it is a heated and incandescent body, habitable only because surrounded with a cool crust, the crust being to it a mere shell, within which the vast internal fires are securely inclosed--and yet not securely perhaps, unless such vents existed as those to which we apply the term volcanoes. Every volcano is a safety valve, ready to relieve the pressure from within when that pressure rises to a certain degree of intensity; or permanently serving for the escape of conflagrations which, if not so provided with escape, might rend the habitable crust to pieces."[88]

The investigations which have been made, and the evidence which has been brought together, render its undeniable that the lower and inner parts of the earth are on fire. Of the intensity of the combustion no practical idea can be formed; it is fearful beyond comparison. The lava thrown out from a volcano in Mexico "was so hot that it continued to smoke for twenty years, and after three years and a half a piece of wood took fire in it, at a distance of five miles from the crater." In different parts. of the world islands of various magnitudes have been thrown up from the depths of the sea, in a red-hot glowing condition, and so intensely heated, that after being forced through many fathoms of salt water, and standing in the: midst of it, exposed to wind and rain for several months, have not been sufficiently cooled for persons to approach and remain upon them." Cotopaxi threw its fiery rockets 3000 feet above its crater; the blazing mass roared like a furnace, so that its awful voice was heard at a distance of 600 miles. Tanguragun flung out torrents of mud which dammed up rivers, opened new lakes, and in valleys of 1000 feet wide made deposits 600 feet deep. Vesuvius has thrown out more than forty millions, and Etna nearly one hundred millions of cubic feet of solid matter; some of it was not thoroughly cooled and consolidated ten years after the event. A block 100 cubic yards in volume has been projected a distance of 9 miles, and Sumbawa, in 1815, sent its ashes as far as Java, a distance of 300 miles."[89]

---

87 "The Quiver", for October 5, 1861. (p.138).
88 "Recreative Science," article "Volcanoes," (p.138).
89 "Recreative Science," article "Volcanoes," (p.139).

"During the eruption of Timboro Mountain, in 1814, Mr. Crawford witnessed some of the effects. At a distance of 300 miles it was pitch dark for three days. The ashes were carried by the monsoon to a distance of 1200 miles from the mountain, and for ten days he was obliged to write by candle light."[90]

Thus it is certain from the phenomena connected with earthquakes, submarine and inland volcanoes, which exist in every part of the earth, from the frozen to the tropical regions, hot and boiling springs, fountains of mud and steam, lakes of burning sulphur and other substances, jets and blasts of combustible destructive gases, the choke and fire-damps of our coal mines--that at only a few miles below the surface of the earth there exists an extensive region of combustion; a vast fiery gulph extending in all directions for thousands of miles: and the intensity and power of the chemical and electric action going on in this almost boundless subterranean furnace are utterly indescribable, and cannot be compared with anything within the range of human experience.

This condition of the earth is represented in diagram 69, which may be called a sectional view, supposing it to be cut through the centre of its whole length, and the water in the front cleared away. N, the northern centre, S. S. the usual sea level, and the figures 1, 2, 3, 4, 5, 6, representing volcanic craters, or outlets of the great fiery gulph below.

Fig. 69

Having shown that the earth is a large and irregular floating mass, having within it a vast region of fire burning with a fierceness and intensity utterly immeasurable, we have now to inquire respecting its position in relation to the rest of the Universe.

FIRST. The earth floats on the waters of the "great deep."

That it thus floats is concluded from the fact that it is surrounded with water, in which it

90 "Times" newspaper, June 10, 1863.

fluctuates; and that if limited in extent, water could not surround it without also gathering underneath it. If not limited in extent, then it extends downwards for ever. If so, it could not fluctuate in a limited mass of water. It does fluctuate, therefore it floats, and hence there must be "waters under the earth."

SECONDLY. What supports the waters?

If the waters are limited in extent there must be some-thing below them; if not limited in extent then they extend downwards for ever. Then indeed would the "great deep" be the "mighty deep," the "fathomless deep" the "great abyss of waters," the "illimitable depths;" and further inquiry would be useless, for the earth simply floats on the surface of the illimitable fathomless deep. It is in fact and literally...

> *"Founded on the seas, and*
> *Established on the floods."*

Just as at present we fail to learn anything respecting the lateral extent of the south; we only know that frost, destroying storm, and darkness, bar the progress of the most daring navigators, so are we incapable, by direct inquiry, of knowing anything as to the downward extent of the "great deep." Does it extend southwards and downwards *ad infinitum*? Is it, in fact, a mighty, an infinite world of waters, an aqueous "world without end?" Or is "the cloud the garment thereof; and thick darkness its swaddling band?"

As "with all our getting to get understanding" is one of our greatest privileges, we may, with advantage and satisfaction, seek to know that which at first sight may seem an impossibility. The Zetetic process will never fail us if we can gather sufficient facts to form, as it were, a fulcrum, or resting place for the lever of investigation and logical induction. The following facts will help us to an answer:--

- 1st. Sea water consists of chlorides of sodium, potassium and magnesium; carbonates of lime and magnesia; sulphates of lime, magnesia and potash; bromides and iodides of sodium, &c., &c.

- 2nd. Immense volumes of sulphuretted hydrogen gas abound in many parts of the ocean, extending for hundreds of miles, which cannot be traced to local causes.

- 3rd. The water nearest the beds of different seas contains more saline matter than that of the surface.

- 4th. The water of open seas is *not saturated* with saline ingredients.

- 5th. The chlorine, sulphur, iodine, and bromine, found in combination with magnesia, potash, soda, lime, &c., are not found, except in mere traces, in our atmosphere, nor, in a free state, in the compounds of which the earth is formed, nor to any extent in the numerous elements detected in the sun and stars by the beautiful and delicate process of spectrum analysis; hence we are driven to seek for their source, not in the luminaries of our firmament, nor in the higher, or middle, or lower regions of the air, nor in the sea itself--the *compounds only* of these elements entering into the composition of sea water.

- 6th. The union of chlorine, sulphur, iodine, and bromine, with oxygen, hydrogen, sodium, potassium, magnesium, and calcium, would of necessity constitute intense pyrogenous or fiery action.

- 7th. Such action is not to be found in the atmosphere, nor in the earth-- not even in the volcanic combustion which exists in almost every part of it--nor in the sea. It is not above, nor upon, nor within, but still it exists. Where? Above, upon, within, and below, are all that can possibly exist; but since it is not above, nor upon, nor within, *below only* remains. Therefore it exists below the lowest depths of the great stratum of waters which constitute the "foundations of the earth." This terrible subaqueous world of fire, acting upon the under surface of the water, decomposes or separates its elements, fixing its oxygen, and liberating its hydrogen, which holding in solution sulphur and other elements, forming sulphuretted hydrogen, permeates the waters, and in many parts of the world escape into the atmosphere, thus rendering vast regions, otherwise fertile and agreeable, unfit for the habitation of man.

- 8th. When chemical action is so intense as to constitute combustion, it is repulsive to aqueous compounds, water in bulk cannot come in direct contact with it--partial decomposition and volatilisation will occur. And thus below the ocean there must be a stratum of watery vapour, and oxygen and hydrogen gases, holding in solution and combination the elements which are seeking to unite, and which are afterwards found in combination, and dissolved as the constituents of ordinary sea water.

A simple experiment will convey an idea of the manner of the sea's suspension over a region of elemental fire. Partially fill a long glass tube with water, and invert the open end over an intense fire; the water will trickle down the tube, but as it approaches the fire it will be converted into steam and thrown upwards, where it will again condense, again descend, and again volatilise, as long as the experiment is continued. There will always be a given space, between the upper stratum of water and the fire, filled with watery vapour.

Another illustration is furnished by the large smelting furnaces in action during rain. The drops of rain, snow, or hail, as they approach the fire suddenly boil away, with loud explosive sounds, and are driven back in the form of steam; or if, on account of the rain being unusually heavy, any portion of it reaches the flames, it is quickly decomposed, and its elements--its oxygen and hydrogen gases, instead of diminishing--greatly increase the intensity of the combustion.

During a great conflagration also it is often observed that a small supply of water instead of extinguishing the fire is partly driven off as steam, and in part decomposed, and, as well known to firemen, its oxygen and hydrogen increase the combustion.

If we are anxious to inquire into the nature of the region above the earth, we find sufficient evidence to force us to definite conclusions. As we ascend we find the atmosphere becoming more and more attenuated, caloric decreasing, and cold rapidly increasing; moisture gradually diminishing, and absolute dryness prevailing; sound becomes more intense, and as we ascend higher and higher positive electricity is more and more abundant.

As there is no heat and no moisture, everything remains in a state of preservation, decomposition and decay cannot take place. Electricity more and more prevailing, all bodies at a great altitude are imponderable; and as the sun and other luminaries are constantly eliminating metallic and other elements in a state of electric solution, it is evident that every object in the higher regions, peculiar conditions excepted, must glow with electric many-coloured light, as shown by metallic spectra, and by the variable and brilliantly-coloured stars which shine so beautifully in every part of the firmament.

> "By the aid of the telescope, have been discovered in the starry vault, in the celestial fields which light traverses, as in the corollas of our flowering plants, and in the metallic oxides, almost every gradation of prismatic colour, between the two extremes of refrangibility. . . . In a cluster near the Southern Cross, above a hundred small stars of different colours--red, green, blue, and blueish green--appear in large telescopes like gems of many colours, like a superb piece of fancy jewellery."[91]

As the sun and moon, as well as comets and stars of every kind, can be proved by direct trigonometrical processes, to be within a few hundred miles of the earth's surface, and, as we have seen, in such a region bodies must be without gravity self-luminous and self-sustaining; we cannot refrain from asking "How far above the earth, and laterally, does such a region extend?" So also in reference to the region of fire below the earth and ocean, the same question must obtrude itself. The only answer, however, which can here be given is, that whereas the region above may and must, for aught man can at present prove to the contrary, extend upwards and laterally without end; so must the region below extend downwards and laterally ad infinitum. Can the earth and the southern external or outer cold and darkness stretch out for ever like an endless diaphragm between the infinitely extending worlds above and below?

---

91 Humboldt.

The actual position of the earth in the universe, as evolved by the Zetetic process of investigation, is represented in the following diagram, fig. 70.

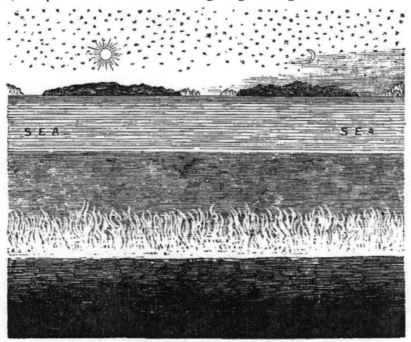

Fig. 70.

Were it not that this work is avowedly astronomical and philosophical, it could easily be shown here that far above the sun, moon, and stars, and beyond the region of electric, magnetic, and other active subtleties, there is a fountain, an infinite conservatory of realities, as much more subtle than electric and magnetic entities, as these are than, the solid elements of the earth; and from which man receives all that makes him better than a demon, and enables and helps him to a god-like existence, whilst below the concrete world of earth and water, a region of fiery decomposition and destruction exists, and whence originate realities--subtleties more subtle than gaseous and electric elements, and which pollute and ruin the great bulk of humanity. The author is inexpressibly sorry to leave this mighty subject undeveloped in the pages of this work.[92] He has entered upon a scientific disquisition, and as scientific men in general have allowed themselves to sink down to the idea that science and philosophy have only to do with the dead and beggarly elements of the world, and that all inquiries into the nature and source of the quickening, ennobling, and perfecting subtleties, which can be proved to exist, are but the dictates of superstition, he will not pursue the subject further--in these pages at least--lest the scientific critics who dread the advent of true and vivifying philosophy should charge him with inconsistency or unwarrantable digression.

92 See his work on the "Life of Christ Zetetically Considered," which is preparing for publication.

Having shown that this earth is but a stage, a platform of concrete, precipitated, ponderable elements between infinity above and infinity below, the subject demands, and is incomplete without an inquiry as to its possible and probable duration. That its origin is comparatively recent is deducible from the fact that all its constituent elements are in a secondary state, that is, thrown out of solution in the all-pervading subtlety which we have agreed to call electricity; and that the processes of precipitation, concretion, and stratification, must of necessity have been rapid and symmetrical, and all the confused conditions now visible to us quickly subsequent to and sequent upon abnormal changes, is evident from the manner in which we can experimentally imitate such changes by urging the electric and chemical forces with which every philosopher is or ought to be familiar. The comparative sluggishness of growth, development, and change of elementary conditions which now exists, is not to guide us in our judgments of the intensity of the forces and processes of the past.

When we consider the composition of the earth, and its aqueous foundations--that it is a vast structure of metallic oxides, sulphurets, and chlorides, intermingled with immense strata of compounds of carbon and hydrogen; and that, as we have already shown, a great portion of the lower parts of the earth is in a molten incandescent state, the earth itself an extended plane, resting in and upon the waters of the "great deep," fitly comparable to a large vessel or ship floating at anchor, with its hold or lower compartments beneath the water-line filled with burning materials, our knowledge of the nature and action of fire does not enable us to understand in what way the combustion can be prevented from extending when these burning materials are known to be surrounded with highly inflammable substances. Wherever a fire is surrounded with heterogeneous materials-- some highly combustible and others partially or indirectly so--it is not possible, in the ordinary course of nature, for it to remain continually in the same condition, nor to diminish in extent and intensity, it must necessarily increase and extend itself. That this is the case is corroborated by many phenomena. The total of volcanic action is greater than it has ever been since man commenced to observe and record his observations.

> "In the caves beneath the Paris observatory, during the last seventeen years, the thermometer standing there has risen. very nearly 0°·4."[93]

> "Bonssingault found in 1823 that the thermal. springs of Las Trincheras (Venezuela) had risen 12° during the twenty-three years that had intervened since my travels in 1800."[94]

> "The perpetual fire in or near Deliktash, in Lycia, was recently found to be as brilliant as ever, and even somewhat increased."[95]

---

93 Humboldt's "Cosmos," p. 166.
94 19 Ibid., p. 219.
95 Ibid., p. 220.

"The Paris papers state that the temperature of the waters flowing from the great Artesian wells at Grenelle and Passy, has increased from 82° to 85° Fahrenheit."[96]

The millions of gallons of petroleum "struck" and drawn from numerous places, indicating increasing heat and therefore increasing distillation of solid carbonaceous matter into combustible oils, and the fearful and increasing explosions in our coal mines also indicate increased and advancing combustion in the earth, giving rise to greater quantities of "choke" and "fire-damps," and the lamentable increase in the loss of life which has occurred within the last few years.

That the fire in the earth is increasing is evident; and that it is surrounded with inflammable materials is matter of certainty. The hundreds of millions of tons of coals which are known to exist in England, America, India, China, Japan, Australia, New Zealand, and many other parts of the earth, the vast quantities of peat, turf, mineral oils, rock tar, pitch, asphalte, bitumen, petroleum, mineral naptha, and numerous other hydro-carbons to be found in all directions, and the great bulk of these combustible carbon compounds existing far down below the earth's surface, prove this condition to exist. The immense volumes of carbon in combination with hydrogen and with oxygen, forming carbonic acid, carbonic oxide, and carburetted hydrogen gases which escape during volcanic action, prove also that these carbon compounds are already in a state of intense combustion.

As the fire is gradually increasing and creeping upwards towards the thousands of miles of veins and strata filled with carbonaceous fuel, it is not possible, unless the "course of nature" is *arrested by some special interference*, for the earth to remain in its present concrete condition. The day is not far distant, nay, even now at any moment some sudden convulsive upheaving of the fiery gulph below, until it reaches and lays bare some of the lower beds of hydro-carbon, which "dip" at various angles from the general strata, may set them on fire. The flames would then rapidly extend; and the fiery action swiftly run along the various and innumerable veins of combustible matter which ramify in every direction throughout the whole earth.

Should such an action once commence, knowing as we do that the rocks and minerals and general constituents of the earth are only oxides of inflammable bases, or of substances directly combustible, and that the affinities of these are greatly altered in the presence of highly-heated carbon and hydrogen, we see clearly that such a chemical action or fire would rapidly increase in intensity, and fiercely rush in all directions, until the whole earth, with everything entering into its composition and dwelling upon and within it, would perish, decompose and volatilise, and burst into one vast indescribable annihilating conflagration; the elements "burning with fervent heat" again dissolving in the great solvent medium, electricity, there to remain until some creative mandate shall

---

96 "English Mechanic," January 4, 1867.

liberate, and again precipitate and stratify them for the formation of another world--perhaps less discordant, and more enduring than the present.

"If we saw a number of persons on some huge raft, tossed up and down on the surface of the ocean, we should naturally feel alarmed for their safety. And if we were told that so far from being apprehensive of danger they fancied their position one of eminent security, that they pointed with pride to the thickness and solidity of the timber under their feet, laughing to scorn every suggestion that their footing might by-and-bye prove less sound than they imagine, we should conclude that their minds must be strangely constituted. Does it not seem extraordinary then that so little should be thought of a position far more perilous, in which all the inhabitants of the earth are continually placed? Their position resembles, more nearly than we most of us think, that of persons floating on the surface of the sea--on a raft of great strength and thickness it is true, but yet not proof against the fury of the waves, and liable to sudden disruption of its parts. The only difference is that the sea on which we are floating is a sea of liquid fire, the molten elements of the main substance of the earth."[97]

---

97 "The Quiver," October 5, 1861.

For my take on some of what is being discussed in Chapter 14 concerning the issue of ship's hulls allegedly "disappearing over the curve" please see the following:

It's a small ball after all? Or is it just an optical illusion?

Ships do NOT go over any curve!

**The Chicago Skyline Expanded Edition - Part 1:
Refraction, Magnification or Curvature?**

CHAPTER XIV

EXAMINATION OF THE SO-CALLED "PROOFS" OF THE EARTH'S ROTUNDITY

WHY A SHIP'S HULL DISAPPEARS BEFORE THE MAST- HEAD

IT has already been proved that the astronomers of the Copernican school merely assumed the rotundity of the earth as a doctrine which enabled them to explain certain well-known phenomena. "What other explanation can be imagined except the sphericity of the earth?" is the language of Professor de Morgan, and it expresses the state of mind of all who hold that the earth is a globe. There is on their part an almost amusing innocence of the fact, than in seeking to explain phenomena by the assumption of rotundity, another assumption is necessarily involved, viz., that nothing else will explain the phenomena in question but the foregone and gratuitous conclusion to which they have committed themselves. To argue, for instance, that because the lower part of an outward-bound vessel disappears before the mast-head, the water must be round, is to assume that a round surface only can produce such an effect. But if it can be shown that a simple law of perspective in connection with a plane surface necessarily produces this appearance, the assumption of rotundity is not required, and all the misleading fallacies and confusion involved in or mixed up with it may be avoided.

Before explaining the influence of perspective in causing-the hull of a ship to disappear first when outward bound, it is necessary to remove an error in its application, which artists and teachers have generally committed, and which if persisted in will not only prevent their giving, as it has hitherto done, absolutely correct representations of natural things, but also deprive them of the power to understand the cause of the lower part of any receding object disappearing to the eye before any higher portion--even though the surface on which it moves is admittedly and provably horizontal.

In the first place it is easily demonstrable that, as shown in the following diagrams, fig. 71, lines which are equi-distant.

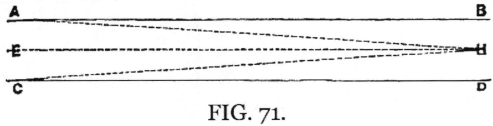

FIG. 71.

> "The range of the eye, or diameter of the field of vision, is 110°; consequently this is the largest angle under which an object can be seen. The range of vision is from 110° to 1°. . . . The smallest angle under which an object can be seen is upon an average, for different sights, the sixtieth part of a degree, or one minute in space; so that when an object is removed from the eye 3000 times its own diameter, it will only just be distinguishable; consequently the greatest distance at which we can behold an object like a shilling of an inch in diameter, is 3000 inches or 250 feet."[98]

The above may be called the *law of perspective*. It may be given in more formal language, as the following:. when any object or any part thereof is so far removed that its greatest diameter subtends at the eye of the observer, an angle of one minute or less of a degree, it is no longer visible.

From the above it follows:--

1. That the larger the object the further will it require to go from the observer before it becomes invisible.

2. The further any two bodies, or any two parts of the same body, are asunder, the further must they recede before they appear to converge to the same point.

3. Any distinctive part of a receding body will be-come invisible before the whole or any larger part of the same body.

The first and second of the above propositions are self-evident. The third may be illustrated by the following diagram, fig. 73.

---

98 "Wonders of Science," by Mayhew, p. 357.

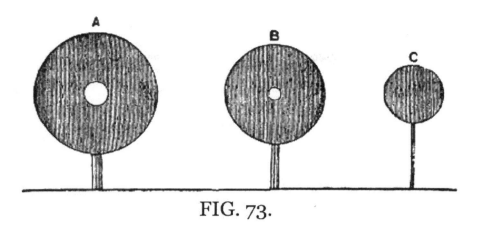

FIG. 73.

Let A represent a disc of wood or card-board, say one foot in diameter, and painted black, except one inch diameter in the centre. On taking this disc to about a hundred feet away from an observer at A, the white centre will appear considerably diminished--as shown at B--and on removing it still further the central white will become invisible, the disc will appear as at C, entirely black. Again, if a similar disc is coloured black, except a segment of say one inch in depth at the lower edge, on moving it forward the lower segment will gradually disappear, as shown at A, B, and C, in diagram fig. 74. If the disc is allowed to rest on a board D, the effect is still more striking. The disc at C will appear perfectly round--the white segment having disappeared.

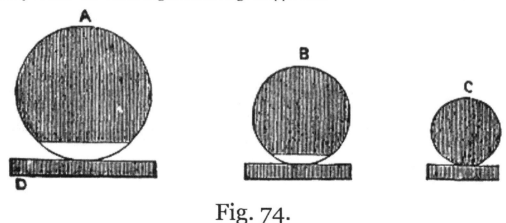

Fig. 74.

The erroneous application of perspective already referred to is the following:--It is well known that on looking along a row of buildings of considerable length, every object *below* the eye appears to *ascend* towards the eye-line; and every thing *above* the eye appears to *descend* towards the same eye-line; and an artist, wishing to represent such a view on paper, generally adopts the following rule:--draw a line across the paper or canvas at the *altitude of the eye.*

223

To this line, as a vanishing point, draw *all other lines* above and below it, irrespective of their distance, as in the diagram 75.

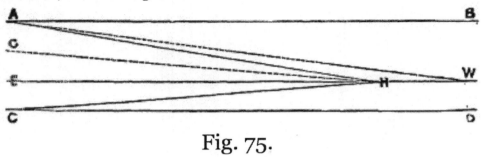

Fig. 75.

Let A, B, and C, D, represent two lines parallel but not equi-distant from the eye-line E, H. To an observer at E, the vanishing point of C, D, would be at H, *because* the lines C, D, and E, H, would come together at H, at an angle of *one minute* of a degree. But it is evident from a single glance at the diagram that H cannot be the vanishing point of A, B, *because* the distance E, A, being greater than E, C, the angle A, H, E, is also greater than C, H, E--is, in fact, considerably *more* than one minute of a degree. Therefore the line A, B, cannot possibly have its vanishing point on the line E, H, unless it is carried forward towards W. Hence the line A, W, is the true perspective line of A, B, forming an angle of one minute at W, which is the true vanishing point of A, B, as H is the vanishing point of C, D, and G, H, because these two lines are equidistant from the eye-line.

The error in perspective, which is almost universally committed, consists in causing lines dissimilarly distant from the eye-line to converge to one and the same vanishing point. Whereas it is demonstrable that lines most distant from an eye-line must of necessity converge less rapidly, and must be carried further over the eye-line before they meet it at the angle one minute, which constitutes the vanishing point.

A very good illustration of the difference is given in fig. 76. False or prevailing perspective would bring the lines A, B, and C, D, to the same point H; but the true or natural perspective brings the line A, B, to the point W, because there and there only does A, W, E, become the same angle as C, H, E. It must be the same angle or it is not the vanishing point.

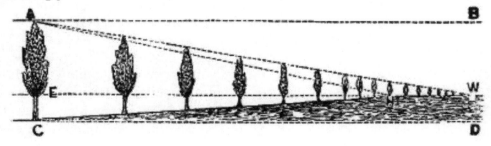

Fig. 76.

The law represented in [fig. 76] is the "law of nature." It may be seen in every layer of a long wall; in every hedge and bank of the roadside, and indeed in every direction where lines and objects run parallel to each other; but no illustration of the contrary perspective is ever to be seen in nature. In the pictures which abound in our public and private collections, however, it may too often be witnessed, giving a degree of distortion to paintings and drawings--otherwise beautifully executed, which strikes the observer as very unnatural, but, as he supposes, artistically or theoretically correct.

The theory which affirms that *all* parallel lines converge to one and the same point on the eye-line, is an error. It is true only of lines equi-distant from the eye-line; lines more or less apart *meet the eye-line at different distances*, and the point at which they meet is that only where each forms the angle of one minute of a degree, or such other angular measure as may be decided upon as the vanishing point. This is the true law of perspective as shown by nature herself; any idea to the contrary is fallacious, and will deceive whoever may hold and apply it to practice.

In accordance with the above law of natural perspective, the following illustrations are important as representing actually observed phenomena. In a long row of lamps, standing on horizontal ground, the pedestals, if short, gradually diminish until at a distance of a few hundred yards they seem to disappear, and the upper and thinner part of the lamp posts appear to touch the ground, as shown in the following diagram, fig. 77.

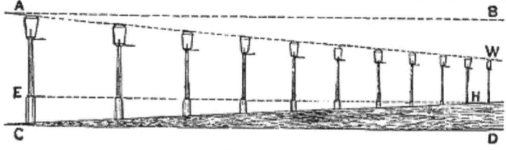

Fig. 77.

The lines A, B, and C, D, represent the actual depth or length of the whole series of lamps, as from C to A. An observer placing his eye a little to the right or left of the point E, and looking along the row will see that each succeeding pedestal appears shorter than the preceding, and at a certain distance the line C, D, will appear to meet the eye-line at H--the pedestals at that point being no longer visible, the upper portion of each succeeding lamp just appears to stand without pedestal. At the point H where the pedestals disappear the upper portions of the lamps seem to have shortened considerably, as shown by the line A, W, but long after the pedestals have entered the vanishing point, the tops will appear above the line of sight E, H, or until the line A, W, meets the line E, H, at an angle of one minute of a degree. A row of lamps such as that above described may be seen in York Road, which for over 600 yards runs across the south end of Regent's Park, London.

On the same road the following case may at any time be seen.

Fig. 78.

Send a young girl, with short garments, from C on towards D; on advancing a hundred yards or more (according to the depth of the limbs exposed) the bottom of the frock or longest garment will seem to touch the ground; and on arriving at H, the vanishing point of the lines C, D, and E, H, the limbs will have disappeared, and the upper part of the body would continue visible, but gradually shortening until the line A, B, came in contact with E, H, at the angle of one minute.

If a receding train be observed on a long, straight, and horizontal portion of railway, the bottom of the last carriage will seem to gradually get nearer to the rails, until at about the distance of two miles the line of rail and the bottom of the carriage will seem to come together, as shown in fig. 79.

Fig. 79.

The south bank of the Duke of Bridgewater's canal (which passes between Manchester and Runcorn) in the neighbourhood of Sale and Timperley, in Cheshire, runs parallel to the surface of the water, at an elevation of about eighteen inches, and at this point the canal is a straight line for more than a statute mile. On this bank eight flags, each 6 ft. high, were placed at intervals of 300 yards, and on looking from the towing path on the opposite side, the bank seemed in the distance to gradually diminish in depth, until the grass and the surface of the water converged to a point, and the last flag appeared to stand not on the bank but in the water of the canal, as shown in the diagram fig. 80.

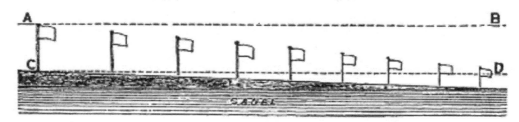

Fig. 80.

The flags and the bank had throughout the whole length the altitude and the depth represented by the lines respectively A, B, and C, D.

Shooting out into Dublin Bay there is a long wall about three statute miles in length, and at the end next to the sea stands the Poolbeg Lighthouse. On one occasion the author sitting in a boat opposite "Irish Town," and three miles from the sea end of the wall, noticed that the lighthouse seemed to spring from the water, as shown in the diagram fig. 81.

Fig. 81.

The top of the wall seemed gradually to decline towards the sea level, as from B to A; but on rowing rapidly towards A the lighthouse was found to be standing on the end of the wall, which was at least four feet vertical depth above the water. as seen in the following diagram, fig. 82.

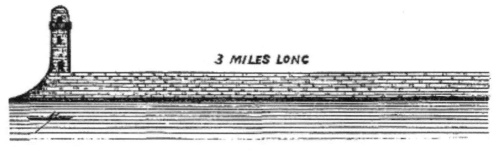

Fig. 82.

From the several cases now advanced, which are selected from a great number of instances involving the same law, the third proposition (on page 203) that "any distinctive part of a body will become invisible before the whole or any larger part of the same body," is sufficiently demonstrated. It will therefore be readily seen that the hull of a receding ship obeying the same law must disappear on a plane surface, before the mast head. If it is put in the form of a syllogism the conclusion is inevitable:--

Any distinctive part of a receding object becomes invisible before the whole or any larger part of the same object.

The hull is a distinctive part of a ship.

Ergo, the hull of a receding or outward bound ship must disappear before the whole, inclusive of the mast head.

To give the argument a more practical and nautical character it may be stated as follows:

That part of any receding body which is nearest to the surface upon which it moves, contracts, and becomes invisible before the parts which are further away from such surface--as shown in figs. 63, 64, 65, 66, 67, 68, 69, and 70.

The hull of a ship is nearer to the water--the surface on which it moves-- than the mast head.

Ergo, the hull of an outward bound ship must be the first to disappear. This will be seen mathematically in the following diagram, fig. 83.

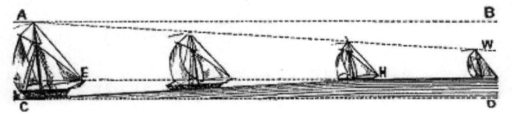

Fig. 83.

The line A, B, represents the altitude of the mast head; E, H, of the observer, and C, D, of the horizontal surface of the sea. By the law of perspective the surface of the water appears to ascend towards the eye- line, meeting it at the point H, which is the horizon. The ship appears to ascend the inclined plane C, H, the hull gradually becoming less until on arriving at the horizon H it is apparently so small that its vertical depth subtends an angle, at the eye of the observer, of less than one minute of a degree, and it is therefore invisible; whilst the angle subtended by the space between the mast-head and the surface of the water is considerably more than one minute, and therefore although the hull has disappeared in the horizon as the vanishing point, the mast-head is still visible above the horizon. But the vessel continuing to sail, the mast-head gradually descends in the direction of the line A, W, until at length it forms the same angle of one minute at the eye of the observer, and then becomes invisible.

Those who believe that the earth is a globe have often sought to prove it to be so by quoting the fact that when the ship's hull has disappeared, if an observer ascends to a higher position the hull again becomes visible. But this, is logically premature; such a result arises simply from the fact that on raising his position the eye-line recedes further over the water before it forms the angle of one minute of a degree, and this includes and brings back the hull within the vanishing point, as shown in fig. 84.

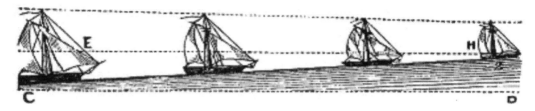

Fig. 84.

The altitude of the eye-line E, H, being greater, the horizon or vanishing point is formed at fig. 2 instead of at fig. 1, as in the previous illustration.

Hence the phenomenon of the hull of an outward bound vessel being the first to disappear, which has been so universally quoted and relied upon as proving the rotundity of the earth, is fairly, both logically and mathematically, a proof of the very contrary, that the earth is a plane. It has been misunderstood and misapplied in consequence of an erroneous view of the laws of perspective, and the unconquered desire to support a theory. That it is valueless for such a purpose is now completely demonstrated.

PERSPECTIVE ON THE SEA

We have now to consider a very important modification of this phenomenon, namely, that whereas in the several instances illustrated by diagrams Nos. 71 to 84 inclusive, when the lower parts of the objects have entered the vanishing point, and thus disappeared to the naked eye, a telescope of considerable power will restore them to view; but in the case of a ship's hull a telescope fails to restore it, however powerful it may be. This fact is considered of such great importance, and so much is made of it as an argument for rotundity by the Newtonian philosophers, that it demands in this place special consideration. It has been already shown that the law of perspective, as commonly taught in our schools of art, is fallacious and contrary to every thing seen in nature. If an object be held up in the air, and gradually carried away from an observer who maintains his position, it is true that all its parts will converge to one and the same point--the centre, in relation to which the whole contracts and diminishes. But if the same object is placed on the ground, or on a board, as shown in diagram 74, and the lower part made distinctive in shape or colour, and similarly moved away from a fixed observer, the same predicate is false. In the first case the *centre* of the object is the *datum* to which every point of the exterior converges; but in the second case the ground or board practically becomes the *datum* in and towards which every part of the object converges in succession--beginning with the lowest, or that nearest to it.

INSTANCES--A man with light trowsers and black boots walking along a level path, will appear at a certain distance as though the boots had been removed and the trowsers brought in contact with the ground. On one occasion the author and several friends witnessed a kind of review or special drill of infantry in the open space behind the Horse Guards, at Whitehall. It was in the month of July, and the soldiers had on their summer clothing, all their "nether garments" were white, and when near to them the black well-polished boots were visible to the depth of three or four inches, standing distinctly between the white cloth of the trowsers, and the brown or yellowish gravel and sand of the parade ground. On moving a few hundred feet away, along one of the walks in St. James's Park, the three or four inches depth of black boots subtended an angle at the eye so acute that they were no longer visible, and the almost snow white trowsers of a line of men seemed to be in actual contact with the ground. Every man when turned away or whose back was towards the spectators, seemed to be footless. The effect was remarkable, and formed a very striking illustration of the true law of perspective. After observing the manœuvres for a short time a party of soldiers were "told off" to relieve guard at St. James's and Buckingham Palaces, and on following then, down the avenue of the park we again noticed the perspective phenomenon of a line of soldiers marching apparently without feet.

A small dog running along will appear to gradually shorten by the legs, which at a distance, of less than half-a-mile will be invisible, and the body or trunk of the animal will appear to glide upon the earth.

Horses and cattle moving away from a given point upon horizontal ground, will seem to lose their hoofs, and to be walking on the bony extremities or stumps of the limbs.

Carriages similarly receding will seem to lose that portion of the rim of the wheels which touches the earth. The axles also will seem to get lower, and at the distance of one or two miles, according to the diameter of the wheels, the body of the carriage will appear to drag along in contact with the ground.

A young girl, with short garments terminating ten or twelve inches above the feet, will, on walking forward, appear to sink towards the earth, the space between which and the bottom of the frock will appear to gradually diminish, and in the distance of half-a-mile or less the limbs which were first seen for ten or twelve inches will be invisible--the bottom of the garment will seem to touch the ground. The whole body of the girl will, of course, gradually diminish as she recedes, but the depth of the limbs, or the lower part, will disappear before the shoulders and head--as illustrated in diagram 78.

These instances which are but a few selected from a great number which have been collected, will be sufficient to prove beyond the power of doubt, or the necessity for controversy, that upon a plane or horizontal surface the *lowest parts* of bodies receding from a given point of observation *necessarily* disappear *before the highest.*

This would be a sufficient explanation of the disappearance of a ship's hull before the rigging and mast-head; but as already stated in every one of the instances given, except that of the ship at sea, a telescope will restore to view whatever has disappeared to the naked eye. It would be the same in the case of the ship's hull were all the conditions the same. If the surface of the sea had no motion or irregularity, or if it were frozen and therefore stationary and uniform, a telescope of sufficient power to magnify at the distance, would at all times restore the hull to sight. On any frozen lake or canal, notably on the "Bedford Canal," in the county of Cambridge, in winter and on a clear day, skaters may be observed several miles away, seeming to glide along upon limbs without feet-- skates and boots quite invisible to the unaided eye, but distinctly visible through a good telescope. But even on the sea, when the water is very calm, if a vessel is observed until it is just "hull down," a powerful telescope turned upon it will restore the hull to sight. From which it must be concluded that the lower part of a receding ship disappears through the influence of perspective, and not from sinking behind the summit of a convex surface. If not so it follows that the telescope either carries the line of sight through the mass of water, or over its surface and down the other side. This would indeed be "looking round a corner," a power which, nor that of penetrating a dense and extensive medium like water, has never yet been claimed for optical instruments of any kind.

Upon the sea the law of perspective is modified because the leading condition, that of *stability in the surface* or *datum* line, is changed. When the surface is calm the hull of a vessel can be seen for a much greater distance than when it is rough and stormy. This can easily be verified by observations upon fixed objects at known distances, such as light- ships, light-houses, sea walls, head-lands, or the light-coloured masonry of batteries, such as are built on the coast in many parts of the world.

In May, 1864, the author, with several gentlemen who bad attended his lectures at Gosport, made a number of observations on the "Nab" light- ship, from the landing stairs of the Victoria Pier, at Portsmouth. From an elevation of thirty-two inches above the water, when it was very calm, the greater part of the hull of the light vessel was, through a good telescope, plainly visible. But on other occasions, when the water was much disturbed, no portion of the hull could be seen from the same elevation, and with the same or even a more powerful telescope. At other times, when the water was more or less calm, only a small portion of the hull, and sometimes the upper part of the bulwarks only, could be seen. These observations not only prove that the distance at which objects at sea can be seen by a powerful telescope depends greatly on the state of the water, but they furnish a strong argument against rotundity. The "Nab" light- ship is eight statute miles from the Victoria pier, and allowing thirty-two inches for the altitude of the observers, and ten feet for the height of the bulwarks above the water line, we find that even if the water were perfectly smooth and stationary, the top of the hull should at all times be fourteen feet below the horizon. Many observations similar to the above have been made on the north-west light-ship, in Liverpool Bay and on light-vessels in various parts of the sea round; Great Britain and Ireland.

It is a well known fact that the light of Eddystone lighthouse is often plainly visible from the beach in Plymouth Sound, and sometimes, when the sea is very calm, persons sitting in ordinary rowing boats can see the light distinctly from that part of the Sound which will allow the line of sight to pass between "Drake's Island" and the western end of the Breakwater. The distance is fourteen statute miles. In the tables published by the Admiralty, and also by calculation according to the supposed rotundity of the earth, the light is stated to be visible thirteen nautical or over fifteen statute miles, yet often at the same distance, and in rough weather, not only is the light not visible but in the day time the top of the vane which surmounts the lantern, and which is nearly twenty feet higher than the centre of the reflectors or the focus of the light, is out of sight.

A remarkable instance of this is given in the Western Daily Mercury, of October 25th, 1864. After lectures by the author at the Plymouth Athenæum and the Devonport Mechanics' Institute, a committee was formed for the purpose of making experiments on this subject, and on the general question of the earth's form. A report and the names of the committee were published in the Journal above referred to; from which the following extract is made.

"OBSERVATION 6TH.--*On the beach, at five feet from the water level*, the Eddystone was entirely out of sight."

At any time when the sea is calm and the weather clear, the light of the Eddystone may be seen from an elevation of five feet above the water level; and according to the Admiralty directions, it "maybe seen thirteen nautical (or fifteen statute), miles,"[99] or one mile further away than the position of the observers on the above-named occasion; yet, *on that occasion*, and at a distance of only fourteen statute miles, notwithstanding that it was a very fine autumn day, and a clear background existed, not only was the

---

99 "Lighthouses of the World," p. 36.

lantern, which is 80 feet high, not visible, but the *top of the vane*, which is 100 feet above the foundation, was, as stated in the report *"entirely out of sight."* There was, however, a considerable "swell" in the sea beyond the breakwater.

That vessels, lighthouses, light-ships, buoys, signals, and other known and fixed objects are sometimes more distinctly seen than at other times, and are often, from the same common elevation, entirely out of sight when the sea is rough, cannot be denied or doubted by any one of experience in nautical matters.

The conclusion which such observations necessitate and force upon us is, that the law of perspective, which is everywhere visible on land, is *modified* when observed in connection with objects on or near the sea. But *how* modified? If the water were frozen and at perfect rest, any object on its surface would be seen again and again as often as it disappeared and as far as telescopic or magnifying power could be brought to bear upon it. But because this is not the case--because the water is always more or less in. motion, not only of progression but of fluctuation and undulation, the "swells" and waves into which the surface is broken, operate to prevent the line of sight from passing absolutely parallel to the horizontal water line.

At page [110] it is shown that the surface of the sea appears to rise up to the level or altitude of the eye; and that at a certain distance, less or greater, according to the elevation of the observer, the line of sight and the surface of the water appear to converge to a "vanishing point," which is in reality "the horizon." If this horizon were formed by the apparent junction of two perfectly stationary parallel lines, it could, as before stated, be penetrated by a telescope of sufficient power to magnify at the distance, however great, to which any vessel had sailed. But because the surface of the sea is not stationary, the line of sight must pass over the horizon, or vanishing point, at an angle at the eye of the observer depending on the amount of "swell" in the water. This will be rendered clear by the following diagram, fig. 85.

Fig. 85.

Let C, D, represent the horizontal surface of the water. By the law of perspective operating without interference from any local cause, the surface will appear to ascend to the point B, which is the horizon, or vanishing point to the observer at A; but because the water undulates, the line A, B, of necessity becomes A, H, S, and the angular direction of this line becomes less or greater if the "swell" at H increases or diminishes. Hence when a ship has reached the point H, the horizon; the line of sight begins to cut the rigging higher and higher towards the mast-head, as the vessel more and more recedes. In such a position a telescope will enlarge and render more visible all that part of the rigging which is above the line A, H, S, but cannot possibly restore that part including the hull, which is below it. The waves at the point H, whatever their real magnitude may be, are magnified and rendered more obstructive by the very instrument (the telescope), which is employed to make the objects beyond more plainly visible; and thus the phenomenon is often very strikingly observed, that while a powerful telescope will render the sails and rigging of a ship beyond the horizon H, so distinct that the different kinds of rope can be readily distinguished, not the slightest portion of the hull, large and solid as it is, can be seen. The "crested waters" form a barrier to the horizontal line of sight as substantial as would the summit of an intervening rock. And because the watery barrier is magnified and practically increased by the telescope, the paradoxical condition arises, that the greater the power of the instrument the less can be seen with it.

Thus have we ascertained by a simple Zetetic process, regardless of all theories, and irrespective of consequences, that the disappearance of the hull of an outward bound vessel is the natural result of the law of perspective operating on a plane surface, but modified by the mobility of the water; and has logically no actual connection with the doctrine of the earth's rotundity. All that can be said for it is, that such a phenomenon would exist if the earth were a globe; but it cannot be employed as a proof that the assumption of rotundity is correct.

If it is argued that "there are times when the surface of the sea is perfectly calm, and that at such times at least, if the earth is a plane, the telescope ought to restore the hull of a ship, irrespective of distance, providing its power is great enough to magnify it," the reply is that practical experiments have proved that during what is called a "dead calm," the undulations or waves in the water amount to more than 20 inches, as will be seen from the following extracts:--

ON THE DIMENSIONS OF OCEAN WAVES

"This interesting subject was very fully entered into at a recent meeting of the Academy of Sciences, by Admiral Coupvent de Bois:

"It is not easy to ascertain the height of the waves of the ocean; nevertheless, the method adopted for the purpose is capable of affording sufficiently exact results. The point in the shrouds corresponding with a tangent to the tops of the highest waves is ascertained by gradually ascending them, and making observations until it is reached. That point being determined, the known dimensions of the ship give the height of the waves above the line of flotation, which corresponds with the horizon of the sea, in the trough of the wave. In this way the following results were obtained:--

With	a smooth sea	the waves were	1.97	feet.
"	fair weather	"	3.28	"
"	a slight swell	"	4.921	"
"	a full swell	"	7.546	"
"	a great swell	"	10.827	"
"	a very great swell	"	15.42	"
"	a heavy sea	"	20.67	"
"	a very heavy	"	28.543	"

"The lengths of the waves have also been measured, and it has been found that, for example, waves of 27 feet in height, are about 1640 feet in length."

It is well known that even on lakes of small dimensions and also on canals, when high winds prevail for some time in the same direction, the ordinary ripple is converted into comparatively large waves. On the "Bedford Canal," during the windy season, the water is raised into undulations so high, that through a powerful telescope at an elevation of 8 inches, a boat two or three miles away will be invisible; but at other times, through the same telescope the same kind of boat may be seen at a distance of six or eight miles.

During very fine weather when the water has been calm for some days and become as it were settled down, persons are often able to see with the naked eye from Dover the coast of France, and a steamer has been traced all the way across the channel. At other times when the winds are very high, and a heavy swell prevails, the coast is invisible, and the steamers cannot be traced the whole distance from the same altitude, even with a good telescope.

Instances could be greatly multiplied, but already more evidence has been given than the subject really requires, to prove that when a telescope does not restore the hull of a distant vessel it is owing to a purely special and local cause.

HOW THE EARTH IS CIRCUMNAVIGATED

Another "proof" of the earth's rotundity is supposed to be found in the fact that mariners by sailing continually due east or west, return home in the opposite direction. This is called "The Circum-navigation of the Globe." Here, again, a supposition is involved, viz., that on a globe only can a ship continue to sail due east and come home from the west, and vice versâ. But when the process or method adopted is understood, it will be seen that a plane can as readily be circum- navigated as a sphere.

In the following diagram, fig. 86, let N, represent the. northern centre, near to which lies the "magnetic pole."

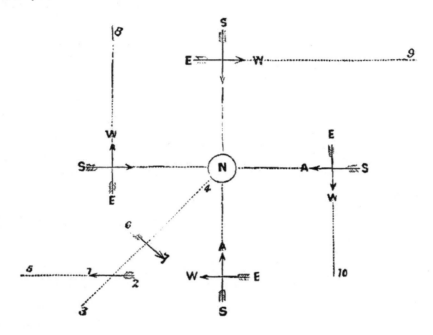

Fig. 86.

Then the several arrows marked A, S, are all pointing northwards; and those marked E, W, are all due east and west. It is evident from the diagram, that A, S, are absolute directions--north and south; but that E, W, east and west, are only relative, that is they are directions at right angles to north and south. If it were not so then, taking the line N, A, S, as representing the meridian of Greenwich, and W, E, on that meridian as due east and west, on moving due west to the meridian 3, 4, N, it is evident that a vessel represented by the arrow 1, 2, would be at angle with the meridian 3, 4, N, much greater than 90 degrees, and if it continued to sail in the same straight line 2, 1, 5, it would get farther and farther away from the centre N, and therefore could never complete a path concentric with N. East and west, however, are directions relative to north and south. Hence, on a mariner arriving at the meridian 3, 4, N, he must of necessity turn the head of his vessel in the direction indicated by the arrow 6, 7, and thus continuing to keep the vessel's head square to the compass, or at right angles to north and south, he will at length arrive at 90 degrees of meridian from N, A, S, when the head of the vessel will be in the direction of E, W, 8. Continuing his course for 90 degrees more his path will be E, W, 9. The same course continued will in the next 90 degrees become E, W, 10, and on passing over another 90 degrees the ship will have arrived again at the meridian of Greenwich N, A, S, having then *completed a circle.*

East-West circumnavigation works ***exactly*** the same on the "circle of the Earth" as it does on a globe. Frankly, it is rather embarrassing that this actually has to be explained to people. For more on this, please see my video *Debunking # 4 of the "Top Ten Reasons Why We (allegedly) Know the Earth is a Globe + A CHALLENGE*:

Simply put: East and West are determined by pointing a compass such that North is 90 degrees off to either side of the direction you wish to travel. If you are going East, you orient yourself so that North is 90 degrees off to the left. If going West, put North 90 degrees off to the right. On the "circle of the Earth," North is in the center. Thus, to go East or West, one simply circumnavigates "around" this center point like a needle on a record player.

Hence it is evident that sailing westerly, or in a direction square to the compass, on passing from one meridian to another, the path must of necessity be an *arc of a circle.* The series of arcs on completing a passage of 360 degrees form a circular path concentric with the magnetic pole, and necessarily, on a plane surface, brings the ship home from the east; and on the contrary, sailing out east, the vessel cannot do otherwise than return from the west.

A very good illustration of the circumnavigation of a plane will be seen by taking a round table, and fixing a pin in the centre to represent the magnetic pole. To this central pin attach a string drawn out to any distance towards the edge of the table. This string may represent the meridian of Greenwich, extending due north and south. If now a pencil or other object is placed across, or at right angles to the string, at any distance between the centre and the circumference of the table, it will represent a vessel standing due east and west. Now move the pencil and the string together in either direction, and it will be seen that by keeping the vessel (or pencil), square to the string it must of necessity describe a circle round the magnetic centre and return to the starting point in the opposite direction to that in which it first sailed.

If it is borne in mind what is really meant by sailing due east or due west, which practically is neither more nor less than keeping the head of a ship at right angles to the various meridians over which it sails, there can be no difficulty in understanding how it is that the path of a circumnavigator is the circumference of a circle, the radius of which is the latitude or distance of the ship from the centre of a plane. But if, in addition to this, the leading facts connected with the subject are considered, it will be seen that the circumnavigation of a globe by the mariners' compass is an impossibility. For instance, it is known that the "dipping needle" is horizontal or without "dip" at the equator; and that the "dip" increases on sailing north and south: and is greatest at the magnetic centre.

Let C, fig. 87, represent a dipping needle on the "equator" of a globe. A mere inspection of the diagram is sufficient to make it demonstrated that the needle C cannot be horizontal, and at the same time pointing towards the north pole N. If a ship sailed east or west on the equator where the compass is horizontal, it is evident that its north or south end would describe a circle in the heavens equal in magnitude to the circumference of the earth at the equator--as shown by D, E, F.

If any small object to represent a ship is placed on the equator of an artificial globe and kept at right angles to the meridian lines, it will at once be seen that it cannot be otherwise than as above stated; and that the two facts that the compass always points towards the pole and yet on the equator lies without dip, cannot possibly co-exist on a globe.

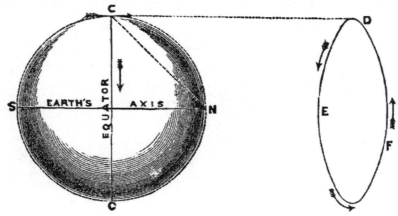

FIG. 87

They do co-exist in nature, and are well ascertained and easily proved to do so, ***therefore the earth cannot possibly be a globe***. They can co-exist on a plane with a northern or central region: they do beyond doubt co-exist, *therefore*, beyond doubt ***the earth is a plane***. So far, then, from the fact of a vessel sailing due west coming home from the east, and vice versâ, being a proof of the earth's rotundity, it is simply a result consistent with and dependent on its being a plane. Those who hold that it is a globe because it has been circumnavigated, have an argument which is logically incomplete and fallacious. This will be seen at once when it is placed in the syllogistic form:--

> A globe *only* can be circumnavigated.
> The earth has been circumnavigated.
> *Ergo*--The earth is a globe.

It has been shown that a *plane* can be circumnavigated, and therefore the first or major proposition is false; and being so, the conclusion is equally false.

This part of the subject furnishes a striking instance of the necessity of at all times proving a proposition by direct and independent evidence; instead of quoting a given result as a proof of what has previously been only assumed. But a theory will not admit of this method; and therefore the Zetetic process--inquiry before conclusion--is the only course which can lead to simple unalterable truth. Whoever creates or upholds a theory, claims or adopts a monster which will sooner or later betray and enslave him, and make him ridiculous in the eyes of practical observers.

LOSS OF TIME ON SAILING WESTWARD

Captain Sir J. C. Ross, at p. 132 of his "Antarctic Voyages," says:--

> "November 25th. Having by sailing to the eastward gained 12 hours, it became necessary, on crossing the 180th degree, and entering upon west longitude, in order to have our time correspond with that of England, to have two days following of the same date, and by this means lose the time we had gained, and still were gaining as we sailed to the eastward!"

The gaining and losing of time on sailing "round the world" east and west, is generally referred to as another proof of the earth's rotundity. But it is equally as fallacious as the argument drawn from circumnavigation, and from the same cause, namely, the assumption that on a globe only will such a result occur. It will be seen by reference to the following diagram, fig. 88, that such an effect must arise equally upon a plane as upon a globe.

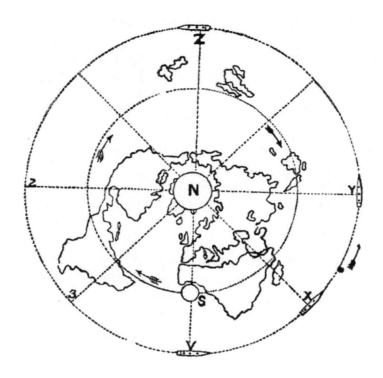

FIG. 88.

Let V, represent a vessel on the meridian of Greenwich V, N; and ready to start on a voyage eastward; and S, represent the sun moving in an opposite direction, or westward. It is evident that the vessel and the sun being on the same meridian on a given day, if the ship should be stationary the sun would go round in the direction of the arrows, and would meet it again in 24 hours. But if, during the next 24 hours, the ship has sailed to the position X, say 45 degrees of longitude eastward, the sun in its course would meet it three hours earlier than before, or in 21 hours--because 15 degrees of longitude correspond to one hour of time. Hence three hours would be gained. The next day, while the sun is going its round the vessel will have arrived at Y, meeting it 6 hours sooner than it would have done had it remained at V, and, in the same way, continuing its course eastward, the vessel would at length meet the sun at Z, twelve hours earlier than if it had remained at V; and thus passing successively over the arcs 1, 2, and 3, to V, or the starting point, 24 hours, or one day will have been gained. But the contrary follows if the ship sails in the opposite direction. The sun having to come round to the meridian of Greenwich V, S, N, in 24 hours, and the ship having in that time moved on to the position fig. 3, will have to overtake the ship at that position, and thus be three hours longer in reaching it. In this way the sun is more and more behind the meridian time of the ship as it proceeds day after day upon its westerly course, so that on completing the circum-navigation the ship's time is one day later than the solar time, reckoning to and from the meridian of Greenwich.

DECLINATION OF THE POLE STAR

Another phenomenon supposed to prove rotundity, is thought to be the fact that Polaris, or the north polar star sinks to the horizon as the traveller approaches the equator, on passing which it becomes invisible. This is a conclusion fully as premature and illogical as that involved in the several cases already alluded to. It is an ordinary effect of perspective for an object to appear lower and lower as the observer goes farther and farther away from it. Let any one try the experiment of looking at a light- house, church spire, monument, gas lamp, or other elevated object, from a distance of only a few yards, and notice the angle at which it is observed. On going farther away, the angle under which it is seen will diminish, and the object will appear lower and lower as the distance of the observer increases, until, at a certain point, the line of sight to the object, and the apparently uprising surface of the earth upon or over which it stands, will converge to the angle which constitutes the "vanishing point" or the horizon; beyond which it will be invisible.

What can be more common than the observation that, standing at one end of a long row of lamp-posts, those nearest to us seem to be the highest; and those farthest away the lowest; whilst, as we move along towards the opposite end of the series, those which we approach seem to get higher, and those we are leaving behind appear to gradually become lower.

This lowering of the pole star as we recede southwards; and the rising of the stars in the south as we approach them, is the necessary result of the everywhere visible law of perspective operating between the eye-line of the observer, the object observed, and the plane surface upon which he stands; and has no connection with or relation whatever to the supposed rotundity of the earth.

THE "DIP SECTOR"

One of the most plausible and yet most fallacious arguments for the earth's rotundity is that supposed to be drawn from observations with an instrument called a "Dip Sector." Sir John F. W. Herschel,[100] considers it one of the most important proofs afforded by geometry; and therefore it must be specially examined. The following are his words:--

"Let us next see what obvious circumstances there are to help us to a knowledge of the *shape* of the earth. Let us first examine what we can actually see of its shape. . . . If we sail out of sight of land, whether we stand on the deck of the ship or climb the mast, we see the surface of the sea--not losing itself in distance and mist, but terminated by a sharp clear, well-defined line, or *offing* as it is called, which runs all round us in a circle, having our station for its centre. That this line

---

100 "Treatise on Astronomy," pp. 15 to 18.

is really a circle we conclude, first, from the perfect apparent similarity of all its parts: and, secondly, from the fact of all its parts appearing at the same distance from us, and that evidently a moderate one; and, thirdly, from this, that its apparent *diameter*, measured with an instrument called the *dip sector*, is the same, in whatever direction the measure is taken, properties which belong only to the circle among geometrical figures. If we ascend a high eminence the same holds good. . . From Ætna, Teneriffe, Mowna Roa, in those few and rare occasions when the transparency of the air will permit the real boundary of the horizon, the true sea-line to be seen--the very same appearances are witnessed, but with this remarkable addition, viz.: that the angular *diameter* of the visible area, as measured by the dip sector, is materially less than at a lower level; or in other words, that the *apparent size* of the earth has sensibly diminished as we have receded from its surface, while yet the *absolute quantity* of it seen at once has been increased. The same appearances are observed universally in every part of the earth's surface visited by man. Now the figure of a body which, however seen, appears *always circular* can be no other than a sphere or globe. A diagram (which is here simplified from the original) will elucidate this. Suppose the earth to be represented by the sphere L, H, N, Q, fig 89.

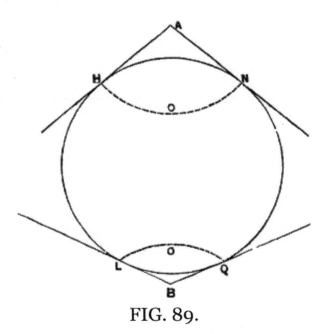

FIG. 89.

Let A, B, be two different stations at different elevations. From each of them let lines be drawn, tangents to the surface, as A, H, and A, N; B, L, and B, Q; then will these lines represent the visual rays along which the spectators at A, and at B, will see the visible horizon; and as the tangent A, H, sweeps round from H, through O, to N, the circle formed is the portion of the earth's surface visible to a spectator at A, and the angle H, A, N, included between the two extreme visual rays, is the measure of its apparent angular diameter. This is the angle measured by the dip sector. Now it is evident, that as A, is more elevated than B, the visible area, and the distance of the visible horizon A, H, or A, N, are greater than the area and horizon represented by B, L, or B, Q, and that the angle H, A, N, is less obtuse than L, B, Q, or in other words the apparent angular diameter of the earth is less, being nowhere so great as 180°, or two right angles, but falling short of it by some sensible quantity; and that more and more the higher we ascend."

The above quotation involves two distinct phenomena. First, that "from the deck of a ship we see the surface of the sea, and the sharp, clear, well- defined line called the offing running round us in a circle, having our station for its centre;" and secondly, that the "dip" to the offing or horizon increases with increase of altitude. The first statement is simply a truism; but as it has been shown by several experiments that the apparent rising of the water to a level of the eye is the result of a law of perspective operating in connection with a plane surface; it is logically and geometrically a proof that the water is horizontal, and a disproof of convexity. The second statement is the very reverse of all the practical observations [e.g. experiments 10,11 and 15] of this work. At every altitude where special observations have been made, the sea surface has been found to ascend to a line of sight at right angles to a plumb line; and that unless some telescopic instrument is used *no dip whatever is required to meet the sea horizon*. Here then are two directly antagonistic statements; and it would be well if all the affirmations found in scientific works were brought to the same condition face to face with fact and experiment. Truth and falsehood are always of this distinctly opposite character; and it only requires that practical as against theoretical evidence be obtained to distinguish one from the other.

VARIABILITY OF PENDULUM VIBRATIONS

Many contend that because a pendulum vibrates more rapidly in the northern region than "at the equator," the earth is thereby proved not only to be a globe, but to have axial motion, and because the variation in the velocity is that of gradual increase as the north pole is approached, it is concluded that the earth's true shape is that of an oblate spheroid--the diameter through the poles being less than that through the equator. The difference was calculated by Newton to be the 235th part of the whole diameter; or that the polar was to the equatorial diameter as 680 to 692. Huygens gave the proportion as 577 to 875, or a difference of about one- third of the whole diameter. Others have given still different proportions; but recently the difference of opinion, each the result of calculation, has become so great that many have concluded that the earth is really instead of oblate, an oblong spheroid.

243

It is argued that as the length of a pendulum vibrating seconds at the equator is 39,027 inches, and at the north pole 39,197 inches, that the earth, like an orange, has a globular form, but somewhat flattened at the "poles." But this so-called argument proceeds and depends upon the assumption that the earth is a globe having a "centre of attraction of gravitation," towards which all bodies gravitate or fall, and as a pendulum is essentially a falling body under certain restraint, the fact that when of the same length it oscillates or falls more rapidly at the north than at the equator is a proof that the northern surface is nearer to the "centre of attraction," or centre of the earth, than the equatorial surface: and of course if nearer the radius must be shorter, and therefore the "earth is a spheroid flattened at the poles."

The above is very ingenious and very plausible, but unfortunately for its character as an argument, the evidence is wanting that the earth is a globe at all; and until proof of convexity is given, all questions as to its being oblate, oblong, or entirely spherical, are logically out of place.

It is the duty of those who, from the behaviour of a pendulum at different latitudes, contend that the earth is spherical, to first prove that *no other cause* could operate besides greater proximity to a centre of gravity in producing the known differences in its oscillations. This not being done, nor attempted, the whole matter must be condemned as logically insufficient, irregular, and worthless for its intended purpose.

M. M. Picart and De la Hire, two celebrated French savans, as well as many other scientific men, have attributed the variations of the pendulum to differences of temperature at different latitudes. It is certain that the average changes of temperature are more than sufficient to bring about the variations which have been observed. The following quotation will show the practical results of these changes:--

> "All the solid bodies with which we are surrounded are constantly undergoing changes of bulk, corresponding to the variations of temperature. . . . The expansion and con-traction of metals by heat and cold form subjects of serious and careful attention to chronometer makers, as will appear by the following statements:--The length of the pendulum vibrating seconds, in vacuo, in the latitude of London (51° 31' 8" north) at the level of the sea, and at the temperature of 62° Fahrenheit, has been ascertained with the greatest precision to be 39.13929 inches; now, as the metal of which it is composed is constantly subject to variation of temperature, it cannot but happen that its length is constantly varying, and when it is further stated that if the 'bob' be let down 1-100th of an inch, the clock will lose ten seconds in twenty-four hours; that the elongation of 1-1000th of an inch will cause it to lose one second per day; and that a change of temperature equal to 30° Fahrenheit will alter its length 1-5000th part, and occasion an error in the rate of going of

244

eight seconds per day, it will appear evident that some plan must be devised for obviating so serious an inconvenience."[101]

"The mean annual temperature of the whole earth at the level of the sea is 50° Fahrenheit. For different latitudes it is as under:--

Latitude (Equator)		0 =	Length of 39.072		
			84.2° Pendulum		
"	"	10 =	"	"	"
			82.6°		
"	"	20 =	"	"	"
			78.1°		
"	"	30 =	"	"	"
			71.1°		
"	"	40 =	"	" 39.139	
			62.6°		
"	London	50 =	"	"	"
			53.6°		
"	"	60 =	"	"	"
			45.0°		
"	"	70 =	"	"	"
			38.1°		
"	"	80 =	"	"	"
			33.6°		
"	Pole	90 =	"	"	
			00.0°	39.197	

From the above table[102] from the equator towards the pole, which would of necessity contract the substance of the pendulum, or starting it and cause it to vibrate more rapidly.

Besides the temperature of a given latitude the pressure and density of the air must be taken into account. In numbers 294 and 480 of the "Philosophical Transactions," Dr. Derham records a number of experiments with pendulums in the open air, and in the receiver of an air-pump, which he summarises as follows:--

"The arches of vibration in vacuo were larger than in the open air, or in the receiver before it was exhausted; the enlargement or diminution of the arches of vibration

---

101 Noad's "Lectures on Chemistry," p. 41. (p. 176).
102 2 "Million of Facts," by Sir Richard Phillips, p. 475.

were constantly proportional to the quantity of air, or rarity, or density of it, which was left in the receiver of the air-pump. And as the vibrations were longer or shorter, so the time were it is seen that the temperature gradually decreases accordingly; viz., two seconds in an hour when the vibrations were longest, and less and less as the air was re-admitted, and the vibrations shortened."

Thus it is evident that two distinct and tangible causes necessarily operate to produce variability in the oscillations of a pendulum at different latitudes, without having recourse to a flattening at the poles of an imaginary globe. First the gradual diminution of temperature as the pendulum is carried from the equator to the polar region, tends to shorten its length, and thus to increase its number of vibrations per hour or day; and secondly, as the polar centre is approached the air is colder, therefore denser, and therefore the "arches of vibration" shorter, and the times of oscillation less, or in other words the number of vibrations greater in a given period. It has also been ascertained that the pendulum is influenced--other conditions being the same, by electric and magnetic states of the atmosphere. When intense electric conditions exist the arches and times of vibration are less than during the existence of opposite conditions. Hence if in different latitudes pendulum experiments are made in vacuo, at the same temperature, and always at the level of the sea, different electric and magnetic conditions prevailing, will induce variable results. The attention of some of the most accurate and patient observers has been directed to this mode of proving the oblate spheroidal form of the earth, but the results have never been satisfactory, nor such as were expected, or that the theory of rotundity should produce. The following remarks upon this subject are interesting:

"Newton was the first person who made a calculation of the figure of the earth on the theory of gravitation. He took the following supposition as the only one to which his theory could be applied. He assumed the earth to be fluid. This fluid matter he assumed to be equally dense in every part. . . . For trial of his theory he supposed the fluid earth to be a spheroid. In this manner he inferred that the form of the earth would be a spheroid in which the length of the shorter is to the length of the longer or equatorial diameter, in the proportion of 229 to 230."[103]

"The following table comprises the results of the most reliable pendulum experiments which have thus far been made, and among which the extensive series of observations by General Sabine holds the first place."

(Particulars are here given of sixty-seven experiments made in every latitude north of the equator, from 0° 1′ 49″ north to 79° 49′ 58″ north; and of twenty-nine experiments in the south from latitude 0° 1' 34″ south, to Cape Horn, 55° 51′ 20″ south, and South Shetland. 62° 56′ 11″ south.) We have here before us the results of fifty-five observations of the seconds pendulum, and of seventy-six

103 Professor Airey's "Six Lectures on Astronomy." Edit. 4, p. 194.

observations of the invariable pendulum; in all 131 experiments; which number, however, includes eight of the former and fifteen of the latter kind, *differing to a remarkable extent*, as compared with the results generally from the computed values. General Sabine observes of these discrepancies that 'they are due in a far greater degree to local peculiarities than to what may be more strictly called errors of observation.' And already Mr. Bailey (in Memoirs of the Royal Astronomical Society, vol. 7), had expressed the opinion 'that the vibrations of a pendulum are powerfully affected, in many places, by the local attraction of the substratum on which it is swung, or by *some other direct influence* at present *unknown to us*, and the effect of which far exceeds the errors of observation."

"General Sabine himself relates:--'Captain Foster was furnished with two invariable pendulums of precisely the same form and construction as those which had been employed by Captain Kayter and myself. Both pendulums were vibrated at all the stations, but *from some cause*, which Mr. Bailey was unable to explain, the observations with one of them were *so discordant* at South Shetland as *to require their rejection*'".[104]

From the foregoing remarks and quotations it is obvious that the assumption of Sir Isaac Newton that the earth is an oblate spheroid, is not confirmed by experiments made with the pendulum.

ARCS OF THE MERIDIAN

The discrepancies and anomalies so often observed in pendulum experiments, have led the followers of Newton to seek the desired evidence in measurements of arcs of the meridian; but here again they are even more unfortunate than in their efforts with the pendulum. It is certain that the question when attempted to be answered by such measurements, is less satisfactory than was expected, and in many respects the results are contradictory.

"The determination of the exact figure of the earth (M. Biot remarks) has, for the last century and a half, been one of the constant aims of the labours of the French Academy of Sciences. From the time of the first measure of a degree by Picard, which enabled Newton to establish the law of universal gravitation, the highest efforts of astronomy and analysis have been directed to the consolidation of all the elements of that great phenomenon; and to the development of all the consequences, which they allow us to draw, not only as to the figure, but also as to the interior condition of the terrestrial spheroid."

Notwithstanding that every possible phase of human ingenuity has been brought to bear on this operation, which was expected to furnish positive proof of the Newtonian

104 "Figure of the Earth," by Johannes Von Gumpach; 2nd Edit., pp. 229 to 244. Hardwicke, London, 1862.

assumptions, the whole has been, geodetically and mathematically, a provoking failure. This will be evident from the following explanation of the process adopted, and quotations of opinions respecting it:--

"If we conceive a great circle in the heavens, the 360 radii of which converge towards and meet in the centre of the earth, this will be the normal circle by which true degrees are, and alone can be, determined on the terrestrial surface, intersected by those radii. Practically the points of intersection are determined by the plumb-line. Supposing now the earth to be a perfect sphere, . . . all plumb-lines or normals prolonged would meet in the earth's centre, and consequently coincide with the radii of the normal circle, determining in a direct manner true degrees on the terrestrial surface; and therefore *assuming* the figure of the earth to slightly deviate from that of a perfect sphere, it is natural to conclude, without a positive proof or reason to the contrary, that the plumb-lines would continue to be directed to the earth's centre all the same. Astronomy, however, not only without any proof or reason whatever, assumes that they do not; but, moreover, starting on the *assumption* that the *imaginary shape* lent to the earth by Sir Isaac Newton's theory, is its *real shape*, gives to the plumb-lines such imaginary directions as are needed in order to adopt the empirical results of geodetic measurements to the earth's *imagined form*. . . . That the direction of the plumb-lines or normals to any given point on the earth's surface is perpendicular to a tangent to that point, or to the plane of its horizon is, as I have already shown, and as appears also distinctly from Sir John Herschel's own words, *a mere assumption*, unsupported by even the shadow of a reason; for what possible connection can there be between the positive force or 'law of nature' which determines the directions of the plumb-line, and the imaginary line and plane, which astronomers term 'a tangent' and 'the horizon?'"[105]

The actual results of these repeated efforts will be seen in the following quotations. In the ordnance survey of Great Britain, which was conducted by the Duke of Richmond, Colonel Mudge, General Roy, Mr. Dalby and others, base lines were measured on Hounslow Heath and Salisbury Plain, with glass rods and steel chains; "when these were connected by a chain of triangles and the length computed, the result did not differ more than one inch from the actual measurements--a convincing proof of the accuracy with which all the operations had been conducted. The two stations of Beachy Head in Sussex, and Dunnose in the Isle of Wight, are visible from each other, and more than sixty-four miles asunder, nearly in a direction from east to west, their exact distance was found by the geodetical operations to be 339,397 feet (sixty- four miles and 1477 feet). The azimuth, or bearing of the line between them with respect to the meridian, and also the latitude of Beachy Head, were determined by astronomical observations. From these data the length of a degree perpendicular to the meridian was computed,

---

105 "Von Gumpach," pp. 38-53.

and this, compared with the length of a meridional degree in the same latitude, gave the proportion of the polar to the equatorial axis. The result thus obtained, however, *differed considerably* from that obtained by meridional degrees. It has been found *impossible to explain the want of agreement in a satisfactory way.* . . . By comparing the celestial with the terrestrial arcs, the length of degrees in various parallels was determined as in the following table:[106]

	Latitude of Middle Point.			Fathoms.
Arbury Hill and Clifton	52°	50′	29.8″	60.766
Blenheim and Clifton	52	38	56.1	60.769
Greenwich and Clifton	52	28	5.7	60.794
Dunnose and Clifton	52	2	19.8	60.820
Arbury Hill and Greenwich	51	51	4.1	60.849
Dunnose and Arbury Hill	51	35	18.2	60.864
Blenheim and Dunnose	51	13	18.2	60.890
Dunnose and Greenwich	51	2	54.2	60.884

Notwithstanding the "accuracy with which all the operations had been conducted," the skill and ingenuity and perfection of the instruments employed were such that after measuring base lines far apart and triangulating from summit to summit of the hills, between the stations the actually measured and the mathematically calculated results "did not differ more than one inch." Such exactitude was never scarcely contemplated, and certainly could not be surpassed, if at all equalled, by the ordnance officers or practical surveyors of any other country in the world; and yet they failed to corroborate the assumption of polar depression or diminution in the axial radius of the earth. "For instead of the degrees *increasing* as we proceed from north to south, they appear to *decrease*, as if the earth were an *oblong* instead of an *oblate* spheroid."[107]

---

106 "Encyclopedia of Geography," by Hugh Murray, and several Professors of the University of Edinburgh.(p. 182)
107 Ibid.

The fallacy involved in all the attempts to prove the oblate spheroidal form of the earth, is, that the earth is first assumed to be a globe, the celestial surface above it to be concave, and the plumb-lines to be radii. If this were the true condition of things, then all the degrees of latitude would be the same in length; and if the earth were really "flattened at the poles," the degrees would certainly shorten in going from the equator towards the north. If, however, the celestial surface is not concave, but horizontal, two plumb-lines suspended north and south of each other would be parallel, and would indicate equal length in all the degrees of latitude, thereby spewing the earth to be parallel with the celestial surface, and therefore a plane. The differences required by a globe are not found in practice, but such as a plane would produce are invariably found. Hence the failure of geodesy becomes evidence against rotundity, but demonstrating that the earth is parallel to the horizontal heavens, and therefore of mathematical and logical necessity A PLANE. It is ever the case, when falsehood is tested in the crucible of experiment, that its value is diminished or destroyed, whilst the contrary is the case with truth, which, like gold, the more intense the fire of criticism the more brilliant it appears.

> "When we come to compare the measures of meridional arcs made in various parts of the earth, the results obtained exhibit discordances far greater than what we have shown to be attributable to error of observation, and which render it evident that the hypothesis (of flattened rotundity) in strictness of its wording is untenable. The lengths of the degree of the meridian were astronomically determined from actual measurement made with all possible care and precision, by commissioners of various nations, men of the first eminence, supplied by their respective governments with the best instruments, and furnished with every facility which could tend to ensure a successful result."[108]

The first recorded measurement of a degree of latitude is that by Eratosthenes, 230 B.C.

	Toises
Ptolemy A.D. 137, measured a degree and made it	56.900
Fennel in 1528, measured a degree near Paris, and found it to be	56.746
The Caliph Abdallah Almamoran made a degree to be 56⅔ miles, of 4000 cubits each. How much is the cubit?	
Snell, in 1617, made it	55.100
Picard, in 1669, made it	57.060
Maupertius, in 1729, made it	57.183
Others at different times made a degree in France to be respectively	56.925 57.422
The arc measured by Picard in 1669, between Paris and Amiens, was again measured in 1739, and found to be instead of 57.060 toises	57.138

---

108 "Treatise on Astronomy," by Sir J. F. W. Herschel.

The arc 56.925 measured in 1752 was again measured some years afterwards, and found to be				56.979
				English Feet
The measurement by the Swedish Government, in latitude 66° 20′ 10″ was				365.782
By the Russian Government, in latitude 58° 17′ 37″				365.368
By the English, in latitude 52° 35′ 45″				364.971

	deg.	min.	sec.	English feet
The French, in	46	52	2	364.872
	44	51	2	364.535
The Roman, in	42	59	0	364.262
The American, United States, in	39	12	0	363.786
Peruvian in	1	31	0	362.808
Indian in	16	8	22	363.044
	12	32	21	363.013
Africa (Cape of Good Hope) in	35	43	20	364.059

The arc measured by Sweden was	1	37	19
Russia	3	35	5
England	3	57	13
France, 1st	8	20	0
2nd	12	22	13
Rome	2	9	47
America	1	28	45
Peru	3	7	3
India, 1st	15	57	40
2nd	1	34	56
Africa (Cape of Good Hope)	3	34	35

It may be interesting to state here a few of the instances of the great care and accuracy manifested by the English ordnance surveyors; from which we may conclude that their published results may be implicitly relied on.

"A base on Salisbury Plain was measured in 1794 with steel chains, and was found to be 36574.4 feet long, and the length, as obtained by triangulation from the Hounslow Heath base, being 36574.3, exhibited therefore a difference of little more than an inch in a length of nearly seven miles."[109]

109 "Professional Papers of the Corps of Royal Engineers." By Major General Colby; vol. iii., p. 10.

"The measurement of this base (on Belhelvie Sands in 1817) occupied from May 5 to June 6, and Ramsden's steel chain was again the instrument used. Its length, when compared with the unit ordnance standard bar O, is found to be 26.516.66 feet, and the length as deduced (in 1827) from the Lough Foyle base, is 26.518.99 feet."

"Hounslow Heath base, measured with glass rods, when reduced to the ordnance standard, 1784, was 27.405.06 feet; the same measured with steel chains, in 1791, gave 27.405.38 feet. Deduced by computation from Lough Foyle base, in 1827, was 27.403.83 feet."

"Salisbury Plain base, measured by steel chains (1794), was 36.575.64 feet. By Colby's compensation bars (1849), it was found to be 36.577.95 feet. Computed from Lough Foyle base (1827), 36.577.34 feet."[110]

Thus it will be seen that the least error between actual measurement of base lines, and the results by triangulation and computation from distant bases was 0.1 foot, a shade more than 1 inch, and the greatest error 2.33 feet.

"These measurements are the most correct that, perhaps, have ever been made on the face of the earth. Men of the greatest skill have been employed; instruments of the most perfect construction have been used; every precaution has been adopted to avoid error, and all that science could do has been done."[111]

How strange it appears, that one of the most ingenious mathematicians the world ever produced, assumed for certain purposes that the earth was a globe, that it revolved, that its revolutions caused the fluid and plastic matter of its substance to determine towards the equator-- causing it to "bulge out" to a greater extent than the diameter in the direction of the axis, and therefore the circumference at the equator must be greater than the circumference at right angles, or in the direction of latitude; or, in other words, that the degrees of latitude must diminish towards the poles, and yet "men of the greatest skill," with "instruments of the most perfect construction," having availed themselves of "all that science can do," have succeeded in making measurements the most exact "ever made on the face of the earth," have found results the very reverse of all that the Newtonian theory deemed essential to its consistency and perfection! Instead of the degrees *diminishing* towards the pole they were found to increase; as if the earth were egg-shaped or prolonged through its axis, and not, like an orange, flattened at the sides--"as if;" to use more scientific language, "the earth were an *oblong* instead of an *oblate* spheroid."

Well may such language as the following be used by practical writers!

---

110 "Professional Papers of Royal Engineers," new series; vol. iii,, p. 27.
111 "The Earth," p. 20, by Captain A. W. Drayson, Royal Artillery.

"The geodetic operations carried out during the last century and a half for the purpose of determining the figure and the dimensions of the earth have, up to this time, led to no satisfactory results. Having been performed by the most eminent astronomers, with the most perfect instruments, in short with all the resources of modern science, it would seem that they ought to have led to a final solution of this most interesting problem; such, however, is by no means the case. Every new measure of a meridian arc has but added, and adds, to the existing doubts, and want of concordance, nay to the positive contradictions which the various operations exhibit, as compared with one another."[112]

"The remarkable circumstance to which I would direct attention is, that in the middle of the nineteenth century, and at a time when astronomy and analysis celebrate their most brilliant triumphs, the ground itself on which the truth of all their practical observations and theoretical deductions mainly rests, continues a subject of doubt and perplexity as much as ever it was in the almost forgotten days of Sir Isaac Newton. After 150 years of unceasing efforts astronomy has yet to discover whether the terrestrial equator forms an ellipse or a circle. After a century and a half of unsuccessful calculation, analysis is still seen toiling to invent empirical formulas for the purpose of establishing a tolerable accordance between the geodetic measurements of today and those of yesterday."[113]

Had it been seen in the days of Newton, or even a century ago, that the surface of standing water was not convex, and therefore that the earth could not be a globe at all, the great expense and labour, and the inconceivable anxiety which astronomers have experienced through the contradictions and inconsistencies developed during their attempts to reconcile the facts of nature with the fancies of speculative mathematicians, would have been avoided, and society saved from the infliction of an education which, in the most confused manner, includes a system of astronomy at variance with every perception of the senses, contrary to every day experience, and demonstrably false both in its groundwork and in its principal ramifications.

SPHERICITY INEVITABLE FROM SEMI-FLUIDITY

An argument for the earth's rotundity is thought, by many, to be found in the following facts:

"Fluid or semi-fluid substances in a state of motion invariably assume the globular form, as instanced in rain, hail, dew, mercury, and melted lead, which, poured from a great height, as in the manufacture of small shot, becomes divided into spherical masses."

---

112 "Memoirs of the Imperial Academy of Sciences of St. Petersburg." By General Von Schubert. St. Petersburg, 1859.
113 "Figure of the Earth," p. 3, by von Gumpach.

"There is abundant evidence, from geology, that the earth has been a fluid or semi-fluid mass, and it could not, therefore, continue in a state of motion through space without becoming spherical."

In the first place, in reply to the above, it is denied that hail is always globular. On examination immediately after or during a hail-storm, the masses present every variety of form, and very few are found perfectly globular. Rain and dew cannot so well be examined during their fall, but when standing on hard surfaces in minute quantities, they generally appear spherical, a result simply of "attraction of cohesion." The same of mercury; and in reference to the formation of shot, by pouring melted lead from the top of a very high tower into cold water, it is a mistake to suppose that all, or even a large proportion, is converted into truly spherical masses. From twenty to fifty per cent. of the masses formed are very irregular in shape, and have to be returned to the crucible for re- melting. In addition to which it may be remarked, that the tendency in falling fluids to become globular is owing to what, in chemical works, is called "attraction of cohesion" (not "attraction of gravitation"), which is very limited in its operation. Its action is confined to small quantities of matter. If, in the manufacture of shot, the melted metal is allowed to fall in masses of several ounces or pounds, instead of being divided (by pouring through a sieve or "cullender" with small holes) into particles weighing only a few grains, it will never take a spherical form. Shot of an inch diameter could not be made by this process; bullets of even half an inch can only be made by casting the metal into spherical moulds. In tropical countries the rain, instead of falling in drops, or small globules, often comes down in large irregular masses or gushes, which have no approximation whatever to sphericity. So that it is manifestly unjust to affirm, of large masses like the earth, that which attaches only to minute portions, or a few grains, of matter.

Without denying that the earth has been, at some former period, or was, when it first existed, in a pulpy or semi-fluid state, it is requisite to prove beyond all doubt that it has a motion through space, or the conclusion that it is therefore spherical is premature, and very illogical. It should also be proved that it has motion upon axes, or it is equally contrary to every principle of reasoning to affirm that the equatorial is greater than the polar diameter, as the inevitable result of the centrifugal force produced by its axial or diurnal rotation. The assumption of such conditions by Sir Isaac Newton, as we have seen when speaking of the measurement of arcs of the meridian, was contrary to evidence, and led to and maintains a "muddle of mathematics" such as philosophers will, sooner or later, be ashamed of. The whole matter, taken together, entirely fails as an argument for the earth's rotundity. It has been demonstrated that axial and orbital motion do not exist, and, therefore, any argument founded upon and including them as facts is necessarily fallacious.

DEGREES OF LONGITUDE

Another argument for the globular form of the earth is the following:-- The degrees of longitude, radiating from the north, gradually increase in extent as they approach the equator; beyond which they again converge, and gradually diminish in extent towards the south. To this it is replied, that no actual, direct, or trigonometrical measurement of a degree of longitude has ever been made south of the equator: therefore, no geodetic evidence exists that the degrees are either less or more. The following is the true state of the question:--If the earth is a globe, it is certain that the degrees of longitude are less on both sides of the equator than upon it. If the degrees of longitude are less *beyond*, or to the south of the equator, than upon it, then it is equally certain that the earth is globular; and the only way to decide the matter, and place it beyond all doubt, is to actually *measure* a distance, to the south of the equator, at right angles to a given meridian, with non-expanding rods or chains, such as are used by the English Ordnance surveyors, and between two points where the sun is vertical at an interval of four minutes of solar time. Or, in other words, as one degree is a 360th part of the sun's whole path over the earth, so is the period of four minutes a 360th part of the whole twenty-four hours which the sun requires to complete its course: therefore, whatever space on the earth is contained between any two points, where the sun is on the meridian at twelve o'clock and at four minutes past twelve, will be one degree of longitude. If we know the proximate distance between any two places, in the south, on or about the same latitude, and have the difference of solar time at these two places, we can calculate, accordingly, the length of a degree of longitude at that latitude. Such elements we have from the map, recently published, of New Zealand, in the "Australian Handbook, Almanack, and Shippers' and Importers' Directory, for the Year 1872."[114] It is there stated that the distance (mail route) between Sydney and Nelson is 1400 miles (sea measure), equal to 1633 statute miles. From this distance it is proper to deduct fully 50 miles for the distance in rounding Cape Farewell and sailing up Tasman Bay, at the head of which Nelson is situated. But if we allow 83 miles, which is more than sufficient, we have the straight-line distance, from the meridian of Sydney to the meridian of Nelson, as 1550 statute miles. The two places are nearly on the same latitude, and the difference in longitude is 22° 2′ 14″.[115] The whole matter now becomes a mere arithmetical question: if 22° 2′ 14″ give 1550 statute miles, what will 360° give? The answer is 25,182 miles. Hence, a 360th part of this distance is *one degree*; and the length of such degree is nearly 20 miles. But upon a globe, such as modern astronomers affirm the earth to be, the length of a degree at the latitude of Sydney would be 49.74 nautical miles, or 58 statute miles. Hence we find that the actual length of a degree of longitude at the latitude of Sydney is nearly 12 miles *longer* than it could possibly be if the earth is a globe of 25,000 miles' equatorial or maximum circumference; and the distance round the earth, at that latitude, is 25,182 statute miles, instead of 20,920, the difference between theory and fact being 4262 miles.

---

114 Published by Gordon & Gotch, 85, Collins Street West, Melbourne, and 121, Holborn Hill, London.
115 Communicated by Captain Stokes, of H.M.S. Albion, to the "Australian Almanack for 1859," p. 118..

If, now, we take, from the same map, the distance between Melbourne and Bluff Harbour, South New Zealand--1400 nautical, or 1633 statute miles--and take the difference of longitude between the two places, allowing 50 statute miles for the angular or diagonal direction of the route to Bluff Harbour, we find the degrees of longitude fully 70 statute miles; whereas, at the average latitude of the two places, viz., 42° S., the degrees, if the earth is a globe, would be less than 54 statute miles; thus showing that in the south, where the length of a degree of longitude should be 54 miles, it is really 70 miles, or 16 miles longer than would be possible according to the theory of the earth's rotundity.

From the above two cases we also find that the degrees of longitude at the latitude of Bluff Harbour, on the southern point of New Zealand, are somewhat longer than the degrees between Sydney and Nelson, where they ought to be--if the earth is globular--several miles less; and also that, according to the same doctrine, there is an excess of 7466 statute miles in the whole circumference.

The following table of longitudes at different latitudes will be useful, to enable the reader to make calculation; for himself:--

That [these] calculations are proximately correct, is corroborated by the results obtained from the datum furnished by the Atlantic Cable between Valencia and Newfoundland. In Chapter IV. of this work it is shown that the earth being a plane, the circumference at the latitude of Cape Town, South Africa, must be 23,400 statute miles. Now, the latitude of Cape Town is 34 °, of Sydney 33½°, and of the entrance to Tasman Bay, going to Nelson, about 40°. If we take the average latitude of the mail steamer route between Sydney and Nelson, we find the distance round the earth at such latitude to be 24,776 miles; and, at the average or medium latitude between Melbourne and Bluff Harbour, still farther south, 25,200. The proximate agreement between these results of calculation, from given base-lines north and south of the equator, is perfectly consistent with the fact that the earth is a plane.

	Degrees.		Nautical Miles.
Latitude	0 Longitude =		60.00
"	1	" =	59.99
"	10	" =	59.09
"	20	" =	56.38
"	30	" =	51.96
(Cape Town)	34	" =	49.74
Latitude	40	" =	45 9G
"	45	" =	42.45
"	50	" =	38.57
(Cape Horn)	56	" =	33.55
Latitude	60	" =	33.00
"	65	" =	25.36
"	70	" =	20.52
"	75	" =	15.53
"	80	" =	10.42
"	85	" =	5.53
"	86	" =	4.19
"	87	" =	3.14
"	88	" =	2.09
"	89	" =	1.05
"	90	" =	0.00

The following diagrams, figs. 90 and 91, will show the difference, in regard to degrees of longitude, between theory and fact.

FIG. 90.

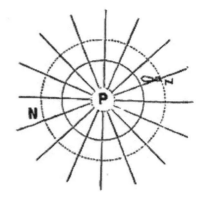

FIG. 91.

According to fig. 90, the circumference at the latitude of Bluff Harbour, south end of New Zealand, shown by the line N, Z, should be about 17,600 statute miles; but it is practically ascertained that the distance round, as shown by the dotted line N, Z, in fig. 91, P being the polar centre, is 25,200 statute miles--a difference between fact and theory of 7600 statute miles.

The above calculations are, as already stated, only proximate; but as liberal allowances have been made for irregularities of route, etc., they are sufficiently accurate to prove that the degrees of longitude, as we proceed south-wards, do not diminish, as they would upon a globe, but expand or increase, as they must if the earth is a plane; or, in other words, the farthest point, or greatest latitude south, must have the greatest circumference and degrees of longitude. But actual measurement--in Australia, or other southern lands, of the space contained between two points east and west of each other, where the difference in the solar time amounts to four minutes, can alone place this matter beyond dispute. The day is surely not far distant when the scientific world will undertake to settle this question by proper geodetic operations; and this not altogether for the sake of determining the magnitude of the southern region, but also for the purpose of ascertaining the cause of the many anomalies observed in its navigation, and which have led to the loss of many vessels and a fearful sacrifice of life and property.

> "In the southern hemisphere, navigators to India have often fancied themselves east of the Cape when still west, and have been driven ashore on the African coast, which, according to their reckoning, lay behind them. This misfortune happened to a fine frigate, the Challenger, in 1845."[116]

> "How came Her Majesty's Ship Conqueror, to be lost? How have so many other noble vessels, perfectly sound, perfectly manned, perfectly navigated, been wrecked

---

116 "Tour through Creation," by Rev. Thomas Milner, M.A.

in calm weather, not only in a dark night, or in a fog, but in broad daylight and sunshine--in the former case upon the coasts, in the latter, upon sunken rocks--from being 'out of reckoning,' under circumstances which until now, have baffled every satisfactory explanation." [117]

"Assuredly there are many shipwrecks from alleged errors in reckoning which may arise from a somewhat false idea of the general form and measurement of the earth's surface; such a subject, therefore, ought to be candidly and boldly discussed."[118]

Surprise at the frequency and the sadness of such losses will naturally subside when it is seen that the degrees of longitude beyond the equatorial region gradually increase with the southern latitude. A false hypothesis, a merely supposed sphericity of the earth and of gradually diminishing lines of longitude on each side of the equator is the true cause of the greater number of these sad catastrophes which have so often startled and appalled the public mind. To this fallacious doctrine of rotundity may be traced not only the source of these terrible losses and sufferings, but also of the fact that mariners are unable to see the true cause of the disasters, and are therefore unable to benefit by experience, and to guard against them in future voyages. They have been led to attribute all the fearful dangers of southern waters to imaginary causes, the chief of which is the prevalence of direct and counter currents. One of the most common peculiarities in these regions is the almost constant confusion in the "reckoning;" as will be seen by the following quotations:--

"We found ourselves every day from 12 to 16 miles by observation in advance of our reckoning."[119]

"By our observations at noon we found ourselves 58 miles to the eastward of our reckoning in two days."[120]

"February 11th, 1822, at noon, in latitude 65.53. S. our chronometers gave 44 miles more westing than the log in three days. On 22nd of April (1822), in latitude 54.16. S. our longitude by chronometers was 46.49, and by D.R. (dead reckoning) 47° 11′: On 2nd May (1822), at noon, in latitude 53.46. S., our longitude by chronometers was 59° 27′, and by D.R. 61° 6′. October 14th, in latitude 58.6, longitude by chronometers 62° 46′, by account 65° 24′. In latitude 59.7. S., longitude by chronometers was 63° 28′, by account 66° 42′. In latitude 61.49. S., longitude by chronometers was 61° 53′, by account 66° 38′."[121]

---

117 Von Gumpach. "Figure of the Earth," p. 256.
118 "The Builder." Sept. 20th, 1862.
119 "South Sea Voyages." By Sir J. C. Ross, p. 96, vol. i.
120 "South Sea Voyages." By Sir J. C. Ross, p. 27. (p. 193)
121 "Condensed Navigation," p.130. Whittaker and Co., London. (p. 193)

The commander of the United States exploring expedition, Lieutenant Wilkes, in his narrative, says that in less than 18 hours he was 20 miles to the east of his reckoning in latitude 54° 20′ S. He gives other instances of the same phenomenon, and, in common with almost all other navigators and writers on the subject, attributes the differences between actual observation and theory to currents, the velocity of which, at latitude 57° 15′ S., amounted to 20 miles a day.[122]

The commanders of these various expeditions were, of course, with their education and belief in the earth's rotundity, unable to conceive of any other cause for the differences between log and chronometer results than the existence of currents. But one simple fact is entirely fatal to such an explanation, viz., that when the route taken is east or west the same results are experienced. The water of the southern region cannot be running in two opposite directions at the same time; and hence, although various local and variable currents have been noticed, they cannot be shown to be the cause of the discrepancies so generally observed in high southern latitudes between time and log results. The conclusion is one of necessity--is forced upon us by the sum of the evidence collected that the degrees of longitude in any given southern latitude are larger than the degrees in any latitude nearer to the northern centre; thus proving the already more than sufficiently demonstrated fact that the earth is a plane, having a northern centre, in relation to which degrees of latitude are concentric, and from which degrees of longitude are diverging lines, continually increasing in their distance from each other as they are prolonged towards the great glacial southern circumference.

"SPHERICAL EXCESS"

As a proof of the earth's rotundity, many place great reliance upon what is called the "spherical excess," which has been observed on making trigonometrical observations on a large scale.

> "The angles taken between any three points on the surface of the earth by the theodolite are, strictly speaking, spherical angles, and their sum must exceed 180 degrees; and the lines bounding them are not the chords as they should be, but the tangents to the earth. This excess is inappreciable in common cases, but in the larger triangles it becomes necessary to allow for it, and to diminish each of the angles of the observed triangle by one-third of the spherical excess. To calculate this excess, divide the area of the triangle in feet by the radius of the earth in seconds, and the quotient is the excess:"[123]

> "The theodolite used to measure the angles (in the English survey) surpassed in its dimensions and elaborate workmanship, every instrument of the kind that

---

122 "Condensed Navigation," p. 130. Whittaker and Co., London.
123 "Treatise on Levelling." By Castle.

had been seen in Europe; it measured angles with such precision, that it became necessary, in the calculation of the triangles, to take into consideration the excess of three spherical angles above two right angles, a quantity that had hitherto been too minute to be ascertained by any instrument, and was only known by theory to have any existence. The amount of the total error in the sum of the three angles never exceeded three seconds, so that the angles. generally must have been measured to the nearest second."[124]

In this so-called argument for rotundity we have another instance of the manner in which the most practical men of science are led astray. Just as the differences observed in the reading of chronometers as compared with those of the logs and dead reckonings when sailing in the southern regions, navigators, having had an education which involved the doctrine of rotundity, could not possibly see the real explanation which demonstrable truth afforded, but were forced to adopt the idea that ocean counter currents existed, overlooking altogether, and not daring to face the obvious fact that the differences were observed whether sailing east or west, and therefore that they were parties to the contradictory notion that the currents of the sea were moving in contrary directions carrying ships right and left, or backward and forward, at the same time; so the most skilful observers connected with the ordnance survey of Great Britain and Ireland, could not see that the angles which were too large for agreement with their general operations were the result of slight divergence in the rays of light passing through the lenses of their telescope; but, contrary to every principle of reasoning, assumed that the tops of the high places on and to which observations were made, were divergent from the common centre of a globular earth, and hence the so- called "spherical excess," for which they made such allowances as were necessary to make their observations agree with the theory of rotundity. Had they known that such a theory was contrary to fact, and that the earth was a plane, they would have sought an explanation of discrepancies in the proper quarter. They would have recognised the influence of refraction or "collimation" in their instruments; for they could not be ignorant of the optical peculiarities which necessitate so many observations upon the same point before they could decide upon the "average of errors" as their proper reading. The rule that the greater the number of observations made "averaging the errors," the more correct the deductions, ought to have led them to seek the "spherical excess" only in the optical character of the telescopes employed. In the operations connected with the Mont Cenis Tunnel the leading observations were many times repeated before the proper angles were ascertained. Mr. Francis Kossuth, one of the Royal Commissioners of Italian Railways, in his report on the tunnel, after describing the processes adopted in surveying over the mountain, says:--

"The whole system consisted of 28 triangles; and 86 was the number of measured angles. All of these were repeated never less than 10 times, the greater part 20, and the most important as many as 60 times."[125]

124 Dr. Rees's "Cyclopœdia," article "Degree."
125 "Marine Advertiser," Sept. 19th 1871.

In many of the triangulations connected with the British ordnance survey, the observations were repeated upwards of a hundred times, in order to diminish the personal and instrumental errors to which all such operations are liable. In page 41 of this work it is shown that a levelled theodolite pointed towards the sea represents the horizon as below the horizontal cross-hair, on account of what is technically called "collimation," or "a slight divergence of the rays of light from the axis of the eye on passing through the several glasses of the theodolite." The same "collimation" exists in connection with the vertical cross-hair; and hence the slight excess of the three angles over 180 degrees so often observed when taking very long sights--such, for instance, as those between Kippure and Donard, in Ireland, and Precelly, in Wales.

THEODOLITE TANGENT

IF a spirit-level or a theodolite is "levelled," and a given point be read on a graduated staff at the distance of say 100 chains, this point will have an altitude slightly in excess of the altitude of the cross-hair of the theodolite; and if the theodolite be removed to the position of the graduated staff, again levelled, and a back sight taken of 100 chains, another excess of altitude will be observed; and this excess will go on increasing as often as the back and fore sight observations are repeated. From this it is argued that the line of sight from the theodolite is a tangent, and, therefore, the surface of the earth is spherical. The author has made experiments similar to the above, and found it to be as stated; but the cause is not that the line of sight is a tangent, but the same "collimation" as that referred to in the section on "Spherical Excess."

TANGENTIAL HORIZON

IF a theodolite is placed on the sea shore, "levelled," and directed towards the sea, the line of the horizon will be a given amount below the cross-hair, and a certain "dip" or inclination from the level position will have to be made to bring the cross-hair and the sea-horizon together. If the theodolite is similarly fixed, but at a greater altitude, the space between the cross-hair and the sea horizon, and the dip of the instrument to bring them together, is also greater. From the above, which is perfectly true, it has been concluded that the surface of the earth is convex, and the line of sight over the sea tangential. As a proof that such is not the case, the following experiment may be tried:--

Place a theodolite on an eminence near the sea. "Level," and direct it over the water, when the horizon will be seen a little below the cross-hair or centre of the telescope, as shown in the diagram, fig. 30, and from the cause there assigned, viz., collimation, or refraction. Now let the instrument be inclined downwards until the cross-hair touches the horizon, as shown in fig. 31, and in the following diagram, fig. 92.

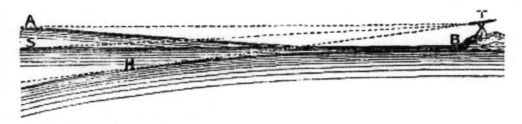

FIG. 92.

If the theodolite had a simple tube without lenses, instead of a telescope, which causes the appearance shown in , the horizon would be seen in a line with the cross-hair, or axis of the eye, as at A, fig. 92, and the amount of "dip" required to bring the cross-hair and the horizon in contact with each other will be represented by the angle A, T, S, to which must be added the collimation. In every instance where the experiment has been specially tried, the dip without the collimation only amounted to the angle A, T, S; thus proving that the surface of the sea, S, B, is horizontal, because parallel to the line A, T. If the water is convex, the line of sight, A, T, would be a tangent, and the dip to the horizon would be T, H, represented by the angle A, T, H. This angle, A, T, H, is never observed, but always A, T, S, plus collimation or divergence produced by the lenses in the telescope of the theodolite. Hence the surface of the waters is everywhere horizontal.

The words "collimation," "divergence," "refraction," &c., have many times been used in connection with this part of the subject, and the following very simple experiment will both exhibit what is meant, and show its influence in practice.

Take a "magnifying glass," or a convex lens, and hold it over a straight line drawn across a sheet of paper. If the line is drawn longer than the diameter of the lens, that part of it which is outside the lens will have a different position to that seen through it, as shown in the following diagram, fig. 93.

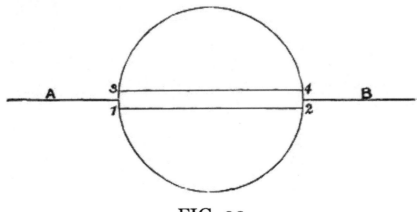

FIG. 93.

Instead of the line going uninterruptedly through the lens in the direction A, B, it will diverge, and appear at 1, 2; or it will appear above the line A, B, as at 3, 4, if the lens is held to the slightest amount above or below the actual centre.

A lens is a magnifying glass because it *dilates*, or spreads out from its centre, the objects seen through it. The infinitesimal or mathematical point actually in the centre is, of course, not visibly influenced, being in the very centre or on the true axis of the eye, but any part in the minutest degree out of that abstract centre is dilated, or diverged, or thrown further away from it than it would be to the naked eye; hence its apparent enlargement or expansion. Whatever, therefore, is *magnified*, is really so because thrown more or less *out of the centre*, and the more or less magnifying power of the lens is really the more or less divergence of the pencils of light on passing through the substance of which it is composed. In the telescope of a theodolite, or spirit-level, the spider's web of which the cross hair is made is placed in the actual centre; hence, in an observation, the point absolutely opposite to it is not seen, but only some other point minutely distant from it, but the distance of which is increased by the divergence caused by the lenses; and this divergence is what is called the "magnifying power." This is the source of those peculiarities which have been so very illogically considered to be proofs of the earth's rotundity. It is from this peculiarity that several gentlemen prematurely concluded that the water in the Bedford Canal was convex.

On the 5th of March, 1870, a party, consisting of Messrs. John Hampden, of Swindon, Wilts; Alfred Wallace, of London, William Carpenter, of Lewisham, M. W. B. Coulcher, of Downham Market, and J. H. Walsh, Editor of "The Field" newspaper, assembled on the northern bank of the "Old Bedford Canal," to repeat experiments similar to those described in figs. 2, 3, 4, and 5 of this work. But, from causes which need not be referred to here, they abandoned their original intentions, and substituted the following. On the western face of the Old Bedford Bridge, at Salter's Lode, a signal was placed at an elevation of 13 feet 4 inches above the water in the canal; at the distance of three miles a signal-post, with a disc 12 inches in diameter on the top, was so fixed that "the *centre* of the disc was 13 feet 4 inches above the water-line;" and at the distance of another three miles (or six miles altogether), on the eastern side of the Welney Bridge, another signal was placed, "3 inches above the top rail of the bridge, and 13 feet 4 inches above the water-line."[126]

This arrangement is represented in the following diagram, fig. 94:-- .

---

126 Reports by Messrs. Carpenter and Coulcher, published in "The Field" of March 26, 1870.

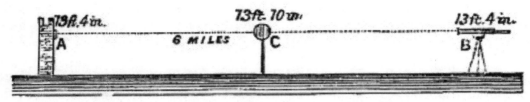

FIG. 94.

A, the signal on the Old Bedford Bridge; B, the telescope on Welney Bridge; and C, the central signal-post, three miles from each end. The object-glass of the telescope was 4½ inches diameter; hence the centre, or true eye-line, was 2¼ inches higher than the top of the signal B, and 3¾ inches below the top of the signal-disc at C. On directing the telescope, "with a power of 50," towards the signal A, the centre of which was 2¼ inches *below* the centre of the telescope, it was seen to be below it; but the disc on the centre pole, the top of which was, *to begin with*, 3¾ inches *above* the centre, or line of sight, from the telescope, was seen to stand considerably *higher* than the signal A. From which, three of the gentlemen immediately, but most unwarrantably, concluded that the elevation of the disc in the field of view of the telescope was owing to a rise in the water of the canal, showing convexity! whereas it was nothing more than simply the upward divergence (of that which was *already* 3¾ inches *above* the line of sight) produced by the magnifying power of the telescope, as shown in the experiment with the lens, on fig. 92.

Why did they omit to consider the fact that 3¾ inches excess of altitude would be made by a magnifying power of 50, to appear to stand considerably above the eye-line, and that a mere hair's-breadth of dip-- an amount which could not be detected--towards the distant signal would by magnifying, diverging, or dilating all above it, make it appear to be lifted up for several feet? Why did they not take care that the *top* of the centre disc was *in a line* with the telescope and the distant signal, A? Why, also, was the centre of the object glass fixed 2¼ inches *higher* than the centre of the object of observation at the other end? There was no difficulty in placing the *centre* of the telescope, the *top* of the middle disc, and the *centre* of the farthest signal mark, *at the same altitude*, and therefore in a straight line. For their own sakes as gentlemen, as well as for the sake of the cause they had undertaken to champion, it is unfortunate that they acted so unwisely; that they so foolishly laid themselves open to charges of unfairness in fixing the signals. Had they already seen enough to prove that the surface of the water was horizontal, and therefore instinctively felt a desire to do their best to delay as long as they could the day of general denunciation of their cherished doctrine of the earth's rotundity? Such questions are perfectly fair in relation to conduct so unjust and one-sided. It is evident that their anxiety to defend a doctrine which had been challenged by others overcame their desire for "truth without fear of consequences;" and they eagerly seized upon the veriest shadow of evidence to support themselves. In the whole history of invention, a more hasty, ill- conceived, illogical conclusion was never drawn; and it is well for civilisation that such procedure is almost universally denounced. It is scarcely possible to draw a favourable conclusion as to their motives in departing from their first intentions. Why did they not confine themselves to the repetition of the experiments, an account of which I had long previously published to the world, and to test which the expedition was first arranged? That of sending out a boat for a distance of six miles, and watching its progress from a fixed point with a good telescope, would have completely satisfied them as to the true form of the surface of the water; and as no irregularity in altitudes of signals, nor peculiarities of instruments, could have influenced the result, all engaged must at once have submitted to the simple truth as developed by the simplest possible experiment. That men should cling to complication, and prefer it to simplicity of action, is difficult to understand, except on the principle, as it was said of old, "Some love darkness better than light." It is certain that many are ever ready to contend almost to death for their mere opinions, who have little or no regard for actual truth, however important in its bearings or sacred in its character.

These same gentlemen tried another experiment, from which they, quite as prematurely and illogically as before, drew the conclusion that the water was convex, and not horizontal.

A 16-inch Troughton level, accurately adjusted, was placed in the same position and height above the water as the large achromatic telescope employed in the last experiment," when the signal-pole, three miles, and the signal-flag on the bridge, six miles, away, were seen as shown in the following diagram, fig. 95.

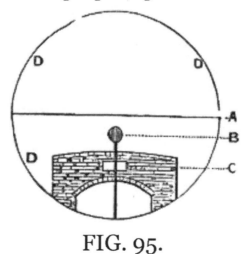

FIG. 95.

A is the cross-hair, B the signal-disc, and C the signal-flag on the Old Bedford Bridge. The telescope, D, D, D, carrying the cross-hair A, is on the bridge at Welney, three miles obverse from B and six from C.

From the above observations, two of the experimenters at once concluded that the cross-hair in the line of sight was a tangent, and the water convex--the appearance of B, and C, resulting from the declination of the surface of the canal. It has been shown already that the best constructed levelling instruments necessarily produce, from the nature and arrangement of the lenses, a refraction or divergence of 1-1000th of a foot in a distance of 10 chains or 660 feet, so that the well-known and admitted refraction inseparable from the instruments employed, is fully sufficient to explain the position of the disc at B, and the flag at C, without demanding that the theory of the earth's rotundity is thereby corroborated. It is the duty of surveyors, and all who have an interest in this subject, to carefully study these peculiarities of levelling instruments, and not only to make themselves thoroughly acquainted with them, but to acknowledge their influence in every one of their operations. Should anyone have the slightest doubt of the effect of lenses in causing divergence of the line of sight, let him simply provide two instruments of precisely the same construction, except that one shall have the lenses taken out. It will then be seen that the instrument with lenses will not read, upon a graduated staff, the same point as that without them. The latter will give the true reading; and the difference between this and the reading of the instrument with lenses, is the amount for which allowance must be made, otherwise the results, however extensive and important, must be fallacious.[127]

In connection with this part of the subject, it will be useful to explain what is the cause of the apparent rise of a plane or horizontal surface towards the axis of the eye. In the following diagram, fig. 96:---

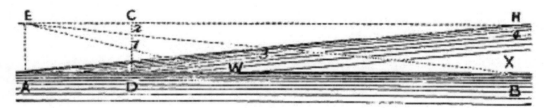

FIG. 96.

Let A, B, represent a plane surface--say several miles over the sea, from the shore, and E, an observer's eye. It is evident that on looking directly downwards, as from E to A, the real and the apparent position of the water-surface will be the same. But if a transparent screen or a plate of glass be erected at some distance from the eye, as at C, D, and the sight be directed over the water to the distance W, the line of sight will cut the screen C, D, at the point 1, and the surface of the water will appear at 3, equal to the altitude of 1.

---

127 The origin and consequences, pecuniary, legal, &c., of the two last-named experiments, may be known by reading several pamphlets written respectively by Mr. Hampden, Mr. Carpenter, and the author of this work, and the reports and subsequent correspondence in "The Field" newspaper.

If the sight is now directed to the point X, the line of sight, E, X, will cut the screen C, D, at the point 2, and the surface of the water will appear to be elevated to the point 4. It is evident, then, that the line of sight may be directed further and further over the water beyond X, and each further line of sight would cut the screen nearer to the line E, C, H, but could never become perfectly parallel with it. In the same way the surface of the water would appear nearer and nearer to the line E, H, at H, but could never come in actual contact with it: the angle H, E, X, becomes more and more acute as the distance increases; but, mathematically, the lines E, X, E, H, might be prolonged ad infinitum, the angle C, E, 2, infinitely acute, and the space H, 4, between the surface of the wafer and the line E, H, immeasurably small, but actual contact is mathematically impossible. Although there is always, at great distances, a minute space between the line of sight and the surface of the water at the horizon, still, for all practical purposes, and to the naked eye, there is no dip required.

The above remarks are made considering the water to be still, as if it were frozen; but as the water of the sea is always in a state of undulation, it is evident that a line of sight passing over a sea horizon cannot possibly continue mathematically parallel to the plane of the water, but must have a minute inclination upwards in the direction of the zenith. Hence it is that often, when the sun is setting over a stormy or heavily swelling sea, the phenomenon of sunset begins at a point on the horizon sensibly less than 90° from the zenith. The same phenomenon may be observed at sunrise, from any eminence over the sea in an easterly direction, as from the summit of the Hill of Howth, and the rock called "Ireland's Eye," near Dublin, looking to the east over Liverpool Bay, in the direction of the coast of Lancashire. This is illustrated by diagram 97:----

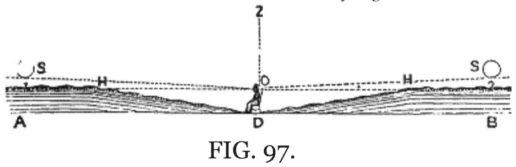

FIG. 97.

A, D, B, represents the horizontal surface of the sea, and D 1, and D 2, the optical or apparent ascent of the water towards the eye-lines O 1, and O 2; O, D, the observer; Z, the zenith; H, H, the horizon; and S, S, the morning and evening sun. It is obvious from this diagram that if the water had a fixed character, as when frozen, the angle Z, O 1, or Z, O 2, would be one of 90 °; but on account of the waves and breakers at the horizon H, H, mounting half their altitudes above the lines O 1, and O 2, the line of sight meets the sun at S, which appears to rise or set on the elevated horizon H, the angle Z, O, S, being less than 90°.

This is evidently the cause of the sun setting and rising at sea, later when the water is calm, and earlier when it is greatly disturbed--a fact well known to observant sea-going travellers and residents on eastern or western shores. It is also the cause of the sun rising later and setting earlier than it would over a smooth plane of earth, or over absolutely still water, or than it ought to do mathematically for its known altitude.

STATIONS AND DISTANCES

"The most complete proof that the earth is a globe consists in the fact that travellers over its surface, whether by sea or land, always find the distance between different stations, exactly such as agree with the calculated distances."[128]

The above sentence is such a compound of childish fable, and either unwarrantable assurance or ignorance, that, were it not that the author is an ardent and extensive, but not a careful or over-scrupulous writer, in defence of the Newtonian astronomy, it would really be unworthy of criticism. It is one of those utterances which indicate a desperate determination to support a cause at all hazards, and without regard to any evidence but such as agrees with a foregone conclusion. So great is the number of those who advocate the earth's rotundity, who do not hesitate to show the same spirit, that it is really a difficult thing to feel that respect for them which persons who merely differ in opinion ought at all times to show and feel towards each other. What can be more misleading, or illogical, or even more the reverse of fact, than to say that "travellers always find the distance between different stations exactly such as agree with the calculated distances, and therefore the earth is a globe?" A mariner at sea, coming in contact with new land, immediately ascertains the latitude by taking the sun's altitude at noon, and the longitude by the local meridian time in relation to the meridian time at Greenwich. Neither the altitude of the sun, nor the time by chronometer, has any logical connection with the shape of the earth. It is true, elements connected with the supposition of the earth's rotundity may be mixed up with the mode of finding latitude and fixing longitude; and anyone may afterwards readily find the places again, by sailing until the sun's altitude and the time by chronometer are the same as those first published, when, of course, they must have arrived at the same position, whether the earth is a globe or a plane. It is altogether wrong to say that places, either on land or sea, are found by calculation, except that when places have already been found, and their latitudes and longitudes given, calculation--which is merely the use of formulæ resulting from previous observation--may be used to find them again. But, primarily and essentially, places are found by observation, and not by calculation. If anyone will read the reports of the leading circumnavigators, and travellers of different countries, they will find many instances where calculation has failed to agree with observations, and where renewed observations have had to be made before anything like the proper position of places in the maps could be fixed. In the majority of instances, where calculation, even when mixed up with some amount of observation, has been relied on, errors have been found.

---

128 "Lessons in Elementary Astronomy;" R. A. Proctor, B.A., F.R.A.S., 1871.

"Assistant surveyor F. Gregory, and Mr. S. Trigg, in a short exploration trip to the eastward of the Geraldine Mine, had succeeded in discovering a large tract of good country, well grassed. . . . Mr. Gregory, in hip report, notes a 'difference of 17 miles in latitude, and something more in longitude, throughout the eastern portion.' between himself and Mr. Austin--a difference for which he cannot account.[129]

"This promontory (North Cape, Prince Edward's Island) we found by good observation to be in latitude 46 ° 53´ S., and longitude 37° 33´ E., agreeing very nearly with Cook in the latitude, but differing considerably in the longitude."[130]

"By noon (March 9, 1840) we were in latitude 64° 20´ S., and longitude 164 ° 20´ E., and therefore about 70 miles north of the land laid down by Lieutenant Wilkes, and not far from the spot from which he must have supposed he saw it; but having now searched for it at a distance varying from 50 to 70 miles from it, to the north, south, east, and west, as well as having sailed directly over its assigned position, we were compelled to infer that it has no real existence."[131]

Either Lieutenant Wilkes or Captain Ross had made a great mistake; or, perhaps the land had disappeared?

In a "Memorandum by Admiral Krusenstern," of the Russian Navy, appended to Lieutenant Wilkes' narrative, several discrepancies respecting true positions are given, and advises that, in addition to the ordinary modes, "absolutely astronomical observations" should be taken. He concludes by saying: "With respect to the coast of South America, Talcahuana, the longitude of which was determined by Captain Beechy to be in 72° 56´59″ W., seems to me a well-determined point. Captain Duperrey is not of that opinion; and it remains to be settled whether the longitude of Talcahuana, or Valparaiso, in 71° 33´ 34″ W., deserves the preference." Here is one of many instances where, in a well-frequented place, a difference exists among nautical calculators, as to its exact position, of 1° 23´ 25″, or (supposing the earth a globe) fully 70 statute miles.

GREAT CIRCLE SAILING

Among landsmen a great amount of misconception prevails as to what is really meant by the so-called "great circle sailing;" and notwithstanding that the subject is very imperfectly understood, the "project" or hypothesis--for it is nothing more--is often very earnestly advanced as an additional proof of the earth's rotundity. But, like all the other "proofs" which have been given, there is no necessary connection between the facts adduced and the theory sought to be proved. Although professional mariners are

---

129 "Australian and New Zealand Gazette" for 1857.
130 "South Sea Voyages," by Captain Ross; vol. i., p. 47.
131 Ibid., p. 285.

familiar with several modes of navigation-- "parallel sailing," "plane sailing," "traverse sailing," "current sailing," "middle latitude sailing," "Mercator sailing," and "great circle sailing," the "Mercator" and "great circle" methods are now the favourites. Nearly all the above systems necessitated the sailing by, or in relation to, Rhumb-lines, or lines at right angles to the meridian lines; and whether the earth is a plane or a globe, these are not geometrically at right angles to lines of latitude, except at the equator. Hence Mercator's projection, on account of its lines of latitude and longitude being square to each other, has been almost universally employed. But previous to the general adoption of Mercator's plan, many leading navigators saw that Rhumb- line sailing upon a globe was practically a series of small circles, and conceived of a method very similar to that which is now called the "great circle" system. As early as 1495 Sebastian Cabot suggested the adoption of this method. It was also advocated in 1537 by Numez, and in 1561, and subsequently by Cortez, Zamarano, and others. After lying dormant for a long time, the system was revived by Mr. Towson, of Devonport, who read a paper before the Society of Arts, in May, 1850, and afterwards presented his "tables to facilitate the practice of great circle sailing," to the Lords Commissioners of the Admiralty, who "ordered them to be printed for the use of all mariners."

Many persons suppose that the words "great circle sailing" simply mean that the mariner, instead of sailing in a direct line from one place to another, on the same latitude, takes a circuitous path to the south or north of this direct line, where the degrees of longitude being smaller, the distance passed over, although apparently greater, is actually *less*. It is then falsely argued that as "the greatest distance round is the nearest path," the degrees of longitude *must* be smaller, and therefore the earth *must* be a globe. This is another instance of the self-deception practised by many of the advocates of rotundity. It is really painful to reflect upon the manner in which a merely fanciful hypothesis has reduced its advocates to mental prostitution. The poor dawdling creature, who vaguely wanders in search of anything or everything which will satisfy her longings, is only a type of the philosophical wanderer who seeks for, and pounces upon, whatever will prove, or only seem to prove, his one idea--his uncontrolled and often uncontrollable longing for something to confirm his notions, and satisfy his desire to be wise and great. The motive which actuates the greater number of modern philosophers, cannot be less or other than the love of distinction. If it were a love of truth and of human progress and welfare they would scrupulously examine the premises on which their theories are founded. But this the advocates of the earth's rotundity and motion have seldom or never done. There is no single instance recorded where even the necessity for doing so is admitted. Hence it is that whilst to question the groundwork is forbidden, they abruptly seize upon everything which gives colour to their assumptions, although in many cases neither pertinent nor logically consistent. In the case before us the contraction or convergence of the degrees of longitude beyond the equator is unproved; and again if they were convergent there could not be a single inch of gain in taking a so-called great circle course between any two places east and west of each other. Let the following experiment be tried in proof of this statement. On an artificial globe mark out a great circle path, between say Cape Town and Sydney, or Valparaiso and Cape Town. Take a strip of sheet lead, and bend it to the form of this path; and after making it straight measure its length as compared with the parallel of latitude between the places. The result will fully satisfy the experimenter that *this* view of great circle sailing is contrary to known geometrical principles. Strictly speaking, it is not "great circle sailing" at all which Mr. Towson and the Lords of the Admiralty have recommended. The words *great circle* are only used in comparison with the *small circles* which are described in sailing upon a Rhumb-line track.

> "The fundamental principle of this method is that axiom of spherical geometry, that the shortest distance between any two points on the surface of a sphere lies on the line of a great circle; or, in other words, of a circle passing through the centre of a sphere. But maps and charts, being *flat* representations of the surface of a *globe*, are of necessity distorted, and are only correct near the equator, the distortion increasing as the poles are approached; and hence it follows that the course which on the *globe* is the *shortest*, is on the chart made to appear very much the longest, and the reverse. This was clearly shown to be the case by the comparison on a chart and on a globe of the course between Van Dieman's Land and Voldivia, on the western coast of South America: the course, which by the chart appeared to be a straight line, when laid down upon the. globe was found to be very circuitous, whilst the line of a great circle, cutting the two points, appeared on the chart as a loop of great length."[132]

> "Mercator and parallel sailing conduct the ship by a *circuitous route* when compared with the track of a *great circle*."[133]

In nautical language Rhumb-line sailing, which was almost universally practised before the recent introduction of great circle sailing, consists in following parallels at right angles to the meridian lines, and as these meridian lines are supposed to be convergent, it is evident that the course of a ship so navigated is not the most direct; a great circle path is one at angles less than 90° north and south of the meridian. If the reader will draw a series of Rhumb-lines on a map of "the globe," he will at once see that the course is circuitous. But if he draws lines at a slight angle north in the northern, and south in the southern region, to the above- named Rhumb-lines, he will readily notice that the ship's course is more direct, and therefore the mariner adopting the so-called "great circle" method, must of necessity save both time and distance, *but only in comparison* with the *Rhumb-line* path. It is not absolutely the shortest route; as the earth is a plane, the degrees of longitude in the south must diverge or expand, and spread out as the

---

132 "From "A Paper on the Principles of Great Circle Sailing," by Mr. J. T. Towson, of Devonport, in the "Journal of the Society of Arts," for May, 1850.

133 "Treatise on Navigation," p. 50. By. J. Greenwood, Esq., of Jesus College, Cambridge. Weale, 59, High Holborn, London.

latitude increases; and the parallels or lines of latitude must be circles concentric with the northern centre. Hence there is in reality a still shorter path than either the Rhumb-line or the great circle course.

This will at once be evident on trying the following simple experiment. Place a light, to represent the sun, at an elevation of say two feet on the centre of a round table. Draw lines from the centre to the circumference to represent meridian lines. Mark any two places to represent Cape Town and Melbourne; now take any small object to represent a ship sailing from one of these places to the other, and, on moving it forward, keeping the light *at the same altitude* all the way the line of latitude or path of the ship will be seen to be an arc of a circle, which practically is a great circle route, whilst the Rhumb-line and greater route would be represented by a series of tangents to the meridian lines between the two places. The nearest route geometrically possible is the chord or straight line joining the ends of the arc which forms the line of latitude. Let this line or chord be drawn, and all argument will be superfluous, the proposition will be immediately self-evident.

Thus we have seen that great circle sailing is not the shortest route possible, but merely shorter than several other routes, which have been theoretically suggested and adopted; and to affirm that the results are confirmatory or demonstrative of the earth's rotundity, is in the highest degree illogical.

MOTION OF STARS NORTH AND SOUTH

It has often been urged that the earth must be a globe, because the stars in the southern "hemisphere" move round a south polar star; in the same way that those of the north revolve round "Polaris," or the northern pole star. This is another instance of the sacrifice of truth, and denial of the evidence of our senses for the purpose of supporting a theory which is in every sense false and unnatural. It is known to every observer that the north pole star is the centre of a number of constellations which move over the earth in a circular direction. Those nearest to it, as the "Great Bear," &c., &c., are always visible in England during their whole twenty- four hours' revolution. Those further away southwards rise north-north- east, and set south-south-west; still further south they rise east by north, and set west by north. The farthest south visible from England, the rising is more to the east and south-east, and the setting to the west and south- west. But *all* the stars visible from London rise and set in a way which is not compatible with the doctrine of rotundity. For in-stance, if we stand with our backs to the north, on the high land known as "Arthur's Seat," near Edinburgh, and note the stars in the zenith of our position, and watch for several hours, the zenith stars will gradually recede to the *north-west*. If we do the same on Woodhouse Moor, near Leeds, or on any of the mountain tops in Yorkshire or Derbyshire, the same phenomenon is observed. The same thing may be seen from the top of Primrose Hill, near Regent's Park, London; from Hampstead

Heath; or Shooter's Hill, near Woolwich. If we remain all night, we shall observe the same stars rising towards our position from the north-east, showing that the path of all the stars between ourselves and the northern centre move round the north pole-star as a common centre of rotation; just as they *must* do over a plane such as the earth is proved to be. It is undeniable that upon a globe zenith stars would rise, pass over head, and set in the plane of the observer's position. If now we carefully watch in the same way the zenith stars from the Rock of Gibraltar, the very same phenomenon is observed. The same is also the case from Cape of Good Hope, Sydney and Melbourne in Australia, in New Zealand, in Rio Janeiro, Monte Video, Valparaiso, and other places in the south. If then the zenith stars of all the places on the earth, where special observations have been made, rise from the morning horizon to the zenith of an observer, and descend to the evening horizon, *not in a plane of the position of such observer, but in an arc of a circle concentric with the northern centre*, the earth is thereby proved to be a plane, and rotundity altogether disproved--shown, indeed, to be impossible.

Here, however, we are met with the positive assertion that there is a very small star (of about the sixth magnitude) in the south, called *Sigma Octantis*, round which all the constellations of the south revolve, and which is therefore the southern polar star. It is scarcely polite to contradict the statements made, but it is certain that persons who have been educated to believe that the earth is a globe, going to the southern parts of the earth do not examine such matters critically. They see the stars move from towards the east towards the west, and they are satisfied. But they have not instituted special experiments, regardless of results, to ascertain the real and absolute movements of the southern constellations. Another thing is certain, that from and within the equator the north pole star, and the constellations *Ursa Major, Ursa Minor*, and many others, can be seen from every meridian simultaneously; whereas in the south, from the equator, neither the so-called south pole star, nor the remarkable constellation of the Southern Cross, can be seen simultaneously from every meridian, showing that all the constellations of the south--pole star included--sweep over a great southern arc and across the meridian, from their rise in the evening to their setting in the morning. But if the earth is a globe, Sigma Octantis a south pole star, and the Southern Cross a southern circumpolar constellation, they would all be visible at the same time from every longitude on the same latitude, as is the case with the northern pole star and the northern circumpolar constellations. Such, however, is strangely not the case; Sir James Clarke Ross did not see it until he was 8° south of the equator, and in longitude 30° W.[134]

MM. Von Spix and Karl Von Martius, in their account of -their scientific travels in Brazil, in 1817-1820, relate that "on the 15th of June, in latitude 14° S, we beheld, for the first time, that glorious constellation of the southern heavens, the Cross, which is to navigators a token of peace, and, according to its position, indicates the hours of the night. We had long wished for this constellation as a guide to the

---

other hemisphere; we therefore felt inexpressible pleasure when we perceived it in the resplendent firmament."

The great traveller Humboldt says:--

"We saw distinctly, for the first time, the cross of the south, on the nights of the 4th and 5th of July, in the 16th degree of latitude. It was strongly inclined, and appeared from time to time between the clouds. . . . The pleasure felt on discovering the Southern Cross was warmly shared in by such of the crew as had lived in the colonies."

If the Southern Cross is a circumpolar cluster of stars, it is a matter of absolute certainty that it could never be in-visible to navigators upon or south of the equator. It would always be seen far above the horizon, just as the "Great Bear" is at all times visible upon and north of the equator. More especially ought it to be at all times visible when the nearest star belonging to it is considerably nearer to the so-called "pole star of the south" than is the nearest of the stars in the "Great Bear" to the pole star of the north. Humboldt did not see the Southern Cross until he was in the 16th latitude south, and then it was "strongly inclined," showing that it was rising in the east, and sharing in the general sweep of the stars from east to west, in common with the whole firmament of stars moving round the pole star of the northern region.

We have seen that wherever the motions of the stars are carefully examined, it is found that all are connected, and move in relation to the northern centre of the earth. There is nowhere to be found a "break" in the general connection. Except, indeed, what is called the "proper motion" of certain stars and groups of stars all move in the same general direction, concentric with the north pole, and with velocities increasing with radial distance from it. To remove every possible doubt respecting the motions of the stars from the central north to the most extreme south, a number of special observers, each completely free from the bias of education respecting the supposed rotundity of the earth, might be placed in various southern localities, to observe and record the motions of the well known southern constellation, not in relation to a *supposed* south pole star, but to the meridian and latitude of each position. This would satisfy a certain number of those who cannot divest themselves of the idea of rotundity, but is not at all necessary for the satisfaction of those who are convinced that the earth is a plane, and that the extreme south is a vast circumference instead of a polar centre. To these the evidence already adduced will be sufficiently demonstrative.

The points of certainty are the following:--

- 1st.--Wherever the experiment is made the stars in the zenith do not rise, culminate, and set in the same straight line, or plane of latitude, as they would if the earth is a globe.

- 2nd.--The Southern Cross is not at all times visible from every point of the southern hemisphere, as the "Great Bear" is from every point in the northern, and as both must necessarily and equally be visible if the earth is globular. In reference to the several cases adduced of the Southern Cross not being visible until the observers had arrived in latitudes 8°, 14°, and 16° south, it cannot be said that they might not have cared to look for it, because we are assured that they "had long wished for it," and therefore must have been strictly on the look out as they advanced southwards. And when the traveller Humboldt saw it "the first time" it was "strongly inclined," and therefore low down on the eastern horizon, and therefore previously invisible, simply because it had not yet risen.

- 3rd.--The earth is a plane, with a northern centre, over which the stars (whether fixed in some peculiar substance or floating in some subtle medium is not yet known) move in concentric courses at different radial distances from the northern centre as far south as and wherever observations have been made. The evidence is the author's own experiments in Great Britain, Ireland, Isle of Man, Isle of Wight, and many other places; the statements of several unbiased and truthful friends, who have resided in New Zealand, Australia, South Africa, Rio Janeiro, Valparaiso, and other southern localities, and the several incidental statements already quoted.

- 4th--The southern region of the earth is not central, but circumferential; and therefore there is no southern pole, no south pole star, and no southern circumpolar constellations; all statements to the contrary are doubtful, inconsistent with known facts, and therefore not admissible as evidence.

CONTINUED DAYLIGHT IN THE EXTREME SOUTH

IF the earth is a revolving globe, moving rapidly in an orbit round the sun, with its axes of revolution inclined to the plane of the ecliptic, as the Newtonian hypothesis affirms, there may be six months' continued light alternating with six months' continued darkness, at both the northern and southern axial or central points. That such is the case in the northern centre is matter of certainty, but that it is so in the south there is no positive evidence. A few irregular statements have been found in the reports of mariners who have endeavoured to circumnavigate the "antarctic circle," which have been seized upon as proofs, but on careful examination they are found to be neither worthy as evidence nor pertinent to the subject in dispute. In the appendix to the narrative of Commander Wilkes, of the United States Navy, the following words occur:

"My time for six weeks was passed on deck, and having all daylight, I of course had constant employment," &c., &c.

The above sentence has been taken as meaning that Captain Wilkes had six weeks uninterrupted daylight; and the words will fairly bear such an interpretation. But the various statements in the body of his narrative show that this was not his meaning, for such was not the case. His ships left Sydney in December, and returned about the end of February. But he only reached latitude 61° S. on the 10th of January, and on February 19th he had returned to latitude 63° S. on his way home, so that he was barely six weeks in the neighbourhood of the "antarctic circle." On the 11th of January he had reached the latitude 64° 11′ 0″ S., when he reports as follows:

> "January 11th, at 101 p.m., we hove to until daylight. The night was beautiful, and everything seemed sunk in sleep. We lay to until 4 o'clock. As it grew light on the 12th a fog set in," &c., &c.

Again, on January 16th, when he had reached latitude 65° 8′ 0″ S., longitude 157° 46′ 0″ E., he says

> "The sun set at a few minutes before 10 o'clock. This night we were beating, with frequent tacks, in order to gain as much southing as possible. Previous to its becoming daylight the fog rendered everything obscure."

> "January 22nd, the effect of sunrise, at a little after 2 a.m., on the 23rd, was glorious."

> "On the morning of the 30th, latitude 63° 30′ 0″ S., the sun rose in great brilliancy."

> "January 28th, latitude 64° 46′ 1″ S., sun set red and fiery."

> "February 2nd, latitude 66° 12′ 0″ S., this evening it was perceptible that the days were becoming shorter, which was a new source of anxiety, for we were often surrounded by numerous ice islands, which the darkness rendered more dangerous."

> "February 6th, latitude 64° 6′ 0″ S., wishing to examine the land closely, I hove to for broad daylight."

> "February 7th, latitude 64° 49′ 0″ S., at 6 p.m., we suddenly found a barrier trending to the southward. I now hauled off until daylight, in order to ascertain the trending of the land more exactly."

> "On the 8th, latitude 65° 3′ 0″ S., at daylight, we again made sail to the southward; at 8 p.m. we were again brought to. The night was dark and unpleasant."

> "February 11th, at 10 p.m., I found it too dark to run, and hove to."

"February 12th, latitude 64° 57′ 0″ S., at 2 a.m. filled away. At 8 p.m. the barrier was within three miles of us; shortly after I hove to for the purpose of awaiting the daylight to continue our observations of the land."

"February 14th, at daylight, we again made sail for the land."

Captain Sir J. C. Ross, in his "South Sea Voyages," p. 252, vol. 1, say

"February 21st, in latitude 71° S., longitude 171 E., as the night was getting very dark, at 9 p.m. we hauled off until day-light appeared."

The above quotations from the narrative show that of the six weeks, from January 10th to February 19th, there was night on the 11th, the 16th, the 22nd, and the 30th of January; on the 2nd, 6th, 7th, 8th, 11th, 12th, and on the 14th of February; so that there can be no possible doubt at! to the meaning of the words in the appendix, that "his time for six weeks was passed on deck, with all daylight." If he meant otherwise than that in the *day time* he had generally good daylight as contra-distinguished from the bad and gloomy weather which so generally prevails in high southern latitudes, we might just as fairly conclude that when he says he "had constant employment for six weeks," he meant that he never slept, but was continually awake, and on active duty for the whole of that period. If any one should still cling to the meaning that he had six weeks' uninterrupted daylight, he will be placed under the disagreeable alternative of admitting that the language of the formal reports given in the narrative is contradicted by that of the appendix; and that Captain Wilkes has, in his study, when writing his work, completely falsified the logs kept during active service.

Bearing on the same subject, several expressions have been quoted from Sir James Clarke Ross' "South Sea Voyages." At page 175, vol. 1, the following words occur:--

"In latitude 65° 22′ 0″ S., longitude 172° 42′ 0″ E., on the 4th of January, at 9 p.m., the sun's altitude was 4°. The setting sun was a very remarkable object, being streaked across by five dark horizontal bands of nearly equal breadth, and was flattened into a most irregular form by the greater refraction of its lower limb, as it touched the horizon at 11° 56′ 51″. Skimming along to the eastward, it almost imperceptibly descended, until its upper limb disappeared exactly 17 minutes and 30 seconds afterwards. . . . The difference in the horizontal and vertical diameter was found by several measurements to amount to only 5′ 21″, the horizontal being 32′ 31″, and the vertical diameter 27′ 10″, that given in the Nautical Almanack being 32′ 34.′″"

Again, at p. 207, vol. 1, it is said:

> "In latitude 74° S., longitude 171° E., on January 22nd, 1841, it was the most beautiful night we had seen in these latitudes. The sky was perfectly clear and serene. At midnight (12 o'clock) when the sun was skimming along the southern horizon, at an altitude of about 2°, the sky over head was remarked to be of a most intense indigo blue, becoming paler in proportion to the distance from the zenith."

In the previous sections of this work the arguments almost universally adduced in favour of rotundity have been clearly enunciated and thoroughly refuted. The unambiguous wording of the evidence in its support has been met by direct and unmistakeable contradiction; but in the above language of Sir James Clarke Ross there is uncertainty of meaning; inconsistency with known collateral phenomena; and, therefore, difficulty in its examination and criticism. If it is true that the earth is a globe revolving on axes inclined 23° to the plane of the ecliptic, it is equally true that all the phenomena described in the above quotations from Captain Ross could, in consequence, occur. And as theorists of every class have confessedly constructed their theories for the express purpose of giving an explanation of phenomena--whether absolutely true or only seemingly true being no question with them--it must be admitted that in the above-named description of appearances in the south they have evidence in their favour--such, at all events, as they ever care to obtain. The Zetetic process which has been adopted throughout this work forbids, however, that, because an assumption of the earth's rotundity and diurnal motion seems to explain certain phenomena, therefore, the assumption becomes, and must be admitted to be, a fact. This is intolerable, even in an abstract sense, but in practice must be unconditionally repudiated. By separate, independent, and absolute evidence, no item of which has been fairly challenged, the earth has been proved to be a plane, without rotary or progressive motion of any kind, and therefore the phenomena observed and described by Captain Ross must be examined with a view to their explanation, not in corroboration of any theory, but in connection with the *demonstrated fact* that the earth is a stationary plane. The first case admits of no difficulty. At 9 o'clock in the evening the sun was 4° above the western horizon; at a few minutes before 12 its lower limb touched the horizon, and in a quarter of an hour after 12 its upper limb disappeared. How long it remained below the horizon, or at what hour it rose again, is not stated. Lieutenant Wilkes, when in the same latitude, and about a week's later date, says:--

> "At 10½ p.m. we hove to until daylight. We lay to until 4 o'clock; as it grew light on the next morning a fog set in."

Three or four days afterwards he says:--"The sun set at a few minutes before 10 o'clock."

From the above quotations we gather that "the sun sets at a few minutes before 10 o'clock," and rises about 4 in the morning. But Captain Ross declares that the sun did not entirely set or disappear until 14 minutes past 12 o'clock. It is evident that the sun in this instance remained above the horizon fully two hours longer than it did to Lieutenant Wilkes a few days later, in consequence of *unusual refraction*. This is corroborated by Captain Ross, who, in the same paragraph, remarks that "the setting sun was a very remarkable object, being flattened into a most irregular form by the *great refraction* of its lower limb*." It is not stated whether the sun was seen in the northern or southern horizon, but as the earth is a plane, and the sun's path is concentric with the northern centre, it is certain that it must have been "skimming along to the eastward" *beyond* or on the *other side* of the northern centre. This will be rendered clear by the following diagram, fig. 98.

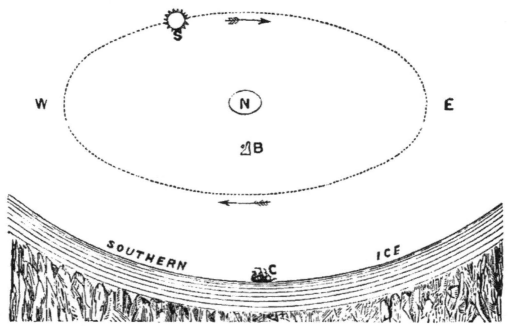

FIG. 98.

Let N represent the northern centre, S the sun moving in the path S, E, W; B the position of Great Britain, and C, the relative position of Captain Ross and Lieutenant Wilkes, at the time the above-named observations were made. The sun rising at E the east, would, during the day, move from east to west (from E to W). But during the night it would be seen, by the operation of great refraction, "skimming along to the eastward," or from W to S and E.

This phenomenon was seen by Captain Ross but not by Lieutenant Wilkes, who reports that the sun set a little before 10 and rose about 4 o'clock. Captain James Weddle was in latitude 74° 15′ 0″ S., on February 20th, 1822, and he expressly states that "the sun was

279

beneath the horizon for more than six hours."[135] Hence we conclude that the sun being visible all the night through was only an occasional phenomenon, arising from unusual refraction. So far the whole matter is clear and easily understood; but in the second case, given by Captain Ross, a word is used which renders the meaning uncertain, and creates a difficulty; that word is "southern." "At midnight, in latitude 74° S., the sun was skimming along the *southern* horizon at an altitude of about 2°." Here, then, is evident confusion. First, it *could not be the southern horizon*, unless the earth is a globe; that *it is not a globe* has been more than sufficiently proved. Secondly, it could not be the *southern horizon*, because when in latitude 65° S., the sun's lower limb, at midnight, touched the horizon, and now being in latitude 74° S., the altitude was only 2°; whereas being 9° of latitude nearer to it, the altitude could not have been less than 11°. Everything is clearly explained except the one word "southern." We must, therefore, look to the absolute meaning of this word, and to its probable perversion or peculiar local application. *Absolutely* the word "south" means the directly reverse of north. *Relatively* it means the direction parallel to the southern extremity of the needle, which, on the compass card, is that end without the fleur-de-lis; and, of course, unless the true south could be determined by known data, the compass would be the mariner's guide. Now we find that the variation of the compass becomes so great in high southern latitudes, that it would not be relied on to determine the position of the sun. The mariner, having been educated to believe the earth to be a globe, with its poles alternately illuminated, could not do other-wise than pronounce the sun, when visible at midnight, to be in the south, whereas in reality it was skimming along from west to east, or from left to right, in that part of the southern region which was on the opposite side to his own position, or beyond the "north pole," across which he was looking. In such a position the light would have to pass through the cold and dense atmosphere of the north, and the heated and rarefied air of the equator, and thus, on certain conditions and in certain directions, unusual refraction would occur, by which the sun would sometimes, but not always, be visible.

We have seen that such was the case, for Captain Ross saw, more than once, what only a few days afterwards was not seen by Lieutenant Wilkes, and which is not mentioned by other antarctic navigators as a constant phenomenon. Clearly, then, there was unusual refraction ("great refraction," as Captain Ross admits, which caused a difference in the horizontal and vertical diameters of the sun of more than five minutes of a degree), which lifted the sun many degrees above its true position, giving an apparent altitude which rendered it visible across the northern centre to the observers on the opposite side of the great southern belt or circumference. This is what *must* of *necessity* have been the case if the earth is a plane; and until this can be experimentally disproved, it is equally a matter of necessity to conclude that Captain Ross made use of the words "southern horizon" simply because in his astronomically educated judgment it could not be otherwise. Had he had the slightest doubt as to the earth's rotundity, and therefore as to the true bearing of the sun at midnight, he would have been able to decide it by a

---

135 "Voyage towards the South Pole," p. 39.

very simple experiment; it is evident that in the daytime the sun would move across the firmament from his right hand to his left, and, keeping himself in the same position, he would see it in the night moving from his left to his right. *This was really the case.* Had the sun been really on the "southern horizon," Captain Ross would have had to turn his face in the opposite direction to that in which he saw the sun at mid- day, and hence the sun's motion would have been from right to left. This simple procedure would have decided the matter. It may be asked how could he have ascertained, in the midst of a waste of waters, that his noon-day position was maintained until midnight? The answer is, that although the variations of the compass rendered it difficult to decide by its means the true bearings of the ship, still the variations would be the same day and night when in the same latitude and longitude. Hence, the direction in relation to the compass of the "look out" during the day could have been maintained by the same relation during the night. It is probable, and much to be desired, that during some future antarctic voyage the above-named means may be taken to place this question beyond dispute. To those, however, who are convinced by experimental demonstration that the earth is a plane, there is no further proof required.

ANALOGY IN FAVOUR OF ROTUNDITY

To those who are not strictly logical, a favourite "argument," in support of the earth's globular form, is "that as all the heavenly bodies are worlds, and visibly round, may, not the earth be so necessarily, seeing that it is one of the same category?"

This is only seemingly plausible. In reality it is a piece of self-deception. It must be proved that the stars are worlds; and to do this, or to make it even possible that they are so, it must be proved that they are millions of miles distant from the earth, and from each other, and are hundreds or thousands of miles in diameter. By plane trigonometry, in special connection with carefully *measured* base lines, it has been *demonstrated--* placed beyond all power of doubt--that the sun, moon, stars, comets, and meteors of every kind, are all within a distance of a few thousand miles from the sea-level of the earth; that therefore they are very small objects, therefore not worlds, and therefore, from analogy, offer no logical reason or pretext for concluding that this world is globular.

LUNAR ECLIPSE A PROOF OF ROTUNDITY

Although the subject of lunar eclipses has already been discussed, it is again briefly noticed because it forms one of the category of supposed evidences of the earth's rotundity. Those who hold that the earth is a globe will often affirm, with marked enthusiasm, that in an eclipse of the moon there is "proof positive" of rotundity. "Is not the shadow of the earth, on the moon, always round?" "Could anything but a globe cast a shadow which at all times, and in all positions, is visibly circular?" "Would not a plane sometimes cast a shadow edgewise, which, on the moon, would appear as a bar or straight line across it?" Notwithstanding the plausibility of these questions, the essential requirements of an argument are wanting. That the eclipsor of the moon is a shadow at all is assumption--no proof whatever is offered. That the moon receives her light from the sun, and that therefore her surface is darkened by the earth intercepting the sun's light, *is not proved*. It *is not proved* that the earth moves in an orbit round the sun, and therefore, by being in different positions, conjunction of sun, earth, and moon, 'Day sometimes occur. The contrary has been clearly proved--that the moon is *not eclipsed by a shadow*; that she is *self-luminous*, and not merely a reflector of solar light, and therefore could not possibly be obscured or eclipsed by *a shadow* from any object whatever; and that the earth is devoid of motion, either on axes or in an orbit through space. Hence to call that an argument for the earth's rotundity, where every necessary proposition is only assumed, and in relation to which direct and practical evidence to the contrary is abundant, is to stultify the judgment and every other reasoning faculty.

Thus we have seen that in every instance where the attempt is made to *prove* the rotundity of the earth, the premises do not warrant the conclusion, which is premature--drawn before the whole subject is fairly stated and examined, and when other and visible causes are amply sufficient to explain the phenomena, for explanation of which the theory of rotundity was originally framed.

The same charge may be made against the few instances which have been adduced as proofs of the earth's motion. To explain day and night, the earth was *assumed* to revolve once in twenty-four hours. The only *direct proofs* offered are the peculiarities attending the oscillations of a long pendulum, and the tendency of railway carriages to be thrown off the rails when running on lines in a due northerly or southerly direction. In the early part of the year 1851 the scientific journals, and nearly all the news-papers published in Great Britain, and on the continents of Europe and America, were occupied in recording and discussing certain experiments with the pendulum, first made by M. Foucault, of Paris; and the public were startled by the announcement that the results furnished a practical proof of the earth's rotation. The subject was referred to in the *Literary Gazette* in the following words:--

> "Everybody knows what is meant by a pendulum in its simplest form, a weight hanging by a thread to a fixed point. Such was the pendulum experimented upon long ago by Galileo, who discovered the well-known law of isochronous vibrations, applicable to the same. The subject has since received a thorough examination, as well theoretical as practical, from mathematicians and mechanicians; and yet, strange to say, the most remarkable feature of the phenomenon has remained unobserved and wholly unsuspected until within the last few weeks, when a young and promising French physicist, M. Foucault, who was induced, by certain

reflections, to repeat Galileo's experiments in the cellar of his mother's house at Paris, succeeded in establishing the existence of a fact connected with it, which gives an immediate and visible demonstration of the earth's rotation.

Suppose the pendulum already described to be set moving in a *vertical plane from north to south*; the plane in which it vibrates, to ordinary observation, would appear to be stationary. M. Foucault, however, has succeeded in showing that this is not the case, but that the plane is itself slowly moving round the fixed point as a centre, in a direction contrary to the earth's rotation, i.e., with the apparent heavens, from east to west. His experiments have since been repeated in the hall of the observatory, under the superintendence of M. Arago, and fully confirmed. If a pointer be attached to the weight of a pendulum suspended by a long and fine wire, capable of *turning round in all directions,* and nearly in contact with the floor of a room, the line which this pointer appears to trace on the ground, and which may easily be followed by a chalk mark, will be found to be slowly, but visibly, and constantly moving round, like the hand of a watch dial. . . . The subject has created a great sensation in the mathematical and physical circles of Paris.

> "It is proposed to obtain permission from the Government to carry on further observations by means of a pendulum suspended from the dome of the Pantheon, length of suspension being a desideratum, in order to make the result visible on a larger scale, and secure greater constancy and duration in the experiments."

Subsequently experiments were made at the Pantheon, and repeated in almost every part of the civilised world, but with results so variable, and in many instances the very contrary to the anticipations suggested by theory, that many of the same Newtonian school of philosophy differed with each other, remained dissatisfied, and raised very serious objections both to the value of the experiments themselves, and to the supposed proof which they furnished of the earth's rotation. One writer in the *Times* newspaper of the period, who signs himself "B. A. C.," says:--

> "I have read the accounts of the Parisian experiment, as they have appeared in many of our papers, and must confess that I still remain unconvinced of the reality of the phenomenon."

THE SUPPOSED MANIFESTATION OF
THE ROTATION OF THE EARTH

In the Liverpool Mercury of May 23, 1851, the following letter appeared:

"SIR,--The French, English, and European continental journals have given publicity to an experiment made in Paris with a pendulum; which experiment is said to have had the same results when made elsewhere. To the facts set forth no contradiction has been given, and it is therefore to be hoped that they are true. The correctness of the inferences drawn from the facts is another matter. The first position of these theorists is, that in a complete vacuum, beyond the sphere of the earth's atmosphere, a pendulum will continue to oscillate in one and the same original plane. On that supposition their whole theory is founded. In making this supposition the fact is overlooked that there is no vibratory motion unless through atmospheric resistance, or by force opposing impulse. Perpetual progress in rectilinear motion may be imagined, as in the corpuscular theory of light; circular motion may also be found in the planetary systems; and parabolic and hyperbolic motions in those of comets; but vibration is artificial and of limited duration. No body in nature returns the same road it went, unless artificially constrained to do so. The supposition of a permanent vibratory motion, such as is presumed in the theory advanced, is unfounded in fact and absurd in idea; and the whole affair of this proclaimed discovery falls to the ground.

"T."

Another writer declared that he and others had made many experiments, and had discovered that the plane of vibration had nothing whatever to do with the meridian longitude, nor with the earth's motion, but followed the plane of the magnetic meridian.

The *Liverpool Mercury,* of May 17th, 1851, contains the following

"A scientific gentleman in Dundee recently tried the pendulum experiment, and he says 'that the pendulum is capable of showing the earth's motion, I regard as a gross delusion; but that, it tends to the magnetic meridian I have found to be a fact.'"

In many cases the experiments have not shown a change at all in the plane of oscillation of the pendulum; in others the alteration has been in the wrong direction, and very often the rate of variation has been altogether different--too fast or too slow--to that which theory indicated. The following is a case in illustration:--

"On Wednesday evening the Rev. H. H. Jones, F.R.A.S., exhibited the apparatus of Foucault to illustrate the diurnal rotation of the earth, in the Library Hall of the Manchester Athenæum. The preparations were simple. A circle of chalk was drawn in the centre of the floor, immediately under the arched skylight. The circle was exactly 360 inches in its circumference, every inch being intended to represent one degree. According to a calculation Mr. Jones had made, and which he produced to the

Philosophical Society six weeks ago, the plane of oscillation of the pendulum would, at Manchester, diverge about one degree in five minutes, or perhaps a very little less. He therefore drew this circle exactly 360 inches round, and marked the inches on its circumference. The pendulum was hung from the skylight, immediately over the centre of the circle, the point of suspension being 25 feet high. At that length of wire it should require 2½ seconds to make each oscillation across the circle. The brazen ball, which at the end of a fine wire constituted the pendulum, was furnished with a point, to enable the spectator to observe the more easily its course. A long line was drawn through the diameter of the circle, due north and south, and the pendulum started so as to swing exactly along this line; to the westward of which, at intervals of three inches at the circumference, two other lines were drawn, passing through the centre. According to the theory, the pendulum should diverge from its original line towards the west, at the rate of one inch or degree in five minutes. This, however, Mr. Jones explained, was a perfection of accuracy only attainable in a vacuum, and rarely could be approached where the pendulum had to pass through an atmosphere subject to disturbances; besides, it was difficult to avoid giving it some slight lateral bias at starting. In order to obviate this as much as possible, the steel wire was as fine as would bear the weight, 1-30th of an inch thick; and the point of suspension was adjusted with delicate nicety. An iron bolt was screwed into the framework of the skylight, into it a brass nut was inserted; the wire passed through the nut (the hollow sides of which were bell-shaped, in order to give it fair play), and at the top the wire ended in a globular piece, there being also a fine screw to keep it from slipping. . . . The pendulum was gently drawn up to one side, at the southern end of the diametrical line, and attached by a thread to something near. When it hung quite still the thread was burnt asunder, and the pendulum began to oscillate to and fro across the circle; before it had been going on quite seven minutes it had reached nearly the third degree towards the west, whereas it ought to have occupied a quarter of an hour in getting thus far from its starting line, even making no allowance for the resistance of the atmosphere."[136]

Besides the irregularities so often observed in the time and direction of the pendulum vibrations, and which are quite sufficient to render them worthless as evidence of the earth's motion, the use which the Newtonian astronomers made of the general fact that the plane of oscillation is variable, was most unfair and illogical. It is true that the advocates of a globular and revolving world had no single fact or experiment which they could point to as proof of their theory, and "a desire has always been felt that some method could be devised of rendering this rotation palpable to the senses. Even the illustrious Laplace participated in this feeling, and has left it on record; 'although,' he says, 'the rotation of the earth is now established with all the certainty which the physical sciences require, still a *direct proof* of that phenomenon ought to interest both geometricians and astronomers.' No man ever knew the laws of the planetary motions

---

136 "Manchester Examiner," supplement, May 24, 1851.

better than Laplace, and before penning such a sentence it is probable that he had turned the subject in his mind, and without discovering any process by which the object could be attained."[137]

This acknowledged absence of any "direct proof" of the earth's rotation evidently created a premature rejoicing when it was announced from Paris that at length an experiment had been hit upon which would render it "palpable to the senses." A trumpet-tone proclaimed to the scientific world that at length, after centuries of groping speculation, a visible proof of the earth's diurnal motion had been discovered; that what had remained for generations a pure assumption, was now found to be a mechanical fact. It was obtruded and commented upon--never logically discussed, in every journal, both scientific and literary, as well as merely miscellaneous, in almost every part of the world. The pride and exultation of astronomers became almost unbounded, and heedless of restraint. But after a time their clamorous triumph over all who had doubted the truthfulness of the Newtonian system suddenly ceased. The blinding meteor had fallen into the sea and become extinguished. A deceptive theory had allured them into a morass of false and illogical reasoning. They had long before assumed that the earth had diurnal rotation; and now, instead of admitting the simple fact that the pendulum, under certain conditions, did not maintain its original plane of vibration, they again, contrary to every principle of justice and reason, recklessly dared to assume that it was not the pendulum at all, but the earth underneath it which "parted company," and moved away to the west.

The motion of the earth was *first assumed* to exist; and when there still was no visible sign of motion, they again *assumed* that their *first* assumption was right, and affirmed that that which really and visibly moved *could not be moving*, because that which could not be seen or proved to move *must* be in motion according to their theory or first assumption! The pendulum, as though a living creature, conscious of unbearable defamation, subsequently became so irregular in its behaviour that the astronomers did and were glad to disown it as an ally or friend of their calumnious philosophy. They struggled fiercely to retain its peculiarities as a proof of their groundless assumptions, but the battle was short and decisive. The pendulum ignored the connection; and the scientific world was compelled to submit to a divorce, and to acknowledge defeat.

Their reasoning had been dexterous, but false and devious. A greater violation of the laws of investigation was never perpetrated. The whole subject, as developed and applied by the theoretical philosophers, was to the fullest degree unreasonable and absurd--not a "jot or tittle" better than the "reasoning" contained in the following letter:--

---

137 "The Scotsman," a scientific article, by the editor, Mr. Charles Maclaren.

"TO THE EDITOR OF 'PUNCH.'

"SIR,--Allow me to call your serious and polite attention to the extraordinary phenomenon demonstrating the rotation of -the earth, which I at this present moment experience, and you yourself, or anybody else, I have not the slightest doubt, would be satisfied of, under similar circumstances. Some sceptical and obstinate individuals may doubt that the earth's motion is visible, but I say from personal observation it's a positive fact. I don't care about latitude or longitude, or a vibratory pendulum revolving round the sine of a tangent, on a spherical surface, nor axes, nor apsides, nor anything of the sort. That is all rubbish. All I know is I see the ceiling of this coffee-room, going round. I perceive this distinctly with the naked eye--only my sight has been sharpened by a slight stimulant. I write after my sixth go of brandy-and-water, whereof witness, my hand.

"SWIGGINS.

"Goose and Gridiron, May 5, 1851.

"P.S.--Why do two waiters come when I only call one?"[138]

The whole matter, as handled by the astronomical theorists, is fully deserving of the ridicule implied in the above quotation. But because great ingenuity and much thought and devotion have been manifested in connection with it, and the general public thereby greatly deceived, it is necessary that the subject should be fairly and seriously examined. What are the facts as developed by numerous, and often-repeated experiments?

FIRSTLY--When a pendulum, constructed according to plan of M. Foucault is allowed to vibrate, its plane of the vibration is often stationary and often variable. The variation is not uniform--is not always the same in the same place; nor the same in its rate, or velocity, or in its direction. This great variability in its behaviour is not compatible with the assumption of an earth or world globular in form and moving with uniform velocity. It cannot therefore be taken as evidence; for that which is inconstant is inadmissible, and not to be relied on. Hence it is not evidence, and nothing is proved or decided by its consideration.

SECONDLY--Admitting the plane of vibration as changeable, where is the connection between such change and the supposed motion of the earth? What principle of reasoning guides the experimenter to the conclusion that it is the earth which moves underneath the pendulum; and not the pendulum which moves over the earth? What logical right or necessity forces one conclusion in preference to the other?

---

138 "Punch," May 10, 1851.

THIRDLY--Why was not the peculiar arrangement of the point of suspension of the pendulum specially considered in regard to its possible influence on the plane of oscillation? Was it not known, or was it overlooked, or was it, in the climax of theoretical revelry, ignored-- thought unworthy of consideration--that a "ball-and-socket" joint, or a globular point of suspension on a plane surface, is one which facilitates *circular* motion more readily than any other, and that a pendulum so suspended (as M. Foucault's) could not, after passing over one arc of vibration, return through the same arc without many chances to one that its globular point of suspension would slightly turn or twist on its bed, and therefore give to the return or backward oscillation a slight change of direction? Changes in the electric and magnetic conditions of the atmosphere, as well as alterations in its density, temperature, and hygrometric state may all tend in addition to the peculiar mode of suspension, to make the pendulum oscillate in irregular directions. So far, then, as we have been able to trace the subject, we are compelled by the evidence obtained to deny that the variations observed in the oscillations of a freely vibrating pendulum have any connection whatever with the motion or non-motion of the surface over which it vibrates.

RAILWAYS, AND "EARTH'S CENTRIFUGAL FORCE."

"Another proof of the diurnal motion of the earth has been made manifest since the introduction of railways. On railways running due north and south in the northern hemisphere, it is found that there is a greater tendency in the carriages to run off the line to the right than to the left of a person proceeding from the north to the south, or from the south to the north in the northern hemisphere. And this is the case in all parts of the world on lines of railways so placed, whether they are long or short."

The above quotation is mostly assertion. The author gives no proof of his statement, and therefore any one has a right to contradict him without giving his reasons. It is true that writers, in their anxiety to furnish some kind of practical evidence in support of their theory of diurnal motion, have occasionally vented their thoughts on this subject in local journals, but they seem to be uncertain whether the few cases they have referred to are really such as would satisfy any scientific investigator. The author has made many inquiries from practical men connected with several of the leading railways which run north and south in Great Britain, but has never received any corroboration of such an idea. In more than one instance the most thoroughly practical men, some who have run hundreds of miles every day for many years, have smiled almost contemptuously at hearing that such a notion had ever entered the head of any reasoning person. It certainly has been found that in some places the winds prevail in one direction more than another, and at such times a tendency to deflection has been noticed; but it has been observed almost as often in one direction as in another, and therefore the possibility of any influence arising from diurnal rotation is looked upon as merely a dream. If the earth really does move on axes, objects in motion on its surface would manifest an unmistakeable degree of deflection from a right line running north and south; but nothing of the kind is practically observable, therefore the earth does not move diurnally. Thus, as ever, theory, when standing against fact, must, sooner or later, be extinguished.

DEFLECTION OF FALLING BODIES

"The falling of bodies from high places is a further proof of the daily rotation of the earth. By this motion everything upon the earth describes a circle, which is larger in proportion as the object is raised above the surface; and as everything moves round in the same time, the greater the elevation of the object, the faster it will travel; so that the top of a house or hill moves faster than its base. It is found then that when a body descends from a high place, say a few hundred feet, it does not fall exactly beneath the spot it left, but a little to the east of it. This could not happen unless the earth had a motion from west to east. Were the earth stationary the body would fall immediately under the place it left."

The above "argument" for the earth's daily motion ought to be anything but satisfactory, even to its propounders; because it is the reverse of another "argument"--advanced for the same purpose [see Chapter 3]; it is not supported by uniform experimental results; the greatest amount of deflection which has ever been observed is a mere trifle compared with that which ought to be found according to the theory of rotation; and, lastly, because special experiment gives evidence directly against the supposition of diurnal motion.

It has been argued already that a body let fall down a coal pit, or from a high tower, *does not deflect*, but falls parallel to the side of the pit or tower, on account of the conjoint action of the earth's centrifugal force, and the force of gravity. It is said that at the moment it is liberated, and begins to fall by gravity, it receives an impulse at right angles to gravity, and therefore really falls in a diagonal direction. Thus what is affirmed in one place is contradicted in another! Inconsistency is ever the companion of falsehood. Again, when experiments have been tried, it has been found that a body has sometimes been out of the vertical a little to the east, sometimes to the west and north and south, and sometimes not at all. The amount, when it has been observed, has been very small, very far less than it ought to have been if it had resulted from the earth's rotation.

About the year 1843, a controversy on this subject had been going on in the *"Mechanics' Magazine"* for some time among persons connected with coal pits in Lancashire. To one of the letters the Editor appended the following remarks:--

"Mathematically speaking, some allowance must no doubt be made for the centrifugal action of the earth; but in the height of 100 yards it is so small as to be *practically inappreciable*. Besides, if the question is to be considered in that light, a farther correction must be made for the latitude of the place at the time of the observation, the surface velocity of the earth varying between London and the equator to the extent of no less than 477 miles."

The subject became very interesting to the scientific world, and during the several following years many experiments were tried. In the Report of the British Association for the Advancement of Science for 1846 appeared "A Letter on the Deviation of Falling Bodies from the Perpendicular, to Sir John Herschel, Bart., from Professor Oerstead," from which the following is an extract:--

"The first experiments of merit upon this subject were made in the last century, I think in 1793, by Professor Guglielmani. He found in a great church an opportunity to make bodies fall from a height of 231 feet. As the earth rotates from west to east, each point in or upon her describes an arc proportional to its distance from the axis, and therefore the falling body has from the beginning of the fall a greater tendency towards east than the point of the surface which is perpendicularly below it; thus it must strike a point lying somewhat easterly from the perpendicular. Still the difference is so small, that great heights are necessary for giving only a deviation of some tenth part of an inch. The experiments of Guglielmani gave indeed such a deviation; but, at the same time, they gave a deviation to the south, which was not in accordance with the mathematical calculations. De la Place objected to these experiments, that the author had not immediately verified his perpendicular, but only some months afterwards.

"In the beginning of this century, Dr. Benzenberg undertook new experiments at Hamburgh, from a height of about 240 feet, which gave a deviation of 3·99 French lines; but they gave a still greater deviation to the south. Though the experiments here quoted seem to be satisfactory in point of the eastern deviation, I cannot consider them to be so in truth; for it is but right to state that these experiments have considerable discrepancies among themselves, and that their mean, therefore, cannot be of great value. In some other experiments made afterwards in a deep pit, Dr. Benzenberg obtained only the eastern deviation, but they seem not to deserve more confidence. Greater faith is to be placed in the experiments of Professor Reich, in a pit of 540 feet, at Freiberg. Here the easterly deviation was also found in good agreement with the calculated result; but a considerable southern deviation was observed. The numbers obtained were the means of experiments which differed much among themselves. After all this, there can be no doubt that our knowledge on this subject is imperfect, and that new experiments are to be desired."

"New experiments" were afterwards made, as will be seen by the following remarks by W. W. Rundell, Esq., secretary to the Royal Cornwall Polytechnic Institution, recorded in the Transactions of that society, and quoted in the "Mechanics' Magazine" for May 20, 1848:--

> "The remarks of Professor Oerstead, at the Southampton meeting of the British Association, on the deflection to the south of falling bodies, and the variety of opinions entertained upon this subject by the most eminent men, not only in regard to its cause, but also as to its real existence, having attracted my attention, it occurred to me that the deep mines of Corn-wall would afford facilities for repeating experiments on this subject which had never before been obtained to the same extent. Professor Reich let bodies fall from a height of 540 feet, while the deep shafts of some of the Cornish mines would allow a fall of two and three times that amount. The man-engine shaft of the united mines was selected. It is perpendicular, and one quarter of a mile deep. . . . Besides the bullets, iron and steel plummets were used, the latter being magnetised. In form these were truncated cones, the lower and larger ends being round. These were suspended by short threads inside a cylinder, to prevent draughts of air affecting them, and, when they appeared free from oscillation, the threads were let go. The number of bullets used was 48, and there were some of each of the following metals:--iron, copper, lead, tin, zinc, antimony, and bismuth. A plumb- line was suspended at each end of the frame, and east and west of each other; to, these were attached heavy plummets, the lower ends pointed. After they had been hanging for some hours in the shaft, a line joining their points was taken as a datum line from which to, measure the deflection. The whole of the bullets and plummets dropped south of this datum line, and so much to the south that only four of the bullets fell upon the platform placed to receive them, the others, with the plummets, falling on the steps of the man-machine, on the south side of the shaft, in situations. which precluded exact measurements of the distances being taken. The bullets which fell on the platform were from 10 to 20 inches south of the plumb-line. . . . There is a real deflection to the south of the plumb-line, and in a fall of one quarter of a mile it is of no small amount."

The above article concludes with a lengthy mathematical explanation, or attempt at an explanation, of the phenomena observed on the supposition of the earth's rotundity and diurnal motion; but it is only one out of many elaborate efforts to reconcile facts and theories which are visibly opposed to each other. Several other mathematicians make strenuous efforts to "explain," and one writer, after a long algebraical article, in which special formulæ are advanced, finds fault with some of the efforts of others, and concludes as follows:--

"In recapitulating, then, we find that falling bodies may have either north, south, east, or west deflection from the plumb-line, and that the first two deflections may be combined with either of the latter two, and that each may exist separately, or not at all, depending on the circumstances of height fallen through, and the weight, size, and form of the bodies used."[139]

Thus it is admitted that deflection from a height of 300 feet "is so small as to be practically inappreciable;" that "great heights are necessary for giving only a deviation of one-tenth part of an inch;" that when this amount was observed, "at the same time deviation to the south was given, which was not in accordance with the mathematical calculations;" that "the experiments have considerable discrepancies among themselves;" that "the experiments differed very much;" that "after all there can be no doubt that our knowledge on this subject is imperfect;" that on repeating the experiments with the utmost possible care down a shaft of 1320 feet in depth, the bullets did not fall easterly at all from the plummets, "but from 10 to 20 inches south of the plumb-line," and out of forty-eight bullets, forty-four fell "on the south side of the shaft, in situations which precluded exact measurements of the distances being taken;" and, finally, that puzzled mathematicians, with their ever ready ingenuity to make facts agree with the wildest of theories, even with those of a directly opposite character, conclude that "falling bodies may have either north, south, east, or west deflection from the plumb-line." What value can such uncertain and conflicting evidence possess in the minds of reasoning men? They are shameless logicians, indeed, who contend that, from such results, the earth is proved to have a diurnal rotation!

GOOSE ROASTING BY REVOLVING FIRE

As an instance of the logical dilemma produced by theory and false doctrine, it may be mentioned that when it is proved by the most direct and practical evidence that the earth is stationary, and that the sun and stars move over its surface in concentric paths, immediately, and regardless of all considerations but defence of opinion and hypothesis, the cry is raised--Is it likely, is it consistent with all that we see and know of economy in the application of power, that a vast body like the sun, 850,000 miles in diameter, should revolve round a mere speck like the earth? If, in roasting a goose, the "spit" were made fast, and the fire so contrived as to be carried round it, would not such an arrangement be sheer folly? And would not the great sun revolving round the little insignificant earth be quite as foolish and improbable? The author of a recently published pamphlet advances the subject a little more learnedly, perhaps, in the following words:--

"It is certain, from the change in the appearance of the starry heavens at different seasons of the year, that either the sun moves round the earth once in twelve

---

139 "Mechanics' Magazine" for July 1, 1848, p. 13.

months, or the earth round the sun. After what we have ascertained of the enormous magnitude of the sun as compared with the earth, 850,000 against less than 8000 miles, we shall be prepared to admit that it is infinitely more reasonable that the little dark earth should move round the great and glorious sun, than that that magnificent and self-luminous globe should have to revolve round our small, and comparatively insignificant, planet. It would be, according to the old homely simile, making the whole fire-place and kitchen and house turn round the joint of meat."

Another writer (Arago) says:--

"In the first place, if we compare the earth, we shall not say merely with the globes of our system, but with the infinity of stars which, as we have seen, are nothing else than suns at least as large as ours, and probably centres of as many planetary systems, we must own that it is but an imperceptible point when contrasted with these enormous masses; and it will no doubt appear monstrous that an atom should be the centre round which circulate so many immense globes. Our amazement will be vastly enhanced if we think of the incredible velocity with which these bodies must move to describe, in such brief times, incommensurable circles; and as this velocity must augment with the distance, it will be necessary to admit that the earth attracts all the stars with a force the greater the further they are from it. We must, therefore, abandon a notion which would lead to such conclusions as these, and put the question to ourselves, whether this apparent revolution of the heavens may not be the effect of an illusion of our senses. Thus we shall be led to suppose the movement of the earth; and this *supposition* being *admitted*, the phenomena will be explained logically and easily."

The only argument contained in the above remarks is that founded upon analogy and probability. It certainly would seem very foolish, and contrary to creative genius and consistency to make a body 850,000 miles in diameter, and, at a distance of 91,000,000 of miles, move round an object only 8000 miles in diameter, merely for the purpose of giving it light and heat, and causing day and night. But when it is demonstrated that such distance and magnitude are purely fanciful, that the sun is only a few hundred miles from the earth, and is, therefore, much the smallest object, all such tawdry notions and counterfeit reasonings must fall to the ground.

DIFFERENCE IN SOLAR AND SIDEREAL TIMES

It is found by observation that the stars come to the meridian about four minutes earlier every twenty-four hours than the sun, taking the solar time as the standard. This makes 120 minutes every thirty days, and twenty-four hours in the year. Hence all the constellations have passed before or in advance of the sun in that time. This is the simple fact as observed in nature, but the theory of rotundity and motion on axes and in an orbit has no place for it. Visible truth must be ignored, because this theory stands in the way, and prevents its votaries from understanding it. What is plain and consistent with every known fact, and with the direct evidence of our senses, must be interpreted or translated into theoretical language--must be called "an illusion of our senses," and affirmed to be an apparent result only; the real cause being the earth's progressive motion round the sun in what is called the ecliptic, the plane of which is assumed to be inclined to the equator 23° 28´.

STATIONS AND RETROGRADATION OF PLANETS

The planets are sometimes seen to move from east to west, sometimes from west to east, and sometimes to appear stationary, and it is contended that "the hypothesis of the earth's motion is the natural and easy explanation; and that it would be in vain to seek it from any other system." To those who have adopted the Newtonian theory the above language is quite natural; but when the very foundation of that system is proved to be erroneous, we must seek for the cause as it really exists in the heavens, regardless of every hypothesis and consequence. Careful observation has shown that the advance, apparent rest, and retrogradation of a planet is a simple mechanical result. All the orbits are above the earth; and whenever a spectator stands in such a position that a planet is moving from right to left, he has only to wait until it reaches the end or part of its orbit nearest to him, when, as it turns to traverse the other side of the orbit, it will, for a time, pass in a direction to which the line of sight is a tangent. A good illustration will be found in an elliptical or circular race-course. A person standing at some distance outside the course would see the horses come in from the right, and pass before him to the left; but on arriving at the extreme arc they would for a time pass in the direction of, or parallel to, his line of sight, and would, therefore, appear for a time not to progress, but on entering the other side of the course would appear to the spectator to move from. left to right, or in a contrary direction to that in which they first passed before him. The following diagram, fig. 99, will illustrate this.

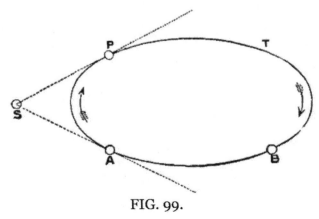

FIG. 99.

Let S be the place of the spectator. It is evident that a body passing from A to P, would pass him from right to left; but during its passage from P to T it would seem not to move across the field of view. On arriving, however, at T, and passing on to B, it would be seen moving from left to right; but from B to A it would again appear to be almost stationary.

TRANSMISSION OF LIGHT

"The progressive transmission of light being established, let us deduce from it our demonstration of the earth's rotation. If the earth is immoveable we ought not to see the stars the moment they arrive at the horizon or at the meridian, but only after the time acquired for the rays they emit to reach us. If, on the contrary, the earth turns, we ought to see the stars the moment they arrive, either at the horizon or at the meridian; for in consequence of the rotary motion, the eyes will fall into the line of the rays which had set out some time before from the stars, and which now arrive at the points of space traversed by our horizon. Now we do see the stars the instant of their arrival. The proof of this is, that the culminations of Mars, for instance, would be more or less advanced or retarded according as that planet approached or receded from us, if we did not see it the moment it arrived at the meridian, but no appearance of the kind is noticed; the earth, therefore, must turn."[140]

It is difficult to understand in what way the language of the above paragraph can be applied to prove the motion of the earth that does not equally apply to the proof of sidereal motion. The Newtonian astronomers, however, felt the necessity for practical proof of their leading assumptions; and hence have always been anxious to seize upon whatever could, by any kind of treatment, be made to appear like an argument in their favour.

In the above case they have been as premature and unfortunate as they have notoriously been in connection with other phenomena.

PRECESSION OF THE EQUINOXES

The Copernican or Newtonian theory of astronomy requires that the "axis of the earth is inclined 23° 28′ to that of the ecliptic."

"And from observation it is found that the sun does not every year cut the equator in the same point. If on a certain day he cuts the equator at a certain point, on the same day in the next year he cuts it at another point situated 50″.103 west of the former, and thus arrives at the equinox 20′ 23″ before having completed his revolution in the heavens, or passed from one fixed star to another. Thus the tropical year, or the true year of the seasons, is shorter than the sidereal year. . . . Retrograding every year 50″.103 to the west, the equinoxes make a complete revolution in

---

140 "Lecture on Astronomy," p. 105, by M. Arago.

25,868 years. Thus the first point of Aries which formerly corresponded to the vernal equinox, is now 30°· more to the west, though by a convention amongst astronomers it always answers to the equinox. . . . This change in the obliquity of the equator to the ecliptic is confirmed by the observations of ancient astronomers, and by calculation. We can convince ourselves of it by comparing the actual situation of the stars with respect to the ecliptic to that which they occupied in the earliest times. Thus we find that those which, according to the testimony of the ancients, were situated north of the ecliptic, near the summer solstice, are now more advanced towards the north, and have receded from this plane; that those which were south of the ecliptic, near the summer solstice, have approached this plane; and that some have passed into it, and even beyond it, on their course northward. The contrary changes take place near the winter solstice."[141]

That the sun does not "cut the equator" every year in the same point, and that "the stars which were, in earliest times, situated north of the summer solstice, are now, in relation to the sun's position, more advanced towards the north," cannot be doubted; but because the earth is not a globe, and neither rotates on axes nor moves in an orbit round the sun, these changes cannot be attributed to what has been called the "precession of the equinoxes, It has been found, [as stated in Chapter 6 of this work], that the path of the sun is always over the earth, and concentric with the northern centre, and that the distance of the annual path has been gradually increasing ever since observations have been made--more than a quarter of a century. And when we consider that in Great Britain, and countries still more to the north, evidences have been found of a more tropical condition having once existed, we are forced to the conclusion that this gradual enlargement of the sun's course has been going on for centuries; and that at a former period the northern centre, and places such as Greenland, Iceland, Siberia, &c., at no great distance from it, have been tropical regions.

"People have dug down in the earth in Scotland, and in Canada--colder still--nay, even on the icy shores of Baffin's Bay; and on Melville Island, the most northern region of the earth that has ever been reached by man, there have been found-- what? magnificent buried forests, and gigantic trees, which could only live now in the warmest countries of our earth-- palm trees, and immense ferns, which, in our day, have scarcely light and heat enough to grow, even in the torrid zone."[142]

"It is well known, as a matter of history, that when Green-land was discovered, it possessed a much warmer climate than it does at present. The ice packs have been extending south from the polar regions for some centuries. The cause of this is not well understood, the fact only is known."[143]

---

141 "Lectures on Astronomy," by M. Arago.
142 "Professor L. Gaussen "World's Birthday," p. 174.
143 "London Journal," February 14, 1857.

As a natural result of the same enlargement of the sun's path, the south must have been gradually changing--its frost and darkness diminishing; and many have declared that such is really the fact.

> "This climate appears to be in general much more temperate now (1822) than it was forty years ago. . . . Immense bodies of ice were then annually found in the latitude of 50° S. During the three voyages which I have made in these seas, I have never seen southern ice drifting to the northward of South Georgia (54° S.) Great changes must therefore have taken place in the south polar ice."[144]

When comparing the accounts of voyages, both to the north and south, made by the earliest navigators, with the statements made by those of recent periods, many incidental proofs are found of the increase of cold in the arctic regions, and corresponding decrease in the antarctic. Hence we find that the various changes which have been attributed to the "procession of the equinoxes," are really due to the sun's gradually increasing distance from the northern centre, and his advance towards the south. How long the sun's path has been moving southwards, or how near it was to the polar centre when the advance commenced, or whether it was once vertical there, are questions which cannot yet be answered. If ever the sun had a vertical position over the northern centre there could not, of course, be alternations of heat and cold, or day and night, but one perpetual day and tropical summer. It is evident then that ever since day and night commenced, the sun must have moved in a concentric path at some distance from the polar centre; but because the path was much nearer than it is at the present day, the whole of the northern region must have been tropical, with long days, and scarcely darkness during the nights; but long continued day, gently gliding into evening or twilight, and summer alternating with spring and autumn, but never with darkness and winter. Hence, with so much day and so little night, such gentle alternations of temperature, and the sun-light almost continually playing at a considerable altitude, this region must have teemed with animal and vegetable life of the most beautiful character. Everything must have been developed with the most perfect structure, the most brilliant colours, the greatest physical powers, and the most intense moral and mental capacities. Such a region could not be less than a paradise, as beautiful and perfect as any ever recorded in the sacred books of ancient theologists, or of which it is possible for the human mind even now to conceive. There are frequent and singular references to be found in the sacred books, legends, and poems, of various nations, to the north as having been the abode of happy, powerful, and highly intelligent beings.

THE PLANET NEPTUNE

For some years the advocates of the earth's rotundity, and of the Newtonian philosophy generally, were accustomed to refer, with an air of pride and triumph, to the supposed

---

144 "Voyages to the South," by Captain James Weddell, F.R.S.E., p. 95.

discovery of a new planet, to which the name of "Neptune" was given, as an undeniable evidence of the truth of their system or theory. The existence of this luminary was said to have been predicated from calculation only, and for a considerable period before it was seen by the telescope. The argument was, "That the system by which such a discovery was made, must, of necessity, be true." An article which appeared in the "Illustrated London Almanack," for 1847, contained the following words:--

> "Whatever view we take of this noble discovery, it is most gratifying, whether at the addition of another planet to our list, whether at the proving the correctness of the theory of universal gravitation, or in what view soever, it must be considered as a splendid discovery, and the merit is chiefly due to theoretical astronomy. This discovery is perhaps the greatest triumph of astronomical science that has ever been recorded."

If such things as criticism, experience, and comparative observation did not exist, the tone of exultation in which the above-named writer indulges might still be shared in by the astronomical student; but let the following summary of facts and extracts be carefully read, and it will be seen that such a tone was premature and unwarranted.

> "In the year 1781, Uranus was discovered by Sir William Herschel. . . . Between 1781 and 1820, it was very frequently observed; and it was hoped that at the latter time sufficient data existed to construct accurate tables of its motions. . . .It was found utterly impossible to construct tables which would represent all the observations. . . . Consequently it was evident that the planet was under the influence of some unknown cause. Some persons talked of a resisting medium, others of a great satellite which might accompany Uranus; some even went so far as to suppose that the vast distance Uranus is from the sun caused the law of gravitation to lose some of its force; others thought of the existence of a planet beyond Uranus, whose disturbing force caused the anomalous motions of the planet; but no one did otherwise than follow the bent of his inclination, and did not support his assertion by any positive considerations. Thus was the theory of Uranus surrounded with difficulties, when M. Le Verrier, an eminent French mathematician, undertook to investigate the irregularities in its motions. . . . The result of these calculations was the discovery of a new planet in the place assigned to it by theory, whose mass, distance, position in the heavens, and orbit it describes round the sun, were all approximately determined before the planet had ever been seen, and all agrees with observations, so far as can at present be determined."[145]

The first paper by M. Le Verrier appeared on the 10th of November, 1845, and a second on June 1st, 1846; and "on the 23rd of September, Dr. Galle, at Berlin, discovered a star of the eighth magnitude, which was proved to be the planet," so it was thought;

---

145 "Illustrated London Almanack" for 1847.

and hence, had it been true, the Newtonian philosophers had good cause to be proud of the theory which had apparently led to such grand results; and, as in the other "great discovery" by the celebrated French mathematician, M. Foucault, of the earth's motion by the vibrations of a pendulum, the peals of triumph rung by mathematicians were for months ringing in the ears of the whole civilised community. The whole of this scientific rejoicing was, however, suddenly arrested by the appearance, two years afterwards, of a paper by M. Babinet, read before the French Academy of Sciences, in which great errors in the calculations of M. Le Verrier were disclosed, as will be seen by the following letter:--

"Paris, September 15, 1848.

"The only sittings of the Academy of late in which there was anything worth recording, and even this was not of a practical character, were those of the 29th ult., and the 11th inst. On the former day M. Babinet made a communication respecting the planet Neptune, which has been generally called M. Le Verrier's planet, the discovery of it having, as it was said, been made by him from theoretical deductions which astonished and delighted the scientific public. What M. Le Verrier had inferred from the action on other planets of some body which ought to exist was verified--at least, so it was thought at the time--by actual vision. Neptune was actually seen by other astronomers, and the honour of the theorist obtained additional lustre. But it appears, from a communication of M. Babinet, that this is not the planet of M. Le Verrier. He had placed his planet at a distance from the sun equal to thirty-six times the limit of the terrestrial orbit. Neptune revolves at a distance equal to thirty times of these limits, which makes a difference of *nearly two hundred millions of leagues*! M. Le Verrier had assigned to his planet a body equal to thirty-eight times that of the earth; Neptune has only one-third of this volume! M. Le Verrier had stated the revolution of his planet round the sun to take place in two hundred and seventeen years; Neptune performs its revolutions in one hundred and sixty-six years! Thus, then, Neptune is not M. Le Verrier's planet, and all his theory as regards that planet falls to the ground! M. Le Verrier may find another planet, but it will not answer the calculations which he had made for Neptune.

"In the sitting of the 14th, M. Le Verrier noticed the communication of M. Babinet, and to a great extent admitted his own error. He complained, indeed, that much of what he said was taken in too absolute a sense, but he evinces much more candour than might have been expected from a disappointed explorer. M. Le Verrier may console himself with the reflection that if he has not been so successful as he thought he had been, others might have been equally unsuccessful; and as he has still before him an immense field for the exercise of observation and calculation, we may hope that he will soon make some discovery which will remove the vexation of his present disappointment."[146]

---

146 "Times" Newspaper of Monday, September 18, 1848.

"As the data of Le Verrier and Adams stand at present, there is a discrepancy between the predicted and the true distance, and in some other elements of the planet. . . . It 'would appear from the most recent observations, that the mass of Neptune, instead of being, as at first stated, one nine thousand three hundredth, is only one twenty-three thousandth that of the sun; whilst its periodic time is now given with a greater probability at 166 years, and its mean distance from the sun nearly thirty. Le Verrier gave the mean distance from the sun thirty-six times that of the earth, and the period of revolution 217 years."[147]

Thus we have found that "a discovery which was incontestably one of the most signal triumphs ever attained by mathematical science, and which marked an era that must be for ever memorable in the history of physical investigation," and which "some years ago excited universal astonishment,"[148] was really worse than no discovery at all; it was a great astronomical blunder. An error of six hundred millions of miles in the planet's distance, of two thirds in its bulk, and of fifty-one years in its periodic time, ought at least to make the advocates of the Newtonian theory less positive, less fanatical and idolatrous--for many of them are as greatly so as the followers of Juggernauth--and more ready to acknowledge what they ought never to forget--that, at best, their system is but hypothetical, and must sooner or later give place to a practical philosophy, the premises of which are demonstrable, and which is, in all its details, sequent and consistent. Will they never learn to value the important truth, that a clear practical recognition of one single fact in nature is worth all the gew-gaw hypotheses which the unbridled fancies of wonder-loving philosophers have ever been able to fabricate?

MOON'S PHASES

It has been shown that the moon is not a reflector of the sun's light, but is self-luminous. That the luminosity is confined to one-half its surface is sufficiently shown by the fact that at "new moon" the entire circle or outline of the whole moon is often distinctly visible, but the darker. outline or circle is always apparently less than the segment which is illuminated. It is a well ascertained fact that a luminous body appears larger, or subtends a greater angle at the eye, than a body of exactly the same magnitude, but which is not luminous. Hence, it is logically fair to conclude that as the part of the moon which is non-luminous is always of less magnitude than the part which is luminous, that luminosity is attached to a part only. From this fact it is easily understood that "new moon," "full moon," and "gibbous moon," are simply the different proportions of the illuminated surface which are presented to the observer on earth. A very simple experiment will both illustrate and imitate these different phases. Take a wooden or other ball, and rub one half its surface with a solution of phosphorus in olive oil. On slowly turning this round in a dark room, all the quarters and intermediate phases of the moon will be most beautifully represented.

---

147 "Cosmos," by Humboldt, p.
148 "How to Observe the Heavens," by Dr. Lardner, p. 173.

MOON'S APPEARANCE

Astronomers have indulged in imagination to such a degree that the moon is now considered to be a solid, opaque spherical world, having mountains, valleys, lakes, or seas, volcanic craters, and other conditions analogous to the surface of the earth. So far has this fancy been carried that the whole visible disc has been mapped out, and special names given to its various peculiarities, as though they had been carefully observed, and actually measured by a party of terrestrial ordnance surveyors. All this has been done in direct opposition to the fact that whoever, for the first time, and without previous bias of mind, looks at the moon's surface through a powerful telescope, is puzzled to say what it is really like, or how to compare it with anything known to him. The comparison which may be made will depend upon the state of mind of the observer. It is well known that persons looking at the rough bark of a tree, or at the irregular lines or veins in certain kinds of marble and stone, or gazing at the red embers in a dull fire will, according to the degree of activity of the imagination, be able to see many different forms, even the outlines of animals and of human faces. It is in this way that persons may fancy that the moon's surface is broken up into hills and valleys, and other conditions such as are found on earth. But that anything really similar to the surface of our own world is anywhere visible upon the moon is altogether fallacious. This is admitted by some of those who have written on the subject, as the following quotations will show:--

> "Some persons when they look into a telescope for the first time having heard that mountains are to be seen, and discovering nothing but these (previously described) unmeaning figures, break off in disappointment, and have their faith in these things rather diminished than increased. I would advise, therefore, before the student takes even *his first view* of the moon through a telescope, to form as clear an idea as he can how mountains, and valleys, and caverns, situated at such a distance *ought to look*, and by what marks they may be recognised. Let him seize, if possible, the most favourable periods (about the time of the first quarter), and *previously learn from drawings and explanations* how to interpret everything he sees."[149]

> "Whenever we exhibit celestial objects to inexperienced observers, it is usual to precede the view with good drawings of the objects, accompanied by an explanation of what each appearance exhibited in the telescope indicates. The novice is told that mountains and valleys can be seen in the moon by the aid of the telescope; but on looking he sees a confused mass of light and shade, and nothing which looks to him like either mountains or valleys. Had his attention been previously directed to a plain drawing of the moon, and each particular appearance interpreted to him, he would then have looked through the telescope with intelligence and satisfaction."[150]

---

149 "Mechanism of the Heavens," by Dr. Olmsted, LL.D., Professor of Natural Philosophy and Astronomy in Yale College, United States.
150 Mitchell's "Orbs of Heaven," p. 232.

"It is fresh in our remembrance that when showing a friend the moon at an advanced phase, 'Is this the moon?' he said, 'why I see nothing but clouds and bubbles!'--a very graphic description of a first view by an uneducated eye. None of the wonderful beauties of the landscape scenery that are so striking to the beholder, can either be recognised or appreciated under such circumstances. It is only after a careful training of the eye, that the peculiarities of the full moon can be truly apprehended."[151]

Thus it is admitted by those who teach, that the moon is a spherical world, having hills and dales like the earth, that such things can only be seen in imagination.

"Nothing but unmeaning figures" are really visible, and "the students break off in disappointment, and have their faith in such things rather diminished than increased, until they previously learn from drawings and explanations how to interpret everything seen."

But who first made the drawings? Who first interpreted the "unmeaning figures" and the "confused mass of light and shade?" Who first declared them to indicate mountains and valleys, and ventured to make drawings, and give explanations and interpretations for the purpose of biassing the minds, and fixing or guiding the imaginations of subsequent observers? Whoever they were, they, at least, had "given the reins to fancy," and afterwards took upon themselves to dogmatise and teach their bold, crude, and unwarranted imaginings to succeeding investigators. And this is the kind of "evidence and reasoning" which is obtruded in our seats of learning, and spread out in the numerous works which are published for the "edification" of society.

MOON TRANSPARENT

It is more than three centuries and a half since Fernando de Magulhane observed that the moon, during a solar eclipse, was not perfectly opaque. He says:--

"On the forenoon of October 11th, 1520, an eclipse of the sun was expected. At eight seconds past ten a.m. the sun, having then reached the altitude of 42°, began to lose its brightness, and gradually continued so to do, changing to a dark red colour, without any cloud intervening that could be perceived. No part of the body of the sun was hid, but the whole appeared as when seen through a thick smoke, till it passed the altitude of 44½°, after which it recovered its former lustre."[152]

During a partial solar eclipse the sun's outline has many times been seen through the body of the moon. But those who have been taught to believe that the moon is a solid opaque sphere, are ever ready with "explanations," often of the most inconsistent

---

151 "The Moon," by W. R. Birt, F.R.A.S., in the "Leisure Hour" for July, 1871, p. 439.
152 "Discoveries in the South Sea," p. 39, by Captain James Burney. 2 "Description of the Heavens," p. 354, by Alex. von Humboldt.

character, rather than acknowledge the simple fact of semi-transparency. Not only has this been proved by the visibility of the sun's outline through segments, and sometimes the very centre, of the moon, but often, at new moon, the outline of the whole, and even the several shades of light on the opposite and illuminated part have been distinctly seen. In other words we are often able to see through the dark side of the moon's body the light on the other side.

> "In this faint light the telescope can distinguish both the larger spots, and also bright shining points, and even when more than half the moon's disc is illuminated, a faint grey light can still be seen on the remaining portion by the aid of the telescope. These phenomena are particularly striking when viewed from the high mountain plateaus of Quito and Mexico."[153]

Many have laboured hard to make it appear that these phenomena are the result of what they have assumed to be light reflected from the earth- -"Earth light," "the reflection of a reflection." The sun's light thrown back from the moon to the earth and returned from the earth to the moon! It seems never to have occurred to these "students of imagination" that this so-called "earth-light" is most intense when the moon is youngest, and therefore illuminates the earth the least. When the operating cause is least intense, the effect is much the greatest!

Besides the fact that when the moon is only a few hours old, and sometimes until past the first quarter, the naked eye is able to see through her body to the light shining on the other side, both fixed stars and planets have been seen through a considerable part of her substance, as proved by the following quotations:

> "On the 15th of March, 1848, when the moon was seven and a half days old, I never saw her *unillumined* disc so beautifully. . . . On my first looking into the telescope a star of about the 7th magnitude was some minutes of a degree distant from the moon's dark limb. I saw that its occultation by the moon was inevitable. . . . The star, instead of disappearing the moment the moon's edge came in contact with it, apparently glided on the moon's dark face, as if it had been seen *through a transparent moon*; or, as if a star were between me and the moon. . . .I have seen a similar apparent projection several times. . . . The cause of this phenomenon is involved in impenetrable mystery."[154]

> "Occultation of Jupiter by the moon, on the 24th of May, 1860, by Thomas Gaunt, Esq. 'I send you the following account as seen by me at Stoke Newington. The observation was made with an achromatic of 3.3 inches aperture, 50 inches focus; the immersion with a power of 50, and the emersion with a power of 70. At the

153 "Description of the Heavens," p. 354, by Alex. von Humboldt. (p. 246).
154 Sir James South, of the Royal Observatory, Kensington, in a letter in the "Times" newspaper of April 7, 1848.

immersion I could not see the dark limb of the moon until the planet appeared to touch it, and then only to the extent of the diameter of the planet; but what I was most struck with was the appearance on the moon as it passed over the planet. It appeared as though the planet was a dark object, and glided on to the moon instead of behind it; and the appearance continued until the planet was hid, when I suddenly lost the dark limb of the moon altogether.'"[155]

"Occultation of Jupiter by the moon, May 24, 1860, observed by T. W. Burr, Esq., at Highbury. The planet's first limb disappeared at 8h. 44m. 6.7s., the second limb disappeared at 8h. 45m. 4.9s. local sidereal time, on the moon's dark limb. The planet's first limb reappeared at 9h. 55m. 48s.; the second limb reappeared at 9h. 56m. 44.7s., at the bright limb. The planet was well seen, notwithstanding the strong sunlight (4h. 34m. Greenwich mean time), but of course without any belts. The moon's dark limb could not be detected until it touched the planet, when it was seen very sharply defined and black; and as it passed the disc of Jupiter in front appeared to brighten. So that the moon's limb was preceded by a bright band of light, doubtless an effect of contrast."[156]

"Occultation of the Pleiades, December 8, 1859, observed at the Royal Observatory, Greenwich; communicated by the Astronomer Royal. Observed by Mr. Dunkin with the alt-azimuth, the disappearance of 27 *Tauri* was a most singular phenomenon; the star appeared to *move a considerable time along the moon's limb*, and disappeared behind a prominence at the first time noted (5h. 34m.); in a few seconds it re-appeared, and finally disappeared at the second time noted (5h. 35m.)."

"Observed by Mr. Criswich, with the north equatorial, 27 *Tauri* was *not occulted at all*, though it passed so close to some of the illuminated peaks of the dark limb as hardly to be distinguished from them."[157]

In the "Philosophical Transactions" for 1794 it is stated:--

Three persons in Norwich, and one in London, saw a star on the evening of March 7th, 1794, in the dark part of the moon, which had not then attained the first quadrature; and from the representations which are given the star must have appeared very far advanced upon the disc. On the same evening there was an occultation of Aldebaran, which Dr. Maskelyne thought a singular coincidence, but which would now be acknowledged as the cause of the phenomenon."[158]

---

155 Monthly Notices of Royal Astronomical Society, for June 8, 1860.
156 Monthly Notices of Royal Astronomical Society, for June 8, 1860.
157 Monthly Notices of Royal Astronomical Society, December 9, 1859.
158 Rev. T. W. Webb in Monthly Notice of Royal Astronomical Society for May 11, 1860.

The [previous] quotations are only a few from many cases which have been recorded; and if, with the evidence advanced in the chapter on eclipses, they are insufficient to prove that the moon is not an opaque reflecting body but is really a semi-transparent, self-luminous structure, to such minds evidence is valueless, and reasoning a vain pretension. Nothing could possibly for a moment prevent such a conclusion being at once admitted, except the pre-occupation of the mind by a strabismic presumptuous hypothesis, which compels its votaries to yield assent to its details, even if directly contrary to every fact in the natural world, and to every principle of mental investigation.

SHADOWS ON THE MOON

There seems to be a thorough conviction in the minds of the Newtonian theorists that many of the dark places on the moon are the shadows of mountains, and very graphic descriptions are given of the manner in which these dark places lengthen and shorten, and change their direction, as the sun is high or low, or on the right or left of certain parts. Hitherto, or in the preceding pages of this work, a spirit of antagonism has been maintained towards the Newtonian astronomers. The Zetetic process has forced a direct denial of every part of their system; but in the present instance there are certain points of agreement. There is at present no reliable evidence against the statements of the following quotation:

> "As the moon turns towards the sun, the tops of her mountains being the first to catch his rays, are made to stand out illuminated, like so many bright diamonds on her unilluminated black surface. And if watched with a pretty good telescope the light of the sun may be seen slowly descending the mountain sides, and at length to light up the plains and valleys below; thus making those parts which but a short time before were intensely black, now white as the snows of winter. And in those basin-like mountains (the craters) the shadows on one side may be seen descending far down on the opposite side, thereby revealing their vast proportions and mighty depths. As the time of the full moon approaches the shadows shorten, and when the rays of the sun fall perpendicularly on her surface (as, at full moon) they cease altogether. But now, if still watched, just the opposite appearances will take place, as the enlightened face of the moon begins to turn from the sun the lower parts are the first to lose his rays and pass into darkness, which will be observed to creep gradually up the mountain sides, and at last their tips will appear to pass out of the sun's light as the last spark of a lighted candle. The enlightened parts of the moon, however, no sooner begin to turn from the sun than the shadows of the mountains again come into view, but on the opposite side to that on which they were seen when the moon was on the increase, and gradually to increase in length so long as the parts up which they are thrown are in the light of the sun."[159]

---

159 "Spherical Form of the Earth, a reply to 'Parallax,' by J. Dyer, p. 34.

That such changes of light and shade in the varying positions of the moon, as those above described, are observed may be admitted; but that they arise from the interposition of immense mountain ranges is of necessity denied. If the Newtonians would be logically modest, the only word they could use would be that *prominences* exist on the moon's surface. To say that mountains and valleys and extinct volcanic craters exist, is to insult the understanding and the common sense of mankind. What possibility of proof exists that such is the character of the moon? Let them be content with that which is, alone warranted by the appearances which have been observed--that the moon's surface is irregular, having upon it prominences and indentations of various forms and sizes, and running in many different directions. This is the common property of all observers, and is not to be seized and perverted, or interpreted by any one class of philosophical arrogants as proving an essential part of their illogical hypothesis.

It has been demonstrated by more than sufficient matter-of-fact evidence that the moon is self-luminous, semi-transparent, admitted to be globular, observed to have prominences and irregularities upon her surface, and moves in a path always above the earth, and at a distance less than that of the sun, and, therefore, that she is a comparatively small body, and simply a satellite and light-giver to the earth. If we choose to reason at all from the facts which appear in evidence, we must necessarily conclude that the moon is a cold, semi-transparent, crystalline mass, more like a spherical ice-berg than anything else, shining with a peculiar delicate phosphorescent light of her own, but, in certain positions, her own light is overcome by the stronger and more violent light of the sun, which causes her protuberances to darken the various indentations adjoining them. This is all that any human being can possibly say without presuming on the ignorance of his fellow men, and daring to obtrude his own wild imaginings where only fact and reason and modest anxiety to know the simple truth ought to exist. This said and submitted to, we are able to illustrate and corroborate it by corresponding facts on earth. It is a well-known fact that often, when passing over the sea during a summer's night, the wake of a vessel--of a steam-ship in particular--is strongly luminous as far as the eye can see. It is also a fact often observed that some kinds of fish will shine with a peculiar light for hours after they are taken out of the water; and it is known that, collect this light by concave reflectors to what extent we may, it will not, to whatever degree of brilliancy we may bring it by concentration to a focus, increase the temperature, as indicated by the most delicate thermometer. This is precisely what we find as to the character of moon-light. The following experiment will also illustrate the subject:-- Take a partially transparent ball, such as are prepared and sold by the cautchouc toy manufacturers, or a very thin bladder well blown out until it is semi-transparent. To represent the many protuberances, &c., place small patches of gum arabic or isinglass in various directions over one half its surface. Now rub the whole of this half surface with a solution of phosphorus in oil of almonds, and carry it into a dark room. It will give, by turning it slowly round, all the peculiar appearances and phases of the moon; but now bring into the apartment a lighted ordinary tallow candle, and at certain distances it will not overcome the comparatively feeble phosphorescent light, but will cause the places immediately behind the gum arabic or isinglass protuberances to be darkened, on account of the light of the candle being intercepted; thus imitating all the peculiarities which are known to belong to the moon. Hence, it is repeated, that observation, fact, experiment, and consistent reasoning, all lead us to the conclusion that the moon is a comparatively small body, only a few hundred miles above the earth, that her surface is irregular, that her substance is crystalised and semi-transparent, and that she shines with a delicate phosphorescent light of her own, but is subject to the action of the light of the sun, which, when in certain positions, causes those peculiar manifestations of light and shade which dreamy and prepossessed philosophers have assigned to the interposition of immense and peculiar mountain structures. Surely the night of dreams is coming to an end, and the sleepers will awake ere long to open their eyes and apply their talents, not for the interpretation of what they have for so long a period been simply dreaming, but for the discovery of the real and tangible causes of the numerous beautiful phenomena constantly occurring in the world around them.

CONCLUSION

Every point of importance has now been fairly considered, and shown to be either unconnected or inconsistent with the assumption of the earth's rotundity and diurnal and orbital motions. It is most important to the reader that he should thoroughly understand the bearings of the various explanations which have been given of the phenomena which the Newtonian philosophers have hitherto relied on as proofs of their hypothesis. They have assumed certain conditions to exist in order to explain certain phenomena; and because the explanations of such phenomena have appeared plausible, they have thought themselves justified in concluding that their assumptions must be looked upon as veritable facts. The contrary, or Zetetic process, has necessitated that the foundations be demonstrated; that the earth be proved by special and direct experiments to be a plane, irrespective of all consequences, regardless of whether numerous or any phenomena can be understood in connection with it or not. An endeavour has been made in the preceding pages to explain the various phenomena without assumption, but in connection with the undoubtedly demonstrated fact that *water is horizontal*, and that the earth as a whole is not a globe, but a vast "discular" plane. The reader must properly bear in mind that if any one, or even the whole, of these explanations are unsatisfactory to him, he is not to jump abruptly to the conclusion that therefore the earth cannot be a plane, but must be a globe. Apart from, and totally independent of, all consequences or success in explaining phenomena, the proposition of the earth's plane or discular form must be admitted, or shown to be fallacious. Wherever doubt shall exist as to the sufficiency of the phenomenal explanations offered, the mind must at once fall back upon the grand reserved proposition that water is horizontal, and, therefore, any want of satisfaction in explaining phenomena must be met by further efforts in that direction, and not by the mentally suicidal process of denouncing a proved foundation.

Once for all it may be said that, whatever explanation is proved, or thought to be, unsatisfactory, a better must be sought for, but still in connection with the same ground-work or datum. Whoever objects to this procedure, and is unable to see its logical justice and necessity, is most certainly not a reasoner, and, quite as clearly, cannot be a philosopher.

CHAPTER XV
GENERAL SUMMARY - APPLICATION - CUI BONO

IN the preceding chapters it has been shown that the Copernican or Newtonian theory of astronomy is an "absurd composition of truth and error;" and, as admitted by its founder, "not necessarily true nor even probable;" that instead of its being a general conclusion derived from known and admitted facts, it is a heterogeneous compound of assumed premises, isolated truths, and variable appearances in nature. Its advocates are challenged to show a single instance wherein a phenomenon is explained, a calculation made, or a conclusion advanced without the aid of an avowed or implied assumption! The very construction of a theory at all, but especially such as the Copernican, is a complete violation of that natural and legitimate mode of investigation to which the term "Zetetic" has been applied. The doctrine of the universality of gravitation is a pure assumption, made only in accordance with that "pride and ambition which has led philosophers to think it beneath them to offer anything less to the world than a complete and finished system of nature." It was said, in effect, by Newton, and has ever since been insisted upon by his disciples: "Allow us, without proof, which is impossible, the existence of two universal forces--centrifugal and centripetal, or attraction and repulsion, and we will construct a theory which shall explain all the leading phenomena and mysteries of nature." An apple falling from a tree, or a stone rolling downwards, and a pail of water tied to a string and set in motion were assumed to be types of the relations existing among all the bodies in the universe. The moon was assumed to have a tendency to fall towards the earth, and the earth and moon together towards the sun. The same relation was assumed to exist between all the smaller and larger luminaries in the firmament; and it soon became necessary to extend these assumptions to affinity.

The universe was parcelled out into systems--co-existent and illimitable. Suns, planets, satellites, and comets, were assumed to exist infinite in number and boundless in extent; and to enable the theorists to explain alternating and constantly recurring phenomena, which were everywhere observable, these numberless and for-ever-extending objects were assumed to be spheres. The earth we inhabit was called a planet, and because it was thought to be reasonable that the luminous objects in the firmament, which were called planets, were spherical and had motion, so it was only reasonable to suppose that, as the earth was a planet, it must also be spherical and have motion--ergo, the earth is a globe and moves upon axes, and in an orbit round the sun! And as the earth is a globe and is inhabited, so again it is only reasonable to conclude that the planets are worlds like the earth, and are inhabited by sentient beings.

What reasoning! what shameful perversion of intellectual gifts! The very foundation of this complicated theory is false, incapable of proof, and contrary to known possibilities. The human mind cannot possibly conceive of its truth and application. To assume the existence of two opposite equal universal forces is to seek to make true things or ideas which are necessarily contradictory; to make black and white, hot and cold, up and down, life and death, and truth and falsehood, one and the same. Can any one by any known possibility conceive of two opposite equal powers acting simultaneously, producing change of position or motion in that which is thus acted upon? Do not two opposite forces, when equal in intensity and operating at the same moment, neutralise each other? There is nothing in practical science to gainsay this conclusion; and in the earliest days of the Newtonian astronomy this contradiction was quickly perceived, but as the assumption was an essential part of the system it was not rejected. An attempt was made to overcome the fatal objection that from two opposite equal forces, acting simultaneously on the earth, no motion whatever could arise, by the further assumption that, when the earth was first made, the Creator threw it out into space, at right angles to the two forces which had been assumed to exist universally, and that then the conjoint action of attraction and repulsion, with the "primitive impulse," resulted in a parabolic orbit round the sun.

> "It will scarcely be believed that La Place (La Place le Grand) actually entered into an elaborate calculation, with a view to determine at what particular point the Creator held the earth at the time of giving the grand push; and that after a most profound investigation he arrived at the sublime and never to-be-forgotten conclusion, that when the 'primitive impulse was imparted, the earth was held exactly twenty-five miles from the centre, 'and hence,' quoth La Place, 'the earth revolved upon her axis in twenty-four hours.' If she had been held a little nearer to the centre, our days would have been longer, and if a little further off, she would have revolved with greater velocity, and our days would have been shorter."[160]

---

160 "Electrical Theory of the Universe," by T. S. Mackintosh.

All efforts to reconcile the various inconsistencies with which the system abounds have necessarily failed. In the above instance it cannot be denied that the two assumed forces of necessity destroy each other; and that therefore the assumed "Primitive Impulse" given at right angles to them must operate alone. There might as well be no other forces operating, for out of the three two are suspended by mutual opposition, and the "Primitive Impulse" alone is left to produce a parabolic circuit. Let geometry and practical mechanics be questioned as to the possibility of such a thing. Can a parabola be described by a moving body if acted on by one force only? If so, then the assumption of the existence of the two other forces was unnecessary.

To assume that attraction and repulsion exist universally is also illogical and inconsistent. In the sense in which the word universal is used in astronomy we cannot separate it from the idea of boundless existence-- existence without limit--eternity and infinity. But infinity, or infinite ex- tent, necessarily implies unity or oneness of existence. There cannot be anything--not an atom, nor a hair's-breadth in addition to whatever is infinite--hence both practically and in the abstract there can only be one infinity, one eternity, one universe. To say then that two equal universal powers exist, is to say that there exist two infinities, two eternals, two everythings! But that which is infinite and eternal, or universal, is alone and is itself all and every-thing, to. which no addition can be made or imagined.

Thus we see that this Newtonian philosophy is devoid of consistency; its details are the result of an entire violation of the laws of legitimate reasoning, and all its premises are assumed. It is, in fact, nothing more than assumption upon assumption, and the conclusions derived therefrom are wilfully considered as things proved, and to be employed as truths to substantiate the first and fundamental assumptions. Such a "juggle and jumble" of fancies and falsehoods extended and intensified as in theoretical astronomy is calculated to make the unprejudiced inquirer revolt with horror from the terrible conjuration which has been practised upon him; to sternly resolve to resist its further progress; to endeavour to over-throw the entire edifice, and to bury in its ruins the false honours which have been associated with its fabricators, and which still attach to its devotees. For the learning, the patience, the perseverance and devotion for which they have ever been examples, honour and applause need not be withheld; but their false reasoning, the advantages they have taken of the general ignorance of mankind in respect to astronomical subjects, and the unfounded theories they have advanced and defended, cannot be otherwise than regretted, and ought to be by every possible means uprooted.

It has become a duty, paramount and imperative, to meet them in open, avowed, and unyielding rebellion; to declare that their reign of error and confusion is over; and that henceforth, like a falling dynasty, they must shrink and disappear, leaving the throne and the kingdom of science and philosophy to those awakening intellects whose numbers are constantly increasing, and whose march is rapid and irresistible. The soldiers of truth and reason have drawn the sword, and ere another generation has been educated and grown to maturity, will have forced the usurpers to abdicate. Like the decayed and crumbling trees of an ancient forest, rent and shattered by wind and storm, the hypothetical philosophies, which have hitherto cumbered the civilised world, are unable to resist the elements of experimental and logical criticism; and sooner or later must succumb to their assaults. The axe is uplifted for a final stroke--it is about to fall, and the blow will surely "cut the cumberer down."

The earth a globe, and it is necessarily demanded that it has diurnal, annual, and various other motions; for a globular world without motion of rotation and progression would be useless--day and night, winter and summer, the half-year's light and darkness at the pole, and other phenomena could not be explained by the supposition of rotundity without the assumption also of rapid and constant motion. Hence it is assumed that the earth and moon, and all the planets and their satellites, move in relation to each other; and also in different planes round the sun. The sun, and its system of revolving bodies, are now assumed to have a general and all-inclusive motion in common with an endless series of other suns and systems round a point which has been assumed to be a "central sun," the true axis and centre of the universe. These assumed general motions, with the particular and peculiar motions which are assigned to the various bodies in detail, together constitute a system so confused and complicated that it is almost impossible, and always difficult to comprehend by the most active and devoted minds. The most simple and direct experiments, however, prove that the earth has no progressive or circular motion whatever; and here, again, the advocates of this interminable and entangling arrangement of the universe are challenged to produce a single instance of so-called proof of these motions which does not involve an assumption--often a glaring falsehood--but always a point which is not, and cannot be, demonstrated.

The magnitudes, distances, velocities, and periodic times which these assumed motions eliminate are all glaringly fictitious, because they are only such as a false theory requires and creates a necessity for. It is geometrically demonstrable that all the visible luminaries in the firmament are within a distance of a few thousand miles from the earth, not more than the space which stretches between the North Pole and the Cape of Good Hope; and the principle of measurement--that of plane triangulation with, invariably, an accurately measured base line--which demonstrates this important fact is one which no mathematician claiming to be a master in the science will for, a moment deny. All these luminaries, then, and the sun itself, being so near to us, cannot be other than very small as compared with the earth we inhabit. They are all in motion over the earth, which is alone immovable; and, therefore, they cannot be anything more than secondary and subservient structures continually ministering to this fixed world and its inhabitants. This is a plain, simple, and in every respect demonstrable philosophy, agreeing with the evidence of our senses, borne out by every fairly instituted experiment, and never requiring a violation of those principles of investigation which the human mind has ever recognised and depended upon in its every-day life. The modern or Newtonian astronomy has none of these characteristics. The whole system taken together constitutes a most monstrous absurdity. It is false in its foundation; irregular, unfair, and illogical, in its details; and, in its conclusions, inconsistent and contradictory. Worse than all, it is a prolific source of irreligion and of atheism, of which its advocates are practically supporters. By defending a system which is directly opposed to that which is taught in connection with the Jewish and Christian religion they lead the more critical and daring intellects to question and deride the cosmogony and general philosophy contained in the sacred books. Because the Newtonian theory is held to be true they are led to reject the Scriptures altogether, to ignore the worship, and doubt and deny the existence of a Creator and Supreme Ruler of the world. Many of the primest minds are thus irreparably injured, robbed of those present pleasures, and that cheering hope of the future which the earnest Christian devotee holds as of far greater value than ail earthly wealth and grandeur; or than the mastery of all the philosophical complications which the human mind ever invented. To the religious mind this matter is most important--it is, indeed, no less than a sacred question, but to the dogged atheist, whose "mind is made up" not to enter into any further investigation, and not to admit of possible error in his past conclusions, it is of little more account than it is to the lowest animal in creation. He may see nothing higher, more noble, more intelligent, or beautiful than himself; and in this his pride, conceit, and vanity, find an incarnation. To such a creature there is no God; for he is himself, in his own estimation, an equal with, and equal to, the highest being he has ever recognised, or the evidence of which he has seen the possibility. Such atheism exists to an alarming extent among the philosophers and deep thinkers of Europe and America; and it has been mainly created and fostered by the astronomical and geological theories of the day. Besides which, in consequence of the differences between the language of Scripture and the teachings of modern astronomy, there is to be found in the very hearts of Christian and Jewish congregations a sort of "smouldering scepticism," a kind of "faint suspicion," which causes great numbers to manifest a cold and morbid indifference to religious requirements. They frigidly believe, and are not wanting in formalities and outward signs arid professions, but in their deepest thoughts a speculative, hypercritical, doubting, and chilling irreverence prevails. It is this confusion and want of certainty as to the absolute truths of religious teachings which creates a love of display and outward manifestation of religion, instead of that "cheerful solemnity" and quiet, unobtrusive good-will and devotion which solid convictions of the truthfulness of Christianity never fail to produce. It is this, too, which has led thousands to openly desert the cause of earnest, practical, active devotion, to seek consistency and satisfaction in scepticism, which has led many of them gradually onwards to utter hopelessness and atheism; and great numbers of those who still remain in the ranks of religion try to console themselves with the declaration "that the Scriptures were not intended to teach correctly other than moral and spiritual doctrines; that the references so often made to the physical world, and to natural phenomena generally, are given in language not pretending to be true, but to suit the prevailing notions and the ignorance of the people."

A Christian philosopher, who wrote almost a century ago, in reference to remarks similar to the above, says:

"Why should we suspect that Moses, Joshua, David, Solomon, and the later prophets and inspired writers, have counterfeited their sentiments concerning the order of the universe from pure complaisance, or being in any way obliged to dissemble with a view to gratify the prepossessions of the populace? These eminent men being kings, law-givers, and generals themselves, or always privileged with access to the Courts of sovereign princes, besides the reverence and awful dignity which the power of divination and working of miracles procured to them, had great worldly and spiritual authority. They had often in charge to command, suspend, revert, and otherwise interfere with the course and laws of Nature, and were never daunted to speak out the truth before the most mighty potentates on earth, much less would they be overawed by the vox populi."

To say that the Scriptures were not intended to teach science truthfully is, in substance, to declare that God Himself has stated, and commissioned His prophets to teach things which are utterly false!

Thus, I have some major issues with the Doctrine of Accommodation. For starters:

Numbers 23:19 *God is not a man, that he should lie; neither the son of man, that he should repent: hath he said, and shall he not do it? or hath he spoken, and shall he not make it good?*

Psalm 119:160 *Thy word is true from the beginning: and every one of thy righteous judgments endureth for ever.*

Psalm 8:1 *O Lord, our Lord, how excellent is thy name in all the earth! who hast set thy glory above the heavens.*

Psalm 138:2 *I will worship toward thy holy temple, and praise thy name for thy lovingkindness and for thy truth: for thou hast magnified thy word above all thy name.*

According to the above Scriptures, we are told that God does not lie. We are told that His word is "true from the beginning." We are told that even though His name is excellent and His glory is above the heavens, He has magnified His word above His name. This leads to a massive problem for all of you who claim the Bible as your (literal) source for truth and yet still cling to the spinning, heliocentric, globular model of our world.

In response to this problem, "theologians" came up with the ridiculously absurd doctrine of "accommodation," which states that YHWH "accommodated" the ignorance of man, and used it to get a "theological message" across, rather than deal with the lies they apparently believed. John Calvin is generally credited with coming up with this concept in response to the discoveries in the natural sciences of his day – most notably that of Copernicus' theory of heliocentrism, which clearly conflicted with the obvious, geocentric model of Scripture. The concept of accommodation thus became an alternative method of Bible interpretation, in contrast to the tradition of literal Biblical interpretation. The rationale generally goes something like this:

Accommodation (or condescension) is the theological principle that God, while being in His nature unknowable and unreachable, has nevertheless communicated with humanity in a way which humans can understand and respond to. The concept is that scripture has accommodated, or made allowance for, the original audience's language and general level of understanding. Thus, Divine accommodation means that the infinite God has accommodated various truths about Himself and the world in such a way that they can be comprehended by the finite human mind.[1]

This makes YHWH an accomplice in those lies by not correcting them, but rather instead effectively endorsing them by describing His creation in the same exact terms upon which the alleged lies were based. This doctrine therefore puts YHWH in agreement with lies instead of being the alleged source for truth upon which we can and should place our trust to combat them.

Here is the problem: If the spinning, heliocentric, globular model of our world is true, then Divine inspiration and inerrancy of Scripture is demonstrably false and all such notions must therefore, of necessity, be forever abandoned. So, which "sacred cow" are we willing to let go of in order to maintain our beliefs? You can't have both. A choice must be made.

If you attempt to go the route that Scripture does in fact, somehow support a spinning, heliocentric, globular view of our world (as many are now trying to do), at best, you will only demonstrate the extreme levels of cognitive dissonance you are suffering from and telegraph how little research you have actually done on the subject for all to see (please don't do that), or at worst, you will be blatantly lying through your teeth.

Biblical scholars who are being intellectually honest with themselves, the text and indeed the whole of ancient history recognize the indisputable fact that the Bible is, without a doubt, a flat Earth book. But if "accommodation" is true, then how can we trust anything we read? What if half (or more) of Scripture is based on the condescension of an allegedly Holy and truthful God accommodating in agreement with lies believed by ignorant sheep herders and fishermen? Could not statements that YHWH is true and He cannot lie also be an "accommodation" of the fallacious ideas of finite men about what an infinite, Holy and perfect God should be? How would you even know what is being "accommodated" and what is not?

---

1 Paraphrased from the Wikipedia entry on Accommodation (religion)

The Apostle Peter said:

2 Peter 1:21 *For the prophecy came not in old time by the will of man: but holy men of God spake as they were moved by the Holy Ghost.*

Along similar lines, the Apostle Paul said:

2 Timothy 3:16 *All scripture is given by inspiration of God, and is profitable for doctrine, for reproof, for correction, for instruction in righteousness:*

In Romans 3:4, Paul also said that we should "let God be true, but every man a liar." Well, how can we do that if YHWH Himself accommodates the lies? If, as Peter states, "holy men of God spake as they were moved by the Holy Ghost" and they wrote those words down, then how can we trust Yeshua when He said that the Holy Ghost leads us to all truth?

John 16:13 *Howbeit when he, the Spirit of truth, is come, he will guide you into all truth: for he shall not speak of himself; but whatsoever he shall hear, that shall he speak: and he will shew you things to come.*

The Apostle John said that we have no need of a (human) teacher, but that the Holy Spirit should be our teacher:

1 John 2:27 *But the anointing which ye have received of him abideth in you, and ye need not that any man teach you: but as the same anointing teacheth you of all things, and is truth, and is no lie, and even as it hath taught you, ye shall abide in him.*

How can we trust the "anointing" (of the Holy Ghost) to teach us "all things" that are supposedly "truth," wherein there "is NO lie" if the Holy Ghost of YHWH accommodates the lies of those who are inspired to write Scripture? Indeed, those who wish to subscribe to the Doctrine of Accommodation are reducing Divine inspiration to little more than cosmic indigestion and are promoting ideologies that obliterate any notion of the inerrant nature of Scripture by advocating such an insane doctrine.

In a blog titled, *Christians Who Believe the Earth is Really Flat - Does It Get Any Dumber Than This?*[161] Dr. Michael Heiser rips into people like me, then goes on to write:

What Mike Thinks

I'm appalled that people who follow Christ are this dumb (or so easily led astray into embracing beliefs that are demonstrably contrary to reality). This level of willful ignorance dishonors God. The stupidity of modern flat earth belief is transparent in today's world. Space flight (really, flight between hemispheres), satellite communications, space photography (any photography showing the

---

161 http://drmsh.com/christians-who-believe-the-earth-is-really-flat-does-it-get-any-dumber-than-this/

earth's curvature), etc. show the idea to be utter nonsense. And that's before getting into the nuts-and-bolts science. Yet some people think they need to believe it to have a "true" Bible. This is mindless, simplistic literalism at its worst. (Well, maybe it can get worse … keep reading).

* * *

I can already hear the comeback. "Let God be true and every man a liar!" Let me just say God isn't a liar. He knows (and knew) the earth is a globe. It just happens that the people he chose to produce this thing we call the Bible didn't know that. And God couldn't have cared less. The writers God used to produce the Bible were not inspired to write about things of the natural world that were beyond their own worldview and knowledge base. And to argue (as normal 24-hour day creationists do) that God gave them advanced scientific knowledge, or that such advanced knowledge is encrypted in the biblical text, means that what they wrote could never have communicated that important knowledge to their original audience (or any audience prior to recent centuries). These approaches are absurd and undermine the communicative purpose of the Bible. What we read in Genesis (and elsewhere) reflects a common ancient Near Eastern perspective about cosmology with one crucial difference: the credit for creation is given exclusively to the God of Israel against all other gods. That is its truth claim with respect to creation. That Israelite cosmology is quite consistent with wider ancient Near Eastern cosmology is easy to demonstrate.1 That God chose people of a certain time, a certain place, with a certain (limited) knowledge base was up to him. We dishonor His choices when we impose our questions and our context on the biblical writers. Precisely the same limitations would be in place if God chose a scientist today to write Genesis 1000 years from now people would chuckle at how primitive he/she was ("Can you believe this is what they thought?"). This is why the Bible intentionally transcends science discourse — science always changes with new discovery and knowledge. Who the creator was never changes.

Sorry Mike. If the "Creator never changes," then He continues to accommodate lies according to this absurd rationale. Furthermore, this whole idea of the Biblical explanation of Creation reflecting "a common ancient Near Eastern perspective about cosmology with one crucial difference: the credit for creation is given exclusively to the God of Israel against all other gods. That is its truth claim with respect to creation," has YHWH effectively taking credit for being the cause of Creation, while simultaneously endorsing the (according to Mike) erroneous method for how He did so, which was apparently in perfect alignment with the "false" cosmology of the Ancient Near East.

Personally, I have never in my life been given any reason to doubt the truth of Scripture. Never. Time and time again, the Bible has proven to be a "living Word," which has not once let me down. It has always proven itself to be 100% true in every detail and thus completely trustworthy to be my "compass" in a world filled with lies. Therefore, you are free to believe whatever you want, but for me, to imagine that the Scriptures would in any way accommodate those lies in an effort to convey truth is an unthinkable, logical fallacy and a patently absurd idea.

I'm in agreement with the Apostle Paul: Let God be true and every man a liar (Rom. 3:4).

Those Newtonian philosophers who still hold that the Sacred Volume is the word of God are thus placed in a fearful dilemma. How can the two systems, so directly opposite in character, be reconciled? Oil and water alone will not combine--mix them by violence as we may, they will again separate when allowed to rest. Call oil oil, and water water, and acknowledge them to be distinct in nature and value, but let no "hodge- podge" be attempted, and passed off as a genuine compound of oil and water. Call Scripture the Word of God, the Creator and Ruler of all things, and the Fountain of all truth; and call the Newtonian or Copernican system of astronomy the word and work of man--of man, too, in his vainest mood--so vain and conceited as not to be content with the direct and simple teachings of his Maker, but must rise up in rebellion, and conjure into existence a fanciful complicated fabric, which, being insisted upon as true, creates and necessitates the dark and horrible interrogatives--**Is God a deceiver? Has He spoken direct and unequivocal falsehood?** Can we no longer indulge in the beautiful and consoling thought that God's justice, and love, and truth, are unchanging and reliable for ever?

Let Christians at least--for sceptics and atheists may be left out of the question--to whatever division of the Church they belong, look to this matter calmly and earnestly. Let them determine to uproot the deception which has led them to think that they can altogether ignore the plainest astronomical teachings of Scripture, and yet indorse a system to which it is in every sense opposed.

The following language is quoted as an instance of the manner in which the doctrine of the earth's rotundity and the plurality of worlds interferes with Scriptural teachings:--

> "The theory of original sin is confuted (by our astronomical and geological knowledge), and I cannot permit the belief, when I know that our world is but a mere speck, a perishable atom in the vast space of creation, that God should just select this little spot to descend upon and assume our form, and clothe Himself in our flesh, to become visible to human eyes, to the tiny beings of this comparatively insignificant world. . . . Thus millions of distant worlds, with the beings allotted to them, were to be extirpated and destroyed in consequence of the original sin

of Adam. No sentiment of the human mind can surely be more derogatory to the divine attributes of the Creator, nor more repugnant to the known economy of the celestial bodies. For, in the first place, who is to say, among the infinity of worlds, whether Adam was the only creature who was tempted by Satan and fell, and by his fall involved all the other worlds in his guilt?"[162]

The difficulty experienced by the author of the above remarks is clearly one which can no longer exist when it is seen that the doctrine of a plurality of worlds is an impossibility. That it is an impossibility is shown by the fact that the sun, moon, and stars, are very small bodies, and very near to the earth; this fact is proved by actual non-theoretical measurement; this measurement is made on the principle of plane trigonometry; this principle of plane trigonometry is adopted because the earth is experimentally demonstrated to be a plane, and all the base lines employed in the triangulation are horizontal. By the same practical method of reasoning, all the difficulties which, upon geological and astronomical grounds, have been raised to the literal teachings of the Scriptures may be completely destroyed.

> This was a big one for me. It's what kept me awake for *many, many* nights in the first year of my research, but indeed it is what compelled me to continue on; to keep digging, researching, studying and comparing what "science" has been trying to force upon me with the truths of Scripture. When you do this, you come to the inescapable conclusion that **modern science and Scripture are simply not compatible** in any way, shape or form.

The doctrine that the earth is a globe has been proved, by the most potent evidence which it is possible for the human mind to recognise, that of direct experiment and observation, to be *unconditionally false*. It is not a question of degree, of more or less truth, but of *absolute falsehood*. That of its diurnal and annual motion, and of its being one of an infinite number of revolving spheres, is equally false; and, therefore, the Scriptures, which negative these notions, and teach expressly the reverse, must in their astronomical philosophy at least be ***literally true***. In practical science, therefore, atheism and denial of Scriptural teaching and authority have no foundation. If human theories are cast aside, rejected as entirely worthless, and the facts of nature and legitimate reasoning alone relied on, it will be seen that religion and true science are not antagonistic, but are strictly parts of one and the same great system of sacred philosophy.

To the religious mind this matter is most important--it is indeed no less than a sacred question; for it renders complete the evidence that the Jewish and Christian Scriptures are absolutely true, and must have been communicated to mankind by an anterior and supernal Being. If after so many ages of mental struggling, of speculation and trial, of

---

162 "Encyclopædia Londinensis," p. 457, vol. 2.

change and counterchange, we have at length discovered that all astronomical theories are false; that the earth is a plane, and motionless, and that the various luminaries above it are lights only and not worlds; and that these very facts have been declared and recorded in a work which has been handed down to us from the earliest times--from a time, in fact, when mankind had lived so short a period upon the earth that they could not have had sufficient experience to enable them to criticise and doubt, much less to invent and speculate--it follows that whoever dictated and caused such doctrines to be recorded and preserved to all generations must have been superhuman, omniscient, and to the earth and its inhabitants pre-existent. That Being could only be the Creator of the world, and His truth is recorded in the Sacred Writings. The Scriptures-- the Bible, therefore, cannot be other than the word and teaching of God. Let it once be seen that such a conclusion is a logical necessity; that the sum of the purely practical evidence which has been collected compels us to acknowledge this, and we find ourselves in possession of a solid and certain foundation for all our future investigations.

Dr. John Walton is the Professor of Old Testament Studies at Wheaton College in Illinois. In a lecture titled, *Understanding Genesis 1-3* given July 17, 2013 he lays the foundation for how we should read the Bible, stating:

"We have to start with the authority of the text."

He goes on to say that YHWH has invested His authority into human beings who wrote the Scriptures down.

"That means that those human communicators are our access to God's authority."

He tells us that we must get to know the ancient world; to understand the culture and beliefs of those who wrote the Bible, not impose our culture and understanding upon the text. We need to strip away our own cultural baggage in order to understand the ancient world, and thus the context in which the Scriptures were written.

"[I]f we're going to understand their texts, we have to think about the world the way that they thought about the world. We can't afford to just kind of freelance it and read it the way we want; reading those words to mean anything that we want them to mean. Can't do that. We have to read it the way the Israelites meant it. You cannot read the text more seriously - more literally - than to read it according to what that ancient author meant to say. It's the only way to do it. So we have to read the text the way they meant it. We cannot take a text like 'God stretched out the heavens' and say that that refers to the Big Bang and the expanding universe. It didn't mean that to the author and cannot mean what it never meant. It means what it means and that's what the author intended to say and that has authority.

We're not free to read new meanings into those text. On what authority would we do that?[1]

I am in complete agreement with Dr. Walton here. Now I must point out that he is *not* a flat Earther. However, he is at least being intellectually honest with the text in insisting that the original author was inspired by YHWH's Holy Spirit to write and thus the text has authority. Our only choice then is to either believe it or disbelieve it (or make up excuses such as the Doctrine of Accommodation). We do not have the authority to change the text into meaning things that support our world view—cosmological or otherwise.

1 For more of his speech, see my YouTube video *How the Bible MUST be read if we consider it to be an authoritative text*: https://youtu.be/fQtEwY9Tl1c

That everything which the Scriptures teach respecting the material world is ___literally true___ will readily be seen. It is a very popular notion among modern astronomers that the stellar universe is an endless congeries of systems, of suns and attendant worlds, peopled with sentient beings analogous in the purpose and destiny of their existence to the inhabitants of this earth.

Ironically enough, it was Sir Isaac Newton who once wrote:

*"About the Time of the End, a body of men will be raised up who will turn their attention to the Prophecies, and insist upon their **literal interpretation**, in the midst of much clamor and opposition."*

Anyone who studies prophecy will eventually see this quote show up. Assuming Newton did say this, I find it odd that so many in "prophecy ministries" like to use this quote about insisting upon the *literal* interpretation of Scripture pertaining to prophecy, but be against a literal interpretation concerning cosmology. If the front of the book is in error, what possible reason do we have to trust the back of the book or anything else in between for that matter?

This doctrine of a plurality of worlds, although it may be admitted to convey most magnificent ideas of the universe, is purely fanciful, and may be compared to some of the "dreams of the alchemists," who laboured with unheard of patience and enthusiasm to discover a "philosopher's stone," to change all common metals into gold and silver; an elixir vitæ to prevent and to cure all the disorders of the human frame; and the "universal solvent" which was deemed necessary to enable them to make all things homogeneous, as preliminary to precipitation, or concretion into any form desired by the operator. However grand the first two projects might have been in their realisation, it is known that they were never developed in a useful and practical sense. They depended upon the third--the discovery of a solvent which would dissolve everything. The idea was suddenly and most unexpectedly destroyed by the few remarks of a simple but critical observer, who demanded to know what service a substance could be to them which would dissolve all things; seeing that it would dissolve every thing, what would they keep it in? It would dissolve every vessel wherein they sought to preserve it! The alchemists had never "given a thought" to such a thing. They were entirely absorbed with the supposed magnitude and grandeur of their purposes. The idea never struck them that their objects involved inconsistency and impossibility; but when it did strike, the blow was so heavy that the whole fraternity of alchemists reeled almost to destruction, and alchemy, as a science, rapidly expired.

The idea of a "plurality of worlds" is as grand and romantic as that of the "universal solvent," and is a natural and reasonable conclusion drawn from the doctrine of the earth's rotundity. It never occurred to the advocates of sphericity and infinity of systems that there was one great and overwhelming necessity at the root of their speculations. The idea never struck them that the convexity of the surface of the earth's standing water required demonstration. The explanation its assumption enabled them to give of natural phenomena was deemed sufficient. At length, however, another "critical observer"--one almost born with doubts and criticisms in his heart, determined to examine practically, experimentally, this fundamental necessity.

The great and theory-destroying fact was quickly discovered that the surface of standing water was perfectly horizontal! Here was another death-blow to the unnatural ideas and speculations of pseudo- philosophers. Just as the "universal solvent" could not be preserved or manipulated, and therefore the whole system of alchemy died away, so the necessary proof of convexity in the waters of the earth could not be found, and therefore the doctrine of rotundity and of the plurality of worlds must also die. Its death is now merely a question of time.

Just as in bygone times a voice was heard to say that "a universal solvent cannot be held," so now an unostentatious, but terribly dangerous and destructive, cry has been raised that water is not convex but horizontal, which will work a revolution in science greater than the world has yet seen. It will do what has never yet been done, destroy the vain and flimsy structures of human ingenuity, and turn the hearts of philosophers and all grades of men of learning to the wisdom and consistency and demonstrable truths contained in the "Word of God," the Scriptures of the all-wise, long-patient, and, by philosophers, almost forgotten Creator of the world. A reverence for, and solemn attention to, the teachings of His dictated Word will rapidly grow and spread in all directions, and our men of science and learning will become the servants of their Creator, and the true friends of their fellow-men. Vain systems of science and false honours and applause will be swallowed up in an ever-spreading, all-influencing, all-inclusive, and reverential philosophy--which will become to all progressive minds the long-hoped-for true and universal religion.

Let us now inquire earnestly, and in all respects fairly, whether the philosophical teachings of the Scriptures are consistent with those of Zetetic Astronomy; or, in other words, are descriptive of that which is, both in nature and in principle, demonstrably true.

In the Newtonian astronomy, continents, oceans, seas, and islands, are considered as together forming one vast globe of 25,000 English statute miles in circumference. This assertion has been shown to be entirely fallacious, and that it is contrary to the plain literal teaching of Scripture will be clearly seen from the following quotations:

> "And God said, Let the waters under the heaven be gathered together unto one place, and let the dry land appear. And God called the dry land earth; and the gathering together of the waters called He seas."-- Genesis i., 9-10.

Instead of the word "earth" meaning both land and water, only the dry land is called earth, and the seas the gathering or collection of the waters in vast bodies. Earth and seas--earth and the great body of waters, are described as two distinct and independent regions, and not as together forming one great globe which modern astronomers call "the earth." This description is confirmed by several other passages of Scripture:

> "The earth is the Lord's and the fulness thereof; the world and they that dwell therein; for He hath founded it upon the seas, and established it upon the floods."--Psalm xxiv., 1-2.

> "O give thanks to the Lord of lords, that by wisdom made the heavens, and that stretched out the earth above the waters."--Psalm cxxxvi., 6.

> "By the word of God the heavens were of old, and the earth standing out of the water and in the water."--2nd Peter iii., 5.

> "Who with the word of His strength fixed the heavens; and founded the earth upon the waters."--Hermes, N. T. Apocrypha.

That the surface of water is horizontal is a matter of absolute truth, and as the earth is founded upon the seas, and stretched out above the waters, it is of necessity a plane; and being a concrete mass of variable elements and compounds, with different specific gravities, it must be a floating structure, standing in and out of the waters, just as we see a ship or an iceberg.

Many have argued that the Scriptures favoured the idea that the earth is a globe suspended in space, from the following language of Job (xxvi., 7):--

> "He stretched out the north over the empty place, and hangeth the earth upon nothing."

Dr. Adam Clark, although himself a Newtonian philosopher, says, in his commentary on this passage, the literal translation is, "on the hollow or empty waste;" and he quotes a Chaldee version of the passage, which runs as follows:--

"He layeth the earth upon the waters, nothing sustaining it."

It is not that he "hangeth the earth upon nothing," an obviously meaningless expression, but "layeth it upon the waters," which were previously empty or waste or unoccupied by the earth--in fact, on and in which there was nothing visible before the dry land appeared.[163]

This is in strict accordance with the other expressions of Scripture that the earth was stretched out above the waters, and founded upon the seas--where nothing had before existed.

If the earth is a globe, it is evident that everywhere the water of its surface--the seas, lakes, oceans, and rivers--must be sustained or upheld by the land, which must be underneath the water; but being a plane "founded upon the seas," and the land and waters distinct and independent of each other, then the waters of the "great deep" must sustain the land as it does a ship, an ice-island, or any other flowing mass, and there must, of necessity, be waters below the earth. In this particular, as in all others, the Scriptures are beautifully sequential and consistent.

> "The Almighty shall bless thee with the blessing of Heaven above, and blessings of the deep that lieth under."--Genesis xliv., 25.

> "Thou shalt not make unto thee any likeness of anything in heaven above, or in the earth beneath, or in the waters under the earth."-- Exodus xx., 4.

> "Take ye, therefore, good heed unto yourselves, and make no similitude of anything on the earth, or the likeness of anything that is in the waters beneath the earth." --Deuteronomy iv., 18.

> "Blessed be his land, for the precious things of heaven, for the dew, and for the deep which croucheth beneath."--Deuteronomy xxxiii., 13.

The same fact was acknowledged by the ancient philosophers. In "Ovid's Metamorphoses" Jupiter, in an "assembly of the gods," is made to say:--

"I swear by the infernal waves which glide under the earth."

As the earth is a distinct structure, standing in and upheld by the waters of the "great deep," it follows, unless it can be proved that something solid and substantial sustains the waters, that "the depths" are fathomless. As there is no evidence whatever of anything

---

163 For an additional in-depth look at Job 26:7 and the issue of the Earth allegedly "hanging upon nothing," please see: http://www.testingtheglobe.com/pillars.html.

existing except the fire consequent upon the rapid combination and decomposition of numerous well-known elements, we are compelled to admit that the depth is boundless--that beneath the waters which glide under the lowest parts of the earth there is nothing of a resisting nature. This is again confirmed by the Scriptures:--

> "Thus saith the Lord, which giveth the sun for a light by day, and the ordinances of the moon and stars for a light by night, which divideth the sea when the waves thereof roar, the Lord of Hosts is His name. If these ordinances depart from before me, saith the Lord, then the seed of Israel also shall cease from being a nation before me for ever. Thus saith the Lord: if heaven above can be measured and the foundations of the earth searched out beneath, I will also cast off all the seed of Israel."-- Jeremiah xxxi., 37.

From the above it is certain that God's promises to His people can no more be broken than can the height of heaven be measured, or the depths of the mighty waters--the earth's foundations--searched out or determined. The fathomless character of the deep beneath, upon which the earth is founded, and the infinitude of heaven above, are here given as emblems of the boundlessness of God's power, and of the certainty that all His ordinances will be fulfilled. When God's power can be limited, heaven above will be no longer infinite; and the "mighty waters," the "great deep," the "foundations of the earth," may be fathomed. But the Scriptures plainly teach us that the power and wisdom of God, the heights of heaven, and the depth of the "waters under the earth," are alike boundless and unfathomable.

Jeremiah 31 is a *very* interesting passage of Scripture, which may shed some light on the "motive" for the global lie. Here we see that if either the sun, moon or stars were to depart or change their ordinances before YHWH, then (true) Israel will cease to exist forever. Israel is the Bride of the God (see the books of Exodus; Jeremiah; Hosea; Romans 7-11; Revelation 21). If Satan can cause a problem with the various Heavenly Luminaries, then he can cause YHWH to obliterate His own Bride.

Please note:

1) While NASA and other space agencies apparently can't do much against the sun or the stars, they did (allegedly) bomb the moon a few years ago.

2) NASA and monkey-man science has claimed to "measure the heavens" going so far as to claim to know the exact details of the first micro-second of the Big Bang, and thereby extrapolating the extent of the universe's expansion.

3) Monkey-man science has given us picture after picture (or I should say, artist renderings) of the core of our world. They claim to know the exact composition of Earth's "foundations" (when in fact, no one has actually been able to go deeper than about 12 miles). But again, we have "science" claiming to have "searched out the Earth

---

beneath" and to have conclusively defined it (every text book on the Earth shows cutaway pictures depicting the various layers of the Earth from the upper atmosphere right down to the "inner core."

If monkey-man science was true, then according to the above, Israel (the ONLY Bride of the Divine listed in Scripture) would have to be "cast off" and "cease" to exist.

Fortunately for all of us natural or grafted in olive tree branches, we are finding more and more that NASA and monkey-man science are lying to us.

That the earth is stationary, except the fluctuating motion referred to in the chapter on the cause of tides, has been more than sufficiently demonstrated; and the Scriptures in no instance affirm the contrary.

The progressive and concentric motion of the sun over the earth is in every sense practically demonstrable; yet the Newtonian astronomers insist upon it that the sun only *appears* to move, and that this appearance arises from the motion of the earth; that when, as the Scriptures affirm, the "sun stood still in the midst of heaven," it was the *earth* which stood still and not the sun; that the Scriptures therefore speak falsely, and the experiments of science, and the observations and applications of our senses are never to be relied upon![164]

Some try to argue that when Joshua commanded the sun and moon to stand still (in Joshua 10:12-14), that it was really just a perspective issue from Earthbound observer's points of view. To be fair, I've made some of the exact same arguments in the past myself. But now I see there are several problems with this view:

1. The text says Joshua commanded the sun and the moon, **not the Earth** to stand still. He took **legal** authority with his words. Words mean things, but even more so in a legal framework. If one is going to take legal authority over the natural world, then the words used should be quite accurate and very definitive. YHWH did not say, "Oh well, I know my servant is an ignorant moron, so I'll do what is necessary to make his command come true. I know what he meant to say, so I'll go ahead and stop the Earth and suspend a host of post-Copernican 'laws' in order to make it happen."

2. Yes, if you stop the Earth in the current post-Copernican model, the sun would appear to stop in the sky. However, the text says the moon stopped too. This presents another problem for anyone who refuses to simply take the Bible at its word. The moon is allegedly in orbit around our world, both spinning itself (in a fashion that just so happens to keep the same "face" pointed toward us all the time) as well as moving around us.

---

164 The Chinese have said: "We have better philosophers, and men of higher intelligence than any you have ever been able to produce. You tell us that the earth goes round the sun, when we know by our senses that it does not. If you won't use your eyes, and believe what you see, you must be deaf to all teaching and instruction, and we will have nothing to do with you."--"Times" Newspaper, August 20, 1872.

So, for Joshua's command to work as stated (and understood in the post-Copernican model of the cosmos), YHWH would have had to stop the Earth and the moon. And if He stopped the moon, but didn't stop its rotation too, then how could it remain in sync with the same face pointed toward us precisely as it is?

If the Earth stops rotating, Newton's orbital laws of motion would have to be suspended. In short, you would lose "gravity." The magnetic field would also collapse and you would have to deal with 1,000 mile wind-sheer as the atmosphere would continue to spin even if the Earth stopped, in accordance with the Law of Inertia. The same would be true of the oceans, which would have to totally flood the whole Earth in accordance with the same law. I see no evidence of the Isrealites being drowned in this encounter.

The Earth (allegedly) spins and is as most believe heliocentric, meaning it is going around the sun. But if the sun stood still, there would have to be a suspension of both our orbital movement as well as our rotational movement in order to keep the sun specifically over one location "upon Gibeon." So, where do we see any evidence that the Earth then spun back up to 1,000 mph, and proceeded to move back into its heliocentric orbital speed of 67,000 mph around the sun?

If the moon is allegedly in charge of the tides of our seas, then we'd also have significant tidal issues as it ramped back up to speed doing its thing after being stopped from doing it by Joshua's command.

But since most prefer to agree with modern, monkey-man science over what the Scriptures actually say, I'll direct such people to do some research into what mainstream science has to say concerning the devastating effects, which would result from the Earth and moon suddenly stopping their spinning and orbital motions.

Meanwhile, we also have the issue of Hezikaih and the sun dial going backward. In this case, things get even worse for the Copernican model.

Isaiah 38:
1 In those days was Hezekiah sick unto death. And Isaiah the prophet the son of Amoz came unto him, and said unto him, Thus saith the Lord, Set thine house in order: for thou shalt die, and not live.
2 Then Hezekiah turned his face toward the wall, and prayed unto the Lord,
3 And said, Remember now, O Lord, I beseech thee, how I have walked before thee in truth and with a perfect heart, and have done that which is good in thy sight. And Hezekiah wept sore.
4 Then came the word of the Lord to Isaiah, saying,
5 Go, and say to Hezekiah, Thus saith the Lord, the God of David thy father, I have heard thy prayer, I have seen thy tears: behold, I will add unto thy days fifteen years.
6 And I will deliver thee and this city out of the hand of the king of Assyria: and I will defend this city.
7 And this shall be a sign unto thee from the Lord, that the Lord will do this thing that he hath spoken;

8 Behold, **I will bring again the shadow of the degrees, which is gone down in the sun dial of Ahaz, ten degrees backward. So the sun returned ten degrees, by which degrees it was gone down.**

Here we would have the Earth stop rotating. Then start rotating backward, then reversing again and ramping back up to 1,000 mph again. Really?? Do you have any idea how badly that would jack up all of the oceans, rivers and lakes?? Of course, you could say, "Well, it's called a 'miracle' for a reason Rob. God just made it all work out that way, with no accompanying issues, which would have to occur according to our monkey-man science." Sure. You could use that argument. Or… you could just simply agree with what the Bible says!

At no time whatsoever does the Bible in any way, shape or form even remotely support a spinning, heliocentric ball Earth concept. The sun doesn't even show up until Day 4 of Creation for crying out loud, showing the singular importance of the Earth over the sun. The sun is here to support life on the pre-existing, stationary Earth. The Earth was here first in the Biblical model and – according to Moses – the sun, moon and stars were later placed over us inside the firmament (dome-like, metallic enclosure) that separates the waters above from the waters below. But in the Copernican-Netonian-Einstein model, the firmament is gone and all importance is shifted to the sun and everything quite literally "revolves" around it instead of Earth. The problem for those who want to hold on to both the Bible and monkey-man science is that in Scripture we always see the Earth as center stage, not the sun and it is to the Earth that everything else in the cosmos remains subordinate. You cannot hold onto both the Bible and monkey-man science as they are most certainly diametrically opposing (pardon the pun) viewpoints.

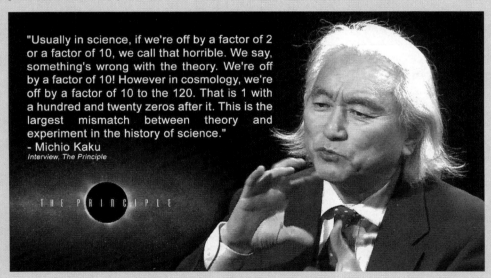

"Usually in science, if we're off by a factor of 2 or a factor of 10, we call that horrible. We say, something's wrong with the theory. We're off by a factor of 10! However in cosmology, we're off by a factor of 10 to the 120. That is 1 with a hundred and twenty zeros after it. This is the largest mismatch between theory and experiment in the history of science."
- Michio Kaku
Interview, The Principle

THE PRINCIPLE

The above quote of Michio Kaku from the documentary, *The Principle* is not taken out of context. The man actually said those words on camera! And elsewhere, we find people like Neil deGrasse Tyson saying that when it comes to our understanding of the universe "we are 96% stupid." So, why are we listening to these people?

Whence comes this bold and arrogant denial of the value of our senses and judgment and authority of Scripture? A *theory* which is absolutely false in its groundwork, and ridiculously illogical in its details, demands that the earth is round and moves upon axes, and in several other various directions; and that these motions are *sufficient to account for* certain phenomena without requiring the sun to move--*therefore*, the sun does *not* move but is a fixed body--his motion is only *apparent*! Such "reasoning" is a disgrace to philosophy, and fearfully dangerous to the best--the religious interests of humanity.

The direct evidence of our senses, actual and special observations, as well as the most practical scientific experiments, all combine to make the motion of the sun over the non-moving earth unquestionable. All the expressions of Scripture are consistent with the fact of the sun's motion. They never declare anything to the contrary, but whenever the subject is required to be named, it is expressly in the affirmative:--

> "In the heavens hath He set a tabernacle for the sun, which is as a bridegroom coming out of his chamber, and rejoiceth as a strong man to *run a race*. His *going forth* is from the end of the heaven, and his *circuit* unto the end of it."
> --Psalms xix., 4-6.

> "The sun also ariseth, and the sun goeth down, and hasteth to his place where he arose."--Ecclesiastes i., 5.

> "Let them that love the Lord be as the sun when he goeth forth in his might."
> --Judges v., 31.

> "The sun stood still in the midst of heaven, and Basted not to go down about a whole day."--Joshua x., 13.

> "Great is the earth, high is the heaven, swift is the sun in his course."
> --1 Esdras iv., 34.

In the religious and mythological poems of all ages and nations the fact of the sun's motion is recognised and declared. Christians especially of every denomination are familiar with, and often read and sing with delight, such poetry as the following:--

> "My God, who makes the sun to know
>   His proper hour to rise,
> And, to give light to all below,
>   Doth send him *round* the skies.

> "When from the chambers of the East,
>   His *morning race* begins,
> He never tires, nor stops to rest,
>   But *round the world* he shines.

"God of the morning, at whose voice
　　The cheerful sun makes haste to rise,
And, like a giant, doth rejoice
　　To *run his journey* through the skies;
He sends the sun *his circuit* round,
　　To cheer the fruits and warm the ground."

"How fine has the day been!
　　How bright was the sun!
How lovely and joyful
　　The *course that he run*!"

The above simple verses are merely examples of what may be found in every hymn-book and collection of sacred poetry throughout the world. The sacred books of all nations, and the perceptions and instincts of the whole human race, completely accord in respect to the motion of the sun and the fixity of the earth; and theoretical astronomy fails to present a single fact or experiment to support the contrary conclusion.

Christian and Jewish ministers, teachers, and commentators, find it a most unwelcome task to reconcile the plain and simple philosophy of the Scriptures with the monstrous and contradictory teachings of modern theoretical astronomy. Dr. Adam Clark, in a letter to his friend, the Rev. Thomas Roberts, of Bath, in replying to questions as to the progress of the commentary he was then writing, and of his endeavours to reconcile the statements of Scripture with the Newtonian astronomy, says:--

> "Joshua's sun and moon standing still have kept me going for nearly three weeks! That one chapter has afforded me more vexation than anything I have ever met with; and even now I am but about half- satisfied with my own solution of all the difficulties, though I am confident that I have removed mountains that were never touched before. Shall I say that I am heartily weary of my work--so weary that I have a thousand times wished I had never written one page of it, and am repeatedly purposing to give it up?[165]

The Rev. John Wesley, in his journal, writes as follows:--

> "The more I consider them the more I doubt of all systems of astronomy. I doubt whether we can with certainty know either the distance or magnitude of any star in the firmament; else why do astronomers so immensely differ, even with regard to the distance of the sun from the earth? some affirming it to be only three, and others ninety millions of miles."[166]

---

165 "Life of Dr. Adam Clark," 8vo. edition.
166 Extracts from the Works of Rev. J. Wesley, 3rd edition, 1849, published by Mason, London; p. 392, vol. 2

In vol. 3 of the same work, p. 203, the following entry occurs:-- "January 1st, 1765.

> "This week I wrote an answer to a warm letter published in the 'London Magazine,' the author whereof is much displeased that I presume to doubt of the modern astronomy. I cannot help it; nay, the more I consider the more my doubts increase, so that at present I doubt whether any man on earth knows either the distance or magnitude, I will not say of a fixed star, but of Saturn or Jupiter--yea, of the sun or moon."

In vol. 13, p. 359, referring again to the subject of theoretical astronomy, he says:--

> "And so the whole hypothesis of innumerable suns and worlds moving round them vanishes into air."

Again, at p. 430 of the same volume, the following words occur:--

> "The planets' revolutions we are acquainted with, but who is able to this day regularly to demonstrate either their magnitude or their distance, unless he will prove, as is the usual way, the magnitude from the distance, and the distance from the magnitude?"

In the same paragraph, speaking of the earth's motion, he says:--

> "Dr. Rogers has evidently demonstrated that no conjunction of the centrifugal and centripetal forces can possibly account for this, or even cause any body to move in an ellipsis."

There are several other incidental remarks in his writings which show that the Rev. John Wesley was well acquainted with the then modern or Newtonian system of astronomy, and that he saw clearly its contradictory and anti-Scriptural character.

Just like the men quoted above, I also struggled immensely with what I was seeing in the Scriptures as I tried desperately to reconcile them with what "modern science" had taught me. Many a night was spent in fervent prayer (often to the point of tears) asking YHWH what I was supposed to do with all of this. His Word clearly contradicted what I was taught to believe my whole life and His only consistent reply to me that whole time was, "I said what I said." He wasn't apologizing, nor was He making any effort to try to show me how His Word could be made to fit my beliefs. This struggle continued from April of 2015 until early July 2016, shortly after returning from my Chicago skyline test[1] with Rick Hummer. After that, His reply to my prayers changed to, "Are you going to believe me now Rob or what?" At that point, I finally yielded and simply said, "Yes." A massive burden was lifted off me that day. And although verbal abuse continues to increase, there has been tremendous blessing in simply accepting YHWH at His Word.

1 See my YouTube video: *Rob Skiba proves the Chicago skyline (as seen from the other side) is NOT a mirage* https://youtu.be/o37t6iBS_q4

The supposition that the heavenly bodies are suns and systems of inhabited worlds is demonstrably false and impossible in nature, and certainly has no counterpart or foundation in Scripture.

"In the beginning God created the heaven and *the earth*."

One earth *only* was created; and, in the numerous references to this world contained in the entire Scriptures, no other physical world is ever mentioned. It is never even stated that *the earth* has companions like itself, or that it is one of an infinite number of worlds which co-exist, and were brought into being at the beginning of creation. It may be remarked also that all the favours and privileges, the promises and threats of God contained in the Scriptures, have sole and entire reference to this on earth and its inhabitants.

Modern science (falsely so-called) tries to tell us that they are actually able to see "Earth-like planets" at staggering distances. In fact, they claim to have found nearly 2,000 such worlds since 1995. On August 6, 2015, just four months into my flat Earth research, Space.com announced *"The 6 Most Earth-like Alien Planets"*[1] which allegedly have been "discovered." They are listed as:

- **Gliese 667Cc** - 22 light-years away and "at least 4.5 times as massive as Earth."
- **Kepler-22b** - 600 light-years away and "about 2.4 times our planet's size."
- **Kepler-69c** - 2,700 light-years away and "about 70% larger than Earth."
- **Kepler-62f** - 1,200 light-years away and "about 40% larger than Earth."
- **Kepler-186f** - 500 light-years away and "at most 10% larger than Earth."
- **Kepler-452b** - 1,400 light-years away and "is the most Earth-like planet found so far."

So, "scientists" claim to be seeing objects ranging in distances from 22 light-years to a whopping 2,700 light-years away. OK. Let's put this into perspective. One light-year is approximately 6 TRILLION miles![2] Anyone believing we have the ability to see 132,000,000,000,000 to a mind boggling 16,200,000,000,000,000 miles away needs to lay off the GMOs, fluoride and aspartame as quickly as possible and immediately get their head examined. Yet "scientists" claim to seeing something 8.4 QUADRILLION[3] (8,400,000,000,000,000) miles away and they have the audacity to declare that not only can they see it, but it is "the most Earth-like planet found so far." Folks, this is beyond insane and more than qualifies for the warning the Apostle Paul gave to Timothy, when he said:

1 Timothy 6:
*20 O Timothy, keep that which is committed to thy trust, **avoiding profane and vain babblings**, and oppositions of **science falsely so called**:*
*21 Which some professing **have erred concerning the faith**. Grace be with thee. Amen.*

1 https://www.space.com/30172-six-most-earth-like-alien-planets.html
2 http://earthsky.org/space/what-is-a-light-year
3 Chart to see the scale of numbers: https://www.thoughtco.com/zeros-in-million-billion-trillion-2312346

The sun, moon, and stars, are described as lights only to give light upon the earth.

> "And God made two great lights; the greater light to rule the day, and the lesser light to rule the night. He made the stars also, and set them in the firmament of heaven to give light upon the earth."--Genesis i., 16-17.

The creation of the world, the origin of evil, and the fall of man; the plan of redemption by the death of Christ, the Day of Judgment, and the final consummation of all things, are, in the Scriptures, invariably associated with *this earth alone*. A great number of passages might be quoted which prove that no other material world is ever, in the slightest manner, referred to by the inspired writers. The expressions in Hebrews (i., 2) "By whom also He made the *worlds*;" and (xi., 3) "Through faith we understand that *the worlds* were framed," are known to be a comparatively recent rendering from the Greek documents. The word in the original which has been translated "worlds" permits of being rendered in the singular quite as well as the plural number, and, previous to the introduction of the Copernican system of astronomy, was always translated *"the world"* [singular]. The Roman Catholic and also the French Protestant Bibles still contain the singular number; and in a copy of the English Protestant Bible, printed in the year 1608, the following translation is given:--

> "Through faith we understand that the world was ordained."

In the later translations either the plural expression "worlds" was used in order to accord with the astronomical theory *then recently introduced*, or it was meant to include the earth--the material world and the spiritual world, as referred to in the following passages:

> "For unto the angels hath He not put in subjection the *world to come?*"
> -- Hebrews ii., 5

> "Far above all principality, and power, and might, and dominion, and every name that is named, not only in *this world*, but also in *that which is to come*."
> --Ephesians i., 21.

> "There is no man that hath left house, or parents, or brethren, or wife, or children, for the Kingdom of God's sake, who shall not receive manifold more in this present time, and *in the world to come* life everlasting."-- Luke xviii., 29-30.

> "Whosoever speaketh against the Holy Ghost it shall not be forgiven him, neither in *this world*, neither in *the world to come*."--Matthew xii., 32.

If by the plural expression "worlds" is not meant the spiritual and the natural world, then the Scriptures have been tampered with; presumptuous men, more in love with their own conceits than with everything else, have perverted them, disputed their original consistency, dared to deny their inspired truthfulness, and challenged the omniscience of their Author.

The Scriptures teach that "the heavens shall pass away with a great noise, and the elements shall melt with fervent heat;" and the "stars of heaven fall unto the earth even as a fig-tree casteth her untimely figs when shaken of a mighty wind." As the stars have been shown to be comparatively minute objects, and very near to the earth, the above language is perfectly consistent with known possibilities; and very expressive of what, from practical observations, is found to be not only probable but inevitable.

Once again, this was a huge revelation for me because Scripture tells us:

Isaiah 34:4 And **all the host of heaven shall be dissolved, and the heavens shall be rolled together as a scroll**: and **all their host shall fall down**, as the leaf falleth off from the vine, and as a falling fig from the fig tree.

Mark 13:25 And **the stars of heaven shall fall**, and the powers that are in heaven shall be shaken.

2 Peter 3:10 But the day of the Lord will come as a thief in the night; in the which **the heavens shall pass away with a great noise, and the elements shall melt with fervent heat**, the earth also and the works that are therein shall be burned up.

Revelation 6:13 And **the stars of heaven fell unto the earth**, even as a fig tree casteth her untimely figs, when she is shaken of a mighty wind.

Here we have Isaiah, Yeshua (the Son of YHWH Himself), Peter and John each telling us that **all of the stars** are going to fall to Earth and that the heavens shall pass away. This is massively huge. And it means someone is lying to us. Either Copernicus, Galileo, Kepler, Newton, Sagan, Tyson, Kaku and company or the Holy Spirit inspired authors of Scripture. I don't know about you, but I'm not prepared to say it's Isaiah Yeshua, Peter and John.

The Newtonian system of astronomy declares that the stars and planets are mighty worlds--nearly all of them larger than the earth we inhabit. The fixed stars are considered to be suns, equal if not greater than our own sun, which is affirmed to be more than 800,000 miles in diameter, and nearly 360,000 times the mass of the earth. All this is simply and provably false; but- to those who have been led to believe it otherwise, and yet believe the Scriptures, the difficult question presents itself--How can thousands of stars fall upon this earth, which is hundreds of times less than any one of them? How can the earth, with a supposed diameter of 8000 miles, receive the numerous suns of the firmament, many of which are said to be a million miles in diameter? Can a whale rush down the throat of a herring? or an elephant ride on the back of a mouse? or the great mountain range which runs between France and Italy spring up from the plains and fall down the crater of Vesuvius? How then can the earth receive a downfall of stars and planets--suns and satellites and worlds, the united mass of which is said to be innumerable millions of times greater than itself? Is there anything in the brain of the maddest inmate of Bedlam which is half so contradictory and ridiculous as this and others of the dilemmas into which religious or Scripture-believing Newtonians are brought?

Again, these stars are assumed to have positions so far from the earth that the distance is almost in expressible; figures, indeed, may be arranged on paper, but in reading them no practical idea is conveyed to the mind. Many are said to be so distant that should they fall with the velocity of light, or above 160,000 miles in a second of time, 600,000,000 of miles per hour, they would require nearly 2,000,000 of years to reach the earth!

Considering the order of events and timeline of the "End Times," it seems quite impossible to fit any Biblical notion of *all the stars falling to Earth* within any framework that agrees with "modern science." According to the latter, each one of the stars are far too distant and way too large to ever fall to Earth. So to imagine *all of them* doing so is already an outrageous proposition, even without the added consideration of the speed and time required to make this happen.

Sir William Herschel, in a paper on "The power of telescopes to penetrate into space,"[167] affirms that with his powerful instruments he discovered brilliant luminaries so far from the earth that the light which they emitted "could not have been less than *one million nine hundred thousand years* in its progress!" Here again a difficulty presents itself, viz., if the stars begin to fall today, and with the greatest imaginable velocity, that of light, 160,000 miles in a second,[168] millions of years must elapse before many of them will reach the earth! But the Scriptures declare that these changes will occur suddenly; shall come, indeed, "as a thief in the night."

The same stultifying theory of astronomy, with its false and inconceivable distances and magnitudes,[169] operates to destroy the ordinary common sense and Scripturally authorised chronology. Christian and Jewish commentators--except the astronomically educated--hold and teach, on Scriptural authority, that the earth as well as the sun, moon, and stars, were created about 4000 years before the birth of Christ, or less than 6000 years before the present time. But if many of these luminaries are so distant that their light requires nearly two millions of years to reach the earth; and if, as it is affirmed, bodies are visible to us because of the light which they reflect or radiate then, because we now see them the light from them has already reached us, or they would not be visible, and therefore they must have been shining, and must have been created at least nearly

---

167 Philosophical Transactions for 1800.

168 Note the currently accepted speed of light is 186,282 mps (see: https://www.space.com/15830-light-speed.html). So, clearly either our understanding of the speed of light has changed in the last 100+ years, our equipment for testing it has become more accurate or the speed of light has increased (or perhaps all of the above).

169 This is covered much more in-depth in the book, "Kings Dethroned" by Gerrard Hickson (1922).

two millions of years ago! But the chronology of the Bible, unless by unwarrantable interpretation, indicates that a period of six thousand years has not yet elapsed since "the heavens and the earth were finished and all the host of them."

This has been a constant problem for "Creation Ministries" as they try to reconcile Scripture with "modern science" (falsely so-called). All the more so when they claim to "take the Bible literally" and demand a Creation week consisting of *literal* twenty-four hour days, while simultaneously denying what the same Scriptures have to say concerning the Firmament and the shape and nature of the Earth within it.

Christine Garwood addresses the divide between Creationists and zetetics on pages 357 and 358 in the Epilogue of her book, *Flat Earth: The History of an Infamous Idea* stating:

[T]here are similarities in how leading creationists and zetetics have defined their campaigns. Specifically, the zetetics claim to practice the only true science: utilizing popularist imagery of scientific endeavor, they cast themselves as the legitimate seekers of truth, guided first and foremost by nature, seeking to defend an empirically proven scientific fact, backed by common sense, objective investigation and Biblical authority. Similarly, in the early 1970s, strict six-day creationists began to utilize the labels 'creation science' and 'scientific creationism' to defend their cause. Yet although zetetics and creationists have packaged their respective issues as science, critical differences remain. Most notably, the Creation Research Institute and the zetetics diverge on the issue of Biblical interpretation, for the former reject the contention that the Bible teaches a flat earth. Just as important, the zetetic movement, if it can even be classified as such, never enjoyed the same level of institutionalization or ideological sophistication as the creation-science movement, or a comparable level of public support. Despite the growing strength of Biblical literalism in the United States, there are probably no more than a few thousand flat-earth believers alive in the world today and fewer still who would be willing to publicly declare their conviction. Yet although flat-earth belief is a rare, last-stand defiance against the teachings of science, its grounding in scriptural authority lends it some resonance at a time when a Gallop poll has revealed that 53 per cent [sic] of Americans believe that 'God created human beings in their present form exactly the way the Bible describes it', and a further 31 per cent [sic] of respondents hold that, while human beings have evolved over millions of years from other forms of life, this process was guided by God.

For this reason, the flat-earth idea remains on the peripheries of the debate. Evolutionists have claimed that if the Bible is accepted as an inerrant, infallible, scientifically accurate authority, as creationists argue, then to avoid contradiction they must also believe the earth to be flat. In response, creationists have insisted that the Bible does not teach a flat earth and such claims on the part of evolutionists are evidence of their moral bankruptcy—they are utilizing the flat-earth idea as a slur to disparage the creationist campaign. Further to this, when one critic likened the Creation Research Institute to the Flat Earth Society, a representative of the institute countered that the two organizations did not share any members in common and the linking of them was nothing but a smear. In general, creationists consider flat-earth believers misguided and too extreme, while flat-earth believers consider creationists hypocritical for emphasizing a literal interpretation of the Bible while rejecting the idea that the earth is flat. Biblical interpretation aside, the Creation Research Institute's hostility towards the flat-earth concept set against zetetic disdain for Christians who believe the earth to be a globe illustrates the dangers of lumping together complex belief systems and their adherents, when in reality they may perceive themselves as radically opposed.

Garwood hits the nail on the head with her analysis. Although her book was written over ten years ago (© 2007), so her statistics no longer reflect what is currently (in 2018) happening. The number of 'Flat Earthers' is rapidly increasing. And right along with this growth is an increase in tensions between flat Earth believers (zetetics) and Creationists. In fact, just in the last year alone, various Creation ministries such as I.C.R. (mentioned by Garwood), Answers in Genesis, the ministry of Kent Hovind, and others have been feverishly writing on-line blogs, publishing articles, making videos, etc. to try and refute the claims of Flat Earthers—particularly going after Christians (like me) who proclaim without hesitation that "the Bible is a flat Earth book."

What is so frustrating about this however is you can have otherwise brilliant scholars like Dr. John Walton, Dr. Robert J. Schneider, Dr. Dennis Bratcher, Dr. Michael Heiser and the scholars at Logos Bible Software give an intellectually honest presentation from the text, showing in no uncertain terms how the authors of Scripture clearly had an enclosed, flat world cosmology, turn around and then deny belief in what they just acknowledged the Holy Spirit inspired the authors to write. They will usually do this in favor of the Doctrine of Accommodation to justify us having more of a 'scientific world view' than the ancient Hebrews had. For more on this, please see my YouTube video, *Flat Earth, a Doctor and the Village Idiot*.[170]

---

170 Please note: when I recorded that broadcast, it was very early in my investigation and at that time, I had not yet become convinced of the things I now believe.

Indeed, after becoming *very* frustrated from seeing more and more double-standards within the Creationist community and among Christians in general, I posted the following on my Facebook wall on August 4, 2016:

Upon further study, I feel I must issue the following warning {CAPPING for emphasis only}:

There can simply be NO QUESTION (despite all of the horribly lame attempts some have been trying to make recently to say otherwise) that the Hebrews shared the exact same cosmological world view as their Ancient Near Eastern neighbors. If you think otherwise, you are only telegraphing how little you know about history and how terrible you are at actually researching what the ancients wrote and believed. That being said, here's the warning...

Dear "literal" Bible believing, young Earth Creationist,

You either accept ALL of the Creation account as given in Genesis and elaborated on by the likes of Job (who really predates Moses), David, Solomon, Ezekiel, Isaiah, Yeshua, Peter, Paul and John (among others), or you MUST throw the whole thing in the garbage bin of mythological fairy tales and nonsense written by the likes of other ignorant, primitive, sheep herders, farmers and fishermen from antiquity. You simply can NOT believe in the "LITERAL six day Creation account," without acknowledging the order of events given (e.g. the EARTH being the central character in the cosmos, not the sun, nor the "universe"). You can NOT ignore the fact that the sun, moon and stars showed up on Day 4 and that they were placed INSIDE the FIRMament, which is described throughout the Biblical narrative as well as in NUMEROUS ancient cultures as a HARD, physical structure that is connected to the "circle" of the Earth. You can NOT maintain any notion of the Earth moving, spinning, orbiting, etc., as NO Biblical text supports such an idea. Rather, we find NUMEROUS examples of the Holy Spirit inspired authors describing the sun on a "circuit" and the moon and stars likewise in motion. If you continue to claim to "take the Bible literally" and yet deny what it says, then you are a liar. Plain and simple. Or worse yet, you are calling YHWH and His authors liars, because none of them held to the belief system you do - of a spinning, heliocentric globular Earth hurling through the endless expanse of space, being yanked along by the sun's "gravity."

Such a concept didn't even begin to take root in the minds of men until the pagan sun god worshiping Greeks began to fantasize about such things about 250 years before Christ. Now, the totally pagan Greek god worshiping organization known as NASA has taken up the cause of perpetuating such a belief. And MOST of you "Creationists" are only parroting what NASA feeds you as if it is the truth. You've exchanged the truth of Scripture for the "truth" as given to us from NASA and are now grossly mangling the Biblical text to try and force it to fit what NASA has told you to believe.

If you try to relegate the CLEAR descriptions of the cosmos as all being "figurative" and "symbolic" poetry, then you MUST also drag the creation of Adam from dust into that same category, because it is just as absurd as the rest of the Creation account - especially in this "scientific world view" we tend to associate ourselves with these days. The same with Eve's creation from Adam's side. Such things are just as ridiculous as a "flat Earth cosmology" because we all know that's not how men and women REALLY come into this world. And while you are at it, clearly snakes don't talk, so the "fall of man" must simply be allegorical too. And if it is, then the concept of "original sin" is utter mythological nonsense too. And if that be the case, what need do we have of a miracle-working Savior born of a virgin??

A miracle is something that generally contradicts what we "KNOW" to be true in the natural, so are ALL of the miracles in the Bible now allegorical, figurative, poetry too? Did Lot's wife really turn into a pillar of salt? Did Moses really part the Red Sea? We KNOW that donkey's can't talk, so the story of Balaam's talking donkey must be "poetic" nonsense. Fire burns people, so we can't possibly accept the story of 3 Hebrews surviving INSIDE a fiery furnace. Therefore, it must just be a "good moral tale" to teach our children (kinda like Santa), right? We KNOW that people can not walk on water, so the act of Jesus AND PETER doing so must simply be a parable for us to figure out. Speaking of Peter, since when can a shadow heal people? Yet, we are told his did. Ah, it's probably just more poetic nonsense! And on and on it goes. You enter an EXTREMELY slippery slope by assigning those things you don't understand to the category of "poetry" and/or merely "figurative" and "allegorical language."

Indeed, the more you read the various descriptions of the Creation account, and the subsequent stories of the Bible with the mindset of "allegory" and "poetry," the less meaningful it becomes. The whole thing is then subject to OUR willingness to either accept what it says at face value or to dismiss it altogether because we *claim* to know such and such to be true. In such a completely subjective scenario, what then is truth and can the Bible even offer anything remotely close to it in a science (falsely so-called) dominated world view?

This modern theoretical astronomy also affirms that the moon is a solid, opaque, non-luminous body; that it is, in fact, nothing less than a material world. It has even been mapped out into continents, islands, seas, lakes, volcanoes, and volcanic regions; and the nature of its atmosphere (or its surface, supposing, as many do, that an atmosphere cannot exist) and the character of its productions and possible inhabitants have been as freely discussed and described as though our philosophers were as familiar with it as they are with the different objects and localities on the earth. The light, too, with which the moon beautifully illuminates the firmament is declared to be only borrowed--to be only the light of the sun intercepted and reflected upon the earth. These notions are not only opposed by a formidable array of well- ascertained facts (as shown in previous chapters), but they are totally denied by the Scriptures. The sun, moon, and stars, are never referred to as worlds but simply as *lights*, to rule alternately the day and the night, and to be "for signs and for seasons, and for days and years."

> "And God said let there be *lights* in the firmament of the heaven to divide the day from the night. . . . And God made *two great lights*, the greater *light* to rule the day, and the lesser *light* to rule the night."-- Genesis i., 14-16.

> "O give thanks to Him that made *great lights*: . . . the sun to rule by day, . . . the moon and stars to rule by night."--Psalm cxxxvi., 7-9.

> "The sun is given for a light by day, and the ordinances of the moon and of the stars for a light by night."--Jeremiah xxxi., 35.

> "I will cover the sun with a cloud, and the moon shall not ***give*** her light. All the bright *lights* of heaven will I make dark over thee."--Ezekiel xxxii., 7-8.

> "Praise Him, sun and moon; praise Him all ye *stars of light*."--Psalm cxlviii., 3.

> "The sun shall be darkened in his going forth, and the moon shall not ***cause*** her *light* to shine."--Isaiah xiii., 10.

> "Immediately after the tribulation of those days shall the sun be darkened, and the moon shall not ***give*** her *light*."--Matthew xxiv., 29.

> "The sun shall be no more thy light by day; neither for brightness shall the moon ***give*** *light* unto thee. . . . Thy sun shall no more go down, neither shall thy moon withdraw itself."--Isaiah lx., 19-20.

> "Behold even to the moon, and *it shineth not*."--Job xxv., 5.

> "While the sun, or the light, or the moon, or the stars be not darkened." -- Ecclesiastes xii., 2.

"The light of the moon shall be as the light of the sun, and the light of the sun shall be sevenfold."--Isaiah xxx., 26.

"And for the precious fruits brought forth by the sun, and for the precious things put forth by the moon."--Deuteronomy xxxiii., 14.

The Book of Enoch also *sheds much light* on this topic. I would refer the reader to Chapters 72-82, which deal with the courses of the heavenly luminaries in great detail. See also the following books[1] by Zen Garcia and the associated videos I did with him:

- **Flat Earth as Key to Decrypt the Book of Enoch**
- **Firmament: Vaulted Dome of the Earth**
- **Paradise: Sides of the North and the Mount of Congregation**

TFR - Revolutionary Radio with Zen Garcia: Flat Earth and the book of Enoch

TFR - Revolutionary Radio with Zen Garcia: Flat Earth and the Firmament

1 NOTE: You can get all three books for a discount as a package deal here: https://sacredwordpublishing.com/collections/flat-earth/products/zens-flat-earth-bundle-decrypt-enoch-firmament-paradise

In the very first of the passages above quoted, the fact is announced that various distinct and independent *lights* were created; but that two *great* lights were specially called into existence for the purpose of ruling the day and the night. The sun and the moon are declared to be these great and alternately ruling lights. Nothing is here said, nor is it said in any other part of Scripture, that the sun only is a great light, and that the moon only shines by reflection. The sun is called the "greater light to rule the day," and the moon the "lesser light to rule the night." Although of these two "great lights" one is less than the other, each is declared to shine with its own independent light. Hence, in Deuteronomy xxxiii., 14, it is consistently affirmed that certain fruits are specially developed by the influence of the sun's light; and certain other productions are "put forth by the moon."

That the light of the sun is influential in encouraging the growth of certain natural products, and that the light of the moon has a distinct influence in promoting the increase of certain other natural substances, is a matter well known to those who are familiar with horticultural and agricultural phenomena; and it is abundantly proved by chemical evidence that the two lights are distinct in character and in their action upon various compounds. This distinction is beautifully preserved throughout the Sacred Writings. In no single instance are the two lights confounded or regarded as of the same character. On the contrary, positive statements are made as to their difference in nature and influence. St. Paul affirms emphatically that "there is one glory of the sun and another glory of the moon, and another glory of the stars, for one star differeth from another star in glory."

> "The sun became black as sackcloth of hair, and the moon became as blood."
> --Revelations vi., 12.

If the moon has a light of her own, the above language is consistent; but if she is only a reflector the moment the sun becomes black her surface will be darkened also. She could not remain as blood while the sun is dark and "black as sackcloth of hair."

The same theoretical astronomy teaches that, as the stars are so far away, hundreds of millions of statute miles, they cannot possibly give light upon the earth; that the fixed stars are burning spheres, or suns each to its own system only of planets and satellites; and that millions of miles from the earth their light terminates, or no longer produces an active and visible luminosity. This is an essentially false conclusion, because the proposition is false upon which it depends--that the stars are vast suns and worlds at almost infinite distances. The contrary has been demonstrated by trigonometrical observation; and is again confirmed by the Scriptures.

> "He made the stars also, and set them in the firmament to *give light* upon the earth."--Genesis i., 16-17.

> "For the stars of heaven and the constellations thereof shall not *give their light*."
> --Isaiah xiii., 10.

"I will cover the heaven, and make the *stars* thereof *dark*."--Ezekiel xxxii., 7.

"The sun and the moon shall be dark, and the *stars* shall withdraw *their shining*." --Joel ii., 10.

"Praise Him sun and moon; praise Him all ye *stars of light*."--Psalm cxlviii., 3.

"Thus saith the Lord, which giveth the sun for a light by day, and the ordinances of the moon and of *the stars for a light* by night."--Jeremiah xxxi., 35.

"They that turn many to righteousness shall *shine as the stars* for ever and ever." --Daniel xii., 3.

These quotations place it beyond doubt to those who believe the Scriptures, that the stars were made expressly to shine and influence the firmament, and "to give light upon the earth." We have also the evidence of our own eyes and judgment that the stars give abundant light; at least, sufficient light to prevent the earth, when the sun and moon are absent, from being utterly dark and injurious, or dangerous to its inhabitants. "What beautiful star-light!" is a common expression; and we all remember the difference between a comparatively dark and starless night, or a night when the atmosphere is thick with heavy clouds, and one when the firmament is, as it were, studded with brilliant luminaries. Travellers inform us that in many parts of the world, where the sky is clear and free from clouds and vapours for weeks together, the stars appear both larger and brighter than they do in England, and that their light is often sufficiently intense to enable them to read and write, and to travel with safety through the most dangerous places.

"Such is the general blaze of starlight near the Southern Cross from that part of the sky, that a person is immediately made aware of its having risen above the horizon, though he should not be at the time looking at the heavens, by the increase of general illumination of the atmosphere, resembling the effect of the young moon."[171]

If it be true that the stars and planets are magnificent worlds, for the most part larger than the earth, it is a very proper question to ask "Are they inhabited?" If the answer be in the affirmative, it is equally proper to inquire "Have the first parents in each world been tempted as were Adam and Eve in the Garden of Eden?" If so, "Did they yield to the temptation and fall as they did?" If so, "Have they required redemption?" And "Have they been redeemed?" "Has each different world required the same kind of redemption, and had a separate Redeemer; or has Christ, by His suffering on earth and crucifixion on Calvary, been the Redeemer for all the innumerable myriads of worlds in the universe; or had He to suffer and die in each world successively?" "Did the fall of Adam in this world involve in his guilt the inhabitants of all the other worlds?" "Or was the baneful

---

171 "Description of the Heavens," by A. V. Humboldt, notes p. 45.

influence of the tempter confined to the first parents of this earth?" If so, "Why so?" and, if not, "Why not?" But, and if, and why, and, again, if but it is useless thus to ponder.

Indeed, such questions have been and are still being asked by those in some of the highest positions of the Roman Catholic Church. I actually discussed this in some of my earlier teachings, back in 2011, shortly after the United Nations appointed an "Ambassador to Alien World."[1] A year prior to that, there was talk within the Catholic Church of baptizing aliens (if they need it) as articles began to appear with headlines like the one from The Guardian[2] posted September 17, 2010:

Pope's astronomer says he would baptise an alien if it asked him

Interestingly enough, the article also cites the Pope's astronomer, Guy Consolmagno as dismissing Intelligent Design (as in the fiat Creation of life by YHWH), considering it to be a pseudo-scientific version of creationism:

> *"The word has been hijacked by a narrow group of creationist fundamentalists in America to mean something it didn't originally mean at all. It's another form of the God of the gaps. It's bad theology in that it turns God once again into the pagan god of thunder and lightning."*

Back to the point in question: perhaps aliens do not need to be baptized. Perhaps they never sinned and thus could teach us a thing or two. Jose' Gabriel Funes, the former Jesuit director of the Vatican Observatory said:

> *"[W]e human beings might be the lost sheep, the sinners in need of a shepherd. God became man in Jesus to save us. In that case, even if there were other sentient life forms, **they might not be in need of redemption**. They could have stayed in full harmony with their Creator."*[3]

This idea is nothing new. Back in 1588, Giordano Bruno, an Italian Dominican Friar once wrote:

> *"I can imagine an infinite number of worlds like the earth, with a Garden of Eden on each one. In all these Gardens of Eden, half the Adams and Eves will not eat the fruit of knowledge, but half will. But half of infinity is infinity, so an infinite number of worlds will fall from grace and there will be an infinite number of crucifixions."*[4]

By his logic though, there would also be another "half of infinity" - an infinite number of worlds with sinless aliens who would likely have more to share with us about God than we would with them. Do you see the dangers here? What happens when "ET" shows up proclaiming a new Gospel?

1 https://www.cbsnews.com/news/united-nations-appointing-ambassador-to-alien-world/
2 https://www.theguardian.com/science/2010/sep/17/pope-astronomer-baptise-aliens
3 https://cruxnow.com/global-church/2017/02/23/catholicism-handle-discovery-extraterrestrial-life/
4 In his 5th dialogue of *On the Cause, Principle and Unity*

Do you think that's outrageous? In 2008, Jose' Gabriel Funes also said:

"Why can't we speak of a 'brother extraterrestrial'?" he said. "It would still be part of creation." **Aliens might even be closer to God than us**, *Funes suggested, and humans could be the "lost sheep" of the universe. In other words,* **alien visitors might well have a more advanced religion than ours. Rather than baptising them, we might want to convert to their faith."[1]**

And there is the set up folks. Pope Francis is totally on board with this too. So while the highest levels of the Catholic Church support evolution, deny Intelligent Design and embrace ideas that "our alien brothers" my have a "more advanced religion than ours," I'm looking at the Scriptures and thinking **the flat, enclosed world cosmology it describes immediately nullifies all of this nonsense.** The Earth is the center stage, main attraction. There are no other worlds and everything that is above us is much smaller and way closer than what we have been taught by "science" (falsely so-called) to believe. So the whole notion of 'Ancient Aliens' goes completely out the window. This is just one of the many reasons why I believe this is an important topic to be discussing, and why I believe it has seen an awakening in the 21st century. Could it be that *something* is coming and we will need to have a firm foundation in the Scriptures in order to not be deceived by it? For more on this, please see my YouTube video, *Flat Earth, Aliens, UFOs and the War Against God*:

5 https://www.theguardian.com/science/shortcuts/2014/may/14/pope-francis-baptise-martian-would-they-want-our-religions

The Christian philosopher must be confounded. If his religion be to him a living reality, he will turn with loathing from, or spurn with indignation and disgust as he would a poisonous reptile, a system of astronomy which creates in his mind so much confusion and uncertainty.

But as the system which necessitates such doubts and difficulties has been shown to be purely theoretical, and not to have the slightest foundation in fact, the religious mind has really no cause for apprehension. Not a shadow of doubt remains that this earth is the only material world created; that the Sacred Scriptures contain, in addition to religious and moral doctrines, a true and consistent philosophy; that they were written for the good of mankind by the direct dictation of God Himself; and that all their teachings and promises may be relied on as truthful, beneficent, and conducive to the greatest enjoyment here and to perfect happiness hereafter. Whoever holds the contrary conclusion is the victim of an arrogant and false astronomy; of an equally false and presumptuous geology; and a suicidal method of reasoning--a logic which never demands a proof of its premises, and which, therefore, leads to deductions and opinions which are contrary to nature, to fact, and human experience, and to the direct teachings of God's Word; and, therefore, contrary to the deepest and most lasting interests of humanity.

> "God has spoken to man in two voices--the voice of Inspiration and the voice of Nature By man's ignorance they have been made to disagree; but the time will come, and cannot be far distant, when these two languages will strictly accord; when the science of Nature will no longer contradict the science of Scripture."[172]

In all the religions of the earth, the words up and above are associated with a region of peace and happiness. Not only is this idea taught by the priests and sacred books of all nations, but human nature itself, even when least intelligent, or unbiassed by education, in its deepest sorrows and sufferings, in great bodily pain, and trouble and anguish of mind, seems instinctively to look upwards, as though relief and comfort might, or could only, come from above. No matter of what creed or country, man, in his deepest wretchedness and despair, involuntarily turns his face and eyes in an upward direction, as though it is only from above that help and sympathy can be looked for. In the final struggle for life, if the sufferer has strength to grapple with death, his last convulsive effort is to die with his countenance hopefully and anxiously upwards. This is the case in private life, in hospitals, in shipwrecks, and in the carnage and uproar of the battle-field; in the midst of the clash of arms, the trample and shouting of furious warriors, the roar of cannon, and the hoarse groans of wounded men and horses, the sufferers who have received their death-blows, and are struggling for life, heedless of all else around them, seek to gain a position where the face and eyes may gaze into the space above the earth, that their last thoughts and feelings may be directed upwards.

> "Immediately after the battle of Inkerman many faces of the dead still seemed to smile; . . . some had a funeral posé, as though laid out by friendly hands; . . . many had their hands raised, as if desiring to offer a last prayer."

---

172 Professor Hunt.

"After the battle of the Alma some seemed still writhing in the agonies of despair and death, but the most wore a look of calm and pious resignation. Some appeared to have words floating on their lips, and a smile, as if in a sort of high beatitude. One was particularly so, his knees bent, his hands raised and joined, his head thrown back, murmuring his supreme prayer."

"At Magenta an Austrian died from hæmorrhage; his face and eyes were turned to Heaven, his hands joined and fingers interlaced, evidently in the attitude of prayer."

The same idea is cultivated and sought to be conveyed by the tapering monuments and the pointed railings of all our graveyards and cemeteries, and by the Gothic windows and doorways, and all the towering spires of our churches and cathedrals. Architects in all ages, when raising religious edifices, have had this idea prominently before them; every modification of the cone and the pyramid has been made subservient to the purpose of leading the beholder to direct his thoughts and looks upwards and heavenwards.

In 1841 the author was on board a steamer sailing along the western shores of Scotland, when suddenly the vessel struck upon an unseen rock; all hands were called to aid in working the pumps, but the water gradually gained upon them. After a few hours the captain announced that all hope of safety had passed away, and, being evidently a religious man, he exhorted all on board to shape their thoughts and feelings for a future life. Immediately every knee was bent, and every eye and face upcast towards Heaven. Among the--over one hundred--passengers, male and female, young and old, were several apostles of atheism, who for a time bravely bore the prospect of death, but, as the ship sank deeper and deeper, a calm reflective aspect came over them, and shortly afterwards no eye or face could be seen higher and more imploringly gazing upwards than those who for years had treated with contempt all ideas of Heaven or God or anything other than a boundless universe filled with material globular worlds, and their godless, soulless, hopeless inhabitants.

All that is lofty, noble, loving, soul-expanding, and expressive of purity, wisdom, and every other form of goodness, is invariably associated in the human mind with upwardness and heavenward progression.

All who believe in and speak of Heaven and hell, do so of the former as above and of the latter as below the earth; and we have good reason, nay, positive evidence, that regions answering to such places exist over and under the physical world (the subject, however, in its moral and spiritual aspect cannot be entered upon in a scientific work like this; the reader who may feel an interest will find sufficient to satisfy him in the work entitled the "Life of Christ Zetetically Considered"). And the language of the Scriptures invariably conveys the same idea.

"Look down from Thy holy habitation, from Heaven, and bless Thy people Israel."
--Deuteronomy xxvi., 15.

"And the Lord God came down upon Mount Sinai."--Exodus xix., 20.

For He hath looked down from the height of His sanctuary; from Heaven did the Lord behold the earth."--Psalm cii., 19.

"Look down from Heaven, and behold from the habitation of Thy holiness and of Thy glory."--Isaiah lxiii., 15.

"For as the Heaven is high above the earth."--Psalm ciii., 2.

"And Elijah went up by a whirlwind into Heaven."--2 Kings ii., 11.

"So then after the Lord had spoken unto them He was received up into Heaven."
--Mark xvi., 10.

"How art thou fallen from Heaven, O Lucifer, son of the morning! . . . Thou halt said in thine heart I will ascend into Heaven, I will exalt my throne above the stars of God. . . . I will ascend above the heights of the clouds. "--Isaiah xiv., 13-14.

"And when He had spoken these things He was taken up, and a cloud received Him out of their sight; and while they looked steadfastly toward Heaven, as He went up, two men said unto them, Ye men of Galilee why stand ye gazing up into Heaven? this same Jesus which is taken up from you into Heaven shall so come in like manner as ye have seen Him go into Heaven."--Acts i., 9-11.

"But he, being full of the Holy Ghost, looked up steadfastly into Heaven."
--Acts vii., 55.

And it came to pass while He blessed them He was parted from them, and carried up into Heaven."--Luke xxiv., 51.

"For a fire is kindled in Mine anger, and shall burn unto the lowest hell."--Deuteronomy xxxii., 22.

"It is as high as Heaven, deeper than hell."--Job xi., 8.

"Let death seize upon them, and let them go down quick into hell."
-- Psalm lv., 15.

"If I ascend up into Heaven, Thou art there; if I make my bed in hell, behold, Thou art there."--Psalm cxxxix., 8.

"Her house is the way to hell, going down to the chambers of death." -- Proverbs vii., 27:

"Thou shalt be brought down to hell, to the sides of the pit."--Isaiah xiv., 15.

"Her guests are in the depths of hell."--Proverbs ix., 18.

"The way of life is above to the wise, that he may depart from hell beneath." --Proverbs xv., 24.

"Hell from beneath is moved for thee."--Isaiah xiv., 9.

"I cast him down to hell. . . . They also went down into hell with him." -- Ezekiel xxxi., 16-17.

"The mighty which are gone down to hell with their weapons of war." -- Ezekiel xxxii., 27.

"And thou, Capernaum, which art exalted unto Heaven, shall be brought down to hell."--Matthew xi., 23.

"God spared not the angels that sinned, but cast them down to hell."--2 Peter ii., 4.

"And the angels which kept not their first estate, but left their own habitation, He hath reserved in everlasting chains under darkness, unto the Judgment of the Great Day, even as Sodom and Gomorrah are set forth for an example, suffering the vengeance of eternal fire."--Jude i., 6- 7.

"Wandering stars, to whom is reserved the blackness of darkness for ever." --Jude i., 13.

"And the devil that deceived them was cast into the lake of fire and brimstone.... The sea gave up the dead which were in it; and death and hell delivered up the dead which were in them.... And death and hell were cast into the lake of fire." --Revelations xx., 10-13-14.

"As for the earth, out of it cometh bread; and under it is turned up as it were fire." --Job xxviii., 5.

If the earth is a globe, revolving at the rate of a thousand miles an hour, all this language of Scripture is necessarily fallacious. The terms "up" and "down" and "above" and "below" are words without meaning--at best, are merely relative, indicative of no absolute direction. That which is "up" at noon-day is directly "down" at midnight. Whatever point, and at whatever moment we fix upon as that from which we are looking upwards, in a second we are moving rapidly downwards. Heaven, then, can only be spoken of as "above," and the Scriptures read correctly for a single moment out of the twenty-four hours. Before the sentence "Heaven is high above the earth" can be uttered the speaker is descending from the meridian where Heaven is above him, and in a few seconds his eye will be looking upon a succession of points millions of miles away from his first position. Hence, in all the ceremonials of religion, when the hands and eyes are raised upward, to Heaven, nay, when Christ Himself "lifted *up* His eyes to *Heaven*, and said "Father, the hour is come," his gaze would be sweeping along the firmament at rapidly varying angles, and with such incomprehensible velocity that a fixed point of observation, and a definite position as indicating the seat or throne of "Him that sitteth in the Heavens" would be an impossibility.

Again: the religious world have always believed and meditated upon the word "heaven" as representing an infinite region of joy and safety, of rest and happiness unspeakable; as, indeed, "the place of God's residence, the dwelling-place of angels and the blessed; the true Palace of God, entirely separated from the impurities and imperfections, the alterations and changes of the lower world; where He reigns in eternal peace. . . . The sacred mansion of light and joy and glory." But if there is an endless plurality of worlds, millions upon millions in never-ending succession; if the universe is filled with innumerable systems of burning suns and rapidly revolving planets, intermingled with rushing comets and whirling satellites, all dashing and sweeping through space in directions and with velocities surpassing all human comprehension, and terrible even to contemplate, where is the place of rest and safety? Where is the true and unchangeable "Palace of God?" In what direction is Heaven to be found? Where is the liberated human soul to find its home and resting-place--its refuge from change and motion, from uncertainty and danger? Is it to wander for ever in a labyrinth of rolling worlds?--to struggle for ever in a never-ending maze of revolving suns and systems?- -to be never at rest, but for ever seeking to protect itself--to guard against and to avoid some vortex of attraction--some whirlpool of gravitation? Truly the fact of, as well as the belief in, the existence of Heaven as a region of peace and harmony, "extending above the earth through all extent," and beyond the influence of natural laws and restless elements, is jeopardised, if not destroyed, by a false and usurping astronomy, which has no better foundation than human conceit and presumption. If this ill-founded philosophy, unsupported as it is by fact or Scripture, or any evidence of the senses, is admitted, the religious mind can no longer rejoice in singing:--

> "Far above the sun, and stars, and skies,
>   In realms of endless light and love,
>   My Father's mansion lies."

A system of philosophy which makes such havoc with the human soul; which destroys its hope of future rest and happiness, and renders the existence of Heaven impossible, and of a beneficent, ever-ruling God and Father of creation useless and uncertain, cannot be less than a curse---a dark and dangerous dragon, hell-born and tartarean in its character and influence.

If all who forget God, who deride and repudiate all ideas of creation, and find a sufficiency of ruling power in the self-operating forces of modern astronomy--in its centrifugal and centripetal universalities--are of necessity rejected of Heaven, then indeed have the blinding philosophies of the day done wondrous service in peopling hell, and adding to the horrors of infernal existence.

Great numbers of religious people, keenly recognising the discrepancies between the direct teachings of Scripture and those of modern astronomy, and failing to see the possibility of the existence of a region of perpetual peace and happiness when worlds and systems of worlds extend unlimited in all directions, have concluded that such a region cannot possibly exist as a locality, but must be a state of mind--a condition only; hence the words "heaven" and "hell" are used, not as expressing actual parts of, or places in, the universe, but simply states of the heart. There cannot be a doubt that the human conscience may be calm and heavenly, or disturbed and demoniacal; and that these conditions may be called heaven or hell to the individual. But is this all? In *addition* to this is it as the Scriptures teach? Is not Heaven spoken of as an *abode*--a blissful residence of the accepted with their satisfied Creator; and hell a *place*, an actual *locality*, appointed for the evil- minded and the rejected? Let the distracted believer in Scripture be careful how he parleys with his judgment, and endangers himself by a too exclusive and one-sided conception. That heaven and hell are only *conditions* and *not places* no man is justified in asserting; but that they are *both* is perfectly demonstrable. To adopt one and reject or deny the possibility of the other is utter folly. To admit that both are realities is simply the dictate of reason, and the conclusion which the evidence compels us to acknowledge.

We have seen, from the evidence furnished by practical observation, that the earth is on fire, and that it will ultimately be burnt up and destroyed. Here again the language of Scripture is clear and definite:--

> "All the hosts of heaven shall be dissolved, and the heavens shall be rolled together as a scroll."--Isaiah xxxiv., 4.

351

"For behold the Lord will come with fire, and with His chariots like a whirlwind, to render His anger with fury, and His rebuke with flames of fire.... The new heavens and the new earth, which I will make, shall remain before Me." --Isaiah lxvi., 15-22.

"When the Lord Jesus shall be revealed from Heaven with His mighty angels, in flaming fire, taking vengeance on them that know not God, and that obey not the Gospel of our Lord Jesus Christ."--2 Thessalonians i., 7-8.

"From whose face the earth and the heaven fled away, and there was found no place for them."--Revelation xx., 11.

"The heavens and the earth which are now are kept in store, reserved unto fire against the Day of Judgment and perdition of ungodly men. . . . The day of the Lord will come as a thief in the night, in the which the heavens shall pass away with a great noise, and the elements shall melt with fervent heat; the earth also and the works therein shall be burnt up. . . . All these things shall be dissolved, . . . the heavens being on fire shall be dissolved. Nevertheless we look for new heavens and a new earth, wherein dwelleth righteousness."--2 Peter iii., 10-13.

"A fire is kindled in Mine anger, and shall burn unto the lowest hell, and shall consume the earth with her increase, and set on fire the foundations of the mountains."--Deuteronomy xxxii., 22.

"I saw a new heaven and a new earth, for the first heaven and the first earth were passed away."--Revelations xxi., 1.

The literal teaching of the Old and New Testaments on the subject of the earth's destruction is plain and unmistakeable. Numbers, however, have been led to deny that the Scriptures have any literal signification. But such a denial is unquestionably contrary to fact, and inconsistent with the genius and purpose of all inspiration. It may not be denied that this language will bear a spiritual application; but its primary and essential meaning is literal and practical. It may have both a spiritual, a moral, and a political aspect, but only as a superstructure upon the material and philosophical. Let men beware how they jeopardise their lasting welfare by taking liberties with a book written as the expressed will of Heaven for the guidance of mankind. If they are determined to read with fanciful bearings, let them do so for what pleasure it will afford; but if it is done to the exclusion of practical good and literal application, it is not less than dangerous presumption.

In addition to the numerous quotations from the Scriptures which have here been found to be true and consistent, it may be useful briefly to refer to the following so-called difficulties which have been raised by the scientific objectors to Scriptural authority:--

"As the earth is a globe, and as all its vast collections of water--its oceans, seas, lakes, and rivers--are sustained by the earthy crust beneath them, and as beneath this "crust of the earth" everything is in a red-hot and molten condition, to what place could the excess of waters retire which are said, in the Scriptures, to have once overwhelmed or deluged the whole earth? It could not sink into the centre of the earth, for the fire there is so intense that the water would be rapidly volatilised, and driven back and away as vapour. It could not evaporate. and remain in a state of fluid, for when the atmosphere is charged with watery vapour beyond a certain degree, condensation begins, and the whole would be thrown back in the form of rain. Hence, as the waters could not sink from the earth's surface, and could not remain in the atmosphere, it follows that if the earth had ever been deluged at all it would have remained so to this day. But as it is not now universally flooded, a deluge of the earth, such as the Scriptures describe, never could have occurred, and therefore the account is false."

All this specious reasoning is founded upon the assumption that the earth is a globe, but, as this has been proved to be false, the "difficulties" at once disappear. The earth being a plane "founded on the seas," would be as readily cleared of its superfluous waters as would the deck of a ship on emerging from a storm; or as a rock in the ocean after the waves, which for a time had overwhelmed it, had subsided. The earth being a plane, and its surface standing above the level of the surrounding seas, the waters of the flood would simply and naturally run down by the valleys and rivers into the "great deep" into which "the waters returned from off the earth continually." Here, again, the Scriptures are perfect in their description of what necessarily occurred:--

"Thou coveredst the earth with the deep as with a garment; the waters stood above the mountains. At Thy rebuke they fled; and at the voice of Thy thunder they hasted away . . down by the valleys unto the place which Thou hast founded for them."--Psalm civ., 6-8.

Again, it is urged:

"As the earth is a globe and in continual motion, how could Jesus, on being 'taken up into an exceedingly high mountain, see all the kingdoms of the world in a moment of time? Or when 'He cometh with clouds and every eye shall see Him,' how was it possible, seeing that twenty-four hours would have to elapse before every part of the earth would be turned to the same point?"

It has been demonstrated that the earth is a plane and motionless; and, therefore, it was consistent with geodetic and optical principles to declare that from a great eminence every part of the surface could be seen at the same moment, and that simultaneously every eye should behold Him when "coming in a cloud, with power and great glory."

CUI BONO?

"Of all terrors to the generous soul, that *Cui bono*[173] is the one to be the most zealously avoided. Whether it be proposed to find the magnetic point, or a passage impossible to be utilised, if discovered, or a race of men of no good to any human institution extant, and of no good to themselves; or to seek the unicorn in Madagascar, and when we had found him not to be able to make use of him; or the great central plateau of Australia, where no one could live for centuries to come; or the great African Lake, which, for all the good it would do us English folk, might as well be in the moon; or the source of the Nile, the triumphant discovery of which would neither lower the rents, nor take off the taxes anywhere-- whatever it is, the *Cui bono* is always a weak and cowardly argument; essentially short-sighted, too, seeing that, according to the law of the past, by which we may always safely predicate the future, so much falls into the hands of the seeker for which he was not looking, and of which he never even knew the existence. The area of the possible is very wide still, and very insignificant and minute the angle we have staked out and marked impossible. What do we know of the powers which Nature has yet in reserve, of the secrets she has still untold, the wealth still concealed? Quixotism is a folly when the energy which might have achieved conquests over misery and wrong, if rightly applied, is wasted in fighting windmills; but to forego any great enterprise for fear of the dangers attending, or to check a grand endeavour by the Cui bono of ignorance and moral scepticism, is worse than a folly--it is baseness, and a cowardice."[174]

The above quotation is an excellent general answer to all those who may, in reference to the subject of this work, or to anything which is not of immediate worldly interest, obtrude the *Cui bono*. But as a special reply it may be claimed for the subject of these pages:--

FIRST.--It is more edifying, more satisfactory, and in every sense far better, that we should know the true and detect the false. Thereby the mind becomes fixed--established on an eternal foundation, and no longer subject to those waverings and changes, those oscillations and fluctuations which are ever the result and concomitant of falsehood. To know the truth and to embody it in our lives and purposes, is to render our progress to a higher and nobler existence both safe and rapid and unlimited in ex-tent. None can say to what it may lead, or how or where it may culminate. Who shall dare to set bounds to the capabilities of the mind, or to fix a limit to human progression? Whatever may be the destiny of the human race, truth alone will help to secure its realisation.

SECOND.--Having detected the fundamental falsehoods of modern astronomy, and discovered that the earth is a plane, and motionless, and the only known material world, we are able to demonstrate the actual character of the universe. In doing this,

173 The Latin phrase "cui bono" means "who stands, or stood, to gain? Literally, "to whom is it a benefit?".
174 "Daily News," April 5th, 1865.

we are enabled to prove that all the so-called arguments with which so many scientific but irreligious men have assailed the Sacred Scriptures are absolutely false--not doubtful or less plausible, but unconditionally false; that they have no foundation except in fallacious astronomical and geological theories; and, therefore, must fall to the ground as valueless. They can no longer be wielded by irreverent smatterers as weapons against religion. If used at all, it can only be that their weakness and utter worthlessness will be exposed. Atheism and every other form of infidelity are thus rendered helpless. Their sting is cut away and their poison dissipated. The irreligious philosopher can no longer obtrude his theories as things proved wherewith to test the teachings of Scripture. He must now himself be tested. He must be forced to demonstrate his premises, a thing which he has never yet attempted, and if he fails in this respect, his impious vanity, self-conceit, and utter disregard of truth and justice, will become so clearly apparent that his presence in the ranks of science will no longer be tolerated. All theories must be put aside, and the question at issue decided by independent practical evidence. This has now been done. The process--the *modus operandi* and the conclusions derived therefrom have been given in the early sections of this work; and, as these conclusions are found to be entirely consistent with the teachings of Scripture, we are compelled, by the sheer weight of evidence, by the force of practical demonstration and logical requirement, to declare emphatically that the Old and New Testaments of the Jewish and Christian Church are, in everything which appertains to the visible and material world, strictly and literally true. If, after the severest criticism, and comparison with known causes of phenomena, the Scriptures are thus found to be absolutely truthful in their literal expressions, it is simply just and wise that we take them as standards by which to test the truth or falsehood of all systems or teachings which may hereafter be presented to the world. Philosophy is no longer to be employed as a test of Scriptural truth, but the Scriptures ought and may with safety and satisfaction be applied as the test of all philosophy. They are not, however, to be used as a test of science and philosophy simply because they are *thought* or *believed* to be written or dictated by inspiration, but because their literal teachings in regard to natural phenomena are *demonstrably true*.

It is quite as faulty and unjust for the religious devotee to urge the teaching of Scripture against the theories of the philosopher simply because he *believes* them to be true, as it is for the philosopher to defend his theories against Scripture for no other reason than that he *disbelieves* them. The whole matter must be taken out of the region of belief and disbelief. In regard to elements and phenomena belief and disbelief should never be named. Men differ in their powers of conception and concatenation; and, therefore, what may readily be believed by some, others may find impossible to believe. Belief is a state of mind which should be exerted only in relation to matters confessedly beyond the direct reach of our senses, and in regard to which it is meritorious to believe. But in reference to matter, and material combinations and phenomena, we should be content with nothing less than conviction, the result of special practical experimental investigation. The Christian will be greatly strengthened, and his mind more completely satisfied, by having it in his power to demonstrate that the Scriptures are philosophically true, than he could possibly be by the simple *belief* in their truthfulness unsupported by practical evidence. On the other hand, the atheist or the disbeliever in the Scriptures, who is met by the Christian on purely scientific grounds, will be led to listen with more respect, and to pay more regard to the reasons advanced than he would concede to the purely religious belief or to any argument founded upon faith alone. If it can be shown to the atheistical or unbelieving philosopher that his astronomical and geological theories have no practical foundation, but are fallacious both in their premises and conclusions, and that all the literal expressions in the Scriptures which have reference to natural phenomena are demonstrably true, he will, of necessity, as a truth- seeker, if he should have so avowed himself, and for very shame as a man, be led to admit that, apart from all other considerations, if the truth of the *philosophy* of the Scriptures can be demonstrated, then, possibly, their *spiritual* and *moral* teachings may also be true; and if so, they may, and indeed must, have had a Divine origin; and, therefore, there must exist a Divine Being, a Creator and Ruler of the physical and spiritual worlds; and that, after all, the Christian religion is a grand reality, and that he himself, through all his days of forgetfulness and denial of God, has been guarded and cared for as a merely mistaken creature, undeserving the fate of an obstinate, self-willed opponent of everything sacred and superhuman. He may be led to see that the very discussion of his theories with a Zetetic opponent was a loving and mysterious leading into a purer and clearer philosophy for his own eternal benefit.

He cannot fail to see, and will not be slow to admit, that all the theories which speculative adventurous philosophers have advanced are nothing better than treacherous quick-sands, into which many of the deepest thinkers have been engulphed and possibly lost. By this process of mental concatenation many highly intelligent minds have been led to renounce and desert the ranks of atheism and speculative philosophy, and to rejoin or enlist in the army of Christian soldiers and devotees. Many have rejoiced, almost beyond expression, that the question of the earth's true form and position in the universe had ever been brought before them; and, doubtless, great numbers will yet be induced to return to that allegiance which plain demonstrable truth demands and deserves.

To truthfully instruct the ingenuous Christian mind, to protect it from the meshes of false philosophy, and the snares of specious but hollow illogical reasoning; to save it from falling into the frigid arms of atheistic science; to convince it that all unscriptural teaching is false and deadly, and to induce great numbers of earnest deep-thinking human beings to desert the rebellious cause of atheism; to return to a full recognition of the beauty and truthfulness of the Scriptures, and to a participation in the joy and satisfaction which the Christian religion alone can supply, is a grand and cheering result, and one which furnishes the noblest possible answer to the ever ready *Cui bono*.

A Challenge to the JOHNS HOPKINS University.

ONE HUNDRED PROOFS

THAT

THE EARTH

IS

NOT A GLOBE.

———•———

Dedicated to RICHARD A. PROCTOR, Esq.
"The Greatest Astronomer of the Age."

———•———

By WM. CARPENTER,

*Referee for John Hampden, Esq., in the Celebrated Scientific Wager, in 1870;
Author of 'Common Sense' on Astronomy, (London, 1866;) Proctor's
Planet Earth; Wallace's Wonderful Water; The
Delusion of the Day, &c., &c.*

~~~~~~~

"UPRIGHT, DOWNRIGHT, STRAIGHTFORWARD."

~~~~~~~

BALTIMORE:
PRINTED AND PUBLISHED BY THE AUTHOR,
No. 71 Chew Street.
1885.

INDEX

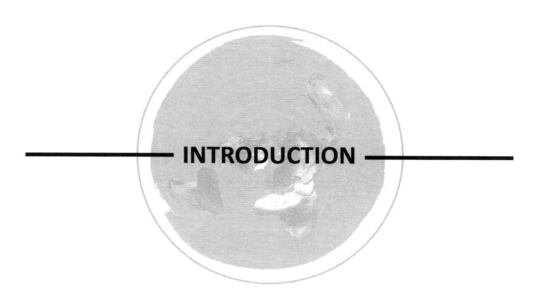

INTRODUCTION

"Parallax," the Founder of the Zetetic Philosophy, is dead; and it now becomes the duty of those, especially, who knew him personally and who labored with him in the cause of Truth against Error, to begin, anew, the work which is left in their hands. Dr. Samuel B. Rowbotham finished his earthly labours, in England, the country of his birth, December 23, 1884, at the age of 89. He was, certainly, one of the most gifted of men: and though his labours as a public lecturer were confined within the limits of the British Islands his published work is known all over the world and is destined to live and be republished when books on the now popular system of philosophy will be considered in no other light than as bundles of waste paper.

For several years did "Parallax" spread a knowledge of the facts which form the basis of his system without the slightest recognition from the newspaper press until, in January, 1849, the people were informed by the "Wilts Independent" that lectures had been delivered by "a gentleman adopting the name of 'Parallax,' to prove modern astronomy unreasonable and contradictory," that "great skill" was shown by the lecturer, and that he proved himself to be "thoroughly acquainted with the subject in all its bearings." Such was the beginning—the end will not be so easily described. The Truth will always find advocates—men who care not a snap of their fingers for the mere opinion of the world, whatever form it may take, whilst they know that they are the masters of the situation and that Reason is King! In 1867, "Parallax" was described as "a paragon of courtesy, good temper, and masterly skill in debate." The author of the following hastily-gotten-up pages is proud of having spent many a pleasant hour in the company of Samuel Birley Rowbotham.

A complete sketch of the "Zetetic Philosophy" is impossible in a small pamphlet; and many things necessarily remain unsaid which, perhaps, should have been touched upon, but which would to some extent have interfered with the plan laid down—the bringing together, in a concise form, "One Hundred Proofs that the Earth is not a Globe." Much may be gathered, indirectly, from the arguments in these pages, as to the real nature of the Earth on which we live and of the heavenly bodies which were created FOR US. The reader is requested to be patient in this matter and not expect a whole flood of light to burst in upon him at once, through the dense clouds of opposition and prejudice which hang all around. Old ideas have to be gotten rid of, by some people, before they can entertain the new; and this will especially be the case in the matter of the Sun, about which we are taught, by Mr. Proctor, as follows: "The globe of the Sun is so much larger than that of the Earth that no less than 1,250,000 globes as large as the Earth would be wanted to make up together a globe as large as the Sun."

Whereas, we know that, as it is demonstrated that the Sun moves round over the Earth, its size is proportionately less. We can then easily understand that Day and Night, and the Seasons are brought about by his daily circuits round in a course concentric with the North, diminishing in their extent to the end of June, and increasing until the end of December, the equatorial region being the area covered by the Sun's mean motion. If, then, these pages serve but to arouse the spirit of enquiry, the author will be satisfied. The right hand of fellowship in this good work is extended, in turn, to Mr. J. Lindgren, 90 South First Street, Brooklyn, E. D., N. Y., Mr. M. C. Flanders, lecturer, Kendall, Orleans County, N. Y., and to Mr. John Hampden, editor of "Parallax" (a new journal), Cosmos House, Balham, Surrey, England.

If man uses the senses which God has given him, he gains knowledge; if he uses them not, he remains ignorant. Mr. R. A. Proctor, who has been called "the greatest astronomer of the age," says: "The Earth on which we live and move seems to be flat." Now, he does not mean that it seems to be flat to the man who shuts his eyes in the face of nature, or, who is not in the full possession of his senses: no, but to the average, common sense, wide-awake, thinking man. He continues: "that is, though there are hills and valleys on its surface, yet it seems to extend on all sides in one and the same general level." Again, he says: "There seems nothing to prevent us from traveling as far as we please in any direction towards the circle all round us, called the horizon, where the sky seems to meet the level of the Earth."

Richard A. Proctor
(1837 - 1888)

"The level of the Earth!"

Mr. Proctor knows right well what he is talking about, for the book from which we take his words, "Lessons in Elementary Astronomy," was written, he tells us, "to guard the beginner against the captious objections which have from time to time been urged against accepted astronomical theories." The things which are to be defended, then, are these "accepted astronomical theories!" It is not truth that is to be defended against the assaults of error—Oh, no: simply "theories," right or wrong, because they have been "accepted!" Accepted! Why, they have been accepted because it was not thought to be worth while to look at them.

Sir John Herschel says: "We shall take for granted, from the outset, the Copernican system of the world." He did not care whether it was the right system or a wrong one, or he would not have done that: he would have looked into it. But, forsooth, the theories are accepted, and, of course, the men who have accepted them are the men who will naturally defend them if they can.

So, Richard A. Proctor tries his hand; and we shall see how it fails him. His book was published without any date to it at all. But there is internal evidence which will fix that matter closely enough. We read of the carrying out of the experiments of the celebrated scientist, Alfred R. Wallace, to prove the "convexity" of the surface of standing water, which experiments were conducted in March, 1870, for the purpose of winning Five Hundred Pounds from John Hampden, Esq., of Swindon, England, who had wagered that sum upon the conviction that the said surface is always a level one. Mr. Proctor says: "The experiment was lately tried in a very amusing way." In or about the year 1870, then, Mr. Proctor wrote his book; and, instead of being ignorant of the details of the experiment, he knew all about them. And whether the "amusing" part of the business was the fact that Mr. Wallace wrongfully claimed the five-hundred pounds and got it, or that Mr. Hampden was the victim of the false claim, it is hard to say. The "way" in which the experiment was carried out is, to all intents and purposes, just the way in which Mr. Proctor states that it "can be tried." He says, however, that the distance involved in the experiment "should be three or four miles."

Now, Mr. Wallace took up six miles in his experiment, and was unable to prove that there is any "curvature," though he claimed the money and got it; surely it would be "amusing" for anyone to expect to be able to show the "curvature of the earth" in three or four miles, as Mr. Proctor suggests! Nay, it is ridiculous. But "the greatest astronomer of the age" says the thing can be done! And he gives a diagram: "Showing how the roundness of the Earth can be proved by means of three boats on a large sheet of water." (Three or four miles.) But, though the accepted astronomical theories be scattered to the winds, we charge Mr. Proctor either that he has never made the experiment with the three boats, or, that, if he has, the experiment did NOT prove what he says it will. Accepted theories, indeed!

Are they to be bolstered up with absurdity and falsehood? Why, if it were possible to show the two ends of a four-mile stretch of water to be on a level, with the centre portion of that water bulged up, the surface of the Earth would be a series of four-mile curves!

But Mr. Proctor says: "We can set three boats in a line on the water, as at A, B, and C, (Fig. 7). Then, if equal masts are placed in these boats, and we place a telescope, as shown, so that when we look through it we see the tops of the masts of A and C, we find the top of the mast B is above the line of sight." Now, here is the point: Mr. Proctor either knows or he ought to know that we shall NOT find anything of the sort! If he has ever tried the experiment, he knows that the three masts will range in a straight line, just as common sense tells us they will. If he has not tried the experiment, he should have tried it, or have paid attention to the details of experiments by those who have tried similar ones a score of times and again. Mr. Proctor may take either horn of the dilemma he pleases: he is just as wrong as a man can be, either way. He mentions no names, but he says: "A person had written a book, in which he said that he had tried such an experiment as the above, and had found that the surface of the water was not curved." That person was "Parallax," the founder of the Zetetic Philosophy.

He continues: "Another person seems to have believed the first, and became so certain that the Earth is flat as to wager a large sum of money that if three boats were placed as in Fig. 7, the middle one would not be above the line joining the two others." That person was John Hampden. And, says Mr. Proctor, "Unfortunately for him, some one who had more sense agreed to take his wager, and, of course, won his money." Now, the "some one who had more sense" was Mr. Wallace. And, says Proctor, in continuation: "He [Hampden?] was rather angry; and it is a strange thing that he was not angry with himself for being so foolish, or with the person who said he had tried the experiment (and so led him astray), but with the person who had won his money!" Here, then, we see that Mr. Proctor knows better than to say that the experiments conducted by "Parallax" were things of the imagination only, or that a wrong account had been given of them; and it would be well if he knew better than to try to make his readers believe that either one or the other of these things is the fact: But, there is the Old Bedford Canal now; and there are ten thousand places where the experiment may be tried! Who, then, are the "foolish" people: those who "believe" the record of experiments made by searchers after Truth, or those who shut their eyes to them, throw a doubt upon the record, charge the conductors of the experiments with dishonesty, never conduct similar experiments themselves, and declare the result of such experiments to be so and so, when the declaration can be proved to be false by any man, with a telescope, in twenty-four hours?

Mr. Proctor:—The sphericity of the Earth CANNOT be proved in the way in which you tell us it "can" be! We tell you to take back your words and remodel them on the basis of Truth. Such careless misrepresentations of facts are a disgrace to science—they are the disgrace of theoretical science to-day! Mr. Blackie, in his work on "Self Culture," says: "All flimsy, shallow, and superficial work, in fact, is a lie, of which a man ought to be ashamed."

That the Earth is an extended plane, stretched out in all directions away from the central North, over which hangs, for ever, the North Star, is a fact which all the falsehoods that can be brought to bear upon it with their dead weight will never overthrow: it is God's Truth the face of which, however, man has the power to smirch all over with his unclean hands. Mr. Proctor says: "We learn from astronomy that all these ideas, natural though they seem, are mistaken." Man's natural ideas and conclusions and experimental results are, then, to be overthrown by—what! By "astronomy?" By a thing without a soul—a mere theoretical abstraction, the outcome of the dreamer? Never! The greatest astronomer of the age is not the man, even, who can so much as attempt to manage the business. "We find," says Mr. Proctor, "that the Earth is not flat, but a globe; not fixed, but in very rapid motion; not much larger than the moon, and far smaller than the Sun and the greater number of the stars."

First, then, Mr. Proctor, tell us HOW you find that the Earth is not flat, but a globe! It does not matter that "we find" it so put down in that conglomeration of suppositions which you seek to defend: the question is, What is the evidence of it?—where can it be obtained?

"The Earth on which we live and move seems to be flat," you tell us: where, then, is the mistake? If the Earth seem to be what it is not, how are we to trust our senses? And if it is said that we cannot do so, are we to believe it, and consent to be put down lower than the brutes? No, sir: we challenge you, as we have done many times before, to produce the slightest evidence of the Earth's rotundity, from the world of facts around you. You have given to us the statement we have quoted, and we have the right to demand a proof; and if this is not forthcoming, we have before us the duty of denouncing the absurd dogma as worse than an absurdity— as a FRAUD—and as a fraud that flies in the face of divine revelation!

Well, then, Mr. Proctor, in demanding a proof of the Earth's rotundity (or the frank admission of your errors), we are tempted to taunt you as we tell you that it is utterly out of your power to produce one; and we tell you that you do not dare even to lift up your finger to point us to the so called proofs in the school-books of the day, for you know the measure of absurdity of which they are composed, and how disgraceful it is to allow them to remain as false guides of the youthful mind!

Mr. Proctor: we charge you that, whilst you teach the theory of the Earth's rotundity and mobility, you KNOW that it is a plane; and here is the ground of the charge. In page 7, in your book, you give a diagram of the "surface on which we live," and the "supposed globe"—the supposed "hollow globe"—of the heavens, arched over the said surface. Now, Mr. Proctor, you picture the surface on which we live in exact accordance with your verbal description. And what is that description? We shall scarcely be believed when we say that we give it just as it stands: "The level of the surface on which we live." And, that there may be no mistake about the meaning of the word "level," we remind you that your diagram proves that the level that you mean is the level of the mechanic, a plane surface, and not the "level" of the astronomer, which is a convex surface!

In short, your description of the Earth is exactly what you say it "seems to be," and, yet, what you say it is not: the very aim of your book being to say so! And we call this the prostitution of the printing press. And it is all the evidence that is necessary to bring the charge home to you, since the words and the diagram are in page 7 of your own book. You know, then, that Earth is a Plane—and so do we.

Now for the evidence of this grand fact, that other people may know it as well as you: remembering, from first to last, that you have not dared to bring forward a single item from the mass of evidence which is to be found in the "Zetetic Philosophy," by "Parallax," a work the influence of which it was the avowed object of your own book to crush!— except that of the three boats, an experiment which you have never tried, and the result of which has never been known, by anyone who has tried it, to be as you say it is!

ONE HUNDRED PROOFS
THAT
EARTH IS NOT A GLOBE

1. The aeronaut can see for himself that Earth is a Plane. The appearance presented to him, even at the highest elevation he has ever attained, is that of a concave surface—this being exactly what is to be expected of a surface that is truly level, since it is the nature of level surfaces to appear to rise to a level with the eye of the observer. This is ocular demonstration and proof that Earth is not a globe.

2. Whenever experiments have been tried on the surface of standing water, this surface has always been found to be level. If the Earth were a globe, the surface of all standing water would be convex. This is an experimental proof that Earth is not a globe.

3. Surveyors' operations in the construction of railroads, tunnels, or canals are conducted without the slightest "allowance" being made for "curvature," although it is taught that this so-called allowance is absolutely necessary! This is a cutting proof that Earth is not a globe.

At the first Flat Earth International Conference in Alberta, Canada, I met a guy who was a surveyor. He sat beside me at dinner one day and showed me his handbook manual, *First Order Measurement Solutions, Inc. Level Book 20-0370*. This is what it said on the page for calculating curvature (note the last two sentences):

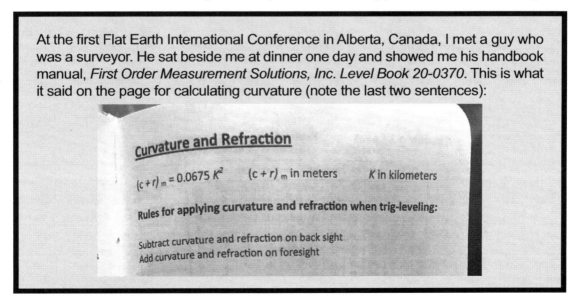

Curvature and Refraction

$$(c+r)_m = 0.0675\,K^2 \qquad (c+r)_m \text{ in meters} \qquad K \text{ in kilometers}$$

Rules for applying curvature and refraction when trig-leveling:

Subtract curvature and refraction on back sight
Add curvature and refraction on foresight

4. There are rivers that flow for hundreds of miles towards the level of the sea without falling more than a few feet— notably, the Nile, which, in a thousand miles, falls but a foot. A level expanse of this extent is quite incompatible with the idea of the Earth's "convexity." It is, therefore, a reasonable proof that Earth is not a globe.

5. The lights which are exhibited in lighthouses are seen by navigators at distances at which, according to the scale of the supposed "curvature" given by astronomers, they ought to be many hundreds of feet, in some cases, down below the line of sight! For instance: the light at Cape Hatteras is seen at such a distance (40 miles) that, according to theory, it ought to be nine-hundred feet higher above the level of the sea than it absolutely is, in order to be visible! This is a conclusive proof that there is no "curvature," on the surface of the sea—"the level of the sea,"—ridiculous though it is to be under the necessity of proving it at all: but it is, nevertheless, a conclusive proof that the Earth is not a globe.

6. If we stand on the sands of the sea-shore and watch a ship approach us, we shall find that she will apparently "rise"— to the extent of her own height, nothing more. If we stand upon an eminence, the same law operates still; and it is but the law of perspective, which causes objects, as they approach us, to appear to increase in size until we see them, close to us, the size they are in fact. That there is no other "rise" than the one spoken of is plain from the fact that, no matter how high we ascend above the level of the sea, the horizon rises on and still on as we rise, so that it is always on a level with the eye, though it be two-hundred miles away, as seen by Mr. J. Glaisher, of England, from Mr. Coxwell's balloon. So that a ship five miles away may be imagined to be "coming up" the imaginary downward curve of the Earth's surface, but if we merely ascend a hill such as Federal Hill, Baltimore, we may see twenty-five miles away, on a level with the eye—that is, twenty miles level distance beyond the ship that we vainly imagined to be "rounding the curve," and "coming up!" This is a plain proof that the Earth is not a globe.

7. If we take a trip down the Chesapeake Bay, in the daytime, we may see for ourselves the utter fallacy of the idea that when a vessel appears "hull down," as it is called, it is because the hull is "behind the water:" for, vessels have been seen, and may often be seen again, presenting the appearance spoken of, and away—far away—beyond those vessels, and, at the same moment, the level shore line, with its accompanying complement of tall trees, towering up, in perspective, over the heads of the "hull-down" ships! Since, then, the idea will not stand its ground when the facts rise up against it, and it is a piece of the popular theory, the theory is a contemptible piece of business, and we may easily wring from it a proof that Earth is not a globe.

8. If the Earth were a globe, a small model globe would be the very best—because the truest—thing for the navigator to take to sea with him. But such a thing as that is not known: with such a toy as a guide, the mariner would wreck his ship, of a certainty! This is a proof that Earth is not a globe.

9. As mariners take to sea with them charts constructed as though the sea were a level surface, however these charts may err as to the true form of this level surface taken as a whole, it is clear, as they find them answer their purpose tolerably well—and only tolerably well, for many ships are wrecked owing to the error of which we speak—that the surface of the sea is as it is taken to be, whether the captain of the ship "supposes" the Earth to be a globe or anything else. Thus, then, we draw, from the common system of "plane sailing," a practical proof that Earth is not a globe.

10. That the mariners' compass points north and south at the same time is a fact as indisputable as that two and two makes four; but that this would be impossible if the thing were placed on a globe with "north" and "south" at the centre of opposite hemispheres is a fact that does not figure in the school-books, though very easily seen: and it requires no lengthy train of reasoning to bring out of it a pointed proof that the Earth is not a globe.

11. As the mariners' compass points north and south at one time, and as the North, to which it is attracted, is that part of the Earth situate where the North Star is in the zenith, it follows that there is no south "point" or "pole" but that, while the centre is North, a vast circumference must be South in its whole extent. This is a proof that the Earth is not a globe.

12. As we have seen that there is, really, no south point (or pole) but an infinity of points forming, together, a vast circumference—the boundary of the known world, with its battlements of icebergs which bid defiance to man's onward course in a southerly direction—so there can be no east or west "points," just as there is no "yesterday," and no "tomorrow." In fact, as there is one point that is fixed (the North), it is impossible for any other point to be fixed likewise. East and west are, therefore, merely directions at right angles with a north and south line: and as the south point of the compass shifts round to all parts of the circular boundary, (as it may be carried round the central North), so the directions east and west, crossing this line, continued, form a circle, at any latitude. A westerly circumnavigation, therefore, is a going round with the North Star continually on the right hand, and an easterly circumnavigation is performed only when the reverse condition of things is maintained, the North Star being on the left hand as the journey is made. These facts, taken together, form a beautiful proof that the Earth is not a globe.

13. As the mariners' compass points north and south at one and the same time, and a meridian is a north and south line, it follows that meridians can be no other than straight lines. But, since all meridians on a globe are semicircles, it is an incontrovertible proof that the Earth is not a globe.

14. "Parallels of latitude" only—of all imaginary lines on the surface of the Earth—are circles, which increase, progressively, from the northern centre to the southern circumference. The mariner's course in the direction of any one of these concentric circles is his longitude, the degrees of which INCREASE to such an extent beyond the equator (going southwards) that hundreds of vessels have been wrecked because of the false idea created by the untruthfulness of the charts and the globular theory together, causing the sailor to be continually getting out of his reckoning. With a map of the Earth in its true form all difficulty is done away with, and ships may be conducted anywhere with perfect safety. This, then, is a very important practical proof that the Earth is not a globe.

15. The idea that, instead of sailing horizontally round the Earth, ships are taken down one side of a globe, then underneath, and are brought up on the other side to get home again, is, except as a mere dream, impossible and absurd! And, since there are neither impossibilities nor absurdities in the simple matter of circumnavigation, it stands, without argument, a proof that the Earth is not a globe.

16. If the Earth were a globe, the distance round its surface at, say, 45 "degrees" south latitude, could not possibly be any greater than it is at the same latitude north; but, since it is found by navigators to be twice the distance—to say the least of it—or, double the distance it ought to be according to the globular theory, it is a proof that the Earth is not a globe.

17. Human beings require a surface on which to live that, in its general character, shall be LEVEL; and since the Omniscient Creator must have been perfectly acquainted with the requirements of His creatures, it follows that, being an All-Wise Creator, He has met them thoroughly. This is a theological proof that the Earth is not a globe.

18. The best possessions of man are his senses; and, when he uses them all, he will not be deceived in his survey of nature. It is only when some one faculty or other is neglected or abused that he is deluded. Every man in full command of his senses knows that a level surface is a flat or horizontal one; but astronomers tell us that the true level is the curved surface of a globe! They know that man requires a level surface on which to live, so they give him one in name which is not one in fact! Since this is the best that astronomers, with their theoretical science, can do for their fellow creatures—deceive them—it is clear that things are not as they say they are; and, in short, it is a proof that Earth is not a globe.

19. Every man in his senses goes the most reasonable way to work to do a thing. Now, astronomers (one after another—following a leader), while they are telling us that Earth is a globe, are cutting off the upper half of this supposititious globe in their books, and, in this way, forming the level surface on which they describe man as living and moving! Now, if the Earth were really a globe, this would be just the most unreasonable and suicidal mode of endeavoring to show it. So that, unless theoretical astronomers are all out of their senses together, it is, clearly, a proof that the Earth is not a globe.

20. The common sense of man tells him—if nothing else told him—that there is an "up" and a "down" in nature, even as regards the heavens and the earth; but the theory of modern astronomers necessitates the conclusion that there is not: therefore, the theory of the astronomers is opposed to common sense—yes, and to inspiration—and this is a common-sense proof that the Earth is not a globe.

21. Man's experience tells him that he is not constructed like the flies that can live and move upon the ceiling of a room with as much safety as on the floor: and since the modern theory of a planetary earth necessitates a crowd of theories to keep company with it, and one of them is that men are really bound to the earth by a force which fastens them to it "like needles round a spherical lodestone," a theory perfectly outrageous and opposed to all human experience, it follows that, unless we can trample upon common sense and ignore the teachings of experience, we have an evident proof that the Earth is not a globe.

22. **God's Truth never—no, never—requires a falsehood to help it along.** Mr. Proctor, in his "Lessons," says: Men "have been able to go round and round the Earth in several directions." Now, in this case, the word "several" will imply more than two, unquestionably: whereas, it is utterly impossible to circumnavigate the Earth in any other than an easterly or a westerly direction; and the fact is perfectly consistent and clear in its relation to Earth as a Plane. Now, since astronomers would not be so foolish as to damage a good cause by misrepresentation, it is presumptive evidence that their cause is a bad one, and—a proof that Earth is not a globe.

23. If astronomical works be searched through and through, there will not be found a single instance of a bold, unhesitating, or manly statement respecting a proof of the Earth's "rotundity." Proctor speaks of "proofs which serve to show … that the Earth is not flat," and says that man "finds reason to think that the Earth is not flat," and speaks of certain matters being "explained by supposing" that the Earth is a globe; and says that people have "assured themselves that it is a globe;" but he says, also, that there is a "most complete proof that the Earth is a globe:" just as though anything in the world could possibly be wanted but a proof—a proof that proves and settles the whole question. This, however, all the money in the United States Treasury would not buy; and, unless the astronomers are all so rich that they don't want the cash, it is a sterling proof that the Earth is not a globe.

24. When a man speaks of a "most complete" thing amongst several other things which claim to be what that thing is, it is evident that they must fall short of something which the "most complete" thing possesses. And when it is known that the "most complete" thing is an entire failure, it is plain that the others, all and sundry, are worthless. Proctor's "most complete proof that the Earth is a globe" lies in what he calls "the fact" that distances from place to place agree with calculation. But, since the distance round the Earth at 45 "degrees" south of the equator is twice the distance it would be on a globe, it follows that what the greatest astronomer of the age calls "a fact" is NOT a fact; that his "most complete proof" is a most complete failure; and that he might as well have told us, at once, that he has NO PROOF to give us at all. Now, since, if the Earth be a globe, there would, necessarily, be piles of proofs of it all round us, it follows that when astronomers, with all their ingenuity, are utterly unable to point one out—to say nothing about picking one up—that they give us a proof that Earth is not a globe.

25. The surveyor's plans in relation to the laying of the first Atlantic Telegraph cable, show that in 1665 miles—from Valentia, Ireland, to St. John's, Newfoundland—the surface of the Atlantic Ocean is a LEVEL surface—not the astronomers' "level," either! The authoritative drawings, published at the time, are a standing evidence of the fact, and form a practical proof that Earth is not a globe.

26. If the Earth were a globe, it would, if we take Valentia to be the place of departure, curvate downwards, in the 1665 miles across the Atlantic to Newfoundland, according to the astronomers' own tables, more than three-hundred miles; but, as the surface of the Atlantic does not do so—the fact of its levelness having been clearly demonstrated by Telegraph Cable surveyors,—it follows that we have a grand proof that Earth is not a globe.

27. Astronomers, in their consideration of the supposed "curvature" of the Earth, have carefully avoided the taking of that view of the question which—if anything were needed to do so—would show its utter absurdity. It is this:—If, instead of taking our ideal point of departure to be at Valentia, we consider ourselves at St. John's, the 1665 miles of water between us and Valentia would just as well "curvate" downwards as it did in the other case! Now, since the direction in which the Earth is said to "curvate" is interchangeable—depending, indeed, upon the position occupied by a man upon its surface—the thing is utterly absurd; and it follows that the theory is an outrage, and that the Earth does not "curvate" at all:—an evident proof that the Earth is not a globe.

28. Astronomers are in the habit of considering two points on the Earth's surface, without, it seems, any limit as to the distance that lies between them, as being on a level, and the intervening section, even though it be an ocean, as a vast "hill"—of water! The Atlantic ocean, in taking this view of the matter, would form a "hill of water" more than a hundred miles high! The idea is simply monstrous, and could only be entertained by scientists whose whole business is made up of materials of the same description: and it certainly requires no argument to deduce, from such "science" as this, a satisfactory proof that the Earth is not a globe.

29. If the Earth were a globe, it would, unquestionably, have the same general characteristics—no matter its size— as a small globe that may be stood upon the table. As the small globe has top, bottom, and sides, so must also the large one—no matter how large it be. But, as the Earth, which is "supposed" to be a large globe, has no sides or bottom as the small globe has, the conclusion is irresistible that it is a proof that Earth is not a globe.

30. If the Earth were a globe, an observer who should ascend above its surface would have to look downwards at the horizon (if it be possible to conceive of a horizon at all under such circumstances) even as astronomical diagrams indicate—at angles varying from ten to nearly fifty degrees below the "horizontal" line of sight! (It is just as absurd as it would be to be taught that when we look at a man full in the face we are looking down at his feet!) But, as no observer in the clouds, or upon any eminence on the earth, has ever had to do so, it follows that the diagrams spoken of are imaginary and false; that the theory which requires such things to prop it up is equally airy and untrue; and that we have a substantial proof that Earth is not a globe.

For example, please see my YouTube video, *A Simple Horizon Test Take 3*:

31. If the Earth were a globe, it would certainly have to be as large as it is said to be—twenty-five thousand miles in circumference. Now, the thing which is called a "proof" of the Earth's roundness, and which is presented to children at school, is, that if we stand on the sea-shore we may see the ships, as they approach us, absolutely "coming up," and that, as we are able to see the highest parts of these ships first, it is because the lower parts are "behind the earth's curve." Now, since, if this were the case—that is, if the lower parts of these ships were behind a "hill of water" at all—the size of the Earth, indicated by such a curve as this, would be so small that it would only be big enough to hold the people of a parish, if they could get all round it, instead of the nations of the world, it follows that the idea is preposterous; that the appearance is due to another and to some reasonable cause; and that, instead of being a proof of the globular form of the Earth, it is a proof that Earth is not a globe.

32. It is often said that, if the Earth were flat, we could see all over it! This is the result of ignorance. If we stand on the level surface of a plain or a prairie, and take notice, we shall find that the horizon is formed at about three miles all around us: that is, the ground appears to rise up until, at that distance, it seems on a level with the eye-line or line of sight. Consequently, objects no higher than we stand—say, six feet—and which are at that distance (three miles), have reached the "vanishing point," and are beyond the sphere of our unaided vision. This is the reason why the hull of a ship disappears (in going away from us) before the sails; and, instead of there being about it the faintest shadow of evidence of the Earth's rotundity, it is a clear proof that Earth is not a globe.

Additionally, for those who make this claim, it should be noted that they must take into account the fact that we do have an atmosphere. And the farther away an object is, the more atmosphere there is through which one must look to see it. Thus, the denser the air, the more things become distorted and obscured. The next time you are in an airplane, just look out at the horizon. You will see how it just fades into a blur and even at 35,000+ feet in altitude, you are quite limited as to how far you can see. So, indeed, as William Carpenter states, those who make this claim are telegraphing exceptional ignorance—ironically enough, usually while attempting to make the flat Earther out to be the stupid one. As for why ships disappear hull first, this is due to perspective, issues with our visual acuity, miraging effects and refraction. For examples on how miraging works to obscure the hulls of ships, please see my YouTube video, *It's a small ball after all? Or is it an optical illusion.*

33. If the Earth were a globe, people—except those on the top—would, certainly, have to be "fastened" to its surface by some means or other, whether by the "attraction" of astronomers or by some other undiscovered and undiscoverable process! But, as we know that we simply walk on its surface without any other aid than that which is necessary for locomotion on a plane, it follows that we have, herein, a conclusive proof that Earth is not a globe.

34. If the Earth were a globe, there certainly would be—if we could imagine the thing to be peopled all round— "antipodes:" "people who," says the dictionary, "living exactly on the opposite side of the globe to ourselves, have their feet opposite to ours:"— people who are hanging heads downwards whilst we are standing heads up! But, since the theory allows us to travel to those parts of the Earth where the people are said to be heads downwards, and still to fancy ourselves to be heads upwards and our friends whom we have left behind us to be heads downwards, it follows that the whole thing is a myth—a dream—a delusion—and a snare; and, instead of there being any evidence at all in this direction to substantiate the popular theory, it is a plain proof that the Earth is not a globe.

I disagree with William Carpenter here. While it is true that those at the antipodes would have their heads pointing opposite to ours and visa versa, it doesn't follow to say the ones opposite to us have their heads pointing "downwards," since on the standard model, the core of the globe is the center of gravity, and thus the ground all over the Earth would be "downward" no matter where you are standing. So technically, no one is upside-down, "hanging with heads downwards whist we are standing heads up."

It is however interesting to note that several of the so-called "Early Church Fathers" (even those who believed in the globe) had issues with the whole idea of people living at the antipodes. For example, St. Augustine denounced the concept of antipodes, stating [emphasis mine]:

*"But as to the __fable that there are Antipodes, that is to say, men on the opposite side of the earth__, where the sun rises when it sets to us, men who walk with their feet opposite ours __that is on no ground credible__. And, indeed, it is not affirmed that this has been learned by historical knowledge, but by **scientific conjecture**, on the ground that the earth is suspended within the concavity of the sky, and that it has as much room on the one side of it as on the other: hence they say that the part that is beneath must also be inhabited. But they do not remark that, although it be supposed or scientifically demonstrated that the world is of a round and spherical form, yet it does not follow that the other*

side of the earth is bare of water; nor even, though it be bare, does it immediately follow that it is peopled. For Scripture, which proves the truth of its historical statements by the accomplishment of its prophecies, gives no false information; and it is too absurd to say, that some men might have taken ship and traversed the whole wide ocean, and crossed from this side of the world to the other, and that thus even the inhabitants of that distant region are descended from that one first man."[1]

Lactantius, a western Christian writer, who preceded Augustine and was an advisor to Emperor Constantine, did not believe the Earth to be a globe. He wrote sometime between 304–313 AD, ridiculing the notion of Antipodes and the philosophers who fancied the Earth a globe,[2] stating [bold emphasis mine]:

How is it with those who imagine that there are antipodes opposite to our footsteps? Do they say anything to the purpose? Or is there any one so senseless as to believe that there are men whose footsteps are higher than their heads? or that the things which with us are in a recumbent position, with them hang in an inverted direction? that the crops and trees grow downwards? that the rains, and snow, and hail fall upwards to the earth? And does any one wonder that hanging gardens are mentioned among the seven wonders of the world, when philosophers make hanging fields, and seas, and cities, and mountains? The origin of this error must also be set forth by us. For they are always deceived in the same manner. For when they have assumed anything false in the commencement of their investigations, led by the resemblance of the truth, they necessarily fall into those things which are its consequences. Thus they fall into many ridiculous things; because those things which are in agreement with false things, must themselves be false. But since they placed confidence in the first, they do not consider the character of those things which follow, but defend them in every way; whereas they ought to judge from those which follow, whether the first are true or false.

What course of argument, therefore, led them to the idea of the antipodes? They saw the courses of the stars travelling towards the west; they saw that the sun and the moon always set towards the same quarter, and rise from the same. But since they did not perceive what contrivance regulated their courses, nor how they returned from the west to the east, but supposed that

---

1 St. Augustine's *The City of God*, Chapter 9: *Whether We are to Believe in the Antipodes*. See also: https://www.ccel.org/ccel/schaff/npnf102.iv.XVI.9.html and Leo Ferrari, *Rethinking Augustine's Confessions, Thirty Years of Discoveries, Religious Studies and Theology* (2000)

2 See http://www.ccel.org/ccel/schaff/anf07.iii.ii.iii.xxiv.html quoting from CHAP. XXIV.—OF THE ANTIPODES, THE HEAVEN, AND THE STARS. of *Ante-Nicene Fathers Volume 7* by Philip Schaff.

the heaven itself sloped downwards in every direction, which appearance it must present on account of its immense breadth, **they thought that the world is round like a ball,** and they fancied that the heaven revolves in accordance with the motion of the heavenly bodies; and thus that the stars and sun, when they have set, by the very rapidity of the motion of the world are borne back to the east. **Therefore they both constructed brazen orbs, as though after the figure of the world, and engraved upon them certain monstrous images, which they said were constellations. It followed, therefore, from this rotundity of the heaven, that the earth was enclosed in the midst of its curved surface. But if this were so, the earth also itself must be like a globe; for that could not possibly be anything but round, which was held enclosed by that which was round.** But if the earth also were round, it must necessarily happen that it should present the same appearance to all parts of the heaven; that is, that it should raise aloft mountains, extend plains, and have level seas. And if this were so, that last consequence also followed, that there would be no part of the earth uninhabited by men and the other animals. **Thus the rotundity of the earth leads, in addition, to the invention of those suspended antipodes.**

But if you inquire from those who defend **these marvellous fictions,** why all things do not fall into that lower part of the heaven, they reply that such is the nature of things, that heavy bodies are borne to the middle, and that they are all joined together towards the middle, as we see spokes in a wheel; but that the bodies which are light, as mist, smoke, and fire, are borne away from the middle, so as to seek the heaven. **I am at a loss what to say respecting those who, when they have once erred, consistently persevere in their folly, and defend one vain thing by another; but that I sometimes imagine that they either discuss philosophy for the sake of a jest, or purposely and knowingly undertake to defend falsehoods, as if to exercise or display their talents on false subjects.** But I should be able to prove by many arguments that it is impossible for the heaven to be lower than the earth, were is not that this book must now be concluded, and that some things still remain, which are more necessary for the present work. And since it is not the work of a single book to run over the errors of each individually, let it be sufficient to have enumerated a few, from which the nature of the others may be understood.

35. If we examine a true picture of the distant horizon, or the thing itself, we shall find that it coincides exactly with a perfectly straight and level line. Now, since there could be nothing of the kind on a globe, and we find it to be the case all over the Earth, it is a proof that the Earth is not a globe.

36. If we take a journey down the Chesapeake Bay, by night, we shall see the "light" exhibited at Sharpe's Island for an hour before the steamer gets to it. We may take up a position on the deck so that the rail of the vessel's side will be in a line with the "light" and in the line of sight; and we shall find that in the whole journey the light will not vary in the slightest degree in its apparent elevation. But, say that a distance of thirteen miles has been traversed, the astronomers' theory of "curvature" demands a difference (one way or the other!) in the apparent elevation of the light, of 112 feet 8 inches! Since, however, there is not a difference of 112 hair's breadths, we have a plain proof that the water of the Chesapeake Bay is not curved, which is a proof that the Earth is not a globe.

37. If the Earth were a globe, there would, very likely, be (for nobody knows) six months day and six months night at the arctic and Antarctic regions, as astronomers dare to assert there is:—for their theory demands it! But, as this fact—the six months day and six months night—is nowhere found but in the arctic regions, it agrees perfectly with everything else that we know about the Earth as a plane, and, whilst it overthrows the "accepted theory," it furnishes a striking proof that Earth is not a globe.

38. When the Sun crosses the equator, in March, and begins to circle round the heavens in north latitude, the inhabitants of high northern latitudes see him skimming round their horizon and forming the break of their long day, in a horizontal course, not disappearing again for six months, as he rises higher and higher in the heavens whilst he makes his twenty-four hour circle until June, when he begins to descend and goes on until he disappears beyond the horizon in September. Thus, in the northern regions, they have that which the traveler calls the "midnight Sun," as he sees that luminary at a time when, in his more southern latitude, it is always midnight. If, then, for one-half the year, we may see for ourselves the Sun making horizontal circles round the heavens, it is presumptive evidence that, for the other half year, he is doing the same, although beyond the boundary of our vision. This, being a proof that Earth is a plane, is, therefore, a proof that the Earth is not a globe.

39. We have abundance of evidence that the Sun moves daily round and over the Earth in circles concentric with the northern region over which hangs the North Star; but, since the theory of the Earth being a globe is necessarily connected with the theory of its motion round the Sun in a yearly orbit, it falls to the ground when we bring forward the evidence of which we speak, and, in so doing, forms a proof that the Earth is not a globe.

> **Psalm 19:**
> 1 *The heavens declare the glory of God; and the firmament sheweth his handywork.*
> 2 *Day unto day uttereth speech, and night unto night sheweth knowledge.*
> 3 *There is no speech nor language, where their voice is not heard.*
> 4 *Their line is gone out through all the earth, and their words to the end of the world. In them hath* **he set a tabernacle for the sun,**
> 5 *Which is as a bridegroom* **coming out of his chamber,** *and rejoiceth as a strong man* **to run a race.**
> 6 **His going forth is from the end of the heaven, and** <u>**his circuit**</u> **unto the ends of it**: *and there is nothing hid from the heat thereof.*

40. The Suez Canal, which joins the Red Sea with the Mediterranean, is about one hundred miles long; it forms a straight and level surface of water from one end to the other; and no "allowance" for any supposed "curvature" was made in its construction. It is a clear proof that the Earth is not a globe.

41. When astronomers assert that it is "necessary" to make "allowance for curvature" in canal construction, it is, of course, in order that, in their idea, a level cutting may be had for the water. How flagrantly, then, do they contradict themselves when they say that the curved surface of the Earth is a "true level!" What more can they want for a canal than a true level? Since they contradict themselves in such an elementary point as this, it is an evidence that the whole thing is a delusion, and we have a proof that the Earth is not a globe.

42. It is certain that the theory of the Earth's rotundity and that of its mobility must stand or fall together. A proof, then, of its immobility is virtually a proof of its nonrotundity. Now, that the Earth does not move, either on an axis, or in an orbit round the Sun or anything else, is easily proven. If the Earth went through space at the rate of eleven-hundred miles in a minute of time, as astronomers teach us, in a particular direction, there would unquestionably be a difference in the result of firing off a projectile in that direction and in a direction the opposite of that one. But as, in fact, there is not the slightest difference in any such case, it is clear that any alleged motion of the Earth is disproved, and that, therefore, we have a proof that the Earth is not a globe.

43. The circumstances which attend bodies which are caused merely to fall from a great height prove nothing as to the motion or stability of the Earth, since the object, if it be on a thing that is in motion, will participate in that motion; but, if an object be thrown upwards from a body at rest, and, again, from a body in motion, the circumstances attending its descent will be very different. In the former case, it will fall, if thrown vertically upwards, at the place from whence it was projected; in the latter case, it will fall behind—the moving body from which it is thrown will leave it in the rear. Now, fix a gun, muzzle upwards, accurately, in the ground; fire off a projectile; and it will fall by the gun. If the Earth traveled eleven-hundred miles a minute, the projectile would fall behind the gun, in the opposite direction to that of the supposed motion. Since, then, this is NOT the case, in fact, the Earth's fancied motion is negatived, and we have a proof that the Earth is not a globe.

44. It is in evidence that, if a projectile be fired from a rapidly moving body in an opposite direction to that in which the body is going, it will fall short of the distance at which it would reach the ground if fired in the direction of motion. Now, since the Earth is said to move at the rate of nineteen miles in a second of time, "from west to east," it would make all the difference imaginable if the gun were fired in an opposite direction. But, as, in practice, there is not the slightest difference, whichever way the thing may be done, we have a forcible overthrow of all fancies relative to the motion of the Earth, and a striking proof that the Earth is not a globe.

45. The Astronomer Royal, of England, George B. Airy, in his celebrated work on Astronomy, the "Ipswich Lectures," says: "Jupiter is a large planet that turns on his axis, and why do not we turn?" Of course, the common-sense reply is: Because the Earth is not a planet! When, therefore, an astronomer royal puts words into our mouth wherewith we may overthrow the supposed planetary nature of the Earth, we have not far to go to pick up a proof that Earth is not a globe.

46. It has been shown that an easterly or a westerly motion is necessarily a circular course round the central North. The only north point or centre of motion of the heavenly bodies known to man is that formed by the North Star, which is over the central portion of the outstretched Earth. When, therefore, astronomers tell us of a planet taking a westerly course round the Sun, the thing is as meaningless to them as it is to us, unless they make the Sun the northern centre of the motion, which they cannot do! Since, then, the motion which they tell us the planets have is, on the face of it, absurd; and since, as a matter of fact, the Earth can have no absurd motion at all, it is clear that it cannot be what astronomers say it is—a planet; and, if not a planet, it is a proof that Earth is not a globe.

47. In consequence of the fact being so plainly seen, by everyone who visits the sea-shore, that the line of the horizon is a perfectly straight line, it becomes impossible for astronomers, when they attempt to convey, pictorially, an idea of the Earth's "convexity," to do so with even a shadow of consistency: for they dare not represent this horizon as a curved line, so well-known is it that it is a straight one! The greatest astronomer of the age, in page 15 of his "Lessons," gives an illustration of a ship sailing away, "as though she were rounding the top of a great hill of water;" and there—of a truth—is the straight and level line of the horizon clear along the top of the "hill" from one side of the picture to the other! Now, if this picture were true in all its parts—and it is outrageously false in several— it would show that Earth is a cylinder; for the "hill" shown is simply up one side of the level, horizontal line, and, we are led to suppose, down the other! Since, then, we have such high authority as Professor Richard A. Proctor that the Earth is a cylinder, it is, certainly, a proof that the Earth is not a globe.

48. In Mr. Proctor's "Lessons in Astronomy," page 15, a ship is represented as sailing away from the observer, and it is given in five positions or distances away on its journey. Now, in its first position, its mast appears above the horizon, and, consequently, higher than the observer's line of vision. But, in its second and third positions, representing the ship as further and further away, it is drawn higher and still higher up above the line of the horizon! Now, it is utterly impossible for a ship to sail away from an observer, under the conditions indicated, and to appear as given in the picture. Consequently, the picture is a misrepresentation, a fraud, and a disgrace. A ship starting to sail away from an observer with her masts above his line of sight would appear, indisputably, to go down and still lower down towards the horizon line, and could not possibly appear—to anyone with his vision undistorted—as going in any other direction, curved or straight. Since, then, the design of the astronomer-artist is to show the Earth to be a globe, and the points in the picture, which would only prove the Earth to be cylindrical if true, are NOT true, it follows that the astronomer-artist fails to prove, pictorially, either that the Earth is a globe or a cylinder, and that we have, therefore, a reasonable proof that the Earth is not a globe.

49. It is a well-known fact that clouds are continually seen moving in all manner of directions—yes, and frequently, in different directions at the same time—from west to east being as frequent a direction as any other. Now, if the Earth were a globe, revolving through space from west to east at the rate of nineteen miles in a second, the clouds appearing to us to move towards the east would have to move quicker than nineteen miles in a second to be thus seen; whilst those which appear to be moving in the opposite direction would have no necessity to be moving at all, since the motion of the Earth would be more than sufficient to cause the appearance. But it only takes a little common sense to show us that it is the clouds that move just as they appear to do, and that, therefore, the Earth is motionless. We have, then, a proof that the Earth is not a globe.

50. We read in the inspired book, or collection of books, called *The Bible*, nothing at all about the Earth being a globe or a planet, from beginning to end, but hundreds of allusions there are in its pages which could not be made if the Earth were a globe, and which are, therefore, said by the astronomer to be absurd and contrary to what he knows to be true! This is the groundwork of modern infidelity. But, since every one of many, many allusions to the Earth and the heavenly bodies in the Scriptures can be demonstrated to be absolutely true to nature, and we read of the Earth being "stretched out" "above the waters," as "standing in the water and out of the water," of its being "established that it cannot be moved," we have a store from which to take all the proofs we need, but we will just put down one proof—the Scriptural proof—that Earth is not a globe.

51. A "Standing Order" exists in the English Houses of Parliament that, in the cutting of canals, &c., the datum line employed shall be a "horizontal line, which shall be the same throughout the whole length of the work." Now, if the Earth were a globe, this "Order" could not be carried out: but, it is carried out: therefore, it is a proof that the Earth is not a globe.

52. It is a well-known and indisputable fact that there is a far greater accumulation of ice south of the equator than is to be found at an equal latitude north: and it is said that at Kerguelen, 50 degrees south, 18 kinds of plants exist, whilst, in Iceland, 15 degrees nearer the northern centre, there are 870 species; and, indeed, all the facts in the case show that the Sun's power is less intense at places in the southern region than it is in corresponding latitudes north. Now, on the Newtonian hypothesis, all this is inexplicable, whilst it is strictly in accordance with the facts brought to light by the carrying out of the principles involved in the Zetetic Philosophy of "Parallax." This is a proof that the Earth is not a globe.

53. Every year the Sun is as long south of the equator as he is north; and if the Earth were not "stretched out" as it is, in fact, but turned under, as the Newtonian theory suggests, it would certainly get as intensive a share of the Sun's rays south as north; but the Southern region being, in consequence of the fact stated, far more extensive than the region North, the Sun, having to complete his journey round every twenty-four hours, travels quicker as he goes further south, from September to December, and his influence has less time in which to accumulate at any given point. Since, then, the facts could not be as they are if the Earth were a globe, it is a proof that the Earth is not a globe.

54. The aeronaut is able to start in his balloon and remain for hours in the air, at an elevation of several miles, and come down again in the same county or parish from which he ascended. Now, unless the Earth drag the balloon along with it in its nineteen-miles-a-second motion, it must be left far behind, in space: but, since balloons have never been known thus to be left, it is a proof that the Earth, does not move, and, therefore, a proof that the Earth is not a globe.

55. The Newtonian theory of astronomy requires that the Moon "borrow" her light from the Sun. Now, since the Sun's rays are hot and the Moon's light sends with it no heat at all, it follows that the Sun and Moon are "two great lights," as we somewhere read; that the Newtonian theory is a mistake; and that, therefore, we have a proof that the Earth is not a globe.

56. The Sun and Moon may often be seen high in the heavens at the same time—the Sun rising in the east and the Moon setting in the west—the Sun's light positively putting the Moon's light out by sheer contrast! If the accepted Newtonian theory were correct, and the Moon had her light from the Sun, she ought to be getting more of it when face to face with that luminary—if it were possible for a sphere to act as a reflector all over its face! But as the Moon's light pales before the rising Sun, it is a proof that the theory fails; and this gives us a proof that the Earth is not a globe.

57. The Newtonian hypothesis involves the necessity of the Sun, in the case of a lunar eclipse, being on the opposite side of a globular earth, to cast its shadow on the Moon: but, since eclipses of the Moon have taken place with both the Sun and the Moon above the horizon, it follows that it cannot be the shadow of the Earth that eclipses the Moon; that the theory is a blunder; and that it is nothing less than a proof that the Earth is not a globe.

58. Astronomers have never agreed amongst themselves about a rotating Moon revolving round a rotating and revolving Earth—this Earth, Moon, planets and their satellites all, at the same time dashing through space, around the rotating and revolving Sun, towards the constellation Hercules, at the rate of four millions of miles a day! And they never will: agreement is impossible! With the Earth a plane and without motion, the whole thing is clear. And if a straw will show which way the wind blows, this may be taken as a pretty strong proof that the Earth is not a globe.

59. Mr. Proctor says: "The Sun is so far off that even moving from one side of the Earth to the other does not cause him to be seen in a different direction—at least the difference is too small to be measured." Now, since we know that north of the equator, say 45 degrees, we see the Sun at mid-day to the south, and that at the same distance south of the equator we see the Sun at mid-day to the north, our very shadows on the ground cry aloud against the delusion of the day and give us a proof that Earth is not a globe.

60. There is no problem more important to the astronomer than that of the Sun's distance from the Earth. Every change in the estimate changes everything. Now, since modern astronomers, in their estimates of this distance, have gone all the way along the line of figures from three millions of miles to a hundred and four millions—today, the distance being something over 91,000,000; it matters not how much: for, not many years ago, Mr. Hind gave the distance, "accurately," as 95,370,000!—it follows that they don't know, and that it is foolish for anyone to expect that they ever will know, the Sun's distance! And since all this speculation and absurdity is caused by the primary assumption that Earth is a wandering, heavenly body, and is all swept away by a knowledge of the fact that Earth is a plane, it is a clear proof that Earth is not a globe.

61. It is plain that a theory of measurements without a measuring-rod is like a ship without a rudder; that a measure that is not fixed, not likely to be fixed, and never has been fixed, forms no measuring-rod at all; and that as modern theoretical astronomy depends upon the Sun's distance from the Earth as its measuring-rod, and the distance is not known, it is a system of measurements without a measuring-rod—a ship without a rudder. Now, since it is not difficult to foresee the dashing of this thing upon the rock on which Zetetic astronomy is founded, it is a proof that Earth is not a globe.

62. It is commonly asserted that "the Earth must be a globe because people have sailed round it." Now, since this implies that we can sail round nothing unless it be a globe, and the fact is well known that we can sail round the Earth as a plane, the assertion is ridiculous, and we have another proof that Earth is not a globe.

63. It is a fact not so well known as it ought to be that when a ship, in sailing away from us, has reached the point at which her hull is lost to our unaided vision, a good telescope will restore to our view this portion of the vessel. Now, since telescopes are not made to enable people to see through a "hill of water," it is clear that the hulls of ships are not behind a hill of water when they can be seen through a telescope though lost to our unaided vision. This is a proof that Earth is not a globe.

64. Mr. Glaisher, in speaking of his balloon ascends, says: "The horizon always appeared on a level with the car." Now, since we may search amongst the laws of optics in vain for any principle that would cause the surface of a globe to turn its face upwards instead of downwards, it is a clear proof that the Earth is not a globe.

65. The Rev. D. Olmsted, in describing a diagram which is supposed to represent the Earth as a globe, with a figure of a man sticking out at each side and one hanging head downwards, says: "We should dwell on this point until it appears to us as truly up,"—in the direction given to these figures as it does with regard to a figure which he has placed on the top! Now, a system of philosophy which requires us to do something which is, really, the going out of our minds, by dwelling on an absurdity until we think it is a fact, cannot be a system based on God's truth, which never requires anything of the kind. Since, then, the popular theoretical astronomy of the day requires this, it is evident that it is the wrong thing, and that this conclusion furnishes us with a proof that the Earth is not a globe.

66. It is often said that the predictions of eclipses prove astronomers to be right in their theories. But it is not seen that this proves too much. It is well known that Ptolemy predicted eclipses for six-hundred years, on the basis of a plane Earth, with as much accuracy as they are predicted by modern observers. If, then, the predictions prove the truth of the particular theories current at the time, they just as well prove one side of the question as the other, and enable us to lay claim to a proof that the Earth is not a globe.

67. Seven-hundred miles is said to be the length of the great Canal, in China. Certain it is that, when this canal was formed, no "allowance" was made for "curvature." Yet the canal is a fact without it. This is a Chinese proof that the Earth is not a globe.

68. Mr. J. N. Lockyer says: "Because the Sun seems to rise in the east and set in the west, the Earth really spins in the opposite direction; that is, from west to east." Now, this is no better than though we were to say—Because a man seems to be coming up the street, the street really goes down to the man! And since true science would contain no such nonsense as this, it follows that the so-called science of theoretical astronomy is not true, and, therefore, we have a proof that the Earth is not a globe.

69. Mr. Lockyer says: "The appearances connected with the rising and setting of the Sun and stars may be due either to our earth being at rest and the Sun and stars traveling round it, or the earth itself turning round, while the Sun and stars are at rest." Now, since true science does not allow of any such beggarly alternatives as these, it is plain that modern theoretical astronomy is not true science, and that its leading dogma is a fallacy. We have, then, a plain proof that the Earth is not a globe.

70. Mr. Lockyer, in describing his picture of the supposed proof of the Earth's rotundity by means of ships rounding a "hill of water," uses these words:—"Diagram showing how, when we suppose the earth is round, we explain how it is that ships at sea appear as they do." This is utterly unworthy of the name of Science! A science that begins by supposing, and ends by explaining the supposition, is, from beginning to end, a mere farce. The men who can do nothing better than amuse themselves in this way must be denounced as dreamers only, and their leading dogma a delusion. This is a proof that Earth is not a globe.

71. The astronomers' theory of a globular Earth necessitates the conclusion that, if we travel south of the equator, to see the North Star is an impossibility. Yet it is well known this star has been seen by navigators when they have been more than 20 degrees south of the equator. This fact, like hundreds of other facts, puts the theory to shame, and gives us a proof that the Earth is not a globe.

72. Astronomers tell us that, in consequence of the Earth's "rotundity," the perpendicular walls of buildings are, nowhere, parallel, and that even the walls of houses on opposite sides of a street are not strictly so! But, since all observation fails to find any evidence of this want of parallelism which theory demands, the idea must be renounced as being absurd and in opposition to all well known facts. This is a proof that the Earth is not a globe.

73. Astronomers have made experiments with pendulums which have been suspended from the interior of high buildings, and have exulted over the idea of being able to prove the rotation of the Earth on its "axis," by the varying direction taken by the pendulum over a prepared table underneath—asserting that the table moved round under the pendulum, instead of the pendulum shifting and oscillating in different directions over the table! But, since it has been found that, as often as not, the pendulum went round the wrong way for the "rotation" theory, chagrin has taken the place of exultation, and we have a proof of the failure of astronomers in their efforts to substantiate their theory, and, therefore, a proof that Earth is not a globe.

In reason #2 of his book, *50 Reasons Copernicus or the Bible*,[1] F.E. Pasche commented on the issue of Foucault's Pendulum, saying:

> Since the rotation of the earth upon its axis, if existing, must be a uniform one, necessarily with all pendulums the deviation should be uniform; but this is not the case. Or does the earth move with different velocity under different pendulums? Dr. Schoepffer, an eye-witness of the experiment, says: "In an introductory speech Dr. Menzzer at Quedlinburg showed that until then there had been no proof for the Copernican hypothesis, the so-called proofs being, after close investigation, just as many confutations, until the Foucault pendulum showed the rotation of the earth uncontrovertibly.
>
> The pendulum was tied, the string was burnt, the swingings began, but the pendulum deviated to the left, instead of to the right. It was hastily brought to rest. New burning of the string. This time the deviation was the one desired, and we were invited again to be present in the church the next morning at eight o'clock, to be convinced that the deviation agrees with the theory. On the following morning, however, we saw that the pendulum during the night had changed its mind, and had from the deviation to the right again re turned to the left.
>
> To me this new proof did not seem to be quite in order. My belief in the Copernican doctrine was shaken by the speech of Dr. Menzzer, and I concluded to go to Berlin for an explanation. After seeing the pendulum-experiment here also and, strangely, again with a deviation to the left, I went to Alexander v. Humboldt, who was indeed ever the first refuge of those seeking information. He received me very friendly and spoke the memorable words:

1 This book will be included in *Testing the Globe: A Zetetic Investigation Volume 2*.

"I have known, too, for a long time, that as yet we have no proof for the Copernican system, but I shall never dare to be the first to attack it. Don't rush into the wasps' nest. You will but bring upon yourself the scorn of the thoughtless multitude."

Furthermore, I have found, by careful experiments, that a skillful experimenter can let the pendulum deviate either to the left or to the right. And we must not overlook the fact that the deviations may be caused by air-currents, electricity, earth-magnetism, special apparatus, and perhaps many other causes. Blunt and Cox observed the most curious and contrary swingings. Phillips of New York found very great hourly deviations in the swinging-line. Walker observed a peculiarly swift deviation when the pendulum swings in the magnetic meridian. D'Oliveira at Rio de Janeiro stated that the pendulum deviates to the right in the direction of the meridian, but to the left in the direction of the parallel.

This deviation, diametrically opposed to the theory, was seen very often. And sometimes the pendulum does not deviate at all. Much more could be said against this "beautiful experiment." Though beautiful it may seem to the theorist, it certainly is far from being irrefragable evidence for the earth's motion.

I also had an interesting encounter at the Griffith Observatory while observing the Foucault Pendulum they have there in the main entrance. For more on this, please see my YouTube video, *Debunking #8 of the Top Ten Reasons Why We (allegedly) Know the Earth is Round (as in a globe)*:

74. As to the supposed "motion of the whole Solar system in space," the Astronomer Royal of England once said: "The matter is left in a most delightful state of uncertainty, and I shall be very glad if anyone can help us out of it." But, since the whole Newtonian scheme is, today, in a most deplorable state of uncertainty—for, whether the Moon goes round the Earth or the Earth round the Moon has, for years, been a matter of "raging" controversy—it follows that, root and branch, the whole thing, is wrong; and, all hot from the raging furnace of philosophical phrensy, we find a glowing proof that Earth is not a globe.

75. Considerably more than a million Earths would be required to make up a body like the Sun—the astronomers tell us: and more than 53,000 suns would be wanted to equal the cubic contents of the star Vega. And Vega is a "small star!" And there are countless millions of these stars! And it takes 30,000,000 years for the light of some of these stars to reach us at 12,000,000 miles in a minute! And, says Mr. Proctor, "I think a moderate estimate of the age of the Earth would be 500,000,000 years!" "Its weight," says the same individual, "is 6,000,000,000,000,000,000,000,000 tons!" Now, since no human being is able to comprehend these things, the giving of them to the world is an insult—an outrage. And though they have all arisen from the one assumption that Earth is a planet, instead of upholding the assumption, they drag it down by the weight of their own absurdity, and leave it lying in the dust—a proof that Earth is not a globe.

76. Mr. J. R. Young, in his work on Navigation, says: "Although the path of the ship is on a spherical surface, yet we may represent the length of the path by a straight line on a plane surface." (And plane sailing is the rule.) Now, since it is altogether impossible to "represent" a curved line by a straight one, and absurd to make the attempt, it follows that a straight line represents a straight line and not a curved one. And, since it is the surface of the waters of the ocean that is being considered by Mr. Young, it follows that this 45 surface is a straight surface, and we are indebted to Mr. Young, a professor of navigation, for a proof that the Earth is not a globe.

77. "Oh, but if the Earth is a plane, we could go to the edge and tumble over!" is a very common assertion. This is a conclusion that is formed too hastily, and facts overthrow it. The Earth certainly is, just what man by his observation finds it to be, and what Mr. Proctor himself says it "seems" to be—flat; and we cannot cross the icy barrier which surrounds it. This is a complete answer to the objection, and, of course, a proof that Earth is not a globe.

78. "Yes, but we can circumnavigate the South easily enough," is often said—by those who don't know. The British Ship Challenger recently completed the circuit of the Southern region—indirectly, to be sure—but she was three years about it, and traversed nearly 69,000 miles—a stretch long enough to have taken her six times round on the globular hypothesis. This is a proof that Earth is not a globe.

79. The remark is common enough that we can see the circle of the Earth if we cross the ocean, and that this proves it to be round. Now, if we tie a donkey to a stake on a level common, and he eats the grass all around him, it is only a circular disc that he has to do with, not a spherical mass. Since, then, circular discs may be seen anywhere—as well from a balloon in the air as from the deck of a ship, or from the standpoint of the donkey, it is a proof that the surface of the Earth is a plane surface, and, therefore, a proof that the Earth is not a globe.

80. It is "supposed," in the regular course of the Newtonian theory, that the Earth is, in June, about 190 millions of miles (190,000,000) away from its position in December. Now, since we can, (in middle north latitudes), see the North Star, on looking out of a window that faces it—and out of the very same corner of the very same pane of glass in the very same window—all the year round, it is proof enough for any man in his senses that we have made no motion at all. It is a proof that the Earth is not a globe.

81. Newtonian philosophers teach us that the Moon goes round the Earth from west to east. But observation—man's most certain mode of gaining knowledge—shows us that the Moon never ceases to move in the opposite direction— from east to west. Since, then, we know that nothing can possibly move in two, opposite directions at the same time, it is a proof that the thing is a big blunder; and, in short, it is a proof that the Earth is not a globe.

82. Astronomers tell us that the Moon goes round the Earth in about 28 days. Well, we may see her making her journey round, every day, if we make use of our eyes—and these are about the best things we have to use. The Moon falls behind in her daily motion as compared with that of the Sun to the extent of one revolution in the time specified; but that is not making a revolution. Failing to go as fast as other bodies go in one direction does not constitute a going round in the opposite one—as the astronomers would have us believe! And, since all this absurdity has been rendered necessary for no other purpose than to help other absurdities along, it is clear that the astronomers are on the wrong track; and it needs no long train of reasoning to show that we have a proof that the Earth is not a globe.

83. It has been shown that meridians are, necessarily, straight lines; and that it is impossible to travel round the Earth in a north or south direction: from which it follows that, in the general acceptation of the word "degree,"—the 360th part of a circle—meridians have no degrees: for no one knows anything of a meridian circle or semicircle, to be thus divided. But astronomers speak of degrees of latitude in the same sense as those of longitude. This, then, is done by assuming that to be true which is not true. Zetetic philosophy does not involve this necessity. This proves that the basis of this philosophy is a sound one, and, in short, is a proof that the Earth is not a globe.

84. If we move away from an elevated object on or over a plain or a prairie, the height of the object will apparently diminish as we do so. Now, that which is sufficient to produce this effect on a small scale is sufficient on a large one; and traveling away from an elevated object, no matter how high, over a level surface, no matter how far, will cause the appearance in question—the lowering of the object. Our modern theoretical astronomers, however, in the case of the apparent lowering of the North Star as we travel southward, assert that it is evidence that the Earth is globular! But, as it is clear that an appearance which is fully accounted for on the basis of known facts cannot be permitted to figure as evidence in favor of that which is only a supposition, it follows that we rightfully order it to stand down, and make way for a proof that the Earth is not a globe.

85. There are rivers which flow east, west, north, and south—that is, rivers are flowing in all directions over the Earth's surface, and at the same time. Now, if the Earth were a globe, some of these rivers would be flowing up-hill and others down, taking it for a fact that there really is an "up" and a "down" in nature, whatever form she assumes. But, since rivers do not flow up-hill, and the globular theory requires that they should, it is a proof that the Earth is not a globe.

86. If the Earth were a globe, rolling and dashing through "space" at the rate of "a hundred miles in five seconds of time," the waters of seas and oceans could not, by any known law, be kept on its surface—the assertion that they could be retained under these circumstances being an outrage upon human understanding and credulity! But as the Earth—that is, the habitable world of dry land—is found to be "standing out of the water and in the water" of the "mighty deep," whose circumferential boundary is ice, we may throw the statement back into the teeth of those who make it and flaunt before their faces the flag of reason and common sense, inscribed with—a proof that the Earth is not a globe.

87. The theory of a rotating and revolving earth demands a theory to keep the water on its surface; but, as the theory which is given for this purpose is as much opposed to all human experience as the one which it is intended to uphold, it is an illustration of the miserable makeshifts to which astronomers are compelled to resort, and affords a proof that the Earth is not a globe.

88. If we could—after our minds had once been opened to the light of Truth—conceive of a globular body on the surface of which human beings could exist, the power—no matter by what name it be called—that would hold them on would, then, necessarily, have to be so constraining and cogent that they could not live; the waters of the oceans would have to be as a solid mass, for motion would be impossible. But we not only exist, but live and move; and the water of the ocean skips and dances like a thing of life and beauty! This is a proof that the Earth is not a globe.

89. It is well known that the law regulating the apparent decrease in the size of objects as we leave them in the distance (or as they leave us) is very different with luminous bodies from what it is in the case of those which are non-luminous. Sail past the light of a small lamp in a row-boat on a dark night, and it will seem to be no smaller when a mile off than it was when close to it. Proctor says, in speaking of the Sun: "his apparent size does not change,"— far off or near. And then he forgets the fact! Mr. Proctor tells us, subsequently, that, if the traveler goes so far south that the North Star appears on the horizon, "the Sun should therefore look much larger"—if the Earth were a plane! Therefore, he argues, "the path followed cannot have been the straight course,"— but a curved one. Now, since it is nothing but common scientific trickery to bring forward, as an objection to stand in the way of a plane Earth, the nonappearance of a thing which has never been known to appear at all, it follows that, unless that which appears to be trickery were an accident, it was the only course open to the objector—to trick. (Mr. Proctor, in a letter to the "English Mechanic" for Oct. 20, 1871, boasts of having turned a recent convert to the Zetetic philosophy by telling him that his arguments were all very good, but that "it seems as though [mark the language!] the sun ought to look nine times larger in summer." And Mr. Proctor concludes thus: "He saw, indeed, that, in his faith in 'Parallax,' he had 'written himself down an ass.' ") Well, then: trickery or no trickery on the part of the objector, the objection is a counterfeit—a fraud—no valid objection at all; and it follows that the system which does not purge itself of these things is a rotten system, and the system which its advocates, with Mr. Proctor at their head, would crush if they could find a weapon to use—the Zetetic philosophy of "Parallax"—is destined to live! This is a proof that the Earth is not a globe.

90. "Is water level, or is it not?" was a question once asked of an astronomer. "Practically, yes; theoretically, no," was the reply. Now, when theory does not harmonize with practice, the best thing to do is to drop the theory. (It is getting too late, now, to say "So much the worse for the facts!") To drop the theory which supposes a curved surface to standing water is to acknowledge the facts which form the basis of Zetetic philosophy. And since this will have to be done—sooner or later,—it is a proof that the Earth is not a globe.

91. "By actual observation," says Schoedler, in his "Book of Nature," "we know that the other heavenly bodies are spherical, hence we unhesitatingly assert that the earth is so also." This is a fair sample of all astronomical reasoning. When a thing is classed amongst "other" things, the likeness between them must first be proven. It does not take a Schoedler to tell us that "heavenly bodies" are spherical, but "the greatest astronomer of the age" will not, now, dare to tell us that The Earth is—and attempt to prove it. Now, since no likeness has ever been proven to exist between the Earth and the heavenly bodies, the classification of the Earth with the heavenly bodies is premature— unscientific—false! This is a proof that Earth is not a globe.

92. "There is no inconsistency in supposing that the earth does move round the sun," says the Astronomer Royal of England. Certainly not, when theoretical astronomy is all supposition together! The inconsistency is in teaching the world that the thing supposed is a fact. Since, then, the "motion" of the Earth is supposition only—since, indeed, it is necessary to suppose it at all—it is plain that it is a fiction and not a fact; and, since "mobility" and "sphericity" stand or fall together, we have before us a proof that Earth is not a globe.

93. We have seen that astronomers—to give us a level surface on which to live—have cut off one-half of the "globe" in a certain picture in their books (See page 6). Now, astronomers having done this, one-half of the substance of their "spherical theory" is given up! Since, then, the theory must stand or fall in its entirety, it has really fallen when the half is gone. Nothing remains, then, but a plane Earth, which is, of course, a proof that the Earth is not a globe.

94. In "Cornell's Geography" there is an "Illustrated proof of the Form of the Earth." A curved line on which is represented a ship in four positions, as she sails away from an observer, is an arc of 72 degrees, or one-fifth of the supposed circumference of the "globe"—about 5,000 miles. Ten such ships as those which are given in the picture would reach the full length of the "arc," making 500 miles as the length of the ship. The man, in the picture, who is watching the ship as she sails away, is about 200 miles high; and the tower, from which he takes an elevated view, at least 500 miles high. These are the proportions, then, of men, towers, and ships which are necessary in order to see a ship, in her different positions, as she "rounds the curve" of the "great hill of water" over which she is supposed to be sailing: for, it must be remembered that this supposed "proof" depends upon lines and angles of vision which, if enlarged, would still retain their characteristics. Now, since ships are not built 500 miles long, with masts in proportion, and men are not quite 200 miles high, it is not what it is said to be—a proof of rotundity—but, either an ignorant farce or a cruel piece of deception. In short, it is a proof that the Earth is not a globe.

95. In "Cornell's Intermediate Geography," (1881) page 12, is an "Illustration of the Natural Divisions of Land and Water." This illustration is so nicely drawn that it affords, at once, a striking proof that Earth is a plane. It is true to nature, and bears the stamp of no astronomer-artist. It is a pictorial proof that Earth is not a globe.

96. If we refer to the diagram in "Cornell's Geography," page 4, and notice the ship in its position the most remote from the observer, we shall find that, though it is about 4,000 miles away, it is the same size as the ship that is nearest to him, distant about 700 miles! This is an illustration of the way in which astronomers ignore the laws of perspective. This course is necessary, or they would be compelled to lay bare the fallacy of their dogmas. In short, there is, in this matter, a proof that the Earth is not a globe.

97. Mr. Hind, the English astronomer, says: "The simplicity with which the seasons are explained by the revolution of the Earth in her orbit and the obliquity of the ecliptic, may certainly be adduced as a strong presumptive proof of the correctness"—of the Newtonian theory; "for on no other rational suppositions with respect to the relations of the Earth and Sun, can these and other as well-known phenomena, be accounted for." But, as true philosophy has no "suppositions" at all—and has nothing to do with "suppositions"—and the phenomena spoken of are thoroughly explained by facts, the "presumptive proof" falls to the ground, covered with the ridicule it so richly deserves; and out of the dust of Mr. Hind's "rational suppositions" we see standing before us a proof that Earth is not a globe.

98. Mr. Hind speaks of the astronomer watching a star as it is "carried across the telescope by the diurnal revolution of the Earth." Now, this is nothing but downright absurdity. No motion of the Earth could possibly carry a star across a telescope or anything else. If the star is carried across anything at all, it is the star that moves, not the thing across which it is carried! Besides, the idea that the Earth, if it were a globe, could possibly move in an orbit of nearly 600,000,000 of miles with such exactitude that the crosshairs in a telescope fixed on its surface would appear to glide gently over a star "millions of millions" of miles away is simply monstrous; whereas, with a FIXED telescope, it matters not the distance of the stars, though we suppose them to be as far off as the astronomer supposes them to be; for, as Mr. Proctor himself says, "the further away they are, the less they will seem to shift." Why, in the name of common sense, should observers have to fix their telescopes on solid stone bases so that they should not move a hair's breadth, if the Earth on which they fix them move at the rate of nineteen miles in a second? Indeed, to believe that Mr. Proctor's mass of "six thousand million million million tons" is "rolling, surging, flying, darting on through space for ever" with a velocity compared with which a shot from a cannon is a "very slow coach," with such unerring accuracy that a telescope fixed on granite pillars in an observatory will not enable a lynx-eyed astronomer to detect a variation in its onward motion of the thousandth part of a hair's-breadth is to conceive a miracle compared with which all the miracles on record put together would sink into utter insignificance. Captain R. J. Morrison, the late compiler of "Zadkeil's Almanac," says: "We declare that this 'motion' is all mere 'bosh'; and that the arguments which uphold it are, when examined with an eye that seeks for TRUTH only, mere nonsense, and childish absurdity." Since, then, these absurd theories are of no use to men in their senses, and since there is no necessity for anything of the kind in Zetetic philosophy, it is a "strong presumptive proof"—as Mr. Hind would say—that the Zetetic philosophy is true, and, therefore, a proof that Earth is not a globe.

99. Mr. Hind speaks of two great mathematicians differing only fifty-five yards in their estimate of the Earth's diameter. Why, Sir John Herschel, in his celebrated work, cuts off 480 miles of the same thing to get "round numbers!" This is like splitting a hair on one side of the head and shaving all the hair off on the other! Oh, "science!" Can there be any truth in a science like this? All the exactitude in astronomy is in Practical astronomy—not Theoretical. Centuries of observation have made practical astronomy a noble art and science, based—as we have a thousand times proved it to be—on a fixed Earth; and we denounce this pretended exactitude on one side and the reckless indifference to figures on the other as the basest trash, and take from it a proof that the "science" which tolerates it is a false—instead of being an "exact"—science, and we have a proof that the Earth is not a globe.

100. The Sun, as he travels round over the surface of the Earth, brings "noon" to all places on the successive meridians which he crosses: his journey being made in a westerly direction, places east of the Sun's position have had their noon, whilst places to the west of the Sun's position have still to get it. Therefore, if we travel easterly, we arrive at those parts of the Earth where "time" is more advanced, the watch in our pocket has to be "put on," or we may be said to "gain time." If, on the other hand, we travel westerly, we arrive at places where it is still "morning," the watch has to be "put back," and it may be said that we "lose time." But, if we travel easterly so as to cross the 180th meridian, there is a loss, there, of a day, which will neutralize the gain of a whole circumnavigation; and, if we travel westerly, and cross the same meridian, we experience the gain of a day, which will compensate for the loss during a complete circumnavigation in that direction. The fact of losing or gaining time in sailing round the world, then, instead of being evidence of the Earth's "rotundity," as it is imagined to be, is, in its practical exemplification, an everlasting proof that the Earth is not a globe. "And what then?" What then! No intelligent man will ask the question; and he who may be called an intellectual man will know that the demonstration of the fact that the Earth is not a globe is the grandest snapping of the chains of slavery that ever took place in the world of literature or science. The floodgates of human knowledge are opened afresh and an impetus is given to investigation and discovery where all was stagnation, bewilderment and dreams! Is it nothing to know that infidelity cannot stand against the mighty rush of the living water of Truth that must flow on and on until the world shall look "up" once more "to Him that stretched out the earth above the waters"—"to Him that made great lights:—the Sun to rule by day—the Moon and Stars to rule by night?" Is it nothing to know and to feel that the heavenly bodies were made for man, and that the monstrous dogma of an infinity of worlds is overthrown forever? The old-time English "Family Herald," for July 25, 1885, says, in its editorial, that "The earth's revolution on its own axis was denied, against Galileo and Copernicus, by the whole weight of the Church of Rome." And, in an article on "The Pride of Ignorance," too!—the editor not knowing that if the Earth had an axis to call its "own"—which the Church well knew it had not, and, therefore, could not admit—it would not "revolve" on it; and that the theoretical motion on an axis is that of rotation, and not revolution! Is it nothing to know that "the whole weight of the Church of Rome" was thrown in the right direction, although it has swayed back again like a gigantic pendulum that will regain its old position before long? Is it nothing to know that the "pride of ignorance" is on the other side? Is it nothing to know that, with all the Bradlaughs and Ingersolls of the world telling us to the contrary—Biblical science is true? Is it nothing to know that we are living on a body at rest, and not upon a heavenly body whirling and dashing through space in every conceivable way and with a velocity utterly inconceivable? Is it nothing to know that we can look steadfastly up to Heaven instead of having no heaven to look up to at all? Is it nothing, indeed, to be in the broad daylight of Truth and to be able to go on towards a possible perfection, instead of being wrapped in the darkness of error on the rough ocean of Life, and finding ourselves stranded at last—God alone knows where?

Baltimore, Maryland, U. S. A.,
August, 1885.

KING'S GATE MEDIA PRESENTS THE WORKS OF:
DAVID SCOTT, FREDERICK PASCHE & GERRARD HICKSON

TESTING THE GLOBE
A ZETETIC INVESTIGATION
VOLUME II

REFORMATTED WITH INTRODUCTION AND COMMENTARY BY
ROB SKIBA

TO BE CONTINUED...

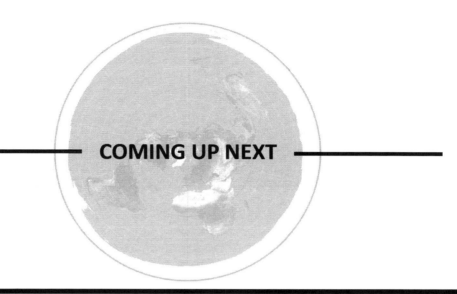

COMING UP NEXT

This volume contained works from the late 19th century. Volume II in this *Testing the Globe: A Zetetic Investigation* series will include the following books from the early 20th century:

- ***Terra Firma: The Earth Not a Planet, Proved From Scripture, Reason, and Fact*** by David Wardlaw Scott (1901).
- ***50 Reasons Copernicus or the Bible*** by Frederick E. Pasche (1915).
- ***Kings Dethroned*** by Gerrard Hickson (1922).

David Wardlaw Scott summarizes what you've read here, while also contributing his own commentary and additional insights along the way. Whereas the books written by Frederick Pasche and Gerrard Hickson deal more with the problems of Copernican/ Newtonian cosmology. Hickson's also addresses the theories of Einstein and the problems with all of modern astronomy, both from a Biblical and practical perspective.

Volume II will also include a new Introduction and further commentary by me, along with an Epilogue describing why I believe this topic is important to be discussing in the 21st century and what I believe the motivation is for lying to us and covering up the true nature of our world and its place in the cosmos.

For more information from my own personal journey of discovery concerning this topic, please be sure to visit my website:

www.testingtheglobe.com

19981357R00234

Made in the USA
Lexington, KY
02 December 2018